A. JAMES REICHLEY

Religion in American Public Life

THE BROOKINGS INSTITUTION
Washington, D.C.

Library of Congress Cataloging-in-Publication Data

Reichley, A. James.
    Religion in American public life.

    Bibliography: p.
    Includes index.
    1. United States—Religion.   2. Religion and
state—United States—History.   I. Title.
BL2525.R44   1985   322'.1'0973   85-21312
ISBN 0-8157-7378-1
ISBN 0-8157-7377-3 (pbk.)

9 8 7 6 5 4

THE BROOKINGS INSTITUTION is an independent organization devoted to nonpartisan research, education, and publication in economics, government, foreign policy, and the social sciences generally. Its principal purposes are to aid in the development of sound public policies and to promote public understanding of issues of national importance.

The Institution was founded on December 8, 1927, to merge the activities of the Institute for Government Research, founded in 1916, the Institute of Economics, founded in 1922, and the Robert Brookings Graduate School of Economics and Government, founded in 1924.

The Board of Trustees is responsible for the general administration of the Institution, while the immediate direction of the policies, program, and staff is vested in the President, assisted by an advisory committee of the officers and staff. The by-laws of the Institution state: "It is the function of the Trustees to make possible the conduct of scientific research, and publication, under the most favorable conditions, and to safeguard the independence of the research staff in the pursuit of their studies and in the publication of the results of such studies. It is not a part of their function to determine, control, or influence the conduct of particular investigations or the conclusions reached."

The President bears final responsibility for the decision to publish a manuscript as a Brookings book. In reaching his judgment on the competence, accuracy, and objectivity of each study, the President is advised by the director of the appropriate research program and weighs the views of a panel of expert outside readers who report to him in confidence on the quality of the work. Publication of a work signifies that it is deemed a competent treatment worthy of public consideration but does not imply endorsement of conclusions or recommendations.

The Institution maintains its position of neutrality on issues of public policy in order to safeguard the intellectual freedom of the staff. Hence interpretations or conclusions in Brookings publications should be understood to be solely those of the authors and should not be attributed to the Institution, to its trustees, officers, or other staff members, or to the organizations that support its research.

*To the memory of my
mother and father*

Foreword

ROBERT BROOKINGS, the St. Louis businessman who came to Washington, D.C., during the First World War and in 1927 founded the Brookings Institution, was concerned with broad social objectives as well as with the efficiency of governmental and economic systems. "Our western civilization," he wrote, "must vindicate its worth if it is to endure." High among the goals by which the American future would be tested, he believed, was "preserving such cherished institutions as the family and the church."

The Brookings Institution has perpetuated its founder's concerns. Although much of their work is devoted to developing means for improving the efficiency of government and the economy, Brookings research fellows have also recently studied such social issues as the rights of women, the quality of life in American cities, and the future direction of American politics. In this book, A. James Reichley, a senior fellow in the Brookings Governmental Studies program, takes up another social issue that is both basic and currently controversial: the role of religion in American public life.

Arguments now abound over the extent to which religious groups should participate in politics or the degree of constitutional separation of church and state that is desirable. These discussions, however, often lack a sense of the historical interplay between religious groups and civil society in the United States or a grasp of the philosophic issues underlying that interplay. This book provides both: it examines the impact of religion on American public life and places religion and politics within a conceptual framework of values in which both are rooted.

The author shows that religion and politics in the United States have long been closely intertwined. The Founding Fathers drew on religious ideals and rhetoric when they formed the new nation. Churches have been active participants in political struggles to abolish slavery, prohibit the sale of liquor, enact Sunday closing laws, and win votes for women. Secular institutions—government and the courts—have affected issues important to religious denominations, such as school prayer, the status of conscientious objectors, and public funding for private education. The ultimate issue that the author examines is how this involvement can be continued without threatening civil liberties and without the secular politicization of religion.

The author is grateful for helpful comments on all or parts of the manuscript by Shlomo Avineri, Robert Benne, Walter Berns, Colin Campbell, Thomas Cavanagh, Christine Compston, John S. Coolidge, Martha Derthick, Anthony Downs, Denis P. Doyle, Ernest Evans, Os Guinness, Stephen Hess, Justice William Hutchinson, Robert A. Katzmann, Herbert Kaufman, Paul Kittlaus, Everett Carll Ladd, Martin E. Marty, Andrew McFarland, Paul E. Peterson, Paul Quirk, Barry Rabe, Donald Robinson, Rustum Roy, Dana Runestad, Gilbert Y. Steiner, James L. Sundquist, and Paul J. Weber. Martin Marty suggested the title.

The author also thanks James Schneider, who edited the book. Judith H. Newman, Julie Bailes Legg, and Joan Milan gave research and secretarial assistance; Diane Hodges provided administrative support; and the staff of the Brookings Library, led by Laura Walker, ran down elusive texts and citations.

The views expressed in this book are the author's alone and should not be ascribed to the persons whose assistance is acknowledged above or to the trustees, officers, or other staff members of the Brookings Institution.

Bruce K. MacLaury
President

August 1985
Washington, D.C.

Contents

ONE

The Religious Issue

THE ROLE of religion in the 1984 national election campaign was unusually intense and visible. President Reagan rarely missed a chance to invoke religious themes in his appeals for support from cultural conservatives. Former Vice-President Walter Mondale, his Democratic opponent, charged that the Reagan administration was undermining the constitutional barrier between church and state and argued that the president was "out to lunch" on the "part of a Christian's responsibility" that called for social justice. Leaders of the Roman Catholic church, the nation's largest denomination, accused Representative Geraldine Ferraro, the Democratic nominee for vice-president and herself a Catholic, of misrepresenting the church's teaching on abortion. And the Reverend Jesse Jackson, the first ordained minister to be a serious candidate for president, campaigned from pulpits of black churches across the nation in his pursuit of the Democratic nomination.

Some church groups constituting the so-called religious new right worked vigorously for a Republican victory in the fall election. Others attacked the administration on issues ranging from nuclear disarmament to school prayer. Mixed with this directly political news, a series of Supreme Court decisions on church-state issues, partly reversing the trend of the past thirty-five years, further focused attention on relations between religion and government.

Americans have always been, as Justice William Douglas repeatedly pointed out in the Supreme Court opinions he wrote on church-state relations in the 1950s, "a religious people." Religion played an important part in motivating colonists to come to the New World and was a major factor in the movement that led to the American Revolution and the formation of the United States. The First Amendment to the Constitution specifically guarantees "free expression" of religion. In the 1980s more than 90 percent of all Americans identify with some religious faith, and on any given Sunday morning more than 40 percent are to be found in church. By most measurable indices the United States is a more religious country than any European nation except Ireland and Poland.[1]

Just how religious commitment should relate to the operations of government and politics, however, has often been a subject of controversy and debate. Along with its tradition of religious belief, the United States has also maintained a strong tradition of separation between church and state. The same First Amendment that guarantees free exercise of religion prohibits Congress from making any law "respecting an establishment of religion." Since the 1940s the Supreme Court has interpreted the Fourteenth Amendment, enacted at the end of the Civil War, to extend this prohibition to the states. Many constitutional experts and ordinary citizens would not go so far as Thomas Jefferson in advocating an unbreachable "wall of separation between church and state," but there can be no doubt that both constitutional authority and social tradition require, at a minimum, that government refrain from sponsoring or regulating religious belief.

The Problem Defined

The extent of political involvement by some religious groups in the 1980s and the widely held perception that these activities differ in kind from earlier instances of church participation in politics have rekindled some apprehensions that Americans have long held. Religion by its very nature touches deep human emotions. If these emotions are introduced directly into political campaigns or legislative debates, some commentators ask, do we not risk the kind of murderous civil conflicts that throughout history have racked societies divided by religiously inspired ideals or prejudices? If a particular religious group through its political exertions wins a share in governmental power, will the United States be safe from repressive measures like those that triumphant religious establishments have frequently imposed? If the churches become deeply involved in politics, will not religion itself eventually be corrupted, as Baptists, among others, have always warned? On the other hand, if religion is virtually excluded from the "public square" and the political arena, as some secularists propose, will not civil life be morally and spiritually impoverished?[2]

Responses to these and related questions provide the bases for four distinguishable points of view. *Separationists* hold that churches should confine themselves to nurturing spiritual and moral values, leaving individual church members to apply these values to concrete public issues. *Social activists* agree that church and state should be kept institutionally separate, but argue that moral imperatives springing from the Judeo-Christian tradition, which provides the common religious heritage of most Americans, require that religious bodies work actively to promote virtuous causes in public life. *Accommodationists* insist that religion should maintain at least a symbolic presence in most areas of public life (like the frieze depicting the Ten Commandments above the Supreme Court dais) and that the church should help set the moral direction of civil society. *Direct interventionists* recommend that the church, or at least its leaders, should plunge into the deals and stratagems of practical politics, winning for the church and its constituents a share of the benefits that issue from public power. (It should not be assumed, as some of their critics do, that the direct interventionists seek power for its own sake or for personal material betterment. The motives of the interventionists may be largely altruistic or moral—based on the observation that if the virtuous abstain from taking steps that lead to tangible political power, the wicked or the foolish may set the course for government.)

On the key questions of separation between church and state and the role of religious institutions in politics, the attitudes represented by these four general points of view may be identified as follows:

	Separation between church and state	*Role of churches in politics*
Separationists	Strict	Small
Social activists	Strict	Large
Accommodationists	Moderate	Moderate
Interventionists	Moderate	Large

Different groups have been drawn to these varying points of view at different times. In the 1980s the separationist position has been expressed by some religious and secular liberals and by a remnant of traditional Baptists. The social activist approach commands the allegiance of much of the leadership of the so-called mainline Protestant denominations (Methodists, Presbyterians, Episcopalians, and some Lutherans, among others) and of some Catholics and most Jews (though Jewish participation in politics is largely carried out through Jewish service agencies rather than through specifically religious bodies). The accommodationist view retains popularity with more traditional Catholics and some conservative mainline Protestants. And direct intervention has many supporters, at the opposite ends of the political spectrum, among the leaders of black Protestant churches and among a growing share of white fundamentalist and evangelical clergy.

These questions and conflicting positions together lead to a recurring and crucial issue of American democracy: What should be the role of religion in public life? Clarification and elucidation of this issue, with a view to working out practical strategies, form the objective of this book.

A Common Source

Religion and politics have both played major roles in human experience from a very early time, the first giving the individual an explanation of his relationship to the totality of existence and a means of transcending his apparently inexorable mortal fate, the second providing techniques and institutions for managing the social units through which humans have always sought material security and emotional satisfaction. The two have usually been closely intertwined. In order to understand how religion and politics relate to each other, it is first necessary to find a common cultural denominator in which both are rooted. This common source, to which chapter 2 devotes some preliminary investigation, lies in the body of human values that motivate and shape all of humanity's religious encounters and political enterprises.

Human values can usefully be analyzed through a theoretic structure of seven value systems around which are organized the drives, hopes, goals, and moral principles that motivate particular individuals and social groups. Four of these systems rely in one way or another on religion: monism, rejecting the apparent world of material reality in favor of a totally spiritualized view of existence; idealism, identifying the goals of the social group, dominant or repressed, with transcendent will; personalism, pursuing transcendence through individual experience; and theist-humanism, discovering transcendent significance in the related experiences of the individual and the group. The other three value systems require no reference to transcendent reality: egoism, reducing all value to the drives and appetites of individual human beings; authoritarianism, basing value entirely on the welfare of the social group; and civil humanism, attempting to balance the rights of the individual against the needs of the group without relating either to transcendent moral law.

A critical question for all modern democracies is whether the three secular value systems, either separately or in some combination, can provide sufficient moral basis to maintain the cohesion and vitality of a free society. If the answer to this question is no, as most of the American founders, including George Washington, John Adams, and much of the time even Thomas Jefferson, argued, then the four value systems based in one way or another on religion must be scrutinized to determine how transcendent moral authority or inspiration can be maintained in a democratic society while minimizing the risks of bigotry, fanaticism, irresponsibility, and obscurantism that some tendencies within religion have all too often fostered.

Monism, based on a completely spiritualized outlook on existence, has never had much cultural impact in the United States (despite brief vogues at various times, such as during the late 1960s, for monistically inclined religions). But the other six value systems have all exerted significant influence and continue to generate attractions of varying intensities within contemporary American society. Theist-humanism, conveyed by the Judeo-Christian tradition, has formed the mainstream of American culture for most ordinary citizens. Tendencies growing out of idealism and personalism, both of which will be defined more fully in the next chapter, have at times effectively rivaled theist-humanism within the religious community, sending shocks through the larger society. Secular egoism has been associated with economic individualism and is aggressively promoted in contemporary American life by themes exalting self-gratification in mass advertising, psychological therapy, and popular entertainment. Secular authoritarianism exerts more influence than is generally recognized within dominant economic structures, both management and union, and has found proponents on the extremes of both the political right and left. Secular civil humanism, though regarded with deep suspicion by the general public, has a distinguished line of advocates stretching back at least to the Enlightenment, and since the 1950s it has provided the basis for what has become almost an established ideology among intellectual and cultural elites.[3]

The contending value systems give shape and direction to religious and political institutions. Current relationships between these institutions are derived in considerable part from trends and constitutional arrangements that developed during the formative years of the American Republic, examined in chapter 3. Puritanism was the strongest cultural force in most of the British colonies in North America during the seventeenth and early eighteenth centuries. By the time of the Revolution, however, the Puritan "way" had been joined by influences stemming from the Great Awakening of the 1730s, the Enlightenment, and several variants of traditional Christianity, including a growing representation of the mighty edifice of Roman Catholicism. This mixture led in time to the religious clauses of the Bill of Rights, which protected free expression of religious values while setting in motion an almost unprecedented experiment in religious and cultural pluralism.

The issue of religion in American public life includes much more than the constitutional relationship between church and state. But the constitutional framework does provide the legal structure within which the larger interaction between religion and civil interests takes place. Chapter 4 studies the evolution of judicial interpretations of the free exercise and establishment clauses. Before the 1940s the Supreme Court rarely took stands on church-state issues. But beginning with the *Cantwell* decision in 1940, which upheld the right of a member of Jehovah's Witnesses to proselytize within a predominantly Catholic neighborhood, even at the risk of provoking public disorder, the Court has gradually defined a broad right to free exercise of religion. Under some circumstances, such as those the Court has held justify the exemption of Amish children from public education beyond the eighth grade, this right even takes precedence over uniform application of civil law. With the *McCollum* decision of 1948, which declared unconstitutional the practice of allowing churches to provide religious instruction during periods of "released time" in the public schools, the Court began applying the establishment clause to eliminate many of the traditional means through which government in the United States has accommodated or acknowledged religion. More recently the Court has seemed to swing back toward an accommodationist position but has stopped far short of a return to earlier practices.[4]

There is nothing in the Bill of Rights to prevent churches from playing an active part in politics (though the courts have held that tax exemptions granted to religious bodies justify limitations on their direct involvement in election campaigns or legislative lobbying). Some denominations, such as the Baptists and the Lutherans, have generally given secular politics a wide berth. But others, especially Methodists, Presbyterians, Congregationalists, Episcopalians, Quakers, and Jews, have vigorously backed such diverse social causes as abolition of slavery, prohibition of the sale of liquor, defense of the gold standard, enactment of women's suffrage, and civil rights for blacks. Up to the First World War the Catholic church pursued its particular interests, such as state aid to parochial schools, but usually avoided taking public positions on broader political issues. In the 1920s the newly organized National Catholic Welfare Council began issuing pronouncements on domestic economic and social questions but still gave little attention to foreign policy. Chapter 5 traces the history of church involvement in politics from the division between evangelicals and socially conservative denominations in the early years of the Republic to the start of the civil rights struggle and the election of John Kennedy as the first Catholic president in 1960.

Since the 1960s most religious denominations have experienced considerable internal ferment, and many have changed their orientations toward public life and their political alignments. The leaderships of most major mainline Protestant denominations, which have formed the core of the Republican party in the North since the Civil War, have moved far to the left on the political spectrum, though survey evidence shows that mainline laities remain moderately conservative in their political views and electoral behavior. Mainline denominations now maintain public policy offices in Washington that lobby determinedly for a wide variety of liberal causes. The Catholic church, led by its increasingly activist bishops, has displayed a growing inclination toward political involvement since the Second Vatican Council in the 1960s. Catholic bishops join political conservatives in their fierce opposition to legalized abortion, while aligning themselves with liberals on issues like nuclear disarmament and expansion of the welfare state. Jews, predominantly liberal and Democratic since the 1930s, have manifested rising dissatisfaction with some of the directions of contemporary liberalism on issues ranging from Middle Eastern politics to affirmative action. Even the leaders of the black Protestant churches, which historically have been major sources of political organization and direction for the black community, have begun to reassess the wisdom of the black community's almost monolithic loyalty to the Democratic party. Most strikingly of all, white evangelical Protestants, who used to be relatively passive politically and were predominantly Democratic to the extent they were active, have switched to political militance and overwhelming support for Ronald Reagan and other conservative Republicans. Chapter 6 examines these changes and their implications for the future influence of the churches on government policy and electoral politics.

The basic question underlying the involvement of religion in American public life remains whether a free society depends ultimately on religious values for cohesion and vindication of human rights. Chapter 7 confronts this question directly, testing the adequacy of the value systems set forth in chapter 2, and then considers some practical and philosophic questions affecting the churches' future participation in the formation of public policy.

The narrative portions of this book deal mainly with the experiences of the mainline Protestant denominations, making up about 30 percent of the total population; the Roman Catholic church, about 25 percent; the white evangelical Protestant churches, about 20 percent; the black Protestant churches, about 8 percent; and the Jews, about 3 percent. Other significant religious groups, such as the Mormons, the Orthodox Christians, the Christian Scientists, the Adventists, and the Black Muslims, are discussed only in passing or in connection with constitutional questions that some of them have raised. More examination of these groups would obviously have produced a more comprehensive picture. The five major groups, however, include all but about 5 percent of the 91 percent of Americans who identify with some religious faith. Because my objective has been to study fundamental issues rather than to construct an inclusive record, I feel reasonably content that the examples offered provide representative instances of the role of religion in American public life.

———————◆———————

TWO

Religion, Politics,
and Human Values

THE CHIEF THING that religion and politics have in common is that both are concerned with the pursuit of values—personal, social, or transcendent. To understand how they relate to each other, therefore, it will be useful to begin with some analysis of the concept of value and examples of how values have shaped actual religious and political institutions in some of the cultures in which modern American society is most directly rooted.

By value I mean more than a simple interest, attraction, or prizing—like a taste for chocolate ice cream or a preference for baseball instead of ice hockey. A value, as I am using the term, includes a component of obligation or entitlement as well as a component of interest. It involves, that is, an "ought" as well as an "is." To say that I value a person or a thing or a form of behavior means that the object of my regard has a claim on me beyond my simply wanting it, or that some quality in my interest demands respect by others—perhaps by the universe. Value, in other words, represents moral authority as well as intellectual interest or physical appetite.

Human values in this sense may be derived from three sources: the individual self; the social group, including entire societies and social subdivisions such as families or communities; and transcendent purpose, shaping or directing the natural world that we know through the senses. These sources may be expressed schematically as:

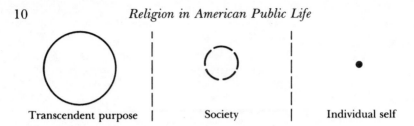

Transcendent purpose | Society | Individual self

It can be shown, I believe, that these three levels are the only plausible primary sources for human values. But because such a demonstration requires considerable space and argument and because my main justification for employing this scheme of classification in this study is its analytic utility, I will proceed directly to a description of the value systems through which transcendence, society, and the self may affect experience.

A Typology of Value Systems

The proposed sources of value may function in actual societies either singly or in combinations of two or three. Some religious philosophies hold that transcendent being, rightly conceived, totally submerges the reality and therefore the moral autonomy of the individual self or society. Some secularists maintain that the self is necessarily the entry point into experience for any particular consciousness and therefore the ultimate source of value for that consciousness. Because it exists, the self, they argue, has a right to exist and enjoys corollary rights to make the terms of its existence as agreeable as is practically possible. Other secularists claim that the true source of all human value is the social group: the tribe, the nation, the class, or the race. Many theorists hold, explicitly or implicitly, that two of the sources or all three together are needed for a full account of value. Each of these views provides the basis for a distinct value system.

The three primary sources, separately or in combination, can form seven possible value systems:

—*Egoism,* based on the individual self alone.
—*Authoritarianism,* based on society alone.
—*Monism,* based on transcendence alone.
—*Idealism,* based on transcendence and society in combination.
—*Personalism,* based on transcendence and the self in combination.

—*Civil humanism,* based on the self and society in combination.
—*Theist-humanism,* based on all three sources: transcendence, the self, and society.

The four value systems that are based in one way or another on transcendent being represent differing tendencies within religion. The three value systems that exclude transcendence are varieties of secularism.

Four additional categories, covering two or more of the value systems, help illuminate the subject of value:

—The two value systems, egoism and personalism, that include the self as a source but exclude society represent types of *individualism.*

—The two value systems, authoritarianism and idealism, that include society but exclude the self represent *collectivism.*

—A tendency within the two kinds of humanism reaching over into egoism expresses *libertarianism.*

—And a tendency within the two kinds of humanism reaching over into authoritarianism embodies *communitarianism.*

The entire typology of value systems is schematically represented in figure 1.

The seven value systems express abstract models that are to be found in no actual societies in pure form. But the ways in which they are brought together go a long way toward determining the kinds of values actual societies serve. To oversimplify at this point, a society that gives an important place to self-interest will tend to emphasize such values as personal freedom, individual initiative, and gratification of the senses. A society that is more devoted to group interests will stress cooperation, discipline, obedience, continuity, and social order. And a society that is most concerned with transcendent purpose will attach particular value to piety, reverence, humility (at least before God), and loving relationships (at least among those who are chosen to carry out the will of God).

Scholars have devoted a great deal of time and effort to discovering how value systems (not necessarily identified as I have defined them) are formed: whether through the influences of religion, or natural environment, or economic competition, or changes in technology, or military encounters, or sexual rivalry. Relatively little attention has been given to the value systems themselves. But these systems, however they are formed, are the factors that most immediately affect rela-

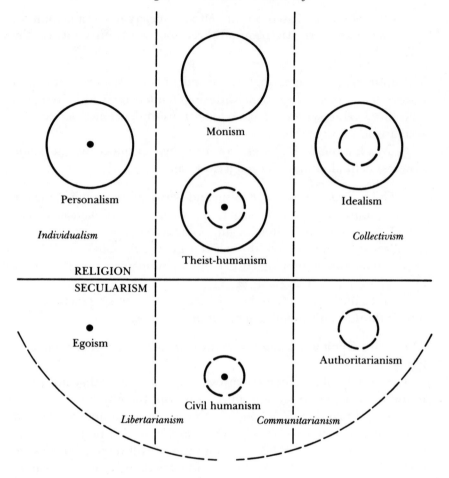

Figure 1. *A Typology of Value Systems*

tionships among social institutions, of which church and state along
with the family are probably the most important, and the characteristics
of each deserve careful examination.[1]

Egoism

The value system that rises most directly from genetically inherited
human nature is egoism. This is not to say that human nature does

not include capacities for sympathy, affection, and even altruism that make social relationships pleasurable, indeed possible. But at least beyond the levels of the family and the primitive hunter group—and some social scientists claim even for these—society is an invention of human intelligence. It evolved to meet needs, including emotional needs for human companionship. The sense of the self, in contrast, is nature's gift—her richest as well as her most dangerous gift—to the human species.

This sense of self is unique. Human nature differs from all other forms of life, not primarily because of such secondary characteristics as the capacity to create language or the ability to manufacture tools but because humans have developed far beyond any other creatures, including other advanced primates, a faculty for holding in consciousness an image of self as distinct from all other beings. Through use of this image of the self as a fulcrum or point of reference, a human is partially freed of dependence on instinct and through pragmatic reason can plot an individual course in the struggle for existence.[2]

Consciousness of self confers incalculable benefits, but it imposes heavy burdens as well. The first of these is a certain fractiousness in social relationships. Human beings seem to be motivated by varying mixtures of natural selfishness and altruism. Desire for personal gratification and innate combativeness are to some extent offset by spontaneous sympathy, a capacity for placing oneself in others' shoes, and instinctual affection. But even the most altruistic individual must recognize a frequent distinction between what he wants and what others want. This awareness of competing interests, which goes beyond instinctual desire, introduces into human affairs an element of tension—generally resolvable, sometimes creative, but a constant source for potential social division and discord.

Second, and even more important, recognition of self-interest must carry with it the realization that over any considerable period of time this interest cannot possibly be fulfilled. For every human life (and for all other life, too, but without the sting of foreknowledge), death must come. During the course of life there will be experiences of frustration, disappointment, and loss of much that is most cherished. Seen purely from a physical perspective, every human life is inherently tragic. "The short space of threescore years," Alexis de Tocqueville wrote, "can never content the imagination of man; nor can the imperfect joys of this world satisfy his heart. Man alone, of all created beings, displays a natural contempt of existence, and yet a boundless desire to exist; he scorns life, but he dreads annihilation."[3] On the basis of physical evidence alone, even the most fortunate of humans must at times find substance in Theodore Dreiser's conclusion that "life is nothing but a God-damned stinking game."

The impact of the human condition on consciousness may produce a variety of reactions: from despair to humanist attempts at adjustment to adoption of otherworldly religion. But the first and most instinctive response appears to be magnification of self-interest as an end in itself—the original sin posited by the authors of the Jewish and Christian religions. "The imagination of man's heart," God told Noah, "is evil from his youth."[4] The consequences of this inclination to pursue selfish ends have provided a theme for observers of human nature throughout history. Ptah-hotep, the first writer whom we know by name, warned in Egypt around 2600 B.C. that "to throw obstacles in the way of the law is to open the way before violence." Hsun-Tze, who lived in China during the third century B.C., wrote, "It thus appears that to follow man's nature and yield obedience to its feelings will assuredly conduct to contentions and robberies, to the violations of the duties belonging to each man's lot, and the confounding of all distinctions, till the issue be a state of savagism. . . ."[5]

Man's relentless fixation on self, Reinhold Niebuhr argued, is the result of "unwillingness to acknowledge his dependence, to accept his finiteness, and to admit his insecurity." Even so optimistic a social theorist as Erich Fromm concedes, "What all people have in common is that they are insatiable and hence never satisfied."[6] To the extent that this tendency toward egoism is rooted in awareness of the human predicament, it springs not from some reptilian remnant within the brain but from the most highly developed level of the neocortex.

Egoism may be relatively passive, prizing self-gratification to the exclusion of other values, or active, motivating self-aggrandizement.

Public moralists in all societies, speaking on behalf of one or another of the competing value systems, have regularly condemned concentration on self-gratification as an end in itself. From earliest times, however, it has attracted champions among writers and other artists (members of hangers-on of privileged elites, no doubt, but almost surely expressing sentiments widely felt). Uninhibited self-gratification was praised by an Egyptian poet around 2200 B.C.: "Celebrate the glad day; be not weary therein. Lo, no man taketh his goods with him; Yea, none returneth again that is gone thither." And by the *Epic of Gilgamesh,* composed in Babylonia before 1000 B.C.:

> When the gods created men,
> upon men did they also impose death. . . .
> Thou, O Gilgamesh, gratify thy flesh;
> Enjoy thyself by day and night;
> Make a feast of joy every day;
> Day and night be wanton and happy.

And by Semonides of Amorgos, around 650 B.C.: "Mortal men have only a short space to be young and to live. But do you learn, and, thinking of the end of life, give yourself some pleasure." And, more passionately, by Euripides:

> When shall I dance once more
> with bare feet the all-night dances,
> tossing my head for joy
> in the damp air, in the dew. . . .[7]

In the modern age, some social philosophers have presented pursuit of self-gratification as the true vocation of humankind. Liberation of the authentic self, to be sure, some proponents of this view have held, requires the overthrow of a false self imposed by a corrupting society. In one version of this argument, man's natural generosity and amiability are said to have been twisted and turned vicious by the effects of social repression. "It is not until relatively late," Wilhelm Reich wrote, "with the establishment of an authoritarian patriarchy, and the beginning of the division of classes, that suppression of sexuality begins to make its appearance. It is at this stage that sexual interests in general begin to enter the service of a minority's interest in material profit; in the patriarchal marriage and family this state of affairs assumes a solid organizational form." Removal of repression, Reich claimed, would bring an end to human conflict, because the "man who attains genital satisfaction is honorable, responsible, grave, and controlled, without making much of a fuss about it." (But where did that "minority's interest in material profit" come from?)[8]

Another version, enthusiastically promoted by some of the social rebels of the late 1960s and early 1970s, maintains that modern technology provides the means for overcoming barriers of scarcity that formerly made competition for limited supplies virtually inevitable. Ernest Mandel, for instance, predicted that "for the first time since man's appearance on earth, the insecurity and instability of material existence will vanish." Charles Reich rejoiced that "Machines can produce enough food and shelter for all," removing economic causes for social conflict.[9] Under such circumstances, Herbert Marcuse judged that intensifying self-gratification will become the only reasonable human concern. "Eros redefines reason in his own terms. Reasonable is what sustains the order of gratification."[10]

Worries about the limits to economic growth and depletion of the earth's natural resources have more recently clouded this optimistic picture. But these concerns, some continue to argue, can be dealt with through social controls that eliminate wasteful consumption. Marcuse, after all, conceded that "many would have to give up manipulated comforts if all were to live a human life."[11]

Pursuit of self-gratification has been a popular source of value, as the above quotations suggest, for some protagonists of the modern political left—the party of equalitarian change. The concept of equality, indeed, assumes some form of individualism because if each individual were not independently valued, there would be no rational or moral justification for regarding or treating as equals persons who are differently endowed. Most segments of the modern left call for at least a transitional stage during which social controls will be more stringent, not less. But much of the emotional appeal of the left— distinct from its practice where it has taken power—is derived from its legitimation of self-gratification, both in the long-run future for humankind as a whole and in short-run personal relationships. As Jerry Rubin put it, the liberated man "can do what he wants whenever he wants to do it."[12]

Adoption of egoism as a conceptual basis for organizing values, however, has by no means been limited to the left. Since the time of Adam Smith, egoism has also been pressed into service by the political right—the party of established order—despite the right's traditional attachment to values like discipline and social continuity. The right has emphasized the active egoism of self-aggrandizement over the passive egoism of self-gratification.

Adam Smith argued that by pursuing his own interest the individual "frequently promotes that of society more effectually than when he really intends to promote it." The entrenched right of eighteenth century European society, founded on class privilege and obedience to established authority, at first resisted Smith's proposal for unleashing individuals, regardless of class, to pursue their own economic interests. But more farsighted political conservatives in England and the United States, like the younger William Pitt and Alexander Hamilton, quickly grasped that a free-market policy would both promote economic growth and provide an ideological justification for private accumulations of wealth. Moreover, by becoming the party of freedom as well as the party of order, conservatives acquired a public stance that has enabled them to compete effectively in modern democracies with parties of the left campaigning under the banner of liberty and equality.

Early advocates of the market system, at least in northern Europe and the United States, usually sought additional legitimation for capitalism through the claim that it contributes to the good of society, as Adam Smith himself argued, or through the concept of stewardship, under which economic success is valued not primarily for its own sake but as an instrument of benevolence, as in John Wesley's famous exhortation to Christians to "gain all you can, save all you can, give all you can."[13]

In more recent times, libertarian theorists like Milton Friedman and Robert Nozick, pursuing a line of argument originated in the seventeenth century by Thomas Hobbes (though Hobbes followed it to different conclusions), have made the case for the market system on the basis of egoism alone. "To the free man," Friedman maintains, "the country is the collection of individuals who compose it, not something over and above it." As a consequence, he insists, the individual should recognize "no national purpose except as it is the consensus of the purposes for which the citizens severally strive." The business corporation, representing a coalition of individual interests, has "one and only one social responsibility—to use its resources and engage in activities designed to increase its profits so long as it stays within the rules of the game." The rules of the game, Friedman makes clear, are the terms of a contract entered into by individuals to advance their separate self-interests.[14]

Some contemporary proponents of capitalism, following the older traditions of Smith or Wesley, still reach beyond egoism for moral legitimacy. George Gilder, for example, seems to suggest that what free-enterprise capitalism mainly unleashes is a religiously inspired spirit of benevolence. "The reason capitalism succeeds is that its laws accord with the laws of the mind. It is capable of fulfilling human needs because it is founded on giving, which depends on sensitivity to the needs of others. . . ." The rigors of economic competition, Gilder claims, "elicit creativity and impel resort to a saving Transcendence." Michael Novak goes so far as to find in the operations of modern business corporations "metaphors for grace, a kind of insight into God's ways in history."[15]

The resort of both glorifiers of private sensuality like Marcuse and defenders of market capitalism like Gilder and Novak to appeals that go beyond egoism indicates their awareness that most human beings insist on acknowledging the authority of values that are not readily reducible to self-interest. To understand the hold and power of these nonegoistic values, we must turn to the other six value systems.

Authoritarianism

While the potentiality for self-awareness is the essential quality of humanness, entrance into full-fledged humanity comes through participation in the social group.

The human species appears to be naturally social in that its members "show definite preference, if not a need, for living in company"; but this preference does not, as with baboons or chimpanzees, carry with it instinctual commitment to a particular kind of social structure. "There is no evidence," Peter Wilson writes, "in any facet of human behavior that biologically determined activities directly produce culture—only that they provide the necessary conditions."[16]

To survive, primitive societies found it necessary to organize their values around a model that ruthlessly suppressed the natural human inclination to pursue self-interest. Jacquetta Hawkes notes that "the last word in any account of early forms of society must be to insist on the subservience of the individual to his tribe. . . . Indeed, the ideal of the free-standing human being was hardly formulated before the Greeks, hardly fulfilled before the Renaissance; for these people it was remote from all experience." Joseph Campbell agrees: "Archaic man was not man at all, in the modern, individualistic sense of the term, but the incarnation of a socially determined archetype."[17]

The program of social indoctrination through which the individual was subordinated to the group was based on the value system I have called authoritarianism. Within the primitive social band, acceptance of authoritarianism was made to seem almost instinctual. Primitive peoples, Jacquetta Hawkes writes, "thought, felt, and acted as members of a group, and in this they were daily confirmed by dancing, initiation, and all other rites that held them in bodily and psychic unison." The Shoshone Indians, who achieved only the simplest level of social organization, were, according to Peter Farb, "circumscribed by customs, rules of behavior, and rituals that in comparison make the Court of Versailles or the Kremlin appear unusually permissive."[18]

As social organization became more complex, particularly after the formation of chiefdoms and kingdoms through military conquest in Egypt and Mesopotamia during the fourth millennium B.C., individual self-interest must have begun to poke its way through the web of authoritarianism, which now disproportionately served the interests of those holding social power. "The gentle man perishes, the bold-faced goes everywhere," laments the writer of a scroll in the Egyptian Middle Kingdom. Expressions of praise for a particularly benevolent ruler give insight into what must have been widely held feelings of resentment among the populace under more usual conditions. "During seven years," according to the inscription on a monument to King Gudea of Lagash, who ruled in Mesopotamia around 2600 B.C., "the maidservant was the equal of her mistress, the slave walked beside his master, and in my town the weak rested by the side of the strong."[19]

Erosion of unquestioning deference to social authority could have several results. One was the development of more sophisticated forms of authoritarianism. Lycurgus, who reformed the government of Sparta in the ninth century B.C., aimed, according to Plutarch, "to make the citizens accustomed to have neither the will nor the ability to lead a private life; but, like the bees, always to be organic parts of their community, to cling together around the leader, and, in an ecstasy of enthusiasm and selfless ambition, to belong wholly to their country." In China three centuries later, Confucius laid the basis for a more subtle and perhaps for that reason far more enduring version of authoritarianism. "The relation between superiors and inferiors," he is reported to have said, "is like that between the wind and the grass. The grass must bend, when the wind blows across it." For the Confucian system, patriarchal rule is the root of social authority: "There is a fundamental agreement between a loyal subject in his service of his ruler and a filial son in his service of his parent."[20]

Authoritarianism has often been associated with religion. Among primitive bands and tribes, religion represented in part worship of the group. As religion became more complex, it conceptualized transcendence in more universal or spiritual terms, and simple authoritarianism had to share social dominance with the value system I will be describing as idealism. Authoritarianism that makes the social group itself the primary source of human value is probably, however, older than religious idealism and may outlive it.

For the West, the Enlightenment of the eighteenth century, which sought emancipation of the human spirit, undermined the prestige of religion and paradoxically gave new life to simple or secular authoritarianism. (In the previous century Hobbes had argued for a form of operational authoritarianism on secular grounds. His ultimate source of value, however, was the individual, whose interests are best served, he believed, by submission to a state with virtually authoritarian powers.) During the French Revolution, Gracchus Babeuf foresaw a left-wing authoritarianism that would "seize upon the new-born individual, watch over his early moments, guarantee the milk and care of his mother, and bring him to the *maison nationale* where he will acquire the virtue and enlightenment of a true citizen."[21]

During the nineteenth century the "soft" left calling for personal liberation was increasingly superseded by a "hard" left promoting authoritarian dictatorship aimed at serving the interest of humanity as a collective species. Karl Marx retained some commitment to humanist values. In the communist society of the future, he wrote, "where nobody has one exclusive sphere of activity but each can become accomplished in any branch he wishes, society regulates the general production and thus makes it possible for me to do one thing today and another tomorrow, to hunt in the morning, fish in the afternoon, rear cattle in the evening, criticize after dinner, just as I have a mind, without becoming hunter, fisher, shepherd, or critic."[22]

Before this euphoric state of affairs could be achieved, however, Marx believed it would be necessary to pass through "a political transition period in which the state can be nothing but the revolutionary dictatorship of the proletariat." Or as he and Friedrich Engels said in the *Communist Manifesto,* "The proletariat will use its political supremacy to wrest, by degrees, all capital from the bourgeoisie, to centralize all instruments of production in the hands of the State, i.e., of the proletariat organized as the ruling class."[23]

The seeming paradox of moving toward liberation through dictatorship was made more acceptable for Marx by his belief that essential human nature lies not in individuality but in participation in *species-being*. "The perfected political state," he wrote, "is, by its nature, the *species-life* of man. . . . Human emancipation will only be complete when the real, individual man has absorbed into himself the abstract citizen; when as an individual man, in his everyday life, in his work, and in his relationships, he has become a *species-being*."[24]

Under Lenin, the Communist party replaced the proletariat as the principal surrogate for species-being. Under Stalin and his successors, the party was converted into an authoritarian structure concerned chiefly with its own survival and the traditional goals of Russian nationalism. "Equalitarianism," Stalin said, "has nothing in common with Marxian socialism."[25]

On the right, after the breakup of medieval Christendom in the sixteenth century, conservative authoritarians began gradually to elevate the nation-state to a position of dominance among the sources of social value. This tendency received encouragement in the nineteenth century from the philosophy of Hegel—although, as Jacques Maritan pointed out, "The modern States were Hegelian in practice long before Hegel and his theory."[26] In the twentieth century, right-wing nationalist authoritarianism led to the collectivist frenzies promoted by fascism and national socialism. "He who speaks of a mission of the German people on this earth," Adolph Hitler wrote in *Mein Kampf*, "must know that it can exist only in the formation of a state which sees its highest task in the preservation and the promotion of the most noble elements of our nationality. . . ."[27]

Authoritarianism emphasizes such values as solidarity, cooperation, discipline, and order, without which human life would be much the poorer—indeed for practical purposes impossible. Some isolated individuals might survive for fairly extended periods in the manner of Robinson Crusoe, but lacking society, the human individual as an existential possibility would quickly disappear. Authoritarianism, however, opens the way to brutal political repression, of which Nazi Germany and the Soviet Union provide only two of the most horrendous examples. Ultimately, moreover, authoritarianism fails to meet the empirical test of experience. Human societies in some ways resemble biological organisms; but society is not finally organic in the sense that the human body, or even a beehive, is organic. To paraphrase Samuel Johnson, individual consciousness, through the

brute fact of its existence, refutes organic authoritarianism. Arguments
for pragmatic authoritarianism, such as those advanced by Hobbes,
cannot be so readily turned aside, but pragmatic authoritarianism, I
shall later maintain, is best understood as a variant of civil humanism.

Monism

Religion, a term coined by Cicero, has been variously defined by
modern theologians, psychologists, and sociologists. William James
viewed it as "the feelings, acts, and experiences of individual men in
their solitude, so far as they apprehend themselves to stand in relation
to whatever they consider divine." For Emile Durkheim, religion was
"a system of beliefs and values related to sacred things." For Max
Weber, "that which finally makes events meaningful." For Paul Tillich,
"whatever is of ultimate concern." Among contemporary writers,
Peter Berger has defined religion as "an aggregation of human
attitudes, beliefs, and actions in the face of two types of experience—
the experience of the supernatural and the experience of the sacred."
Louis Dupré has defined it "a commitment to the transcendent as to
another reality," Daniel Bell as "a set of coherent answers to the
universal existential problems of mankind."[28]

Some of these writers (Weber, Tillich, and Bell) define religion in
ways that do not necessarily require belief in anything beyond the
world we know through the senses—though they do not reject the
possibility of a supernatural level of existence. I will be using the
term in a narrower and more traditional sense. For the purposes of
this book *religion* means belief that the totality of existence includes
objective overall purpose or significance, beyond the "hurrying of
material, endlessly, meaninglessly," that Alfred North Whitehead
pointed out (following Hume and Kant) is all that can ever be
apprehended directly through pure reason or the senses.[29]

Religion of some kind has been with the human species for a very
long time—at least since our Neanderthal cousins began placing
articles in the graves of their dead, presumably for use in the afterlife.
The oldest discovered religious shrine, a stone idol found in northern
Spain in 1981, has been dated to about 12,000 B.C. (The features of
the idol appear to be half those of a smiling man and half those of a
snarling cat.)

Various origins have been suggested for primitive man's belief in the existence of a level of reality transcending his everyday experience. Among those more widely accepted are

—The tribe's need to legitimize and objectify its social authority.

—Encounters with the dead or fantastic images in dreams.

—Groping efforts to name or characterize aspects of man's natural environment—earth, sky, moon, stars, storm, sea, fire.

—Expression of socially repressed sexual drives or other instinctual urges (including, according to Freud, a deep-seated drive to self-destruction).

—Creation of spells to bewitch the object of the hunt. (According to Joseph Campbell, the principal quarry of each tribe's hunt always becomes its sacred totem.)

—Development of rituals to maintain crucial stages in the weather cycle.

—Hope that mortality is not after all the last word on human existence. ("Religion," Tocqueville wrote, "is simply another form of hope, and it is no less natural to the human heart than hope itself.")[30]

—Demand for magic to cure illnesses, attract lovers, and so forth.

—Awe at the majesty and mystery of the universe. ("What first fascinated man," Ernst Cassirer suggested, "were not the objects of his surroundings. Even the primitive mind was much more impressed by the great spectacle of nature as a whole.")[31]

—Intuitive experience of transcendent being. ("Man," William James wrote, "identifies his real being with the germinal higher part of himself. . . . He becomes conscious that this higher part is coterminous and continuous with a MORE of the same quality, which is operative in the universe outside of him, and which he can keep in working touch with, and in a fashion get on board of and save himself when all his lower being has gone to pieces in the wreck.")[32]

—Revelation by God of his presence to those who seek him. ("Ask, and it shall be given you; seek, and ye shall find; knock, and it shall be opened unto you.")[33]

These suggested origins for religion, it will be observed, perform one or another of two kinds of functions: serving practical social needs, such as buttressing political authority or assuring success at the hunt, or providing means to achieve personal spiritual security or fulfillment.

Two kinds of religious specialists, roughly associated with the two kinds of functions, developed in many primitive tribes. Priests were integrated into the tribal hierarchy and helped express the tribe's sense of itself as a collective whole. Shamans, often exotic wild men living on the fringe of the tribe, pursued their personal visions of the supernatural. Though priests helped fill spiritual needs and shamans sometimes performed practical functions (like preparing love potions), priests were generally more closely involved with the practical social aspects of religion and shamans with the more purely spiritual.[34]

The concept of transcendence embodied by most primitive religions did not go much beyond assigning supernatural causes or explanations to natural events, usually within the context of a mythology teeming with otherworldly spirits. The idea that a single transcendent purpose created and governs the whole of existence does not seem to have developed, or at least was not recorded, before Akhenaton, pharaoh of Egypt in the early years of the fourteenth century B.C. Akhenaton apparently had political motives for dislodging the power of the traditional priesthood administering Egypt's polytheistic religion, and he may also have been moved by personal emotions rising out of his relationship with his father, Amenhotep III. For whatever reason, he declared an end to polytheism and put in its place worship of the one, true god, whom he called Aton. "O sole god, whose power no other possesseth," Akhenaton wrote,

> Thou didst create the earth according to thy heart
> While thou wast alone. . . .
> How excellent are thy designs,
> O Lord of eternity. . . .[35]

Akhenaton failed. "The 'teaching of Pharaoh' had but small positive effect on his subjects," Leonard Woolley relates. "They saw the old temples defaced and closed, the state priesthood disestablished and an interdict laid upon the public services of the gods, but there was no one to teach them anything about the new religion, which a royal edict had brought into being; in itself the idea of a 'sole god' did not appeal to them, for they were accustomed to, and liked, gods in plenty; they were therefore driven back more than ever to the minor cults and superstitions which had always meant more to the humble classes of Egyptian society than did the formalized worship of the state."[36] Soon Akhenaton was overthrown; polytheism was restored by his son-in-law and successor, Tutankhamen; the traditional priesthood regained its privileges and power. But perhaps Akhenaton's ideas left some trace. About two centuries later, a young nobleman at the court of another pharaoh cast his lot with an enslaved people from the distant hills of Palestine who clung to worship of their single, all-powerful god, Yahweh.

The idea that the universe is ruled by a single transcendent force or mode of being has been regarded by many in all advanced cultures as the one conclusive solution to humankind's problems of existential loneliness and despair. But the concept raises several questions of its own. How does transcendent being relate to the world of material reality experienced in everyday life or to the world governed by physical laws described by science? If transcendence has a purpose, how can humans know of it? Do humans, either as individuals or as members of a social group, have any special part to play in carrying out transcendent being's plan for the universe?

One way of dealing with these questions is to conclude that *all* of reality is comprehended within transcendent being—that transcendence and the universe are, in effect, identical. This view of reality provides the ontological basis for the value system I have called monism.

If transcendent being is identical with the universe, in what sense is it then "transcendent"? What is left to transcend? How does a universe so conceived differ from the meaningless materialism which Whitehead attributed to natural science? The answer seems to be that identification of the whole of reality with transcendent being introduces a concept of extraphysical unity, producing a certain luminosity and even a sort of ultimate meaning absent from the world conceived by scientific materialism. (Some scientists, however, have been drawn to monism as the form of religion most compatible with natural science's operating assumptions. Robert Oppenheimer was moved to recite a passage from the *Bhagavad-Gita* at the time of the explosion of the first atomic bomb. A kind of psychedelic monism seems to rattle around in the ruminations of Carl Sagan.)

Monism has been a major theme in Eastern religion and philosophy at least since the formulation of what has been called the basic insight of oriental wisdom by the Indian sage, Aruni, around 800 B.C.: "tat tuam asi"—thou art that. Most oriental religions prescribe intellectual and physical exercises to reach unity with what the Upanishads, composed in India sometime before the sixth century B.C., describe as "the unseen Seer, the unheard Hearer, the unthought Thinker, the unknown Knower."

Around 528 B.C., Siddhartha Gautama, a young Indian prince who had subjected himself to all sorts of painful self-denials and ascetic disciplines in pursuit of spiritual enlightenment, concluded in a moment of illumination while sitting beneath the Bodhi tree that his victory, rightly conceived, was already won: "All existence whatever is unsubstantial." The fragmented appearance of reality is illusion. The only thing that truly exists is the immaterial whole. If this is so, no amount of asceticism will make it more or less so. It simply is. With this insight, Gautama became the Buddha.

Hinduism in India, Taoism in China, and the form of Buddhism itself most practiced in Korea and Japan have not usually gone quite so far as the Buddha advised in dismissing material reality. "I am the good sweet smell of the moistened earth," says the *Bhagavad-Gita,* the Hindu epic composed around the time of Jesus:

> I am the fire's red light,
> The vital air moving in all which moves,
> The holiness of hallowed souls, the root
> Undying, Whence hath sprung whatever is. . . .

In this passage, which seems representative of Hinduism to the extent that any particular attitude can be said to be representative of so broad and varied a religion, the creator is identified with the created more thoroughly than we would find in any form of Western theism, but earth, fire, air, and hallowed souls appear to enjoy some measure of distinct existence. The same acknowledgment of at least the reality of the illusion of material existence seems characteristic of Taoism and Mahayana Buddhism. Monism, nevertheless, if not usually in the pure form preached by the Buddha (of which the Buddha himself may have been the only perfect example), has profoundly affected the societies and cultures of the Orient.[37]

In the West, it has been much less influential. Monism has maintained a presence in Western philosophy since Parmenides contended in the fifth century B.C. that being "is universal, existing alone, immovable, and without end"; has sometimes provided themes for art and literature, as in Goethe's "everything transient is but a symbol"; has operated in the underground of religion; and has attracted, as has been noted, some modern scientists. But the busy, striving West, along both its Hebraic and Hellenic strains, has never been content for long with a view of existence that denies the reality of particular things. A saying attributed to the Buddha advises, "If one lives in the midst of company, love of amusement and desire arises; strong attachment for children arises; let therefore one who dislikes separation, which must happen sooner or later from those beloved, walk alone like a rhinoceros." This kind of superhuman detachment has not won significant moral support in Western cultures. The arguments for solitude and contemplation given by John Milton and Henry Thoreau, for example, are very different from those of Buddhism.[38]

Persons convinced of the unreality of worldly goals are not likely to bother much with society's material problems or needs. Although Hinduism and Buddhism have sometimes played active roles in the politics of the East, they have at such times, the experts agree, departed from their underlying natures. More usually, Ernst Troeltsch wrote, Buddhism "presents the opposition to politics in its most acute form." According to Robert Bellah, "In India we find perhaps the most radical of all versions of world rejection, culminating in the great image of Buddha, that the world is a burning house and that man's most urgent need is to escape from it."[39]

Monism exists as one pole toward which all religions are to some extent drawn. It no doubt has insights to impart that its more this-world-oriented competitors have tended to overlook. But to examine more active relationships between religion and public life, we must turn to the other value systems that seek direction from transcendent being.

Idealism

Metaphysical dualism, meaning belief in distinct material and transcendent levels of existence, has been a defining characteristic of all major religious traditions with roots in western Asia, including Judaism, Christianity, and Islam. In recent years Christian dialecticians at all points on the ideological spectrum—from exponents of radical liberation theology in Latin America to advocates of the new religious right in the United States—have found it expedient to hold the corrupting influence of "platonic dualism" responsible for many of the troubles afflicting contemporary Christianity. It is true that the older Hebraic tradition maintained a less rigid distinction between mind and matter, ideas and things, than that associated with Plato and the Hellenistic Platonists. But *all* religions and philosophies that trace existence to a transcendent origin and distinguish between the creator and his creation—which certainly includes Judaism and its offshoots—are, properly speaking, dualistic.

Within the framework established by transcendent being and everyday material reality there are only three possibilities: only transcendent being exists, as is held by the tradition of monism; only natural reality exists, as is held by secular egoists, authoritarians, and humanists; or transcendent being and natural reality somehow exist simultaneously. The third position was chosen not only by Plato and his followers but also by all of the principal figures whose teachings are conveyed by the Old and New Testaments. To the extent that modern churchmen dispute this choice, their quarrel is not so much with Plato or Plotinus as it is with Abraham, Moses, Isaiah, Jesus, and Paul.

To say that a religion is dualistic tells only that it rejects the total spiritualization of reality proposed by monism. Dualistic religions differ in their answers to the next important question: How does transcendent being relate to natural existence? There probably was always a spiritual and personal dimension to primitive religion, expressed mainly by the shaman. But the aspect of primitive religion of which we have most knowledge is, not surprisingly, that which was used by social authority to help carry out society's political, economic, and domestic functions. Many primitive religions, anthropologists claim, are not much more than exercises through which the tribe worships its collective being. "The paramount function of all myth and ritual" among primitive peoples, Joseph Campbell writes, is "to engage the individual, both emotionally and intellectually, in the local organization."[40]

When the goal of transcendent purpose is identified with the welfare of a particular social group (for instance, a nation, a church, or a race), the result is the value system I have called idealism. Idealism may be of two types: absolutist idealism, holding that the objectives of transcendent purpose are served through the established order of society, and utopian idealism, locating the will of transcendence in a model of the social future, often identified with a currently repressed group or class. Utopian idealism that wins social power tends naturally to turn into absolutist idealism.

The early Hebrew religion was based on a shifting mixture of absolutist and utopian idealism, emphasizing the transcendent significance of Jewish history. The promise made by God to Abraham was for the Hebrew nation rather than for individual Jews. Among the holy men of India, Campbell observes, "the proper place for a full experience of the ultimate reach of the mystery is the utter solitude of a Himalayan peak." But among the Hebrews "the participation of the individual in the destiny of the group is stressed to such a degree that for any valid act of public worship not less than ten males above the age of thirteen are required, and the whole reference of the ceremonial system is to the holy history of the tribe."[41] The Ten Commandments promulgated by Moses put the stamp of transcendence on an essentially conservative body of rules and obligations, from which we learn much about duties but almost nothing about rights.

In time Judaism moved toward a more humanistic conception of religion—in part to explain the recurrent suffering and humiliation of God's chosen people. But it retained a capacity for militance. "Blow ye the trumpet in Zion," ordered the prophet Joel, "and sound an alarm in my holy mountain: let all the inhabitants of the land tremble: for the day of the Lord cometh, for it is nigh at hand."[42]

During the fifth century B.C., political and economic strains shook the authoritarian social systems of the ancient world from the Italian peninsula to China. In some cases this opened the way for the first budding shoots of humanism and democracy. But in others it led to formulation of more richly conceived versions of idealism. From this latter track in Athens during the first half of the fourth century came the philosophy of Plato.

Plato's larger philosophy of being holds, as is well known, that material existence reflects a more fundamental reality composed of transcendent ideas. On this foundation, Plato built a social theory proposing that institutions should be shaped to conform to transcendent models. "In heaven," he wrote in *The Republic*, "perhaps, a pattern is laid up for the man who wants to see and found a city on the basis of what he sees. It doesn't make any difference whether it is or will be somewhere. For he would mind the things of this city alone, and of no other."[43]

The individual, Plato believed, has no significance or value except for the contribution he makes to transcendent purpose, reflected in the interest of society as an organic whole. "The supervisor of the universe," he wrote in *The Laws*, "has arranged everything with an eye to its preservation and excellence, and its individual parts play appropriate active or passive roles according to their various capacities. . . . You forget that creation is not for your benefit: *you* exist for the sake of the universe." The individual citizen, Plato prescribed, "must be brought to that which naturally suits him—one man, one job—so that each man practicing his own, which is one, will not become many but one; and thus, you see, the whole city will grow to be one and not many." All social classes have a role maintaining the ideal city, but political power should be monopolized by an intellectual elite who comprehend the interest of the social whole. "Unless the philosophers rule as kings or those now called kings and chiefs genuinely and adequately philosophize, and political power and philosophy coincide . . . there is not rest from ills for the cities . . . nor I think for human kind. . . ."[44]

Idealist tendencies derived from both Hebraic and Hellenic sources exerted significant influence on the early development of Christianity. The apostle Paul, while rejecting dogmatic legalism of the kind represented at Jerusalem by Jesus' brother, James, proposed the idea of an organic community rooted in the transcendent authority of Christ. "For as the body is one," Paul wrote to the church at Corinth, "and hath many members, and all the members of that one body, being many, are one body; so also is Christ. For by one spirit are we all baptized into one body, whether we be Jews or Gentiles, whether we be bond or free; and have been all made to drink into one Spirit."[45]

The human dimension of the community that Paul described was the body of Christian believers, not the state or society at large. He was anxious that the church maintain its internal integrity, which he believed required some separation from the pagan world in which it existed. "Be not conformed to this world," he warned. But the authority of the state, too, he concluded, was ultimately based on God's will, and should be obeyed within the area of its competence. "Let every soul be subject unto the higher powers," he wrote to the church at Rome. "For there is no power but of God: the powers that be are ordained of God. Whosoever resisteth the power, resisteth the ordinance of God: and they that resist shall receive to themselves damnation. For rules are not a terror to good works, but to evil." If church and state should disagree, which Paul realized might easily happen over the issue of monotheism, he hewed uncompromisingly to the directive of Jesus' disciple, Peter: "Obey God rather than men."[46]

Three centuries later, Augustine, the greatest of Christian philosophers, was confronted with the collapse of the Roman state on which Paul had relied to maintain social order. In the meantime a most important change had taken place: in A.D. 313 the emperor Constantine had ended the state's persecution of Christians, and in 383 Theodosius I had established Christianity as the official religion of the Roman Empire. Augustine's solution to the problem, spiritual as well as political and economic, posed by the fall of Rome was twofold. First, he made clear that the church had never expected that salvation would be achieved through actions by civil governments, which he likened to "great robberies." Second, he conceived the institution of the church as the embodiment of God's will on earth. The enduring achievement of Augustine—the base to which Thomas Aquinas as well as Martin Luther and John Calvin returned—was to define the sublime total authority of God's rule, come what may, over all that is. But by glorifying the role of the institutional church, Reinhold Niebuhr wrote, Augustine also began a tradition that encouraged some among his followers to embark on "the great heresy of identifying the church with the Kingdom of God, and of making unqualified claims of divinity for this human, historical, and relative institution."[47]

Augustine's two-part solution directed the church in the West during the Middle Ages along two somewhat divergent paths. (The Eastern church usually accepted direction from the Byzantine state on political matters.) The main institutional church, led by a dynamic papacy and guided by the formulations of scholastic philosophy, conceived the idea of a Christian civilization, based, as Ernst Troeltsch wrote, on the belief that "relative approximation of social institutions to the ideals of Christianity needed only the authority of the church and renewal of the vitality of religious principles." The monastic orders, in contrast, clung to the earlier ideal of a detached community of believers, bound by Paul's injunction to "conform not to this world." The two paths were not necessarily incompatible, but they represented differences in emphasis that were bound to produce tension. Both concepts were based in part on idealist values. The main institutional church assumed that the whole of society could be made to approximate a kind of Platonic ideal of community. The monastic orders aimed to create perfectly disciplined social bodies in which the interests of individual members would be submerged in the whole.[48]

The path taken by the main body of the church had the more direct bearing on secular public life. From the papacy of Innocent

II at the end of the twelfth century to that of Boniface VIII at the beginning of the fourteenth, the church vigorously pursued political power. Even at its most worldly and most militant, the medieval church retained concern for the welfare of the individual human soul, which Jesus had emphasized. But competition with authoritarian civil governments for social power naturally led the church to make its claims to political as well as spiritual authority increasingly comprehensive. "There is one holy catholic and apostolic Church, outside of which there is neither salvation nor remission of sins," proclaimed the bull *Unam Sanctam* issued by Boniface VIII in 1302. "We are told by the word of the gospel that in His fold there are two swords—a spiritual, namely, and a temporal. . . . Both swords, the spiritual and the material, therefore, are in the power of the Church; the one, indeed, to be wielded for the Church, the other by the Church. . . ." Even Thomas Aquinas, who believed that the church should play only a limited role in politics, agreed that "the believer accepts the whole deposit as proposed by the Church."[49]

From the eighth to the fifteenth centuries, Christendom was challenged almost continuously by societies built around the related religion of Islam. The faith based on the teachings of Mohammed includes, like Christianity, a complex constellation of value systems; but the influence of absolutist idealism in Islam has usually been stronger and more nearly paramount than in Christianity. The Koran makes militant loyalty to the faith the chief requisite for salvation: "Say not of those who are slain in fight for the religion of GOD, that they are dead; yea, they are living. . . . Whoso obeyeth GOD and his apostle, GOD shall lead him into gardens wherein rivers flow, they shall continue therein forever."[50]

Except for its first few years, Islam has usually been a state-supported religion. Probably for this reason, and perhaps also because of its stricter interpretation of monotheism, it did not develop a doctrine distinguishing church from state. In theory the political structure dictated by Islam has been theocracy. In practice it often has permitted authoritarian or simply corrupt politicians to use the faith to pursue secular ends.[51]

The tide of Islam had not greatly receded—indeed the last great surge that captured Constantinople in 1453 had only just occurred—when Western Christendom was riven by the Protestant Reformation. The Reformation was directed in part against repressive tendencies within medieval church, but also, and probably more profoundly, against the worldly humanism associated with the Renaissance. Reaching back to Augustine for inspiration, Luther and Calvin decried the willingness of the sixteenth century church to countenance pursuit of this-worldly pleasures and to encourage a doctrine of salvation through works. In so doing, the reformers unleashed a challenge to the church's authority that in time proved propitious to the growth of ideas valuing individual freedom. But Luther and Calvin were not themselves social libertarians or democrats.

Luther, with his doctrine of salvation through faith alone, believed that the most important reality for each human life is the relationship established between the individual soul and God. In keeping with this view, he regarded social concerns as secondary to spiritual imperatives. He did not, however, dismiss social issues as fundamentally insignificant, in the manner of the monists. Besides his spiritual existence, mortal man must also live in a corrupt social environment that is the result of original sin. To deal with this environment, civil government must be prepared to exercise coercive authority, which is both punishment for sin and protection against its material consequences. "The secular sword," Luther wrote, "must be red and sanguinary, for the world will and must be evil." His famous appeal to the German nobility to show no mercy in crushing the Peasants' Rebellion ("Strike, throttle, thrust") sprang from his conviction that civil society tends naturally to corruption and that very strong government therefore is needed to maintain minimum standards of livability while waiting for God's coming.[52]

Luther's conception of the role of civil society was not wholly negative. While good works in themselves do not lead to salvation, the individual who has been moved to salvation through faith will naturally be disposed to love and help his neighbors. "Faith does not ask whether good works ought to be done but does them before there is time to ask; faith is always found in action." Government provides a means for carrying out part of the moral obligations that proceed from faith. The state, as Karl Holl paraphrased Luther, is "bound to proceed in the direction of love, and therefore to eliminate inhuman, cruel, and irrational elements in existing law." Luther's doctrine of Christian vocation linked religious ideals to the practical needs of secular society. "If the activity of the state benefits Christianity, then true Christians not only may but must participate in it—whether as officials, judges, soldiers, or even hangmen."[53]

In practice, Luther's delegation of broad authority over temporal life to civil government contributed to the development of societies in some ways more authoritarian than idealist. But in the background, an idealist value system always hovered. "Lutheranism," Ernst Troeltsch wrote, "was based entirely upon the idea of an ecclesiastical civilization, forcibly dominated by religious ideas."[54] Bismarck, a true heir to the Lutheran tradition, gave high place in his scheme of values to the Prussian and German states, but always regarded the object of his policies as ultimately religious.

Calvin agreed with Luther—as well as with Augustine and Aquinas—on the central importance of spiritual experience to human life. But he went further than his fellow reformer in finding a potentiality for positive value in this-worldly pursuits. "While we are aspiring toward our true country," Calvin wrote, "we be pilgrims on earth, and if such aids [of civil government] are necessary to our pilgrimage, they who take them from man deprive him of his human nature." While Luther viewed temporal life as not much more than a moral sideshow to the real business of spiritual salvation, Calvin urged his followers to enter civil society to produce a "Holy Community." The distinction between spiritual and temporal realities, he argued, should not cause men "to consider the whole system of government as a polluted thing."[55]

Calvin's social philosophy was conservative in the sense that he believed in the need for strong government to counter the effects of original sin. "One country," he wrote, "if it did not inflict the most exemplary vengeance upon murderers, would soon by ruined by murders and robberies." But he did not value punishment for its own sake. "It behooves the magistrate to be on guard against both these errors—that he do not, by excessive severity, wound rather than heal, or, through a superstitious affectation of clemency, fall into a mistaken humanity, which is the worst kind of cruelty, by indulging a weak and ill-judged lenity to the detriment of multitudes."[56]

Calvin's concern for the integrity of the church led him to put more emphasis than Luther had on Peter's injunction to "obey God rather than men." Although he urged that even tyrannical governments should normally be endured, he drew the line at governments that tried to force citizens to violate basic moral laws established by God. "In the obedience we have shown to be due to the authority of governors, it is always necessary to make one exception, and that is entitled to our first attention—that it do not seduce us from obedience to him to whose will the desires of all kings ought to be subject, to whose decrees all their commands ought to yield, to whose majesty all their sceptres ought to submit."[57]

The response of the Catholic church to the Reformation was not only to move against the administrative corruption that had made Luther's criticism immediately plausible but also to turn away from the humanist innovations the church had begun to tolerate and even in some cases sponsor. The result was a church substantially cleansed, but at the same time locked more tightly to an absolutist scheme of social values. The Council of Trent, convened in 1546 to deal with the Lutheran challenge, approved a more rigorous formulation of the doctrine of the infallible authority of the church. Ignatius Loyola, who in 1534 founded the Jesuit order, decreed, "We ought always be ready to believe that what seems to us white is black if the hierarchical Church so defines it."[58]

Idealism thus entered the modern world under both Protestant and Catholic auspices. Since the Enlightenment, religious idealism has given ground, first under attack by several varieties of egoism and humanism, and more recently under repression by modern forms of authoritarianism. But it remains powerful—sometimes under surprising guises. For instance, Edmund Wilson argued that Marxist collectivism is the product of, among other things, Marx's substitution of the proletariat for the Hebrew nation as the chosen instrument of God's will.[59] Marxism is not a religion in the sense I am using the term, but part of its appeal undoubtedly comes, as Joseph Schumpeter and others have pointed out, from its capacity to persuade its followers that they are participating in a cause larger than themselves and related to the fundamental force that moves human history.

Idealism's claim to speak with the authority of transcendent purpose would seem to make it even more threatening than authoritarianism to individual rights or any concept of individual self-determination. So it has sometimes proven to be. Erich Przywaya, a modern Augustinian, has written, "The Dominican order had become, willy-nilly, the servants of the Inquisition, not on account of a sort of fanaticism (the great Dominicans were all men of childlike humility and even tender sensitiveness) but on account of utter abandonment of all individualism to the service of everlasting truth."[60]

By very reason of its dualism, however, religious idealism offers a potential for growth and change not usually achievable under a clearly dominant secular authoritarianism. When the church that speaks for transcendent ideals maintains a measure of independence, as it generally has in the West, social space is opened in which individual conscience and critical intelligence may find room to breathe and function. Frederick Watkins has identified the steady tension between the church and civil government in the Middle Ages as the key to the development of the West. "If dualism has its obvious costs, it also has its compensations. Out of the tensions of an almost impossible ethic, content neither to accept nor reject but striving to transform historic reality, Western man has found the energy to make great strides toward the conquest of his physical environment. Stimulated by the nearly hopeless task of achieving order within a dualistic society, he has created forms of government unique in their dynamic capacity to meet changing needs."[61]

Personalism

Idealism identifies God's purpose with the history of a social group. Its great opposite among value systems based on a dualistic metaphysic, which I call personalism, regards the direct relationship between the individual and transcendent being as the essence of human existence.

Idealism's discovery of transcendent purpose in history may seem more plausible than personalism's claim that the creator of the universe is accessible to each human consciousness. But for many, the spiritual returns from personalism are clearly more exhilarating—particularly when history bears discouraging results or when the larger society seems uncaring or repressive. The existence of shaman-type religious specialists in most primitive societies is evidence of a spiritual hunger that priest-administered official religions often did not satisfy.

Personalism, in the sense I am using the term, has a meaning somewhat similar to that of the religious term *mysticism*. But mysticism may include monism or even some kinds of idealism as well as personalism, and may imply a loss of self different from that to which personalism aspires. Personalism aims to triumph over the natural world and over mortality by opening consciousness to transcendence, but it does not, like monism, regard natural existence as essentially meaningless. "Life is real! life is earnest!" exulted Longfellow, "and the grave is not its goal."

The meaning of personalism is even closer to the term of aesthetic and cultural criticism, *romanticism*. Usually, however, romanticism is applied only to work produced in the West since the romantic revolution at the beginning of the nineteenth century. Through romanticism in the arts, personalism has combated not only formalist idealism but also the rising tide of rationalist humanism. "The artist," Friedrich Nietzsche wrote, "having unveiled the truth garment by garment, remains with his gaze fixed on what is still hidden. Theoretical man [in contrast] takes delight in the cast garments and finds his highest satisfaction in the unveiling process itself, which proves to him his own power. Science could not have developed as it has done if its sole concern had been that one naked goddess."[62]

Scorning worldly wisdom, personalism relies for guidance on feeling and intuition. St. Francis of Assisi in the thirteenth century told his followers, "God said that He wanted me to be a pauper and an idiot— a great fool—in this world, and would not lead us by any other path of science than this." Six centuries later, Soren Kierkegaard similarly concluded: "Faith begins precisely where thinking leaves off."[63] Personalism's intuitions may come from what is conventionally re- garded as the darker side of human nature. "The tigers of wrath," William Blake wrote, "are wiser than the horses of experience."

In both art and religion, personalism esteems two qualities above all others: immediacy and universality. It has no patience with formal exercises or contrivances that separate the individual spirit from transcendence or with the limitations of a particular culture. Person- alist artists from Sappho to Richard Wagner and James Joyce have sought to climb, to soar, to pull free of attachments to a particular time or place, to penetrate to the sublime without wasting effort or attention on the merely beautiful.

Personalism probably first became available to human consciousness through the ministrations of the shamans, as has been suggested. It acquired intellectual content in the Egyptian idea that each human soul will be judged individually at the final judgment. Among the ancient Hebrews, personalism provided an alternative value system through which Elijah and subsequent prophets challenged the idealist religious establishment (though some of the prophets moved toward the synthesis I will later describe as theist-humanism). During the century before Jesus, the world of the eastern Mediterranean teemed with mystery cults based on variants of personalism.

Within Christianity, personalism exercised important influence from the start. Jesus himself directed, "Be ye therefore perfect, even as your Father which is in heaven is perfect." In the early church the personalist tendency was championed by the gnostics, who according to H. Richard Niebuhr attempted "to interpret Christianity as a religion rather than as a church," and ended with "a mystery cult rather than a faith governing all life."[64] Gnosticism was defeated and almost effaced from history by proponents of what became Christianity's orthodox tradition, but it continued within the underground of European culture, passed through the centuries in garments of superstition and myth.

During the Middle Ages, while the main body of the church gravitated toward absolutist idealism, personalism was kept alive within orthodox Christianity by mystics like St. Francis. From time to time, dissident groups attracted by personalism rose in protest: Cathars in the eleventh century, Waldensians in the twelfth, John Wycliffe and the Lollards in the fourteenth. Finally, with the Reformation, personalism burst like a flood across Western society and culture.

The Reformation, as we have seen, had its idealist side, represented within both Lutheranism and Calvinism. But Luther's doctrine of salvation through faith, the theological root of the Reformation, leans profoundly toward personalism. Protestantism, above all, promised a direct relationship between the individual believer and God. "The new movement," Richard Niebuhr wrote, "was impatient not only with the system of mediators of divine rule and grace but also with the deferment of the fulfillment of life's promise. . . . Justification was *now* to be apprehended; assurance of salvation was *now* to be received; the rule of Christ was *now* to become effective."[65]

In Lutheranism and Calvinism, personalism was substantially modified by the influence of other value systems. But in the third great wing of the Reformation, pietism, which was to have particular effect in the future United States, personalism was paramount. Unlike Lutheranism or Calvinism, pietism was not launched by a single originating genius. It represented forces and ideas inherited from earlier movements like the Waldensians and the Lollards. Its emergence as a distinct branch of the Reformation is usually traced to the formation of the first Anabaptist congregation in Zurich in 1523.[66]

Ulrich Zwingli, who had brought the Reformation to Zurich, proposed that a liturgical dispute within the reformed church be settled by appeal to the city council. Simon Stumpf, speaking for a faction that emphasized direct experience of the Holy Spirit by the individual believer, replied, "Master Ulrich, you do not have the right to place the decision on this matter in the hands of my lords, for the decision has already been made, the Spirit of God decides." Those sharing Stumpf's view seceded and took the name Anabaptist.[67]

The Anabaptist designation was derived from the pietists' insistence that baptism should take place after a mature decision to accept Christ rather than as a sacrament performed in infancy. This change reflected the view that the earthly church is a voluntary association of believers rather than a supernaturally established union—a departure that would profoundly influence both the development of individualism in the United States and American constitutional theory on the proper relationship between church and state.

Pietism formed no single church but issued in a multiplicity of sects, ranging from the pacifist Mennonites and Quakers to the militant Levellers and Fifth Monarchy Men of seventeenth century England. All held in common the conviction, expressed by George Fox, founder of the Society of Friends, that they had been "sent to turn people from darkness to the light."[68]

In its purest form personalism would seem to require no necessary political or even social content. If all that really matters in human life is the individual's experience of personal salvation (or pursuit of aesthetic ecstasy or truth), the concerns of civil government and the marketplace may be regarded as essentially irrelevant. Some personalist prophets, artists, and seers have taken just this position.

Personalism understood in this way will of necessity have difficulty enduring through time. If the world is about to end (an idea often associated with personalism), the problem of passing the faith from one generation to the next need not arise. But if the world persists in continuing and if the individual personalist feels obliged to share or pass on his spiritual insight, some kind of institutionalized religion or social structure will shortly be required.

A compromise means for meeting this need is represented by the institution of the sect—an organized social group, but one that aims to avoid the mundane preoccupations of the larger society. Interestingly, the internal structure of the sect often tends toward absolutist idealism—whether in the benign form represented by some Catholic orders or Protestant pietist denominations, or at the horrific extreme of the Jim Jones cult in Guyana that committed mass suicide at the behest of its megalomaniac leader in 1979. The ascetic discipline of the sect, paradoxically, often leads to exceptional worldly success, as in John Wesley's formulation: "Religion must necessarily produce both industry and frugality, and these cannot but produce riches."[69]

Once established, the sect, try though it may to escape involvement with the larger society, almost inevitably must develop social interests. These interests may in part be material, but they may also rise from the spiritual convictions on which the sect is founded. The need to protect its social interests draws it ineluctably toward some degree of participation in politics. The Quakers in seventeenth century England, for example, found it necessary to become effective lobbyists to defend their pacifist convictions (the first instance, according to Quaker historians, of organized lobbying by a special-interest group). The entrance of formerly apolitical fundamentalists into American politics during the 1970s was in part also motivated by this kind of concern.

Along another route, some personalists are attracted to political participation that, far from being reluctant, is enthusiastic and militant. Existing social structures may be interpreted as interfering with personalist spiritual fulfillment. Such structures, some personalists may conclude, must therefore be swept away, by force if necessary. Personalists who follow this route into politics are likely to project their belief in the possibility of individual perfection onto society as a whole. Their position then becomes almost indistinguishable from that of utopian idealism—may indeed be a major source of most of the social movements embodying utopian idealism that are known to history.

Just such a course was followed by those sixteenth century Anabaptists who, as Troeltsch wrote, felt that their spiritual vision "justified setting up the Holy Jerusalem by force." Small rebellions broke out across central and western Europe, most spectacularly at Münster in 1534. For more than a year, the Münster Anabaptists maintained a society based on their idea of the New Jerusalem, featuring common ownership of property and polygamous marriage. The experiment was finally crushed by an army raised by the frightened German nobility, with much bloodshed and cruelty by both sides. In the English Civil War of the next century, the spirit of revolutionary pietism was carried on by, among others, the Fifth Monarchy Men, who believed that God would soon "give them authority and rule over the nations and kingdoms of the world."

Personalism transformed into utopian idealism often finds justification for crushing the very individualism from which it began. But utopian idealists with their roots in personalism generally retain a distinctly romantic view of politics. They instinctively abhor the kind of detailed model for the social future that is attractive to some kinds of authoritarians and absolutist idealists. They believe rather that "the revolution will make itself," as the rebels of the 1960s liked to say. They agree with Nietzsche that "the doing is everything," and their symbol is Delacroix's impassioned painting of Liberty storming the barricades. Their objective is not a perfectly regimented human beehive, but a social environment in which personal ecstasy can be indefinitely prolonged—"a new kind of world for a new kind of human being."

Civil Humanism

Humanism, a term first used by scholars in the sixteenth century to designate the study of Greek and Roman letters, has acquired a wide assortment of meanings, some of them contradictory. I use the term to mean the view that the individual person is a primary source of human value (in contrast to the organic view of authoritarianism and idealism), but that a truly human personality requires cultivation by society (in contrast to the more radical individualism of egoism and personalism). As Aristotle put it, "Man when perfected is the best of animals, but when separated from law and justice, he is the worst of all." Natural, biological man, humanism holds, lacks the moral sense that is an essential attribute of fully developed humanity. Freedom itself is a product of civilization. "Liberty, as a principle," John Stuart Mill wrote, "has no application to any state of things anterior to the time when mankind have become capable of being improved by free and equal discussion."[70]

Humanism divorced from religion I have called civil humanism. "Secular humanism" would do just as well, but in American discourse this term has recently been turned into a scare phrase by some publicists for the religious new right.

Among value systems, both civil humanism and the system I will describe in the next section as theist-humanism are relatively late arrivals in history. Theist-humanism first rose among the Hebrews.

Civil humanism, at least in anything approaching the form we now know it, originated with the ancient Greeks.

Even in Homeric times, the Greeks, while practicing a variant of polytheistic religion, were already devoted to a standard of personal excellence that made them unique among ancient peoples. This standard was not narrowly individualistic. "Nowadays," Werner Jaeger has written, "we must find it difficult to imagine how entirely *public* was the conscience of the Greek." But the concept of public duty was tied in part to fascination with the physical and intellectual potentialities of human nature. For Homeric heroes, Jaeger points out, military courage and traditional piety were no longer enough to reach the highest level of achievement. A reasoned approach to life and fluency in expression were needed to attain true nobility. "Be both a speaker of words and a doer of deeds," the aged counsellor Phoenix tells Achilles in the *Iliad*. Among the warrior aristocracy of the archaic period, the standard of the good life was that set forth in an old Greek definition of happiness cited by Edith Hamilton: "The exercise of vital powers along lines of excellence in a life affording them scope."[71]

In fifth century Athens the archetype of the free citizen was celebrated by politicians, philosophers, and poets. "There is no exclusiveness in our public life," insisted Pericles, "and in our private intercourse we are not suspicious of one another, nor angry with our neighbor if he does what he likes." Protagoras made human reason the sole judge of truth: "Man is the measure of all things—of those that are, that they are, and of those that are not, that they are not."[72]

Humanism in the Periclean age turned away from the traditional Greek religion. For many of the creators of civil humanism, transcendent being was either irrelevant or did not exist. Epicurus, an avowed materialist, wrote, "The gods are not to be feared; death cannot be felt; the good can be won; all that we dread can be conquered."[73] Rejection of the supernatural motivated civil humanists to look out toward the natural world, and away from the inner life of spirit and fantasy. "Greek art," Heinrich Zimmer wrote, "was derived from experiences of the eye, Hindu from those of the circulation of the blood." Humanist artists such as Phidias explored the possibilities of fulfillment through the human body. "Become what you are," urged Pindar.[74]

In politics, civil humanism at first encouraged and then helped to undermine Athens' experiment with democracy. By freeing individual consciousness from automatic obedience to custom, humanism laid a basis for the idea that each man should have a say in determining the laws and administration of his society. But humanism's emphasis on intellectual excellence also nurtured the view that government should be the responsibility of a trained elite. No one would dream, Socrates said, of selecting "a pilot, a mason, a flute player, or any craftsman at all" without regard for their professional skills, "though the shortcomings of such men are far less harmful than those that disorder our government." Aristotle saw merit in democracy, but concluded that the best system of government "must be that which is administered by the best." Public officials should not be paid, he argued, so that "the poor will keep to their work and grow rich, and the notables will not be governed by the lower class."[75]

Athenian democracy did not get much beyond what has been called "the democracy of the club." When Pericles boasted that in Athens "the administration is in the hands of the many and not of the few," he referred only to the many among free citizens. A census taken in the fourth century showed that in a population of 431,000, only 21,000 Athenians were citizens; the rest of the city-state's inhabitants were either aliens, with no role in government, or slaves. Even among the citizens, class struggle was intense. During the period of Athenian prosperity, Jaegar reports, the difference in income between rich and poor steadily increased. Class rivalry led eventually to ruinous civil war.

Greek humanism never developed effective means for dealing with the underlying political and economic problems of the city-state. Indeed, some tendencies within humanism probably helped make some of these problems more serious. A tendency toward egoism, perhaps inherent in civil humanism, eroded the Greeks' willingness to make sacrifices for the common good. Humanism's very liberality of spirit distracted citizens from paying sufficient attention to the strategic perils among which they lived. Lewis Mumford has commented that the fourth century Athenians spent funds on public games and festivals that they should have used to build up their city's defenses against the Macedonian army.[76]

Abandonment of traditional religion seems to have left a moral void at the core of Athenian society. Aristotle's idea of an unmoved mover who set the universe in motion preserved a concept of deity, but Aristotle's god, John Finnis observes, did not offer "sufficient assurance that the uncaused cause of all the good things of this world (including our ability to understand them) is itself a good that one could love, personal in a way that one might imitate, a guide that one should follow, or a guarantor of anyone's practical reasonableness." As a result, Finnis argues, Aristotle was unable to produce a plausible explanation of why one should make sacrifices for a friend, let alone for one's city. Epicurus's consistent materialism provided even less basis for civic virtue.[77]

Finally, secular civil humanism led to spiritual disorientation and loneliness. Greek tragedy embodies, more than anything else, efforts through art to cope with the existential despair felt by men in a world that seemed to have lost purpose. "Alas, poor men, their destiny," Aeschylus wrote. "When all goes well a shadow will overthrow it. If it be unkind one stroke of a wet sponge wipes all the picture out; and that is far the most unhappy thing of all."[78]

After the Macedonians conquered Greece in the fourth century, civil humanism went into gradual decline. It maintained a flickering life during the Hellenistic period, and enjoyed a significant revival in Rome—though the authoritarian quality of Roman culture somewhat muted its expression. Political freedom ended in Rome after the overthrow of the republic by the Caesars, although some personal and economic freedoms continued until the end of the third century A.D. when Diocletian, facing social chaos, introduced rigid controls over the economy.

During the centuries that followed, the Christian church, though restricted by secular authoritarianism and its own tendency toward absolutist idealism, preserved a concept of the sanctity of individual human life. Occasional voices, usually from within the church, upheld the validity of independent observation and analysis. Erigena, for instance, in the ninth century wrote, "Authority sometimes proceeds from reason, but reason never from authority. For all authority that is not approved by true reason seems weak. But true reason, since it rests on its own strength, needs no reinforcement by any authority." (Erigena's liberal ideas did not save him from the effects of a ninth century generation gap—according to legend, he died when "pierced with the iron pens of the boys whom he instructed.") In the twelfth century, William of Conches complained against the credulity and intellectual laziness of his contemporaries: "They say, We do not know how this is, but we know that God can do it. You poor fools! God can make a cow out of a tree, but has he ever done so? Therefore show some reason why a thing is so, or cease to hold that it is so."[79]

Early in the fifteenth century, personal optimism and confidence began to rise again in the West. Giovanni Pico Della Mirandola, a fifteenth century Florentine, wrote, "This is the culminating gift of God, this is the supreme and marvelous facility of man . . . that he can be what he wills to be." According to Kenneth Clark, "the discovery of the individual was made in early fifteenth century Florence."[80]

In the great intellectual flowering known as the Renaissance, man in society, the embodiment of humanist values, became both standard and theme. Artists concentrated on the human figure and painted from the perspective of human vision. Galileo argued that men should think for themselves: "I do not feel obliged to believe that the same God who has endowed us with sense, reason, and intellect has intended us to forego their use."[81]

The Renaissance was for the most part at least nominally respectful toward Christianity, and in fact owned some of its inspiration to the humanist values that had always been part of the Christian message. A few advanced thinkers, however, began to regard traditional Christianity as irrelevant to the human situation, if not downright harmful. Niccolo Machiavelli, particularly, considered himself liberated from the fetters of conventional morality. Christianity, he claimed, had made the world "a prey to the wicked, who have found men readier, for the sake of going to paradise, to submit to blows rather than to resent them." Machiavelli was by no means lacking in public spirit. His distinctive trait was that he acknowledged no moral authority higher than the public good. "Where the very safety of the country depends upon the resolution to be taken," he wrote, "no considerations of justice or injustice, humanity or cruelty, nor of glory or of shame, should be allowed to prevail. But putting all other considerations aside, the only question should be, what course will save the life and liberty of the country?"[82]

Thomas Hobbes and John Locke, writing in the century after Machiavelli, pushed further the emancipation of the individual self as a primary source of value. They did not, however, share Machiavelli's uncritical regard for society as a good in itself. Social authority, they maintained, rests on a contract formed in the state of nature among individuals aiming, in Locke's words, at "the mutual preservation of their lives, liberties, and estates." Hobbes's belief in the innate rapacity of human nature led him to conclude that a rational individual, in order to escape the natural "war of every man against every man," should consent to governmental checks on personal behavior virtually indistinguishable from those justified by authoritarianism (though always with the reservation that the individual should not be prepared to sacrifice his life, the ultimate source of all value, for his society). Locke, beginning from assumptions in some ways similar to those of Hobbes, developed a liberal social philosophy that calls for extensive freedoms for the individual. Locke was able to avoid Hobbes's dour prescription because his view of human nature was considerably more optimistic and because he continued to regard transcendent purpose as the ultimate basis for moral authority in the universe.[83]

The Enlightenment, which paralleled in time and to some extent influenced the founding of the United States, carried on Locke's promotion of the individual as a source of value but tried, without accepting Hobbes's grim political conclusions, to break the ties between humanism and theistic religion. The Enlightenment enterprise was pressed most effectively, as Alasdair MacIntyre has pointed out, not in France, where its expressions were for the most part patterned on other models, but in northern Europe, particularly in Scotland and Germany. The commanding geniuses of the effort to free humanist values from dependence on religion were David Hume and Immanuel Kant. Their influence echoes into our own time. Neither, however, fully solved the problems of finding a secular basis for the defense of human rights against the encroaching power of the state, or of rescuing civil society from Hobbes's "war of every man against every man."[84]

In the end Hume fell back on the bonds of human sympathy as the moral basis for a free society. This was a sentimental makeshift he had earlier rejected and that he continued to regard as unsatisfactory. Kant, like Aristotle, preserved an idea of deity as part of his system, but only to ensure that everything would finally work out all right, not to provide a religious foundation for his humanist ethics. The moral authority for Kant's organizing principle, "Act only on the basis of a moral rule that you can will to become a universal law" (the "categorical imperative"), rests finally on the aesthetic splendor of his ethical system. Kant's system is indeed splendid. But one must doubt that it has ever in itself seriously deterred anyone otherwise bent on murder, theft, adultery, or bearing false witness.

Despite many ups and downs, the influence of secular civil humanism in the West since the Enlightenment has generally followed an ascending course. Even in the United States, where religion remains a powerful social force, civil humanism is now probably the dominant value system within the intellectual community. It thereby exerts strong influence over the entertainment and news industries and over the higher levels of the education system and the government bureaucracy. Leo Pfeffer, a distinguished authority on church-state relations, has written, "Secular humanism [is] a cultural force which in many respects is stronger in the United States than any of the major religious groups or any alliance among them."[85]

Yet the conceptual problems for which Hume and Kant found no adequate answers remain unsolved. Many of the troubles that secular civil humanism could not deal with in the ancient world and may even have aggravated seem increasingly present in our own society. The question of whether civil humanism can meet the spiritual needs of human beings—the central question, no doubt—lies beyond the scope of this book. But short of this final test, there is serious doubt, to be further discussed in chapter 7, that secular civil humanism can supply the values needed for effective performance of society's political, economic, domestic, or even cognitive functions.

Theist-Humanism

Any collection of the six value systems so far discussed may exist simultaneously within a single society or even a single human personality. Such coexistence may occur harmoniously or creatively but often has led to value conflicts, sometimes explosive.

Theist-humanism differs from collections of parallel value systems in that it represents a synthesis of the three primary value sources, individual self-interest, social-group interest, and transcendent purpose, brought together into a unified value system. It combines metaphysical dualism (acknowledging the reality of both the natural world and a transcendent level of being that gives meaning to that world) with social constitutional pluralism (supporting the legitimacy of both individual interests and a common social interest).

Any value system or metaphysic that includes belief in the reality of transcendent purpose must view transcendence as in some sense sovereign. But the Jewish and Christian versions of theist-humanism, as set forth by thinkers from Isaiah to Karl Barth, holds that transcendent being—God—deliberately grants freedom to each human individual, thereby permitting individual consciousness to function as an autonomous, though ultimately dependent, source of value. Since a fully formed human personality is a product of culture as well as of biological nature, organized society, which transmits values from one generation to the next, is also within historic time an autonomous value source. Transcendent purpose maintains ultimate authority over both individual and social interests; but because the natural world, with all its evident suffering and imperfection as well as opportunities for pleasure, is real, and because human beings through their humanity belong to that world, no individual and no social group or institution, including the church, can say with assurance what transcendent purpose may intend in any particular situation. Within theist-humanism, the three value sources may pull in different directions but may also reinforce each other. The freedom and irreducible personal value of the self are traceable to the individual's origin as a creature of God. Society bases its authority not only on practical utility but also on its role as a means through which individuals carry out their God-assigned responsibilities to each other. And transcendent purpose is known through both individual and collective experience.

The possibility of theist-humanism no doubt occurred to individuals in primitive and archaic societies. Some of the Greeks were moving toward it during the social crisis of the fifth century. Sophocles, for example, in his Theban plays examined and found wanting not only the authoritarianism of Creon but also the defiant personalism of Antigone ("your self-sufficiency has brought you down") and the confident civil humanism of the young King Oedipus (perhaps suggested by Pericles, born the year before Sophocles). Reacting to the disparagement of traditional religion by Athenian intellectuals, Sophocles affirmed the authority of transcendent values. The moral and religious framework within which the tragedy of *Oedipus the King* goes forward is established by the chorus:

May destiny ever find me
Pious in word and deed
Prescribed by the laws that live on high:
Laws begotten in the clear air of heaven,
Whose only father is Olympus;
No mortal nature brought them to birth,
No forgetfulness shall lull them to sleep;
For God is great in them and grows not old.[86]

In *Oedipus at Colonus*, Sophocles' last play, written when he was almost ninety, the dying hero utters a beatitude that prefigures part of Christianity:

I know it was hard, my children.—And yet one word
Makes all those difficulties disappear:
That word is love.[87]

What Sophocles lacked, as did Aristotle and Stoic philosophers such as Zeno who also sought a transcendent source of value, was a conception of God not as an impersonal unmoved mover (the unknown god whose altar Paul saw in the marketplace at Athens) but as the loving creator and good shepherd of the universe, continually concerned with the lives of individual human beings.

This lack was filled by the monotheistic religion of the Hebrews. That religion began as a form of absolutist idealism, stressing the obligations placed on Israel by the tribal god, Yahweh, who claimed exclusive authority over the universe. But during the eighth century B.C., possibly at first as an outgrowth of the old quarrel between shamans and members of the official priesthood, a line of inspired holy men—prophets—began expounding the original idea that salvation depends not on performance of rituals pleasing to the deity but on how human beings deal with each other. "I hate, I despise your feast days" proclaimed the prophet Amos, quoting the Lord God. "Take thou away from me the noise of thy songs; for I will not hear the melody of thy viols. But let judgment run down as waters, and righteousness as a mighty stream."[88]

Isaiah's ethical message was even more explicit: "Woe unto them that decree unrighteous decrees . . . to turn aside the needy from judgment, and to take away the right from the poor of my people, that widows may be their prey, and that they may rob the fatherless!"[89] Jeremiah, who seems to have been the son of the reforming high priest, Hilkiah (discoverer of the book of Deuteronomy in the Jerusalem temple), voiced God's wrath against political and social corruption: "Woe unto him that buildeth his house by unrighteousness and his chambers by wrong; that useth his neighbour's service without wages, and giveth him not for his work. . . . Did not thy father [the former king] eat and drink, and do judgment and justice, and then it was well with him? He judged the cause of the poor and the needy; and then it was well with him: was not this to know me?"[90]

As Robert Benne writes, the prophets "progressed from a nationalistic messianism in which God delivers the nation from its enemies to an ethical messianism in which God saves the good who unjustly suffer at the hands of evildoers."[91]

A few of the prophets, like Joel, emphasized the collective mission of the Hebrew nation, but most gave unprecedented attention to the role and importance of the individual. The prophets taught that the fatherless, the widow, and the hungry are distinct human beings, each with rights to justice and compassion. The prophets provided the first clear statements of a value system in which individual rights and social obligations are related through a theistic view of reality. Building on this tradition, as well as on other traditions of idealism, personalism, and humanism percolating through the Mediterranean world at the end of the Hellenistic age, Jesus of Nazareth gave shaping expression to the values of theist-humanism.

The exact significance and meaning of Jesus' life and doctrine have of course been hotly debated among rival churches, denominations, and sects claiming his authority as well as by numerous unbelievers for almost two thousand years. But the main points of his teaching seem clear: man's primary obligation is to love God, the creator and good shepherd of the universe. Love of God leads to caring relationships with other human beings. To "love thy neighbor as thyself," which Jesus called for, was already a moral imperative within theist-humanist and even secular-humanist doctrine. Jesus' distinctive departure, reported in the Gospel of John, was to base this obligation on a relationship between the individual and a personal deity: "Love one another," he commanded, "as I have loved you."[92]

Again and again, Jesus emphasizes the importance of the individual. Each person's salvation, he insists, is of unique value and significance to God. For the Creator, there is no averaging out; though ninety and nine are saved, the Heavenly Father cannot be content if even one is lost. The class, the group, the nation are not what count. What counts is the individual human soul. The "first outstanding characteristic" of the "gospel ethic," Ernst Troeltsch wrote, "is an unlimited, unqualified individualism."

Jesus expressed reverence for the moral law received from Jewish tradition—"Till heaven and earth pass, one jot or one tittle shall in no way pass, till all be fulfilled"—but the law must be directed to serve human needs. "The sabbath," he said, "was made for man, and not man for the sabbath."[93]

The ethical doctrine taught by Jesus goes far beyond what civil humanism holds to be achievable or even desirable: "Love your enemies, bless them that curse you, do good to them that hate you, and pray for them that despitefully use you, and persecute you. . . . Take therefore no thought for the morrow: for the morrow shall take thought for the things of itself. Sufficient unto the day is the evil thereof. Judge not, that ye be not judged."[94]

Jesus seems to have accepted the need for pragmatic authority to deal with political and economic needs. Unlike the idealist Zealots who were his contemporaries in Palestine, he was not a political revolutionary. "Render therefore unto Caesar the things which are Caesar's," he said, "and unto God the things that are God's." While his teaching appeared to have social and political implications, establishment of an earthly utopia through political action was not one of them: "My kingdom is not of this world."[95]

He viewed his mission, however, as one that would bring practical relief, here and now, to "you poor . . . you that hunger now . . . you that weep now. . . ." Quoting Isaiah, he said, "The Spirit of the Lord is upon me, because he hath anointed me to preach the gospel to the poor; he hath sent me to heal the brokenhearted, to preach deliverance to the captives, and recovering of sight to the blind, to set at liberty them that are bruised, to preach the acceptable year of the Lord. . . . This day is this scripture fulfilled in your ears."[96]

The "good news" of which Jesus spoke was interpreted by his followers as the promise that life will be eternal for those who accept his mission. "The hinge on which the faith turned," C. H. Dodd has written, "was the belief that Jesus, having been put to death by crucifixion, 'rose from the dead.' . . . It is the central belief about which the church itself grew, without which there would have been no church and no gospels, at least of the kind we have."[97] The promised salvation requires change in behavior as well as belief. The kingdom of God is to come on earth as well as in heaven. Human participation in the coming of the kingdom necessitates movement toward mutuality in human relationships, acceptance of membership in a common family, bonded by love for God, the eternal "Father in heaven."

The Christian religion that grew up around Jesus' teaching and belief in his resurrection soon developed powerful idealist and personalist tendencies, as we have seen. But the central value system that was returned to repeatedly, whatever their deviations, by Paul, Augustine, Aquinas, Luther, Calvin, and Wesley, among many others, was and has remained theist-humanism.

Judaism, too, along a different path, has continued the pursuit of theist-humanist values first conceived by the Hebrew prophets. The two religious traditions have often been at odds, opening the way to well-known consequences of the utmost tragedy, but the values that both claim to serve retain much in common. "It is the commonality of human suffering," Arthur Cohen writes, "that is the commonality of Christian and Jew; and that must come, as a miracle of grace, a means of expressing that shared experience. . . . Upon one thing Jews and Christians agree: the magnitude of creation and the grandeur and misery of man. Out of such agreement an authentic community, a viable consensus, a meaningful cooperation can emerge—the Judeo-Christian humanism."[98]

Art as well as religion, and sometimes art celebrating religion, has also provided witness to theist-humanist values. The great artists of the Western theist-humanist mainstream—one might name, as examples, Michelangelo, Rembrandt, Shakespeare, Bach, Mozart, Jane Austen, Dickens, Melville, Rodin, Eakins, Dostoevsky, Tolstoy, Mahler, Conrad, Faulkner—have at least three qualities in common: belief that the universe they represent has objective moral significance; attention to the human scale; and attachment to a particular culture that they seek to transfigure, aesthetically and sometimes morally, not to escape.

Theist-humanism solves the problem of balancing individual rights against social authority by rooting both in God's transcendent purpose, which is concerned for the welfare of each human soul. This does not, of course, provide a formula for settling all, or even most, or even any social problems. But it does create a body of shared values through which problems can be mediated.

———————◄•●•►————————

THREE

Intentions of the Founders

THE NEW REPUBLIC that first saw the light of day in Philadelphia in July 1776 represented values derived from both foreign and native sources. Foremost was Europe; and beyond Europe, earlier cultural formations in the Middle East. But Old World traditions had undergone substantial change through experience of America and would undergo more through the act of revolution that the men gathered in Philadelphia were helping to foment.

The political values on which the Republic was based were embodied in the Constitution, composed in 1787, and its subsequent Bill of Rights, enacted in 1791. This charter has provided a legal framework for relations between church and state, which, though altered by interpretation, remains in force to the present day. To understand what the founders had in mind, it is necessary to examine in some detail the values and beliefs upon which they drew when they formulated the nation's fundamental law.

City on a Hill

The single most influential cultural force at work in the new nation was the combination of religious beliefs and social attitudes known as Puritanism. At the time of the Revolution, at least 75 percent of American citizens had grown up in families espousing some form of Puritanism.[1] Among the remainder, more than half had roots in related traditions of European Calvinism. Puritanism was the creed of the Congregational church, officially established in three of the four New England colonies, and also exerted strong influence both in the South, where the Anglican church was established, and in the somewhat more cosmopolitan middle colonies.

Itself representing cultural complexity, Puritanism was the product of the militant second phase of the English Reformation. The first round of Protestantism in England, to the extent that it did not spring from the dynastic designs or sexual whims of Henry VIII, expressed spirits of gathering nationalism and verdant humanism, both directed against the resurgent idealism of the Counter-Reformation Catholic church. Toward the end of Henry's tenure and particularly during the brief reign of his son, Edward VI, the deeper currents of the Reformation, conveying ideas such as predestination and salvation through faith alone, began to rise in England. Protestantism was ruthlessly persecuted under Edward's Catholic half-sister, Mary, but during the long and brilliant reign of Henry's last surviving offspring, Elizabeth, it achieved enduring triumph.

The great idea of Puritanism, as of the entire Reformation, was the total sovereignty and awesome otherness of God, separated from all things human, including the institutional church, by a vast spiritual and moral gulf, crossable only by the infinitude of God's grace and love. Preached by impassioned believers, this idea could cut like a redeeming sword through religious cant and superstition. But pushed almost to the exclusion of other Christian beliefs and values, as both Luther and Calvin at times tended to do, it could carry Protestantism away from Jesus' call to "love one another as I have loved you" and toward a purified, more efficient form of absolutist idealism. In its Lutheran embodiment this tendency encouraged the church to legitimize the political power of the authoritarian state. In its Calvinist manifestation, with which Puritanism was more closely aligned, it fostered a legalistic morality, based on preoccupation with sin. "Calvinism," Ernst Troeltsch wrote, "felt no need at all to adjust its ethical ideal to the law of Christ in the New Testament, or the Sermon on the Mount." Concentration on God's transcendence, Perry Miller observed, "liberated men from treadmill of indulgences and penances, but cast them on the iron couch of introspection."[2]

Following Calvin's lead, mainline Puritanism regarded human society as tainted by sin but nevertheless potentially useful to religion. The biblical model of a "city on a hill" was the relevant goal for political action. Puritan divines called for establishment of a "Holy

Community," governed according to standards derived from Christian principles of morality and justice. "Reform all places, all persons, all callings," commanded Thomas Case, a seventeenth century Puritan minister, preaching to the House of Commons. "Reform the benches of judgment, the inferior magistrates. . . . Reform the universities, reform the cities, reform the countries, reform inferior schools of learning, reform the Sabbath, reform the ordinances, the worship of God. . . ."[3]

The organizing principle of Puritan social thought was the concept of the covenant. The covenant is by no means a contract in the sense of an agreement placing obligations on both sides. It is rather the result of God's free choice, made for his own purpose, like his selection of Abraham in the Old Testament. Individuals are called to the covenant, one by one, through a mature experience of spiritual rebirth, an idea borrowed originally from the Anabaptists (whom the Puritans on other grounds condemned). Those included in the covenant, therefore, formed a "gathered community" held together by shared knowledge of individual salvation.[4]

Strict Calvinists insisted that no human agency could in any way affect God's choice of those who are to be saved. The slightest concession to human autonomy, they maintained, would imply a limit to God's omnipotence, which would appear to make God less than God. It would also, Jonathan Edwards later argued, disrupt the chain of causation in nature, thereby rendering the universe both unintelligible and meaningless. Other Puritans, equally devout, such as Thomas Hooker, claimed that because intelligibility also requires that human consciousness must have a role somehow distinct from that of ordinary matter, it logically follows that God's grace, while irresistible, may welcome "preparation" for salvation among believers. This deviation, though minute, provided an opening for the germ of humanism, which would carry more eclectic Puritans toward the doctrine of Arminianism, the distinctly un-Calvinist view that individual consciousness plays a real, though dependent, part in salvation and therefore in formation of the covenant.

MASSACHUSETTS BAY: PURITAN COMMONWEALTH

Puritanism was an active force in the settlement of virtually all of England's colonies in North America but exerted its most critical influence through the Massachusetts Bay Colony, founded in 1630.

The Puritans who came to the new world were in part driven by renewal of persecution in England under the Stuarts and their ecclesiastical allies but also were positively inspired by a sense that they rode in the vanguard of a great new departure in history. Unlike the more radical Baptists and Quakers, they viewed themselves as still part of the established English national church. But they believed profoundly in the uniqueness of their calling. "We do not go to New-England as separatists from the Church of England," Francis Higginson is said to have cried as the ship bearing his party to Massachusetts passed Land's End, "though we cannot but separate from the corruptions in it: but we go to practice the positive part of Church reformation, and propagate the gospel in America.[5]

Political authority in the Bay Colony was at first monopolized by about a dozen of the founding members. In 1631 political participation was somewhat broadened, but citizenship was limited to members of the Congregational church. (The Congregational church was technically still part of the Church of England but was organized through a system of congregational governance rather than under the authority of an Anglican bishop.) Because only a small minority of even devout Puritans could claim the full experience of individual spiritual regeneration required for church membership, this restriction had the effect of creating a political elite composed of only about 8 percent of the colony's total population in 1640. The structure of government was a form of bicameralism, with an upper body composed of the governor and his council and a lower chamber of local representatives elected by citizens in the towns. Civil authority was given responsibility to "restrain corrupt opinions" that ran counter to church doctrine. All residents were subject to taxes imposed to support the church.[6]

The Massachusetts Puritans had no use for religious tolerance. "Toleration," wrote John Cotton, the most subtle of the early new England divines, "made the world anti-Christian." Nathaniel Ward, the self-titled Simple Cobbler of Agawam (prototype for all later rustic Yankee xenophobes), produced a more homely formulation: "My heart has naturally detested four things: the standing of the Apocrypha in the Bible; foreigners dwelling in my country to crowd out native subjects into the corners of the earth; alchemized coins; [and] tolerations of diverse religions, or of one religion in segregant shapes." The only liberty owed to dissenters, Ward maintained, was the "liberty to keep away from us."[7] In 1644 Baptists, whose radical personalism appeared to challenge Puritan solidarity, were banished from the Bay Colony. Between 1659 and 1661, four Quakers, practitioners of an even more extreme form of personalist heresy, after repeated banishments and whippings had failed to keep them away, were publicly executed by hanging in Boston. (The series of executions was stopped by the government of Charles II, who had his own reasons for disliking Puritans.)

Yet Massachusetts was never a theocracy in the sense of a polity ruled by church officials. Church elders, indeed, were not eligible to serve as civil magistrates. According to George Armstrong Kelly, "Though the vested power of a harsh creed was pervasive, state and church were distinct, and the clergy had less control over politics than anywhere in Europe."[8]

John Cotton's proposal that Massachusetts law be based directly on the Mosaic code attracted little support. The Bible was the "touchstone" for rules of moral conduct in early Massachusetts, but its principles were applied through the mediating structure of English common law—the "cornerstone" of the colony's legal system. Common law, based on "a set of unchanging principles of public law," is said to have enjoyed greater prestige than in England, then engulfed by a "chaotic confusion of laws" stemming from competing ecclesiastical, statutory, and customary sources.[9]

John Winthrop, first governor of Massachusetts Bay, warned that the public has a natural propensity to behave as a "wild beast, which all the ordinances of God are bent against to restrain and subdue it." Winthrop's underlying view, according to Perry Miller, was that the people should be seen and not heard. Nevertheless, by teaching the inherent corruption of all man-made institutions, including the state, Puritanism laid the basis for resistance to autocratic government. Puritanism's "distinctive contribution to democracy," John Coolidge noted, was its "insistence that the civil order is created by human will, and therefore has no claim to worship."[10]

Fatefully for the future of American society, this reservoir of democratic ideas was fed by suspicion of all political authority, rather than by confidence that government elected by popular suffrage can be counted on to serve the public good. "Let all the world learn," John Cotton wrote, "to give mortal men no greater power than they are content they shall use, for use it they will." The Puritans, Richard Niebuhr observed, "recognized that legal power was necessary for

curbing unregenerate power, and therefore agreed to civil government, but [because] the exercise of power tended to corrupt men,
[they] sought limitations by means of constitutionalism, the Scriptures
and 'politic covenants,' and the dispersion of power."[11]

In 1634 a band of Puritans led by Thomas Hooker pulled out of
the Bay colony and trekked to the Connecticut Valley, where they
established a new colony at Hartford. The move was apparently
caused more by land hunger and a personality clash between Cotton
and Hooker than by theological or political differences. But the
Connecticut Colony was somewhat less strict in its test for church
membership and therefore permitted a slightly broader suffrage.
Laying down the rules for election of civil officers, Hooker asserted,
"The choice of public magistrates belongs unto the people by God's
own allowance."[12]

Connecticut's reputation for nascent liberalism, however, has been
exaggerated. Despite his nudge away from strict Calvinism on the
question of the possibility of "preparation" for salvation, Hooker was
essentially orthodox in both politics and theology and in fact became
a staunch defender of the established "New England Way." When
Cotton wavered in response to the so-called antinomian heresy in
1637, Hooker stood firm. By the end of the seventeenth century,
Connecticut had become a bastion of conservative Puritanism against
progressive tendencies cropping out in Massachusetts, a position it
continued to maintain during most of the next two centuries.[13]

On the authority of the Old Testament, the Puritans believed God
wills that man shall acquire mastery over the material world. The
problem, from their perspective, was that such mastery may easily
come to be valued for its own sake. The most dangerous temptation
facing the colony, John Winthrop warned, was that its members
should "fall to embrace this present world and prosecute our carnall
intentions, seekeing great things for our selves and our posterity."
John Cotton's solution was drawn from the teachings of Paul and
others in the New Testament: believers should apply "diligence in
worldly business, and yet deadness to the world." The Puritan, Cotton
maintained, is obliged to pursue material success. "Yet his heart is
not set upon these things, he can tell what to do with his estate when
he hath got it." The world should be loved with "weaned affections."[14]

For a group of zealots within the Bay Colony known as "antinomians," among whom the redoubtable Ann Hutchinson was the most
eloquent and outspoken, this formulation had the stench of theological

compromise. The antinomian controversy, Winthrop later suggested, became so muddled by emotion that "nobody could understand what the dispute was about." But for Mrs. Hutchinson, who first was attracted to New England, she said, by the purity of Cotton's explication of Calvinist doctrine, the root of the antinomian position was clear: man "must see nothing in himselfe, have nothing, doe nothing, onely he is to stand still and waite for Christ to do all for him." The antinomians were headed toward the personalism, even monism, which could result, as it did among the Baptists and the Quakers, from a different slanting of Protestantism's emphasis on the total sovereignty of transcendent will.[15]

The Puritan elite, recalling Münster and other examples of what Anabaptism might produce, found this interpretation of Protestantism incompatible with survival. A court presided over by Winthrop in 1637 concluded that Mrs. Hutchinson's ideas "tend to slothfulness, and quench all indeavor in the creature." Cotton at first hedged, then aligned himself with the orthodox establishment. The court condemned unrepentant antinomians to banishment.[16]

After wandering for several years along the New England frontier, Ann Hutchinson was murdered by Indians in 1643. But memory of her lingered. In 1672, almost thirty years after her death, William Coddington, a surviving antinomian who had shared her banishment, wrote to the governor of Massachusetts, "You may as well withhold the flowing of the Tide into the Massachusetts Bay, as the Working of the God of Truth in the Hearts of his People in the Massachusetts Jurisdiction, or to limit the Holy One to a Company or Tribe of Priests, who make a trade of the scriptures, Keeping People alwayes under their Teachings, and they may be alwayes paying of them."[17]

The governor burned the letter (of which Coddington had kept a copy) without reading it, but the spirit it expressed rolled on, like the tide into Massachusetts Bay, often recurring as a theme in American culture and politics. When George McGovern ran for president in 1972, a social historian described his campaign as "antinomian," and there were parallels to antinomianism in the hippy art and culture of the 1960s and early 1970s. No direct line of descent from Ann Hutchinson to McGovern or the hippies need be claimed, but the antinomians had opened a possibility that, amplified by New England transcendentalism two centuries later, would continue to be heard in America.

In the short run, at least, a far more effective challenge to the New

England Way soon rose from the side of worldliness, expressed by members of the community who were moving toward buoyant humanism of the kind rising in Europe, which John Winthrop had feared and John Cotton had tried to head off. Strict Puritanism would probably have been unsustainable in any case, but the mechanism that began its erosion was political. Many among the colony's prospering class of merchants could not claim the personal experience of spiritual rebirth required for church membership and therefore did not qualify for citizenship. Resentment against the church elite led some of them, paradoxically, to support Ann Hutchinson and her associates in the antinomian controversy. Defeated in this foray, they turned to the more congenial course of pressing for dilution of the test for church membership. In 1657 the consolidated ministerium of Massachusetts and Connecticut approved, over heated minority objection, particularly from those representing the offshoot of the Connecticut Colony in New Haven, a "half-way covenant" under which partial church membership was granted to baptized Christians who had not experienced mystical regeneration.

The Puritan sway was further weakened by the Act of Toleration of 1693, imposed by the English home government as a by-product of the Glorious Revolution of 1688 that had brought William and Mary, representing pragmatic Whiggery, to the throne. Religious toleration was extended to all Protestants, and ownership of property was substituted for church membership as a qualification for political suffrage. Orthodox Puritans, who retained a majority in the colonial legislature, kept the Congregational church effectively established by requiring that each town support "an able, orthodox, and learned minister." But the old severity was giving way. "What is become of the primitive zeal, piety, and holy hearts found in our parents?" asked one conservative. "Who is there left among you that saw these churches in their first glory, and how do you see them now?"[18]

In the closing years of the seventeenth century and the beginning of the eighteenth, the smoothly cultivated Brattle brothers, Thomas, a merchant, and William, a clergyman, led a party within Congregationalism itself, centered on the new Brattle Street Church, that aimed to reorganize the church on "broad and catholick" lines similar to the urbane eclecticism by then dominant in the Church of England. In 1707 the Brattles managed the election of John Leverett, a successful merchant, as president of Harvard College, which had been founded in 1636 to maintain a literate clergy.[19]

While the Brattles represented the politically conservative commercial establishment, a very different kind of humanism was being promoted by John Wise of Ipswich (on Massachusetts' North Shore), a Congregationalist minister who was the first articulate American populist, in the sense of one who seeks to foster economic and social equality through government. General acceptance of "equality among men," Wise wrote, "bears a very great force in maintaining peace and friendship." Moral exhortations by Puritan divines, he observed, had failed to prevent development of a class society. What was needed to break the sway of the Brattles and their like over the class of economically depressed farmers, he concluded, was a political solution: deliberate inflation of the currency. "A plentiful Medium," Wise argued, would give the farmers "Power to Remove those who stand in their Way." Wise's prescription, too, has rolled on to the present time.[20]

Leadership of the defense of the Puritan tradition against both political equalitarianism on the left and fashionable eclecticism on the right fell largely to the indomitable Mathers, Increase and Cotton, father and son. Increase Mather's father, Richard, had been one of the Bay Colony's founders. His son, Cotton, born in 1663 and living until 1728, ensured the continuity of the dynasty. Increase was elected president of Harvard in 1685, a post which he held until he was pushed out by the Brattles in 1701, preparatory to their elevation of Leverett. Both father and son were for many years ministers of Boston's Old North Church.

Neither of the Mathers was in the same intellectual league with John Cotton (Increase's father-in-law). Their pleas that citizens inform against neighbors who swore or blasphemed gave license to busybodyism or something worse. They also hesitantly endorsed the notorious Salem witch trials of 1692, which produced nineteen executions—"a small incident in the history of a great superstition," as Samuel Eliot Morison maintained, but a deep stain on the Puritan record.[21] Yet the Mathers, in their fussy, parochial way, gave an optimistic, energetic, even humanitarian turn to American conservatism that has generally distinguished it from its European counterparts. Ousted from control of Harvard, they played a major role in 1701 in the founding of Yale, which became a seedbed for the humanities and science as well as a bulwark of political conservatism. Cotton Mather's conclusion that "our Faith its selfe will not be found good and profitable if Good Works do not follow upon it" may have strayed

from strict Calvinism, but it offered a formulation through which Calvinist moral force could be related to the realities of the New World
and the coming industrial age. His *Essays to Do Good* influenced the
young Benjamin Franklin, who grew up in Boston while Cotton was
in his prime. Both directly and through reflection in Franklin's writings, Mather's book helped set the moral tone of small-town, middle-
class America. "Sirs," Cotton Mather advised, "You must Get up and
be doing." Millions of Americans were to believe that he was right.[22]

Puritanism, created as part of a protest against one kind of absolutist
idealism, generated an obsessive idealism of its own, contemptuous
of the "cakes and ale" side of human nature, which gives credibility
to H. L. Mencken's comment that it expressed "the haunting fear
that someone somewhere might be happy." But Puritanism also
bequeathed to America a store of moral capital that relentless egoism,
encouraged by both the political right and left, has not yet succeeded
in running down. Samuel Morison's comment that "Puritanism was
a cutting edge which hewed liberty, democracy, humanitarianism,
and universal education out of the black forest of feudal Europe and
the American wilderness," has a ring of smugness, but it is smugness
that is founded in large measure on truth. Christopher Dawson, a
modern Catholic writer with no special fondness for Puritanism,
concludes, "The modern Western beliefs in progress, in the rights of
man, and the duty of conforming political action to moral ideals,
whatever they may owe to other influences, derive ultimately from
the moral ideals of Puritanism and its faith in the possibility of the
realization of the Holy Community on earth by the efforts of the
elect."[23]

PLYMOUTH: "SOME GOOD FOUNDATION"

From the start, Puritanism did not go unchallenged even within
New England as a molder of social values. Ten years before the
arrival of the Puritans in Massachusetts Bay, a small body of Pilgrims—
not so radical as the Baptists but, unlike the Puritans, formally
separated from the Church of England—landed forty miles to the
southeast on the bleak coast of Cape Cod. The Pilgrims, drawn more
from working-class backgrounds than the Puritans, represented the
pietist line of the Reformation. As pietists, they partook of a development in theology that was to have important effects for democracy.

The theist-humanist doctrine of original sin, propounded by both the Hebrew prophets and the writers of the New Testament, suggested the inherent fallibility of all human institutions. After Christianity became the official religion of the Roman empire in A.D. 383, however, Christian theorists were drawn toward the idealist view that the established church holds a monopoly on religious truth that the state is obliged to enforce. As a practical matter the church would tolerate different religions where it lacked the political resources to impose its doctrine. But where it had state support, it regarded imposition of religious orthodoxy as a sacred duty. Religious error had no rights, Catholic theologians argued—no more than false ideas about the material world had a right to equal status with confirmable truths. A responsible state would not permit its citizens to be educated to believe that two plus two equals five, or that theft and murder are compatible with social peace. When the stakes are eternal life and the danger of damnation, the state's obligation to uphold authentic truth is even more clear.

The Protestant reformers challenged parts of the Catholic church's particular version of truth and placed renewed emphasis on the importance of the individual's direct relationship to God, but they did not, for the most part, doubt that truth—their own versions of truth—should be officially enforced. The Peace of Augsburg of 1555, which settled the religious wars rising out of the Reformation, established not religious freedom, but the pragmatic principle that the religion of the prince should determine the religion of his people. Even the pietists, whose personalist values led them to regard the fate of temporal society as essentially insignificant and who suffered beatings and even death rather than accept the slightest socially required modification of the dictates of their inner light, did not at first develop a doctrine that would accommodate the existence of *different* inner lights. Truth, after all, was truth, whether it came from the church, the Bible, or the inner voice of conscience.

The European Anabaptists denied the right of the state to enforce religion because such a right, they recognized, tends to make the state the arbiter of religious truth. But it was left to dissenting pietist sects in seventeenth century England, among which the Pilgrims were one, to raise the question of whether monopolization of truth by a single church is even theoretically valid. God gives "certainty of grace" to those whom he chooses, one dissenting theologian argued, but he does not require "uniformity of profession."[24]

John Robinson, the spiritual leader of the community of Pilgrims that eventually made its way to New England (though he accompanied them only as far as Holland, where they first fled to escape persecution in England), offered an even more startling proposition: "The Lord hath more truth and light yet to break forth." God, Robinson suggested, continues to make known his purpose through history. No single church, therefore—not the Church of Rome, nor the Calvinists, nor the Anabaptists, nor the Pilgrims themselves—can possibly possess detailed knowledge of God's ultimate plan. If God's plan is unknowable to any church, it clearly cannot be made the basis for a program of state-enforced religion. Unlike the Anabaptists, who would make the sect virtually a law unto itself, the Pilgrims did not deny the responsibility of the state to enforce moral behavior. But the values on which morality is based, they believed, lie beyond the state's legitimate jurisdiction. "The magistrate is not by virtue of his office to meddle with religion or matters of conscience," John Robinson wrote, "to force and compel men to this or that form of religion or doctrine; but to leave Christian religion free to every man's conscience and to handle only civil transgressions. . . ."[25]

The Pilgrims carried this modest creed to New England and made it the basis for the small society they founded at Plymouth. They came to America, William Bradford, the colony's elected governor, wrote, "not out of any newfangledness, or other such like giddie humor, by which men are often time transported to their great hurt and danger but for sundrie weightie and solid reasons." Among these reasons were hope for material betterment, concern that their children be removed from contact with worldly temptations present in Holland, and "lastly (and which was not least), a great hope and inward zeal they had, of laying some good foundation, or at least to make some way thereunto, for the propagating and advancing the gospell of the kingdom of Christ in those remote parts of the world; yea, though they should be but even as stepping stones unto others for the performing of so great a work."[26]

Almost at once, the Plymouth Colony came under attack from critics in England, both conservative Anglicans and Puritans, for doctrinal looseness. Bradford, deprived of counsel he might have received from Robinson, whom the English authorities refused to allow to enter the colony, replied, "We may erre, and other churches may erre, and doubtless doe in many circumstances. That honour therefore belongs only to the infallible word of God, and pure

Testamente of Christ, to be propounded and followed as the only rule and pattern for direction to all churches and Christians. And it is too great arrogancie for any man, or churches to thinke that he or they have so sounded the word of God to the bottome, as precislie to sett down the church discipline, without error in substance or circumstance, as that no other without blame may digress or differ in anything from the same."[27]

Perhaps because they were too few in numbers, or because they lacked support in England equivalent to that enjoyed by the Puritans who soon came to Massachusetts Bay, or because the place at which they had settled was less promising, or perhaps in part, too, because the very modesty of their pretensions made them less assertive than their Puritan neighbors, the Pilgrims survived but did not flourish. In 1691 the colony was absorbed into Massachusetts. By that time, however, the pluralist position the Pilgrims represented had been placed on a solid footing elsewhere in New England by one for whom belief in religious tolerance in no way dampened self-confidence: Roger Williams.

PROVIDENCE: EXPERIMENT IN TOLERANCE

Arriving in Massachusetts in 1631 a more-or-less orthodox Puritan, Williams soon was agitating to break the formal tie holding the Congregational church to the Church of England. He next antagonized Boston's Puritan establishment by arguing that the civil authority should not enforce acceptance of the "first table" of the Ten Commandments (dealing with relations between man and God). In 1636 he and a small group of like-minded followers found it advisable to flee the Bay Colony, first to Plymouth and then to unsettled territory at the head of Narragansett Bay, where they purchased land from friendly Indians.

The new settlement, which Williams named Providence, permitted complete freedom of religious worship. The colony took in some of the antinomians who were expelled from Massachusetts as well as Baptists and Quakers. Williams himself for a short time became a Baptist (thereby acquiring a latter-day status as a sort of patron saint for American Baptism) but soon grew dissatisfied with the Baptists' extreme personalism and thereafter designated himself a "Seeker."[28]

Before long, covetous eyes in Massachusetts were directed toward the new settlement. Also, some of the newly arrived antinomians began settling on land claimed by founders of the Providence Colony. Williams decided that his group needed a firmer title to the area than the one they had obtained from the Indians.

In 1643 he returned to England, seeking government backing for his settlement. In response to criticisms of Providence's policy of religious tolerance, Williams issued in 1644 (forty-five years before Locke's *Letter Concerning Toleration*) his classic defense of religious liberty, *The Bloudy Tenent of Persecution for the Cause of Conscience Discussed.* "God," Williams forthrightly maintained, "requireth not an uniformity of Religion." The civil power, he argued, is incapable of touching the inner life of the spirit, which is the paramount concern of religion. "The civil sword," he wrote, "may make a nation of hypocrites and anti-Christians, but not one true Christian." If the church accepts establishment by the state, it puts itself in the position of "appealing to darkness to judge light, to unrighteousness to judge righteousness, the spiritually blind to judge and end the controversy concerning heavenly colors." The argument that a non-Christian state cannot effectively carry out its secular functions is simply false. Statecraft, like seacraft, is a practical skill, unrelated to religious faith. "A pagan or anti-Christian pilot may be as skillful to carry the ship to its desired port as any Christian mariner or pilot in the world, and may perform that work with as much safety and speed."[29]

Fortunately for Williams, the faction then holding the upper hand in the English parliament was not well disposed toward the Puritan establishment of Massachusetts. He returned to Providence with his settlement's land title fully confirmed and with authorization for a union of Providence with smaller settlements at Newport and Portsmouth to form a new colony of Providence Plantations, soon called Rhode Island.

In 1647 an assembly of the colony's freemen approved a charter calling for a "DEMOCRATICAL . . . form of government." This charter established religious liberty not as protection against religion but as a means for giving religion free rein. "Let the saints of the Most High walk in this Colony without molestation, in the name of Jehovah their God, for ever and ever."[30]

Perhaps irritated by Williams's political success, as well as affronted by his unorthodox theology, John Cotton in 1647 issued an attack on Rhode Island's policy of tolerance titled *The Bloudy Tenent Washed and*

Made White in the Bloud of the Lambe. "It is a carnal and worldly and, indeed, an ungodly imagination," Cotton argued, "to confine the magistrate's charge to the bodies and goods of the subject, and to exclude them from the care of their souls." But even if the state's jurisdiction were limited to concern for "bodies and goods," it would still be obliged to practice "watchfulness against such pollutions of religion as tend to apostasy." An irreligious state, Cotton warned, would surely cause God to "visit the city and country with public calamity, if not captivity, for the church's sake."[31]

Williams responded (in 1651) with a broadside titled, *The Bloudy Tenent yet More Bloudy.* Cotton's claim that Massachusetts did not "meddle with the heretic before he has sinned against his own conscience," Williams charged, was sophistry. "Their practice cries, their imprisonments, finings, whippings, banishments, cry in the ears of the Lord of Hosts, and the louder because of such unchristian figleaves, cloakes. . . ." Cotton (who died the following year) was not further heard from.[32]

The primary objective of Williams's policy of religious liberty, Mark DeWolfe Howe has pointed out, was protection of the church against the taint of worldly corruption. "The church of the Jews under the Old Testament," Williams wrote, "and the church of the Christians under the New Testament . . . were both separate from the world." When men "opened a gap in the hedge or wall of separation between the garden of the church and the wilderness of the world, God hath ever broke down the wall itself, removed the candlestick, and made His garden a wilderness, as at this day." To pull free of the wilderness, the church "must of necessity be walled in peculiarly unto Himself from the world," so that "all that shall be saved out of the world are to be transplanted out of the wilderness of the world, and added unto his church or garden." For Williams the wall of separation was to insulate the garden of the church against the wilderness of worldly affairs—a substantially different intention than that which Thomas Jefferson later conveyed through the same metaphor.[33]

Williams's position leaned toward the value system I have called personalism. He did not, however, deny that the state should play a role in maintaining moral discipline. The Rhode Island Colony, with Williams's approval, continued to enforce moral regulations based on the "second table" of the Decalogue (dealing with human social relations). Though he welcomed Quakers to Rhode Island, Williams disapproved the extreme spiritualization of religion that he identified with Quakerism. When George Fox, founder of the Society of Friends, visited Newport in 1672, Williams, though just short of seventy, rowed thirty miles across Narragansett Bay to expose Fox's "heresies." Arriving after Fox had departed, Williams set forth his objections to the extreme otherworldliness of Quakerism in a broadside titled, *George Fox Digg'd Out of His Burrowes.* (Fox responded with *A New England Firebrand Quenched, Being Something in Answer unto a Lying, Slanderous Book, Entitled George Fox Digged Out of His Burrowes.*)[34]

Modern scholars hold that the Rhode Island model had little real influence on the development of American pluralism. Though the colony was one of only three that did not maintain, at least in theory, an established church at the time of the Revolution, its social climate was not much different from that of its Puritan neighbors. Roman Catholics and Jews were denied citizenship. Stage performances judged immoral were banned after 1762. "Although Williams is celebrated as the prophet of religious freedom," Perry Miller wrote, "he actually exerted little or no influence on institutional development in America; only after the conception of liberty for all denominations had triumphed on wholly other grounds did Americans look back on Williams and invest him with his ill-fitting halo."[35]

The availability of Williams as a culture hero, however, at least reinforced support for religious liberty among later generations of Americans. And the theology of continuing revelation, which both the Pilgrims and Williams in different ways represented, provided an ideological foundation on which future attempts at pluralism might grow.

THE VALLEY: EVANGELICAL HARVEST

In the first half of the eighteenth century, a construct of value systems that would influence the American future more directly than those developing in either Boston or Providence was taking shape in the upper reaches of the Connecticut Valley. The village of Northampton, perched on the western bank of the Connecticut River, though politically part of Massachusetts, was setting its own cultural direction responsive to the frontier, which in the coastal towns had already begun to seem distant.

Solomon Stoddard, Northampton's vigorous and dynamic Congregational minister for more than half a century, was, among other things, a prototype of what was to become a classic American figure: the political boss. His primary significance for the future, however, was not political in the narrow sense but cultural and religious. Stoddard grasped that the legalistic church system supported by Boston's Puritan elite, both Matherites and Brattleites, would not work for the frontier. If Christianity remained the exclusive property of a pious elect, Christianity would lose America. Even the half-way covenant, under which partial church membership was made available to all baptized Christians, was in practice too restrictive to fit conditions in Northampton and the Valley. Stoddard's solution was not that of Williams: he saw no special merit in diversity. Nor did he favor a more genial and liberal religion of the kind the Brattles and their friends were introducing in Boston. God would be a God of mercy, Stoddard bluntly held, even "if it had pleased him never to exercise any." Stoddard's religion would be rock-hard Calvinism, but Calvinism that reached out to appeal to the masses. Not more democratic— Stoddard maintained tight discipline through his church elders, who "were not to be over-ruled by the brethren"—but more popular.[36]

The first step was to admit all professing Christians to participation in the Lord's Supper (more important to the Puritans than baptism as a sacrament opening the way to salvation). Let the church include the whole town, Stoddard proposed, and then "let God do the selecting." The essential thing, after all, was not scholastic definition of the requirements for church membership, but the salvation of human souls. The conversion of souls, Stoddard claimed, could best be achieved through the second of his innovations, a style of preaching that appealed not to dry intellect but to living experience, to fear of damnation and hope of heaven. "The word is a hammer," he said, "and we should use it to break the rocky hearts of men."[37]

In a series of evangelical revivals in Northampton, Stoddard tested his conviction that both church members and potential converts should be "thoroughly scared with the dangers of damnation." He did not shrink from breaking new ground. "If the practises of our Fathers in any particulars were mistakes," he said, "it is fit they should be rejected, if they be not, they will bear examination." Five "seasons of harvest" substantially increased church rolls. By imparting the "threatnings of God," Stoddard exulted, he was winning souls to righteousness.[38]

Back in Boston, leaders of the old establishment were appalled both by Stoddard's opening up of church membership and by his unrestrained whipping up of emotion. "Would he bring the Churches in New-England back to the Imperfect Reformation in other Lands," Increase Mather demanded, "and so deprive us of our Glory for ever?" Stoddard was undeterred. "Mr. Mather," he said, "all along intermingles Passionate Lamentations with his Arguments," which "serve to swell the Book and make it more in bulk, but not in Weight." Results, he insisted, justified his method. "There is a necessity of vindicating the Truth, yet we cannot do it without making some disturbance."[39]

Before he died in 1729, Stoddard had the satisfaction of seeing his grandson, Jonathan Edwards, ordained as his successor in Northampton. In time, Edwards would conclude that Stoddard had gone too far in relaxing the formal requirements for church membership and would recommend reinstituting stricter tests for admission to the Lord's Supper, thereby providing his enemies with an excuse through which to drive him from the Northampton pulpit. But Edwards never lost confidence in his grandfather's style of evangelism or in his emphasis on experience as the heart of true religion. The Great Awakening of the 1730s and early 1740s, an event of epochal significance for both religion and politics in America, was the flower of the seed that Stoddard had planted.

Jonathan Edwards has a folk reputation—based largely on his sermon, *Sinners in the Hands of an Angry God,* in which he memorably portrayed mankind held by God "over the spit of hell, much as one holds a spider or some loathsome insect over the fire"—as the quintessence of dour New England Puritanism. Scholars present another Edwards—indeed, one of many facets: the student of science, who is said to have understood Isaac Newton better than anyone else in North America; the lover of nature who tenderly described the sombre beauty of New England; the humanitarian who befriended the Indians; and most of all, the theologian of the first rank who gave coherence and clarity to Puritan doctrine.[40]

The dourness popularly attributed to Edwards's outlook on life certainly reflects a part of the man's character. Fear of damnation hangs over much of his work. "Wickedness," he observed, "is agreeable to the nature of mankind in its present state." In the fallen condition to which men have been carried by original sin, he wrote, "there are no means within reach that can be any security to them." Man's very existence from one moment to the next is sustained only by "the mere arbitrary will, and uncovenanted, unobliged forbearance of an incensed God."[41]

Yet, through God's grace, what a prospect has been opened for mankind. "I am bold to say," Edwards wrote, "that the conversion of one soul . . . is a more glorious work of God than the creation of the whole material universe." The road to salvation is rugged and hard but at the end lies the promised "kingdom of holiness, purity, love, peace, and happiness to mankind."[42]

The scholastic rationalism of the earlier Puritans, Edwards noted, was being converted by the "broad and catholick" clergy of Boston into justification for a religion devoted "almost wholly in benevolence to men," and "little in respect to the divine Being." Edwards would have none of it. His theology "scientifically, deliberately committed Puritanism, which had been a fervent rationalism of the covenant, to a pure passion of the senses, and the terror he imparted was the terror of modern man, the terror of insecurity." Edwards's study of science, Perry Miller observed, was aimed at bringing men "face to face . . . with the divinity of divinity."[43]

Edwards, however, was no antinomian, no radical personalist. Human society, he believed, following Calvin, is inherently corrupt but nevertheless provides a vehicle for God's purpose. Social discipline is needed to provide some protection against the natural selfishness that stems from original sin. Mankind would "scarce be able to subsist in the world" if God had not ordained "civil government to keep men from destroying each other." Beyond that, existing society offers a means for making the first steps toward God's earthly kingdom. The kingdom, Edwards held, "will not be accomplished at once, as by some miracle," but will be "*gradually* brought to pass." The ascent will be difficult, but the direction is clear: it is "God's manner to keep things always progressive."[44]

Edwards took little direct part in politics. In his youth, Alan Heimert reports, he subscribed to "what might be called squirearchical government." Distrust of abstract reason made him suspicious of the political liberalism that broad and catholic Boston clerics like Charles Chauncy and Jonathan Mayhew were grafting onto rationalist theology. Yet an equalitarian spirit, which has something in common with John Wise's equalitarian populism, rises from Edwards's writings and sermons. The social objective of Christians, he maintained, should be "a condition of perfect *brotherhood,* as becomes beings of the same race, the offspring of one God." In nature, he found "so much equality, so much beauty." He did not, however, like Wise, attribute special virtue to a particular class. Progress toward a "happy" Christian commonwealth, he taught, requires suppression of "envy" as well as pride.[45]

Edwards's chief influence on politics came through his role in relating the millennial expectations aroused by the Great Awakening to progressive American nationalism. The Awakening, a blossoming of religious enthusiasm carried out through revivals similar to those that had been organized by Stoddard, began with a series of sermons Edwards preached in Northampton in 1734. As it proceeded, active leadership passed to more naturally exuberant personalities, such as George Whitefield, the celebrated English evangelist, who campaigned up and down the Atlantic coast to become "the first American public figure known from New Hampshire to Georgia," and Gilbert and William Tennent, champions of "New Side" Presbyterianism in the middle colonies. Edwards became disturbed at the emotional extremes that entered some of the later revivals but continued to regard the Awakening as a forerunner of a fundamental change in human affairs.[46]

" 'Tis not unlikely," Edwards wrote, "that this work of God's spirit, that is so extraordinary and wonderful, is the dawning, or at least a prelude, of that glorious work of God often foretold in Scripture, which the progress and issue of it shall renew the world of mankind." From the time of the first settlements in the New World, many had believed that God had selected America for some great work. Now it was clear to the evangelicals what this work must be: development of a model for the "unspeakably happy and glorious" human society that was to precede the last judgment. "The latter-day glory," Edwards predicted, "is probably to begin in America."[47] The Great Awakening "made noncataclysmic millenarianism 'the common and vital possession' of evangelical American Christianity."[48] Belief in progress toward a better society became for eighteenth century evangelicals not simply a secular passion but a conclusion drawn from religious prophecy.

The rationalist clergy viewed the Awakening with predictable scorn. Timothy Cutler, an Anglican priest and former rector at Yale, commented bitterly that when Gilbert Tennent preached in Boston "people wallowed in snow, night and day, for the benefit of his beastly brayings." Charles Chauncy, leader of Boston's "Old Light" Congregational establishment (which a generation earlier had been the new wave pounding the bulwark of orthodoxy guarded by the Mathers), diagnosed revivalism as "properly a disease, a sort of madness." Chauncy's trump card was to identify revivalism with extreme personalist enthusiasm exemplified by Münster: "It has made strong attempts to destroy all property, to make all things common, wives as well as goods." To Edwards's argument that revivalism touched the inner spirit rather than simply the intellect, Chauncy replied that false teachers had "always been very shy of close Reasoning, chusing rather to have their Scheme admitted by the Affections." Young Jonathan Mayhew, observing the Awakening from Harvard Yard, decided that the revivalists were "enlightened Ideots" who made "inspiration, and the Spirit of truth and wisdom, the vehicale of nonsense and contradictions."[49]

By the middle of the 1740s the rationalists were more than holding their own in the seaboard cities and towns. In 1750 triumphant Old Lights in Northampton itself ousted Edwards as minister. (Still a relatively young man, he became a missionary to the Indians in western Massachusetts. In 1758 as he was about to become president of the recently formed college at Princeton, a New Light stronghold, he died as the result of a smallpox inoculation.) The evangelicals, however, remained dominant in large parts of the interior: most of the Connecticut Valley, the Berkshire hills of Massachusetts, central New Jersey, the Great Valley of Pennsylvania and Virginia (a major staging area in later generations for migration to the Middle West), Virginia's northern neck, and the Carolina highlands, among other regions. Rationalists might prevail in the cities and for the time at most of the colleges, but the evangelicals had captured the frontier. And the frontier was to become America.

In the period leading up to the Revolution, the rationalist clergy helped to formulate and popularize a liberal ideology that justified resistance against perceived English oppression. The rationalists were particularly incensed by proposals within the Church of England for appointment of an Anglican bishop for the North American colonies. Such a step, they feared, would have the effect of asserting Anglican authority over the virtually autonomous Congregational bodies. They also, however, were aroused by more general sentiments of nationalism and individualism. Jonathan Mayhew, before his untimely death in 1766, played a leading role in the agitation against the stamp tax.

Charles Chauncy, who lived through the Revolution, ardently backed the patriot cause.

But it was the evangelical New Lights of the interior, viewing nationhood as the essential first step in God's plan for America, who rallied the farmers, mechanics, and small-town merchants whose participation was to prove crucial in the struggle for independence. "What do we mean by the American Revolution?" John Adams asked long afterward. "Do we mean the American war? The Revolution was effected before the war commenced. The Revolution was in the minds and hearts of the people; a change in their religious sentiments. . . ."[50] The change in sentiments that Adams recalled was rooted in the Great Awakening, in the dawn of a new conviction that America, like ancient Israel, was a God-chosen nation, destined, as Edwards wrote, to begin the glorious work that in God's good time would "renew the world of mankind."

Degrees of Diversity

The practice of American pluralism, historians maintain, largely originated in the middle colonies, particularly New York, Pennsylvania, and Maryland. In Pennsylvania and Maryland this development was fed by the philosophic convictions and religious beliefs of the respective founders of these colonies, William Penn and George and Caecilius Calvert. In New York it owed more to circumstance—was in fact resisted by official policy during much of the century preceding the Revolution.

NEW YORK: PLURALISM BY ACCIDENT

The chief political factors contributing to New York's religious pluralism were its origin as a colony of the Netherlands and the tolerant approach favored by James, duke of York, who controlled its governmental authority after the English took over in 1664. These factors, plus the colony's natural advantages as a gateway to the interior, helped attract an unusually cosmopolitan population, which in turn produced an enduring constituency for pluralism.

The seventeenth century Netherlands, though not quite the oasis of social liberalism its reputation has come to suggest, was for its time exceptionally tolerant of religious diversity. Partly for commercial reasons, the dominant merchant class welcomed refugees fleeing persecution by various forms of absolutist idealism. Although the Dutch Reformed church, a Calvinist offshoot, was legally established, and no other religious body was officially entitled to public worship, the law was not strictly enforced. A multiplicity of sects and denominations flourished.

The colony of New Netherlands, descended from Henry Hudson's voyage of exploration in 1609, was managed by a military and commercial establishment that seems to have regarded religion with disdain. One early governor entertained himself while drunk by chasing the colony's Dutch Reformed pastor with a drawn sword, and another regularly fired cannon on the green during church services. Disrespect for organized religion by the colony's rulers had the effect of opening it up to settlement by members of many faiths. A French Jesuit who visited New Netherlands in 1643 observed that there were "besides Calvinists in the Colony Catholics, English Puritans, Lutherans, Anabaptists. . . ."[51]

Besides accommodating religious variety, the colony's administration was permissive toward "alcohol consumption, brawling, and Sabbath desecration." When Peter Stuyvestant arrived as military governor in 1647, he found a state bordering on social anarchy. As part of a program to restore moral discipline, Stuyvestant set out to make the Reformed church the colony's officially established religion in fact as well as in name.[52] The policy of welcoming adherents of other faiths, however, continued. In 1654 a ship carrying Jewish refugees from Brazil entered New Amsterdam harbor. The Netherlands at the time was the only country in western Europe where Jews were officially welcome. As a result, Jews collaborated with Dutch colonial expansion in many parts of the world. The Jewish families that came to New Amsterdam were part of a group that a quarter century before had helped the Dutch take the Brazilian port of Recife from the Portuguese. When the Portuguese reconquered Recife, the Jews had to get out.

The Dutch Reformed minister in New Amsterdam opposed admission of the Jews because "we have here Papists, Mennonites and Lutherans among the Dutch; also many Puritans or Independents, and many Atheists and various other servants of Baal among the English under this Government, who conceal themselves under the name of Christian; it would create still further confusion, if the obstinate and immovable Jews came to settle here."[53] The governing authorities, however, were true to the Dutch tradition, and the Jews were permitted to settle, thereby beginning the life of organized Judaism in the territory that was to become the United States. (A scattering of individual Jews had come earlier to the English colonies.)

In 1664 an English fleet appeared before New Amsterdam. Charles II, implementing a general strategy of global assertiveness he had initiated after the Stuart restoration in 1660, had given his brother, the duke of York, title to a vast area between the Delaware River and the Connecticut Valley that included the Dutch colony. The practical Dutch recognized the military situation as hopeless, and New Netherlands became New York (reverting briefly back again when the military balance temporarily favored the Dutch in 1673–74).

Pursuing the usual Stuart passion for strong executive government, the duke instituted a colonial administration that was much more authoritarian than those dared by the overlords of the other English colonies. Toward religious diversity, however, he was if anything more tolerant than the Dutch had been. There were two reasons for this apparent anomaly. First, he sought political backing from the Dutch patroons, who still controlled large tracts along the Hudson, and therefore found it prudent to avoid antagonizing the formerly established Dutch Reformed church. Second, and more important, he sympathized with the plight of English Roman Catholics, persecuted since Tudor times, whose ranks he was to join as a convert in 1672.

Thomas Dongan, a Catholic appointed by the duke as governor in 1682, brought several Jesuit priests to the colony and actively promoted Catholic immigration. In 1683 Dongan sponsored a bill granting freedom of worship to all Christians. This charter of tolerance was not popular with the colony's Protestant majority, who regarded it as a means for attracting more Catholics. When the duke of York ascended the throne to become James II in 1685, Protestants in New York, as in England, feared a plot to restore Catholicism as the established religion.[54]

The Glorious Revolution of 1688 (as it was shrewdly titled by the victorious Whigs) sent James packing and put the Protestants William and Mary in his place. New York Protestants responded with an uprising of their own, remembered to history as Leisler's Rebellion, after its leader, Jacob Leisler, a German-born Calvinist. The elected assembly called by Leisler suspended "all Roman Catholics from Command and Places of Trust" and authorized arrest of "reputed Papists." Dongan (by now retired but living on Long Island) and the Jesuits who had joined him in New York fled for their lives.[55]

The new government in England, anxious that anti-Catholicism not be confused with hankerings toward democracy, quickly got rid of Leisler, who was hanged. But the governor sent by William was required to sign a declaration condemning key items in Catholic theology. Catholics were denied the right to vote, and "Jesuits and Popish Priests" were prohibited from entering the colony. A small but vigorous Catholic community nevertheless remained, surpassed in numbers only by those in Maryland and Pennsylvania.[56]

From Leisler's Rebellion to the American Revolution, the Church of England, usually with the support of royal governors, steadily insisted that it was the colony's established religion. Dutch Calvinists and Presbyterians, who had become numerous, just as regularly opposed this claim. A law approved by the New York Assembly in 1693 decreed that "a good, sufficient, Protestant Minister" should be supported by public taxes in each of the towns of the four southern counties, New York, Richmond, Westchester, and Queens. But it did not specifically mention the Church of England and left the situation in the rest of the colony ambiguous. In 1731 a court ruled that the town of Jamaica in Queens could select a Presbyterian minister rather than an Anglican for its established church. The true situation was one of "multiple establishment," under which each community was required to support an established church but was left to pick its preferred denomination, so long as the choice was Protestant.[57]

In the middle years of the eighteenth century New York became a center of the resistance against appointment of an Anglican bishop for the colonies (the same issue that helped mobilize the rationalist Old Light Congregationalists of Massachusetts against royal authority). Installation of a bishop in America, Presbyterians and other dissenters argued, would be a step toward enforcing the Anglicans' claim to exclusive establishment. The issue underlay the struggle between Anglicans and Presbyterians for control of King's College (later Columbia) in the 1750s. William Livingston, a prominent Presbyterian lawyer, wrote a series of widely read newspaper polemics that broadened the controversy to a general argument for religious liberty based on the philosophy of natural rights then being popularized in England by disciples of John Locke. "Among the many Instances of the Abuse of Government," Livingston maintained, "there is none more immediately destructive of the natural Rights of Mankind, than the Interposition of the secular Arm in Matters purely religious."[58]

The dispute over establishment was abruptly terminated (in New York though not in some of the other states) by American independence. The New York constitution of 1777 resoundingly proclaimed that "all such parts of the said common law . . . as may be construed to establish or maintain any particular denomination of Christians or their ministers . . . be, and they hereby are, abrogated and rejected." (Note, however, that the revolutionary constitution contained no prohibition against state support for religion in general.) Going beyond simple disestablishment, the constitution further held that "no minister of the gospel or priests of any denomination whatsoever, shall at any time hereafter, under any pretence or deception whatever, be eligible to, or capable of holding any civil or military office or place within this state." Religious pluralism was thus linked to a spirit of hard-nosed anticlericalism that was to have an extended life in New York politics.[59]

PENNSYLVANIA: PLURALISM BY DESIGN

William Penn regarded the colony he founded in 1782 on the west bank of the Delaware River as a "Holy Experiment." In contrast to many such experiments in applied religion, Penn's plan for Pennsylvania envisioned achieving spiritual enlightenment, though not moral regulation, through voluntary acceptance of salvation by individuals instead of through the offices of an established church.

Penn's Quaker faith was among the most extreme of the personalist-leaning offshoots of the pietist branch of the Reformation. The emphasis placed by George Fox, Quakerism's founder, on individual experience of the "inner light" as the essence of religion was condemned by more orthodox Christians (including such constitutional pluralists as Roger Williams) as excessively individualistic and mystical. But in the atmosphere of religious excitement prevailing in England during the Puritan Commonwealth, it won a small but dedicated body of believers.

The Quakers' distinctive insistence on pacifism was not originally part of Fox's doctrine. As an ally of the radical fringe of Puritanism that sought revolutionary transformation of society, Fox at first held no scruple against military means: "To them that do well, the sword is a praise." He urged the leaders of the Puritan army to wage holy war against Protestantism's archenemy: "If ever you Souldiers and true Officers come again into the power of God which hath been lost, never set up your standart until you come to *Rome,* and it be atopt *Rome* then there let your standart stand. . . ." But as Oliver Cromwell's government succeeded in suppressing the radicals, Fox came to believe, as of course he may have done in any case, that violence even in a good cause is contrary to God's will.[60]

By the time of the Stuart Restoration, Fox had led the Quakers to a position of total pacifism. A "Declaration from the harmless and innocent people of God, called Quakers," issued in 1661, rejected "all outward wars and strife and fightings with outward weapons, for any end or under all pretence whatsoever." The Quakers promised obedience to Charles II, but refused to pay taxes for support of the Church of England and would not testify under oath (which they regarded as idolatrous). Official persecution followed.[61]

While fully sharing Fox's belief in the importance of the inner light, Penn was convinced that the light held implications for worldly conduct this side of the millennium. Like Jonathan Edwards later, he considered that the signs of the times indicated a ripeness for preparing at least a model for God's earthly kingdom. Also like Edwards, Penn regarded America, free of the encumbrances of European history, as the likely site for such a departure. Pennsylvania was founded, he wrote, "that an example may be set up to the nations; there may be room there, though not here [in England], for such an Holy Experiment." (Fox, twenty years older than Penn, was not so sure. "My friends," he wrote, "that are gone, and are going over to plant, and make outward plantations in America, keep your own plantations in your hearts, with the spirit and power of God, that your own vines and lillies be not hurt.")[62]

Penn was in no way a secularist. "If we are not governed by God," he wrote, "then we will be ruled by tyrants." But the Quaker emphasis on individual experience helped carry him away from the Puritan view, common to many forms of idealism, that government should be responsible for imposing orthodox religious belief. The organic law of Pennsylvania, enacted in 1690, while assuming a basic theism, held that no person acknowledging "one Almighty God . . . shall in any case be molested or prejudiced for his, or her conscientious persuasion or practice, nor shall hee or shee at any time be compelled to frequent or Maintain anie religious worship, place or Ministry whatsoever Contrary to his, or her mind. . . ."[63]

Religious liberty, however, did not imply a morally permissive society open to exploitation by egoism such as that which had existed in New Amsterdam. Penn's conception of the role of government as a regulator of morals was not far from that of the Puritans. With his approval the Pennsylvania assembly decreed that adulterers "for the first offense be publicly whipt and suffer one whole year's imprisonment in the house of Correction at hard labour" and for any subsequent infraction suffer "imprisonment in manner aforesaid During Life." Blasphemers were to be fined ten pounds or committed to three months' imprisonment at hard labor. On the Sabbath, workers were required to "abstain from their usual and common toil and labour," as a means for assuring that "Looseness, Irreligion, and Atheism may not creep in under the pretence of Conscience in this Province."[64]

At times Penn displayed the disdain for public affairs characteristic of one kind of personalism. "Meddle not with government," he wrote to his children in 1699. "Never speak of it, let others say or do as they please. . . . I have said little to you about distributing justice, or being just in power or government, for I should desire that you should never be concerned therein." But more usually he regarded social action as a natural outlet for religious enthusiasm. "Government," he wrote while actively guiding the colony's development, "seems to me a part of religion itself, a thing sacred in its institutions and purpose."[65]

Others who migrated to Pennsylvania were drawn by religious conviction to address social problems. In 1688 Francis Daniel Pastorius, leader of a group of German pietists who settled at Germantown outside Philadelphia, was joined by three Mennonites in issuing a call for the abolition of slavery—the first such in America and among the first in Western history. "Here is liberty of conscience, which is right and reasonable," Pastorius wrote. "Here ought to be likewise liberty of ye body. . . ." The Quakers and pietists in the colonial assembly followed Penn's example in promoting fair treatment for the Indians.[66]

Quakers other than Penn seem to have been more adept at advocating social reforms than at the pragmatic tasks of building a society, perhaps a further example of the effects of personalism. Digby Baltzell has argued that the extreme otherworldliness of the Quakers' religion undermined their fitness for social leadership (though many of them did well at business).[67] Almost from the colony's inception, Penn found it necessary to recruit tough-minded Anglican soldiers and politicians to fill top administrative posts. Guided by the idea of the covenant, Puritan Boston, Baltzell points out, produced far more distinguished political leaders and social theorists, both in colonial times and during the early years of the Republic, than Quaker Philadelphia. Indeed, Philadelphia's most significant public figure after Penn, Benjamin Franklin, grew up in Boston.

Until the middle of the eighteenth century, the Quakers maintained a majority in the colonial assembly but were increasingly torn by conflict between their religious principles and practical pressures rising out of the long military struggle between England and France for control of North America. Franklin, who became active in Pennsylvania politics in the 1730s, later wrote, "My being many years in the Assembly, a majority of which were constantly Quakers, gave me frequent opportunity of seeing the embarrassment given them by their principles against war, whenever application was made to them, by order of the crown to grant aids for military purposes. They were unwilling to offend the government on the one hand, by direct refusal; and their friends, the body of the Quakers, on the other by a compliance contrary to their principles; using a variety of evasions to avoid complying, and modes of disguising the compliance when it became unavoidable."[68]

During Queen Anne's reign the Quakers in the assembly voted funds "for the Queen's use," knowing the appropriation would be used for military purposes but persuading themselves, as one said, that they were not responsible for "any use she might put it to, that being not our part but hers." At another time, an appropriation was voted for "bread, beef, pork, flour, wheat and other grains" with the tacit understanding that "other grains" would include gunpowder. Finally, in 1756, the colony found itself actually at war with the Delaware and Shawnee Indians. The Quaker assemblymen concluded among themselves that the sham should be preserved no longer and resigned as a group.[69]

After England's victory over France in 1763, the Quakers reentered colonial politics. With Franklin as their agent, they sought alliance with the British crown to offset the power of Penn's descendants, the proprietors, who had returned to the Church of England. The proprietors, for their part, looked for allies among the Scotch-Irish Presbyterians of western Pennsylvania. An election broadside circulated by the proprietary party among the Scotch-Irish called for a common front against "the eastern, Quaker-dominated, pacifist, Indian-coddling, undemocratic Assembly party."[70]

The Quakers never regained their former ascendancy within the colonial government. But the policy of religious pluralism they had initiated was continued. Besides Quakers and German pietists, religious liberty attracted to Pennsylvania numerous Presbyterians and Lutherans and smaller groups of Baptists and Catholics. Anglicans and later Methodists were also well represented. Several of these denominations set up extensive systems of elementary and secondary education. The University of Pennsylvania, growing out of the academy founded in 1740 as America's first nonsectarian college, gave further expression to the pluralist spirit. Though scorned by a contemporary New Englander as a "swamp of sectarianism," Pennsylvania produced a culture and a society that "foreshadowed . . . the variety and lay activism which were later to become characteristic of the whole American religious scene."[71]

In practice Pennsylvania fell well short of pluralist republican standards. The first state constitution of 1776 limited membership in the legislature to Christians. This restriction was removed in the constitution of 1790, but suffrage was still confined to free white males (as it was in all other states). Nevertheless, Penn's colony and the state that grew out of it endeavored with rare persistence to embody in actual institutions the values of constitutional pluralism.

MARYLAND: CATHOLIC HAVEN

A more limited experiment with religious pluralism was briefly attempted in Maryland. George Calvert, Lord Baltimore, a Stuart favorite who had converted to Catholicism, applied to Charles I in 1630 for the grant of a proprietary colony north of the Potomac River that he aimed, like the duke of York later, to make a haven in the New World for fellow English Catholics. Calvert died before the king acted on his petition. But in 1632 the grant was approved to Calvert's son, Caecilius, second Lord Baltimore. Understandably wary in the slippery time that culminated in the English Civil War and the execution of Charles, Caecilius Calvert gave cautious instructions to his colonial administrators. All Christians, he ordered, should have religious freedom in Maryland. But he directed that Catholic worship must be kept "as privately as may be" and that Catholics should not discuss religion in public.[72]

Calvert's plan for Maryland went further than that of any other English colony, in attempting to impose a feudal structure on society. "Nowhere else was the manorial system with its attendant distinctions and privileges and with its aristocratic and seignorial life so fully established and realized."[73] In the first few years the upper class, commanding fertile estates on the eastern shore of Chesapeake Bay, was composed largely of recusant English Catholics. Calvert also turned over large tracts to the Jesuits, who used them as bases for missionary work among the Indians. Within a short time, however, Protestants of a Puritan persuasion formed a majority of the colony's white population.

Reacting to the Puritan victory in England, Calvert pressured the Maryland assembly in 1649 to pass an Act of Toleration that he hoped would preserve religious freedom for Catholics. The act decreed that "noe person or persons whatsoever within this Province . . . professing to believe in Jesus Christ, shall from henceforth bee any waies troubled, Molested or discountenanced for or in respect of his or her religion nor in the free exercise thereof." (The precise language of the last phrase was later used in the First Amendment to the federal Constitution.) Perhaps aiming to allay charges of softness toward irreligion, the assembly at the same time established the death penalty for blasphemers and deniers of the trinity. It further ordered whipping and imprisonment for any person calling another "an heretic, schismatic, idolator, Puritan, Independent, Presbyterian, papish priest, Jesuit, Jesuited papist, Lutheran, Calvinist, Anabaptist, Brownist, Antinomian, Barrowist, Roundhead, Separatist, or any other term in a reproachful manner relating to matters of religion"—which must have had a dampening effect on religious discussion.[74]

Calvert's attempt to provide statutory protection for religious pluralism failed. In 1655 Puritan insurgents routed a force supporting the incumbent administration at the "Battle of the Severn," and installed a firmly Protestant government. The victorious Puritans repudiated the Act of Toleration, seized the Jesuits' estates, exiled all priests from the colony, and executed at least four Catholics. The Cromwell government in England annulled a Maryland act effectively outlawing "the Popish religion" but approved an order excluding Catholics from public office. Calvert maintained a tenuous hold on the proprietorship by agreeing to appoint a Protestant governor.[75]

After the Stuart Restoration in 1660 the Calverts regained some of their lost authority but met continuing hostility from the Protestant majority because of economic and social as well as religious differences. The Glorious Revolution of 1688 led to abrogation of the Calverts' original charter and conversion of the colony into a royal province. The Church of England was established by an act of 1702, making attendance at Anglican services compulsory and providing for church support out of tax revenues. Catholics were prohibited from voting, although after 1712 they were permitted to worship in private. In 1715 the Calvert heir was granted a new charter—two years after his father, the fourth Lord Baltimore, had embraced the Anglican religion.

Catholics nevertheless remained more numerous in Maryland than in any other colony, and some of the old Catholic families continued to prosper. In the 1750s Charles Carroll of Annapolis, reputedly the richest man in British America, threatened to emigrate to French Louisiana when the colonial legislature levied double taxation on Catholics to help finance the war effort against France. (Carroll's son, Charles Carroll of Carrollton, became the only Catholic to sign the Declaration of Independence, and his cousin, John Carroll, was consecrated in 1790 as the first Catholic bishop in the United States.) The Jesuits maintained a presence in Maryland, regaining much of the land they had lost in 1655. When Pope Clement XIV (a Franciscan) dissolved the Jesuit order in 1773, Jesuits in Maryland were able to hold onto some of their land, which was later used, after the order's restoration in 1814, to support Catholic missions in America.

With the coming of national independence the Maryland constitution of 1776 gave authority to the state legislature to "lay a general and equal tax, for the support of the Christian religion; leaving to each individual the power of appointing the payment over of the money, collected from him, to the support of any particular place of worship or minister, or for the benefit of the poor of his own denomination, or the poor in general of any particular county."[76] It was an ingenious device for maintaining what Freeman Butts calls "multiple establishment," a system of state aid to religion now employed by the Federal Republic of Germany and several other countries in Western Europe. Direct state support for religion in Maryland was finally terminated by an amendment to the state constitution in 1810.

The American Enlightenment

If Puritanism was the most important intellectual and cultural force shaping the American mind in the second half of the eighteenth century, the European Enlightenment was unquestionably second. The Enlightenment itself had important roots in the individualism and rationalism fostered by Puritanism. Its main impact in America, however, came, as one writer has observed, not through "the witch-hunting Puritans of New England," but through "the fox-hunting cavaliers of Virginia."

VIRGINIA: WHIG SQUIREARCHY

Virginia, founded in 1607, thirteen years before the Pilgrims arrived on Cape Cod, maintained throughout its colonial existence an officially established Anglican church. Though the colony's early settlers freely acknowledged the commercial and political motives that brought them to the New World, many also were intent, as their charter stated, on ensuring that the "true word and service of God and the Christian faith" should "be preached, planted, and used." In the absence of a resident bishop, the colonial governor exercised quasi-episcopal authority over the Anglican clergy. During most of the seventeenth century, church attendance was required and payment of church rates was compulsory. The governor designated "glebes," tracts of land to be used for the support of the church and its ministers.[77]

As a result of the English Act of Toleration of 1689 (confirmed by a statute approved by the Virginia House of Burgesses in 1699), Protestant dissenters whose ministers and places of worship were registered were given the right to hold public services. Presbyterians and Baptists began to move into the Shenandoah Valley from Maryland and Pennsylvania and gradually to fan eastward through the Piedmont and Tidewater. Formation of non-Anglican evangelical congregations greatly accelerated during the Great Awakening. The Anglican clergy, by all accounts an indolent lot, made some efforts to curb the growth of dissenting denominations through legislation that would "check night meetings, preaching among slaves, and other new dangers," but with little success. By the time of the Revolution, dissenters, according to one estimate, constituted about two-thirds of the white population.[78]

When the Revolution broke out, most of the Anglican clergy stayed loyal to the crown. Disestablishment, nevertheless, was resisted more stubbornly within the newly formed commonwealth than in most of the other states where Anglicanism had been established.

The Anglican planter aristocracy, many of whom subscribed to liberal social ideas received from English Whiggery, dominated the commonwealth government. When a convention gathered in Williamsburg to draft a state constitution in the spring of 1776, George Mason, a liberal Anglican, proposed a bill of rights with a clause granting "the fullest Toleration in the Exercise of Religion." Young James Madison, observing that "toleration" would not necessarily prohibit the kind of establishment that had existed in Virginia since 1699, offered a substitute declaring that "all men are equally entitled to the full and free exercise of religion," and that therefore "no man or class of men ought, on account of religion to be invested with any peculiar emoluments or privileges." Patrick Henry, who seems characteristically to have been moving in several different directions at the same time, supported Madison's amendment, while claiming, illogically, that it contained no implication of disestablishment.[79]

Madison then drafted a second amendment that dropped the clause specifically eliminating "peculiar emoluments or privileges" for a religious class. The language finally included in Virginia's Declaration of Rights, approved a few weeks before the signing of the Declaration of Independence, held that "all men are equally entitled to the free exercise of religion according to the dictates of conscience; and that it is the mutual duty of all to practice Christian forebearance, love and charity toward the other," thereby decreeing religious freedom, while at the same time affirming the foundation of Virginia society on values attributed to the Christian faith.[80]

The practical effect of the Declaration of Rights was at first uncertain. In the autumn of 1776 the Hanover Presbytery, wishing to clarify the status of dissenters, petitioned the legislature to enact a definite statute exempting Virginia citizens "from all taxes for the support of any church whatsoever further than what may be agreeable to their own private choice, or voluntary obligation," the concluding phrase leaving open the possibility that the state might act as a sort of collection agency for voluntary church taxes. The legislature responded with a law making "all dissenters of whatever denomination . . . totally free and exempt from all levies, taxes and impositions whatever toward supporting and maintaining the said [Anglican] church." Church taxes on Anglicans were also temporarily suspended. But when Thomas Jefferson in 1779 proposed a bill that would unequivocally complete disestablishment, the legislature killed it with a tabling motion. The struggle for disestablishment in Virginia, Jefferson later said, was "the severest contest in which I have ever been engaged."[81]

After the Revolution, conservatives among the Virginia leadership, including George Washington, John Marshall, and the volatile Patrick Henry, became convinced that restoration of direct state support for religion was needed to strengthen social stability. In 1784 Henry introduced a bill that would authorize "a moderate tax or contribution annually for the support of the Christian religion, or of some Christian church, denomination or communion of Christians, or for some form of Christian worship." Henry argued that state support for Christianity was justified on purely secular grounds. "The general diffusion of Christian knowledge [has] a natural tendency to correct the morals of men, restrain their vices, and preserve the peace of society. . . ." The proposed legislation would permit each taxpayer to designate the church to which his tax dollars should be paid, or, if he preferred, "for the encouragement of seminars of learning within the Counties where such sums shall arise." George Washington supported the bill, with the proviso that exemptions should be granted to those declaring themselves "Jews, Mahometans, or otherwise."[82] Many of the dissenters, particularly the Baptists, and the liberals, led by Jefferson and Madison, opposed the church subsidy bill. Henry, however, appeared to have the votes.

To rally opposition to the bill among the general public, Madison wrote his famous *Memorial and Remonstrance Against Religious Assessments,* a document, one suspects, now more often cited than read. The *Memorial and Remonstrance* begins with a forthright statement of principle: "The Religion . . . of every man must be left to the conviction and conscience of every man; and it is the right of every man to exercise it as these may dictate. The right is in its nature an unalienable right." From this premise it follows that all men retain an "equal title to the free exercise of Religion according to the dictates of conscience." Public taxation for the support of religion necessarily "violates equality by subjecting some to peculiar burdens." No matter how small, such a tax must be rejected because "the same authority which can force a citizen to contribute three pence only of his property for the support of any one establishment, may force him to conform to any other establishment in all cases whatsoever."[83]

Far from attacking religion, Madison wrote as a Christian believer addressing other Christians, and argued that the principle of religious liberty stems from the inmost nature of Christianity. "Before any man can be considered as a member of Civil Society, he must be considered as a subject of the Governor of the Universe." The duty that each man owes to his particular society must always be subordinated to "his allegiance to the Universal Sovereign." In matters of religion, therefore, "no man's right is abridged by the institution of Civil Society, and . . . Religion is wholly exempt from its cognizance." While Christians "assert for ourselves a freedom to embrace, to profess and to observe the Religion which we believe to be of divine origin, we cannot deny an equal freedom to those whose minds have not yielded to the evidence which has convinced us." To claim that Christianity needs the support of government "is a contradiction to the Christian Religion itself; for every page of it disavows a dependence on the powers of this world: it is a contradiction to fact; for it is known that this Religion both existed and flourished, not only without the support of human laws, but in spite of every opposition from them."[84]

What had come of the long European experiment with an established church? "More or less in all places, pride and indolence in the Clergy; ignorance and servility in the laity; in both superstition, bigotry and persecution." The proposal for taxation to support religion "is adverse to the diffusion of the light of Christianity," because "instead of levelling as far as possible every obstacle to the victorious progress of truth, the Bill with an ignoble and unchristian timidity would circumscribe it, with a wall of defense, against the encroachment of error."[85]

Finally, Madison maintains, in the last of fifteen numbered arguments for rejection of Henry's bill, religious liberty is "the gift of nature." This final argument has led some commentators to conclude that Madison's case for religious liberty is essentially secular. But since he had already indicated his belief that nature is subject to the "Governor of the Universe," his theory of natural rights, like that set forth by Jefferson in the Declaration of Independence, would appear to be rooted in a concept of transcendent moral law.[86]

Soon after the appearance of the *Memorial and Remonstrance*, the bill for religious assessments was killed in committee, with the apparent concurrence of a majority in the legislature. Other factors were involved: Henry, levered upward into the governorship, was otherwise occupied; conservative legislators feared that the church subsidy would require a tax increase. But the effect of Madison's broadside was generally acknowledged to have been decisive.

Taking advantage of the momentum so created, Madison moved quickly to secure passage of Jefferson's bill for religious liberty, which had been tabled by the legislature in 1779. Jefferson, though serving abroad as ambassador to France, followed events closely and gave tactical advice. The statute completing disestablishment finally passed in 1785. (It was not, however, incorporated into the Virginia Constitution until 1830.)

MADISON AND JEFFERSON: RELIGIOUS FREEDOM

Where did the authors of religious liberty in Virginia, particularly Madison and Jefferson, get their ideas? This question is important to our enterprise, since the Virginia model was to prove exceptionally influential in the debate that soon followed at the national level.

Several of the Virginia liberals, including Jefferson, Madison, and Mason, had read widely and imbibed freely at the well of Western culture, particularly the common culture enjoyed by educated Englishmen of their time. Jefferson liked to trace his intellectual origins to the Stoic philosophers of antiquity, like Cicero, Seneca, and Marcus Aurelius, in whom he identified "a conception of patriotism and public duty." He was attracted by the ideas of the European Enlightenment and shared the disdain of the *philosophes* for traditional Catholicism (an attitude reinforced and intensified during his tenure as ambassador to France from 1784 to 1789). "The general spread of the light of science," he wrote, "has already laid open to every view the palpable truth, that the mass of mankind has not been born with saddles on their backs, nor a favored few booted and spurred, ready to ride them legitimately, by the grace of God." He approved the Reformation as a movement for the purification of religion but privately condemned the dogmatic turn he believed it had taken under Calvin (a view that would have surprised and irritated his Presbyterian allies in Virginia politics).[87]

Madison studied at Princeton in the early 1770s under John Witherspoon (later a signer of the Declaration of Independence), who introduced him to the writings of the great figures of Scottish realism: David Hume, Thomas Reid, Adam Smith, and Francis Hutcheson, among others. From these, Madison said, he received "very early and strong impressions in favor of Liberty both Civil and Religious."[88]

The core tradition from which the Virginia liberals drew most of their social ideas was that initiated in England during the previous century by John Locke. The Virginians read Locke, who Jefferson said was one of the three greatest men in history (Francis Bacon and Isaac Newton being the other two), directly and encountered him indirectly through his influence on both Scottish realism and the French *philosophes*.[89]

What did Locke have to say about the relationship between government and religion? In the first of his two treatises on government, he argued at length against the absolutist claim that legitimate monarchs inherit their authority from God's donation of dominion over the earth to Adam. "How Adam's being created, which was nothing but his receiving a being immediately from omnipotency and the hand of God," he wrote, "gave Adam a sovereignty over anything, I cannot see." In his much better known *Second Treatise*, Locke proposed the alternative theory that civil government rises from a contract through which men seek to protect and secure the rights of life, liberty, and property that are theirs in a state of nature.[90]

Locke's contract theory for the origin of civil society has provided a political rationale for one branch of civil humanism ever since. But Locke was not himself a civil humanist, not even of the deist variety that acknowledges a clockmaker God who set the world in motion and then left it to be governed by the laws of mechanics. As Ernst Troeltsch pointed out, Locke constructed his system within a "religious setting," which some later Lockeans abandoned. All human life, Locke held, receives meaning and direction from God's "great design of continuing the race of mankind and the occasion of life." The rights to possess and use property, which drive the Lockean system, are founded on a theistic base: "God gave the world to men in common; but since He gave it to them for their benefit, and the greatest conveniences of life they were capable to draw from it, it cannot be supposed He meant it should always remain common and uncultivated. He gave it to the use of the industrious and the rational (and labor was to be [their] title to it), not to the fancy or covetousness of the quarrelsome and contentious."[91]

Locke's position, moreover, is specifically Christian. The "works of nature," he wrote, "sufficiently evidence a Deity." But before the coming of Christ, members of the human race, even the philosophers, were "like people groping and feeling for something in the dark. . . ." In "this state of darkness and error, in reference to the 'true God,' our Saviour found the world." The "clear revelation he brought with him, dissipated this darkness; made the one invisible true God known to the world."[92]

What then are the respective roles of civil government, created for the advancement of self-interest, and religion, on which both government and self-interest ultimately depend for legitimacy? To this question Locke turned his attention in the *Letter Concerning Toleration* (published in 1689).

Locke's task was eased by the fact that he, like the Puritans, regarded religious salvation as a matter of personal experience rather than as the result of inclusion in a divinely designated race or church. Under this view the church becomes "a voluntary society" whose members join themselves together for "the public worshiping of God in such a manner as they judge acceptable to Him, and effectual to the salvation of their souls." Its primary concerns are spiritual and moral, and "nothing ought nor can be transacted in this society relating to the possession of civil and wordly goods."[93]

Civil government, in contrast, exists to assist men in "procuring, preserving, and advancing" their material interests, which include "life, liberty, health, and indolence of body," as well as "possession of outward things, such as money, lands, houses, furniture, and the like." The authority of civil government "neither can nor ought in any manner to be extended to the salvation of souls." Possession of governmental authority confers no authority over religion, because "it appears not that God has ever given any such authority to one man over another as to compel anyone to his religion." Religion imposed through state coercion is not only oppressive but also ineffective because "though the rigour of laws and the force of penalties were capable to convince and change men's minds, yet would not that help at all to the salvation of their souls." (This view of the soul as a virtually unconditioned entity was not far from that of Locke's contemporary, the Quaker George Fox.)[94]

The church and civil society, however, do not occupy mutually exclusive realms. The two come together as complementary means for achieving "a good life," in which "lies the safety both of men's souls and of the commonwealth." The legitimate interests of religion and civil government, therefore, overlap in concern for "moral actions" that belong "to the jurisdiction both of the outward and inward court; both of the civil and domestic governor; I mean both of the magistrate and conscience." In case of conflict between the two, which Locke thought would be rare in a well-administered society where both church and state tend to their primary tasks, "a private person is to abstain from the action that he judges unlawful, and he is to undergo the punishment which it is not unlawful for him to bear." Moral disagreement with "a law enacted in political matters, for the political good, does not take away the obligation of that law, nor deserve a dispensation."[95]

Locke would place certain practical limits on toleration. Mohammedanism, for instance, is not to be tolerated, because a devout Mohammedan "acknowledges himself bound to yield blind obedience to the Mufti of Constantinople, who himself is entirely obedient to the Ottoman Emperor and frames the feigned oracles of that religion according to his pleasure." Atheism, too, is not to be tolerated, because "promises, covenants, and oaths, which are the bonds of human society, can have no hold upon an atheist." Locke's view of atheism highlights his belief that the argument for religious liberty rests ultimately on religion: "Those that by their atheism undermine and destroy all religion, can have no pretence of religion whereupon to challenge the privilege of toleration." Even those holding proscribed religious beliefs, however, should not be denied the rest of their civil liberties: "Neither Pagan nor Mahometan, nor Jew, ought to be excluded from the civil rights of the commonwealth because of his religion."[96]

George Mason's idea of toleration, embodied in his original draft of the Virginia Declaration of Rights, was close to Locke's. James Madison, motivated like Roger Williams by concern that government unchecked would manipulate religion for its own ends, went further in the direction of advocating complete religious liberty.

Madison's political liberalism coexisted with and to some extent grew out of religious orthodoxy. Exposure to New Side Presbyterianism at Princeton seems to have reinforced a naturally religious temperament (in the sense of one concerned with transcendence). Madison coupled the Calvinist view that "there is a degree of depravity in mankind which requires a certain degree of circumspection and distrust" with a cautiously hopeful conviction that "there are other qualities in human nature which justify a certain portion of esteem and confidence"—the conception of human nature that underlies the system of checks and balances which he, among others, incorporated into the federal Constitution.[97]

Madison's idea of religion, like Locke's, was one of a highly personal relationship between the individual and his maker. Madison went beyond Locke in seeking to prevent "unhallowed perversion" by government "of the means of salvation." But he was less rigid than his friend and political ally, Jefferson, in opposing involvement by the churches in public affairs. As Sidney Mead pointed out, Madison's "line of separation between the rights of religion and the civil authority" was more fluid and realistic than Jefferson's "wall of separation." Madison opposed employment of military chaplains by the state because such a connection might introduce "political authority in matters of religion." But he had no objection to "religious instruction and exhortation" of the military services "from a voluntary source." As president, he vetoed a bill passed by Congress that would have incorporated a church in Alexandria, Virginia, and one granting land for construction of a church in Mississippi because these bills singled out religious institutions for special treatment.[98]

Thomas Jefferson shared many of Madison's conclusions in this as in other areas, but he reached them from a more skeptical turn of mind. During the course of his life, Jefferson's personal religious beliefs underwent considerable change. As a young man he questioned the historical accuracy of some stories in the Bible and soon had ceased to be an orthodox trinitarian Christian. While hotly denying charges by his political opponents that he was an atheist, he moved close to the boundary that separates theist-humanism from secular civil humanism. At various times, he called himself a "deist," a "theist," a "unitarian," and a "rational Christian." He subscribed, he said, to the moral teachings of Jesus but rejected what he took to be Jesus' metaphysics: "It is not to be understood that I am with him in all his doctrines. I am a materialist; he takes the side of Spiritualism." Later, he decided he had got Jesus wrong: "Jesus himself, the founder of our religion, was unquestionably a Materialist as to man." As he grew older, Jefferson became increasingly convinced of the truth of theism. Evidences for the existence of God, he wrote to John Adams in 1823, are "irresistible." Shortly before his death, he expressed the view that it would be a good thing if all Americans believed, without compulsion, that there is "only one God, and he all perfect," and that "there is a future state of rewards and punishments."[99]

While his personal religious beliefs fluctuated, Jefferson seems to have held a settled distrust for the clergy of all denominations. "The Presbyterian clergy are the loudest," he wrote in 1820, "the most intolerant of all sects, the most tyrannical and ambitious, ready at the word of the lawgiver, if such a word could now be obtained, to put the torch to the pile." His suspicion of organized religion led him at one point to advocate barring the clergy from public office, a position from which he was swayed by Madison, who persuaded him that such a prohibition would invade civil liberties.[100]

Distrust of the clergy no doubt contributed to Jefferson's view that church and state should be kept as far apart as was politically feasible. "The legitimate powers of government," he wrote in 1782, "extend only to such acts as are injurious to others. But it does me no injury for my neighbor to say there are twenty gods, or no God. It neither picks my pocket nor breaks my leg." Twenty years later, as president, he wrote to the Baptist Association of Danbury, Connecticut, which had inquired about his interpretation of the Bill of Rights, that the First Amendment raises "a wall of separation between church and state," a metaphor that many Americans have come to regard as almost part of the Constitution. As president he refused to proclaim national days of prayer and thanksgiving, as Washington and John Adams had done during earlier administrations and as Madison was to do after.[101]

Yet Jefferson did not believe that civilized society, particularly a society formed as a republic, can get along without religion. Can "the liberties of a nation be thought secure," he asked in 1781, "when we have removed their only firm basis, a conviction in the minds of the people that these liberties are of the gift of God?" He often used religion to advance political ends, sometimes with a touch of cynicism. When the English closed the port of Boston in 1774, he decided that "a day of general fasting & prayer" would help stir up indignation among the public in Virginia. With some political cronies, he "rummaged over" Puritan documents from the previous century, and "cooked up a resolution, somewhat modernizing the phrases." Responsibility for introducing the bill, he later recalled, was entrusted to a member of the House of Burgesses "whose grave & religious character was more in unison with the tone of our resolution." As wartime governor of Virginia, Jefferson sponsored a Bill for Appointing Days of Public Fasting and Thanksgiving that required that "each minister of the gospel shall on each day so to be appointed . . . preach a sermon, or discourse suited to the occasion, in his church, on pain of forfeiting fifty pounds for every failure, not having a reasonable excuse."[102]

Jefferson's invocation of the Deity in the Declaration of Independence is well known: the nation's right to independence is justified by the "Laws of Nature and Nature's God," and men are "endowed by their Creator" with rights to "Life, Liberty, and the Pursuit of Happiness." He approved the "multiplicity of sects" in Pennsylvania and New York, which he judged "sufficient to preserve peace and order [and] morals." Religion, he wrote, should be regarded as "a supplement to law in the government of men," and as "the alpha and omega of the moral law."[103]

Like Jonathan Edwards, Jefferson turned to the Old Testament for a parallel to the role and destiny of America. "I shall need," he said in his second inaugural address, "the favor of that Being in whose hands we are, who led our fathers, as Israel of old, from their native land and planted them in a country flowing with all the necessaries and comforts of life." (Some commentators have argued that Jefferson's identification of the Deity as a "Being" or "Creator," rather than as God, indicates that he clung to deism. But did the watchmaker God lead "our fathers, as Israel of old"?) When he came to plan the University of Virginia, he proposed that the "religious sects of the state" should be invited to "establish within, or adjacent to, the precincts of the University, schools for instruction in the religion of their own sect," an approach similar to the "released time" system used in many public schools before it was declared unconstitutional by the Supreme Court in 1948.[104]

Some of the positions on the role of religion in public life taken by Jefferson at different times were simply inconsistent, as he himself would probably have acknowledged, attributing the inconsistencies to changes of mind or to pressing political needs of the moment. His overall view, however, though based on two sets of values in natural tension, was not necessarily inconsistent. Jefferson firmly believed that government should be barred from acting in any way as arbiter of religion; but he also believed that a free society, a society that upholds personal freedom while functioning effectively as a social whole, requires moral sustenance from a religious culture. These beliefs, which were largely shared by Madison, can exist together within a consistent social philosophy, though they may pull against each other in ways that require difficult constitutional adjustments.

The need for just such adjustments was high on the agenda of the government that took office under the new federal Constitution in 1789. The debates that had been carried on in Virginia now moved to the national level.

A New Nation

On the eve of the Revolution, only three colonies had no provision for an established church: Rhode Island, Pennsylvania, and Delaware. (Formed out of the southeastern extension of Pennsylvania in 1702, Delaware had continued the pluralist system maintained in the parent colony.) In Massachusetts, Connecticut, and New Hampshire, the Congregational church was established, with various provisions permitting Anglicans and dissenters to form their own churches, sometimes with government subsidies. In New York, New Jersey, and the five southern colonies, the Anglican church was established in one form or another.

With the coming of independence, new state constitutions ended Anglican establishments in New Jersey and North Carolina in 1776 and in New York and Georgia in 1777. Virginia carried out a kind of de facto disestablishment, as we have seen, finally ratified by statute in 1785. The Maryland constitution of 1776 provided for establishment of multiple Christian churches. In South Carolina the constitution of

1778 established "the Christian Protestant religion." Pennsylvania, Delaware, and the four New England states continued under roughly the same arrangements that had existed before the Revolution.[105]

THE LANGUAGE OF INDEPENDENCE

For many of its adherents, the Revolution quickly became a religious crusade. While most of the Anglican clergy remained loyal to the crown, the great majority of Congregational and Presbyterian ministers, leading the two most numerous denominations in the former colonies, actively supported the cause of independence. James Otis (himself the "Martin Luther" of colonial protest according to his friend, John Adams) spoke warmly of the "Black Regiment" of dissenting clergy who backed his early defiance of British authority. In 1770 Thomas Hutchinson, the ill-fated royal governor of Massachusetts, complained, "Our pulpits are filled with such dark covered expressions and the people are led to think they may lawfully resist the King's troops as any foreign enemy." Jonathan Boucher, a loyalist Anglican priest, later recalled, "In America, as in the Grand Rebellion in England, much execution was done by sermons. Those persons who have read any out of the great number of Puritan sermons that were then printed as well as preached, will cease to wonder that so many people were worked up into such a state of frenzy. . . ." William Livingston, governor of New Jersey after the Revolution, proudly remembered in 1790 that the clergy (excepting presumably the Anglicans) had been "almost universally good Whigs."[106]

Catherine Albanese has traced the bursts of "enthusiasm" which moved the colonists toward rebellion during the early 1770s to "the private and personal initiations of the Great Awakening." Mercy Otis Warren of Massachusetts, though not making the direct religious connection, observed at the time, "Perhaps there are no people on earth, in whom a spirit of enthusiastic zeal is so readily enkindled, and burns so remarkably conspicuous as among the Americans." In Connecticut, New Light Congregationalists were identified in 1766 as the core of opposition to the Stamp Act. In western Pennsylvania a loyalist official found Presbyterians "as averse to Kings, as they were in the Days of Cromwell, and some begin to cry out, *No King but King Jesus*."[107]

Jonathan Edwards's idea of America as a chosen nation bred secular parallels. Young John Adams wrote to a friend: "Soon after the Reformation, a few People came over into this new world for conscience sake. Perhaps this, apparently, trivial incident may transfer the great seat of empire in America. It looks likely to me."[108]

We have noted how the proposed appointment of an Anglican bishop for the colonies fanned antagonism toward the London government. "For us in the twentieth century," Carl Bridenbaugh wrote, "it is very, very difficult to recover imaginatively a real understanding of the enormous effect of this controversy on the opinions and feelings of a pious, dissenting people grown accustomed to ecclesiastical self-government and currently engaged in a struggle to protect their liberties in the civil sphere. . . . The agitation over an American episcopate reached its peak by 1770, and the public had grown almost frenzied in the course of it."[109]

After the signing of the Treaty of Paris in 1763, ending the French and Indian Wars, the privileged position granted the Catholic church in Canada inflamed an even more deeply felt grievance attributed by Puritanism to the English crown: softness on Catholicism. Passage in 1774 of the Quebec Act, extending the borders of Canada south to the Ohio River, created a wave of apprehension, economic as well as religious, that Protestants in the coastal colonies would be denied access to the rich lands across the Appalachians.

"Pope Day," celebrated in New England on November 5 since the seventeenth century, had long provided an excuse for rowdy parades climaxed by ritualistic burnings of effigies of the pope. "In Boston a rivalry developed between the north and south ends so that each group carried its own Pope, meeting in a general combat to try to capture the rival effigies." After passage of the Quebec Act, Pope Day spread as far south as Charleston, where "the Pope, Pretender [the Stuart claimant to the throne], and Old Nick were burned in a bonfire of English Tea." Early in the Revolution, the president of Princeton opined that "the common hatred of Popery caused by the Quebec Act [was] the only thing which cemented the divergent religions in the colonies together sufficiently to allow them to make war." Jefferson included the Quebec Act among the specific crimes attributed to George III in the Declaration of Independence.[110]

After war started in 1775 the patriot leaders took every opportunity to identify the struggle for independence with religion. George

Washington's first general order after issuance of the Declaration called on "every officer and man . . . to live and act as becomes a Christian soldier, defending the dearest rights and liberties of his country." In 1777 Congress authorized the importation of 20,000 Bibles. Four years later, a project for printing an American edition of the Bible received official congressional approval. Benjamin Rush observed that the "language" of American independence was "the same as that of the heavenly host that announced the birth of the Saviour of mankind. It proclaims 'glory to God in the highest—on earth peace—good will to man.' "[111]

A study of congressional proceedings led Edward Humphrey to conclude that "the proclamations and other state papers of the Continental Congress are so filled with Biblical phrases as to resemble Old Testament ecclesiastical documents." Humphrey shrewdly put his finger on at least part of the reason for Congress's attachment to religion: "Their extreme insistence upon the religious sanction may be explained in part by the fact that the Government was without definite legislative authority; this deficiency could be remedied in no other way so well as by a reliance upon religion."[112]

The dissenting clergy assured their parishioners that God favored independence. "God requires a people, struggling for their liberties," one instructed his congregation, "to treat such of the community who will not join them, as open enemies, and to reject them as unworthy the privileges which others enjoy." Another rallied American troops before the Battle of Brandywine: "Remember, soldiers, that God is with you! The eternal God fights for you! He rides on the battle-cloud; he sweeps onward with the march, or the hurricane charge! God, the awful, the infinite, fights for you, and will triumph!" Another found that God had enabled the American army to escape from British encirclement on Long Island "by sending a thick fog about two o'clock in the morning which hung over Long-Island, while on New-York side it was clear."[113]

In a nation returned to "a state of nature" (as Patrick Henry described it), many looked to religion as a stabilizing force. Mercy Otis Warren later recalled, "While matters hung in this suspense, the people in all the shire towns collected in prodigious numbers to prevent the sitting of the courts of common laws, forbidding the justices to meet, or the jurors to empanel. . . . Thus were the bands of society relaxed, law set at defiance, and government unhinged throughout the province. Perhaps this may be marked in the annals of time, as one of the most extraordinary eras in the history of man: the exertions of spirit awakened by the severe hand of power had led to that most alarming experiment of levelling all ranks, and destroying all subordination." In Mercy Warren's opinion, the churches held the line against social dissolution. "Religion, viewed merely in a political light, is after all the best cement of society, the great barrier of just government, and the only certain restraint of the passions, those dangerous inlets to licentiousness and anarchy."[114]

Much has been made of the influence of deism, a rationalized, impersonal theism that in Europe became almost indistinguishable from emerging secular humanism, on the American founders. Deism did indeed hold some attraction for some of the revolutionary leadership, particularly at the second and third levels. Rationalist Congregational ministers in Massachusetts, like Chauncy and Mayhew, had edged toward deistic ideas. In 1755 a lectureship in "Natural Religion" was established at Harvard. By the 1770s, even heirs of the Great Awakening like John Witherspoon at Princeton were entertaining rationalist attitudes. "Nature's God" in the Declaration could be given a deist as well as a Christian interpretation. Thomas Paine, the inspired pamphleteer of independence, produced after the war (and after belief in equalitarian ideology had carried him to participation in the French Revolution) *The Age of Reason,* a deist treatise ridiculing Christianity. Ethan Allen, conqueror of the British stronghold at Ticonderoga, argued that "reason ought to control the Bible, in those particulars in which it may be supposed to deviate from reason." Allen's *Reason the Only Oracle of Man* was, according to Timothy Dwight, president of Yale, "the first formal publication, in the United States, openly directed against the Christian religion."[115]

Yet Perry Miller was probably close to the truth when he wrote, "Actually, European deism was an exotic plant in America, which never struck roots in the soil. 'Rationalism' was never so widespread as liberal historians, or those fascinated by Jefferson, have imagined. The basic fact is that the Revolution had been preached to the masses as a religious revival, and had the astounding fortune to succeed." Catherine Albanese found a larger influence for deism, but conceded, "While Jehovah God of Battles, got lost in the war, Nature's God apparently found his armor lying there, put it on, and began to direct events. The language of the God of Nature became inseparable for some from the *actions* of a God of History."[116]

Albanese, among others, identified the Masonic order, which included among its members fifty-two of the fifty-six signers of the Declaration, as an institutional expression of deism. But most Masons, she admits, remained Christians. When Philadelphia was recaptured from the British in 1778, patriotic Masons celebrated with a parade through the city led by General Washington, but the procession ended with a service of thanksgiving at Christ Church.[117]

"A PATRIOT MUST BE A RELIGIOUS MAN"

The views of Madison and Jefferson on the role of religion in public life have already been discussed. Let us now examine briefly the beliefs in this area of the other four among the generally acknowledged front rank of the founders: Benjamin Franklin, George Washington, Alexander Hamilton, and John Adams.

Of all the principal founders, Franklin in style of life and public utterances was farthest from conventional piety. Some of the dogmas of the Presbyterian faith in which he had been raised, he wrote in his *Autobiography*, completed in 1789, "appeared to me unintelligible, others doubtful, and I early absented myself from the public assemblies of the sect, Sunday being my study day." When George Whitefield came to preach in Philadelphia in 1739, Franklin struck up a close friendship, but resisted the evangelist's efforts to bring him to salvation. "He us'd, indeed, sometimes to pray for my conversion but never had the satisfaction of believing that his prayers were heard. Ours was a mere civil friendship, sincere on both sides, and lasted to his death."[118]

Even Franklin, however, was convinced of the practical utility of religion. History, he wrote in 1749 in a plan for educating the youth of Pennsylvania, shows "the Necessity of a *Publick Religion*, from its usefulness to the Publick; the Advantage of a Religious Character among private Persons, the Mischiefs of Superstition, & c. and the excellency of the CHRISTIAN RELIGION above all others antient or modern." The great mass of men and women, he later observed, "have need of the motives of religion to restrain them from vice, to support their virtue, and retain them in the practice of it till it becomes habitual."[119]

Franklin's skepticism toward Whitefield's brand of Christianity, moreover, did not extend to the general truth of a theistic view of reality. "I never was without some religious principles," he wrote in the *Autobiography.* "I never doubted, for instance, the existence of the Deity; that he made the world and govern'd it by his Providence; that the most acceptable service to God was the doing of good to men; that our souls are immortal; and that all crime will be punished, and virtue rewarded either here or hereafter." When the 1787 convention in Philadelphia drafting the new federal Constitution deadlocked, Franklin proposed that one of the local clergy be asked to open each daily session with a prayer. "In the beginning of the contest with Great Britain," he recalled, "when we were sensible of danger, we had daily prayer in this room for the divine protection. Our prayers, sir, were heard, and they were graciously answered. . . . I have lived, sir, a long time, and, the longer I live, the more convincing proofs I see of this truth—that God governs in the affairs of men. And if a sparrow cannot fall to the ground without his notice, is it possible that an empire can rise without his aid? We have been assured, sir, in the sacred writings that 'except the Lord build the house, they labor in vain that build it.' I firmly believe this; and I also believe that without his concurring aid we shall succeed, in this political building, no better than the builders of Babel." (The convention took no action on Franklin's proposal, yielding to arguments by the supposedly more pious Alexander Hamilton and others that calling in the clergy might signal "embarrassments and dissensions within the Convention.")[120]

George Washington, as we have seen, invoked religion to support the war effort during the Revolution, and favored restoration of the established church in Virginia during the 1780s. Scholars have exposed the questionable or wholly fictitious sources for such folk tales as those describing Washington praying on his knees in the snow at Valley Forge or offering dramatic testimony to his religious faith. (There is, on the other hand, no evidence that Washington did *not* pray at Valley Forge, and given his character and convictions, he almost surely did—in the snow or not.) The pattern of Washington's religious behavior uncovered by scholarship is that of a conscientious church member (vestryman in his local Anglican parish for more than twenty years, churchwarden on three occasions), who was a "consistent, if not always regular" attendant at Sunday services but who displayed total disinterest in the doctrinal disputes that preoccupied many ardent churchmen of his time.[121]

Washington was keenly conscious of the public value of religion. As commander of the Continental Army, he called on Congress to authorize the appointment of military chaplains and required church attendance on Sunday by all soldiers "not engaged on actual duty." When he took the oath of office as president in 1789, he added the phrase, "so help me God," a custom followed by all his successors. As president he issued proclamations of thanksgiving addressed to "Almighty God."[122]

Retiring from public life at the end of his second term in 1796, he advised his countrymen in his farewell address to regard "religion and morality" as "indispensable supports" to "political prosperity." Taking up a theme developed by Locke, he went on to say, "Where is the security for property, for reputation, for life, if the sense of religious obligation desert the oaths, which are the instruments of investigation in courts or justice? And let us with caution indulge the supposition that morality can be maintained without religion. Whatever may be conceded to the influence of refined education on minds of peculiar structure, reason and experience both forbid us to expect that national morality can prevail in exclusion of religious principle." Some commentators have argued that the final sentence shows that Washington valued religion *only* for its political utility. This argument rests on the assumption that he meant to include himself among those possessors of "minds of peculiar structure" who believe they can get all the moral guidance they need from "refined education"—in short that he regarded himself as a civil humanist. A more plausible interpretation, given his private as well as public piety, is that he was politely acknowledging but not indicating agreement with the position taken by associates like Jefferson.[123]

While linking the social compact to service of transcendent purpose, Washington emphatically rejected identifying the nation with a particular church or denomination. His public invocations of religion were usually ecumenical rather than specifically Protestant or even Christian. Soon after taking command of the army in 1775, he ordered that no military personnel should participate in "that ridiculous and childish custom of burning the Effigy of the pope"—thereby ending Pope Day in the United States. (His immediate purpose, he candidly stated, was to avoid offending Canadian Catholics, whose support he was courting.) In 1790, while president, he received a message of thanks from a Jewish congregation in Newport, Rhode Island, for his administration's support of civil liberties. He publicly replied: "It is now no more that toleration is spoken of, as if it was by the indulgence of one class of people, that another enjoyed the exercise of their inherent natural rights. For happily the Government of the United States, which gives to bigotry no sanction, to persecution no assistance, requires only that they who live under its protection should demean themselves as good citizens, in giving it on all occasions their effectual support."[124]

Alexander Hamilton, Washington's principal aide in the last phase of the war and a major architect of the national government, believed even more strongly than most of the other founders that religion is a necessary foundation for a cohesive society. Hamilton's approach to relations between church and state, however, was characteristically pragmatic, even cynical. Attracting manufacturers to the new nation— which for Hamilton became almost an end in itself—would, he argued, be promoted by a legal system providing "perfect equality of religious principles." The value of prayer, as we have seen, he judged by coldly utilitarian standards. According to an old anecdote, when a Princeton professor told him after the adjournment of the Constitutional Convention that the Princeton faculty were "greatly grieved that the Constitution has no recognition of God or the Christian religion," he replied, "I declare, we forgot it!"[125]

After Jefferson's Republicans replaced the Federalists in control of the national government in 1801, Hamilton sought to form an alliance between religion and political conservativism, an idea that was to have many progeny in American political history. In 1802 he proposed a "Christian Constitutional Society," with the joint goals of supporting "the Christian religion" and upholding "the Constitution of the United States." The plan was still in the idea stage when he died in a duel with Aaron Burr (a grandson of Jonathan Edwards) in 1804.[126]

As a young man John Adams was impressed by the rationalist humanism preached by his friend, Jonathan Mayhew. He never departed far, however, from the Puritan belief that valid social law depends ultimately on religious sanction. "Statesmen may plan and speculate for Liberty," he wrote to Abigail, his wife, in 1775, "but it is Religion and Morality alone which can establish the principles upon which Freedom can securely stand. A patriot must be a religious man."[127]

The Massachusetts constitution of 1780, which Adams largely wrote, made explicit the obligation of human society to transcendent being: "It is the right as well as the duty of all men in society, publicly and at stated sessions, to worship the SUPREME BEING, the great Creator and Preserver of the universe." The constitution, however, also provided for religious freedom: "No subject shall be hurt, molested, or restrained . . . for worshipping GOD in the manner and season most agreeable to the dictates of his own conscience . . . provided he doth not disturb the public peace, or obstruct others in their religious worship."[128]

Like Jefferson and Franklin, Adams doubted some of the doctrinal tenets of orthodox Christianity, but he believed in the immortality of the human soul and viewed theistic religion as an indispensable basis for republican virtue. "We have no government armed with power capable of contending with human passions unbridled by morality and religion," he wrote in 1789, soon after becoming vice-president. "Our constitution was made only for a moral and religious people. It is wholly inadequate to the government of any other."[129]

Two broad generalizations emerge on the principal founders' beliefs about religion. All were convinced of the need for religion as an underpinning for republican government, and though some were skeptical toward some of the tenets of revealed Christianity, all, except perhaps Jefferson, and he not consistently, shared belief in the view of reality on which theist-humanist values are based.

The founders' conception of human nature was largely derived from the Judeo-Christian belief that man is inherently inclined to sin (that is, to pursue his own ends to the detriment, if necessary, of all others). Madison, for instance, wrote of the "infirmities and depravities of the human character." Hamilton contemplated the "folly and wickedness of mankind." Even Jefferson maintained that "in questions of power, let no more be heard of confidence in man but bind him down from mischief by the chains of the constitution." *Federalist* paper number fifty-one, generally attributed to Madison, states perhaps most memorably the view of human nature that underlies the Constitution: "But what is government itself, but the greatest of all reflections on human nature? If men were angels, no government would be necessary."[130]

James Bryce, writing almost a century after the Constitution was drafted, concluded, "There is a hearty Puritanism in the view of human nature that pervades the instrument of 1787. It is the work of men who believed in original sin, and were resolved to leave open for transgressors no door which they could possibly shut. Compare this spirit with the enthusiastic optimism of the Frenchmen of 1789. It is not merely a difference of race temperaments: it is a difference of fundamental ideas."[131]

Belief in original sin led the founders, as Madison pointed out, to regard government as a necessary check on natural egoism but also to distrust government itself, which they regarded as all too easily subverted by the greed or pride of the gang of politicians holding power at any given time. The positive effects of government could be achieved while avoiding its inherent perils, they believed, in part by positioning each branch of government to check the potential excesses of the others and in part by balancing interest against interest within the larger society. But these constitutional mechanisms, though useful and necessary, would not be enough. "Liberal government [of the kind created by the Constitution] protected the private realm," Walter Berns has written, "but there seems to have been an awareness that the health of liberal government required certain virtuous habits to be preserved in that realm." The principal source for such "virtuous habits," the founders were sure, had to be religion.[132]

THE BILL OF RIGHTS

Though convinced of the need, both spiritual and political, for religion, most of the founders had at the same time concluded that government, at least at the national level, should be kept largely secular.

The first reason for this conclusion was the practical fact of religious pluralism. Although a substantial majority among citizens of the new nation had roots in some form of Puritanism, no single denomination approached majority status. (Only about 6 percent of the population were actual church members at the time of the Revolution. But this statistic reflects mainly the strictness of church standards for membership. Most Americans seem to have identified with some denomination or other.) Congregationalists and Presbyterians, both Calvinist offshoots, were the most numerous denominations when the Constitution was ratified, followed by Baptists, Episcopalians (reconstituted from the Anglican church at the end of the Revolution), Reformeds (Dutch and German Calvinists), Lutherans, and Roman Catholics. There were smaller groups of Quakers, recently organized Methodists (soon to become the most numerous of all American denominations), various German pietist sects, and Jews. Even in New England, where except for Rhode Island the Congregational church was established, Congregationalism was torn between rationalists and evangelicals, a situation soon to produce fission, with some of the rationalists leaving to form an independent Unitarian church. Under the circumstances, designation of a single denomination as the established national church was simply out of the question.

Conviction that the national government should remain secular also resulted from concern, derived from direct experience or from study of history, over the tendency of established churches to produce, in Madison's words, "superstition, bigotry and persecution." While some political leaders, including Washington and Adams, saw merit in government support for religion at the state or local levels, most had decided that even a multidenominational direct relationship between church and state at the national level would be harmful to both.

Finally, the founders held the belief, inherited in varying forms from the Pilgrims, Roger Williams, John Locke, the Baptists, and William Penn, that religious liberty is itself a primary *religious* value within the theist-humanist tradition from which the United States had grown. Coerced religion, they were persuaded, was an impediment rather than an aid to genuine faith.

The founders thus approached the task of constructing a charter of fundamental law with a certain tension in their attitudes on the role of religion in public life. The Constitution agreed to in Philadelphia in 1787, unlike the Declaration of Independence, contains no reference to God—probably because the framers were not yet prepared to resolve this tension and therefore tried to avoid anything that might bring up the issue. The only mention of religion in the original Constitution comes in Article VI, Section 3, which holds, after providing that all federal and state officers "shall be bound by oath or affirmation," that "no religious test shall ever be required as a qualification to any office or public trust under the United States." The motion to prohibit a religious test for public office was made by Charles Pinckney of South Carolina and was opposed only by Roger Sherman of Connecticut, who argued that "prevailing liberality" was "a sufficient security against such tests."[133]

George Mason of Virginia (author of Virginia's Declaration of Rights) proposed that the Constitution should be "prefaced with a

Bill of Rights." (So far as can be learned from Madison's notes, Mason did not explicitly mention religion.) Roger Sherman this time had his way. Speaking against the motion for a Bill of Rights, Sherman pithily commented that he "was for securing the rights of the people where requisite," but that the state declarations of rights "being in force are sufficient." No states voted for the motion; Massachusetts abstained.[134]

Opponents of the proposed Constitution seized upon the absence of a Bill of Rights as an issue through which to urge its rejection by the states. The tactic failed—narrowly in some states—to achieve its immediate objective but did produce a number of resolutions by state conventions demanding that the new government adopt a declaration of fundamental rights. The Virginia convention called specifically for a constitutional amendment stating that "all men have an equal, natural and unalienable right to the free exercise of religion according to the dictates of conscience, and that no particular religious sect or society ought to be favored or established by Law in preference to others." The New York convention passed a resolution with very similar language. Though the New York resolution dropped the word "particular" from the clause dealing with establishment, inclusion of the phrase "in preference to others" in both the Virginia and New York resolutions seemed to leave open the possibility of a multi-denominational establishment.[135]

Madison, elected as a member of the first House of Representatives (over the opposition of Patrick Henry, who had blocked his election to the Senate), moved quickly to seek enactment of a Bill of Rights. Further delay, he warned on June 8, 1789, might "occasion suspicions" among the public that "we are not sincere in our desire to incorporate such amendments in the constitution as will secure those rights which they consider as not sufficiently guarded." Madison introduced nine amendments, the fourth of which included ten clauses conferring specific rights. The first of these clauses read: "The civil rights of none shall be abridged on account of religious belief or worship, nor shall any national religion be established, nor shall the full and equal rights of conscience be in any manner, or any pretext, infringed."[136]

The fifth amendment in Madison's original list of nine was directed at the states. It provided that, among other prohibitions: "No state shall violate the equal rights of conscience. . . ." Irving Brant, Madison's most thorough biographer, and Walter Berns have interpreted this language as a proposal for eliminating the remaining state establishments. This interpretation seems doubtful, however, particularly because none of the defenders of the state establishments, who were numerous in the House, raised the point when the amendment was debated (though the order of the clause was reversed, and the word "violate" was changed to "infringed"). It is true, nevertheless, that Madison spoke of his proposed restriction on the states as "the most valuable amendment in the whole list," and his own disapproval of state establishments as infringements on religious liberty was well known.[137]

The entire package of amendments was referred to a select committee, with Madison among its members. On August 15, the committee brought to the floor a freshly worded amendment, which could be read as applying to both federal and state governments: "No religion shall be established by law, nor shall the equal rights of conscience be infringed." Peter Sylvester of New York was at once on his feet to object that this new formulation "might be thought to have a tendency to abolish religion altogether." Elbridge Gerry of Massachusetts, where the Congregational church was established, pitched in with the suggestion that the amendment be changed to prohibit only establishment of "religious doctrine," which would have limited the reach of the amendment to questions of theology and ecclesiastical organization. Roger Sherman, whose opinion of the need for a Bill of Rights had not changed, found the amendment "altogether unnecessary," because "Congress had no authority whatever designated to them by the Constitution to make religious establishments."[138]

Madison was ready with a soothing interpretation: the words meant only that "Congress should not establish a religion, and enforce the legal worship of it by law, nor compel men to worship God in any manner contrary to their conscience." Benjamin Huntington of Connecticut, another state with an established church, was not satisfied. Might not the amendment, he asked, be construed to prohibit state "support of ministers or building of places of worship?" Huntington favored an amendment "to secure the rights of conscience," but not one worded in a way that would "patronise those who professed no religion at all."[139]

Madison had the solution. Inserting the word "national" before "religion" would make clear that only establishment by the federal government was prohibited. But this provoked the former antifederalists, for whom any mention of the word "national" was anathema. Madison's suggestion, Elbridge Gerry said, reawakened fears among those who had opposed ratification of the Constitution that "this form of Government consolidated the Union." (The contending sides in the earlier struggle, Gerry interpolated, should have been called not "federalists and anti-federalists, but rats and anti-rats.") Samuel Livermore of New Hampshire, another establishment state, moved that the amendment be changed to read: "Congress shall make no laws touching religion, or infringing the rights of conscience." Livermore's motion, which not only limited the restrictive effect of the amendment to Congress but also avoided an outright prohibition of establishment at even the national level, was approved by the House by vote of thirty-one to twenty.[140]

On August 20, Fisher Ames of Massachusetts, an exceptionally conservative Federalist who privately disparaged the whole idea of a Bill of Rights, offered a new version of the amendment that seems to have been agreed upon as a compromise: "Congress shall make no law establishing religion, or to prevent the free exercise thereof, or to infringe the rights of conscience." Ames's version was accepted and passed by the House without further discussion. In a separate action, the House then passed, also without debate, Madison's amendment restricting the states.[141]

The Senate completed action on the package of amendments that became the Bill of Rights on September 9. The separate amendment directed at the states was dropped, probably reflecting resistance in the Senate to even minimal extension of national authority over the states on such matters. The part of Madison's original fourth amendment dealing with religion was combined with a part instituting freedom of speech and the press to form a single amendment—the framework for the First Amendment as we now have it. The part of the new amendment dealing with religion read, "Congress shall make no law establishing articles of faith, or a mode of worship, or prohibiting the free exercise of religion," a clear victory for those, like Patrick Henry's ally, Senator Richard Henry Lee of Virginia, who would leave the state establishments untouched and would allow government support of religion even at the national level, prohibiting only a role by the federal government in matters of theology or forms of worship.[142]

The House asked for a conference. Madison was chairman of the three House conferees (the tough-minded Roger Sherman was one of the others). Brant is sure, without direct evidence, that he dominated the conference committee. In any case the clauses on religion were accepted by the committee, and eventually approved by two-thirds votes in both houses of Congress and ratified by the required three-fourths of the states. The clauses thereby added to the Constitution read, "Congress shall make no law respecting an establishment of religion or prohibiting the free exercise thereof."[143]

What did it mean?—what *does* it mean? Chapter 4 examines at some length later judicial and scholarly interpretations of the clauses on religion finally included in the First Amendment. But consideration of what the original framers had in mind is in order here. The general intent of the free-exercise clause is relatively clear—though questions would inevitably arise over the extent to which "free exercise" might protect behavior otherwise illegal. But what was meant by the prohibition against Congress making any law "respecting an establishment of religion"?

One thing, at least, is clear. The entire amendment applied only to the federal government. The various state establishments were gradually eliminated: South Carolina in 1790, Maryland in 1810, Connecticut in 1818, and New Hampshire in 1819. Finally, in 1833 Massachusetts amended its constitution to end the last state establishment of religion. (Unitarians had gained control of so many local parishes, each of which determined by majority vote what local church should receive the state subsidy, that conservative Congregationalists at last decided that it was better to give up establishment altogether than to continue funding the opposition.) But these acts of state disestablishment were entirely voluntary, carried out without reference to the requirements of the First Amendment.[144]

The religion clauses acquired major significance only long after the Civil War, when some judges, as we shall see, began finding the First Amendment in the clause of the Fourteenth Amendment extending due process to the states. Prohibition against "establishment" was then interpreted by some to mean Jefferson's "wall of separation between church and state." But Jefferson's metaphor, in the sense that he used it, was not coined until more than ten years after the First Amendment was approved, and none of those active in framing the Bill of Rights, including Madison, who consistently took the most separatist position during the debates in Congress, said anything at the time suggesting an intention so drastic.

Still, prohibition of a national establishment meant more than requiring that the federal government distribute whatever aid it gives to religion without discrimination among churches—the interpretation favored by modern accommodationists. The framers of the First Amendment were familiar with the system of multiple establishment, which existed in New York before the Revolution and was provided for in the first state constitutions of Maryland and South Carolina. This was, roughly, the kind of arrangement that would have been permitted under the proposal offered by Elbridge Gerry in the House or under the First Amendment in the form that it first passed the Senate. Because Congress did not finally approve this approach, it must, as Freeman Butts has argued, have intended something different.[145]

Butts's claim, however, that when the founders rejected a national "establishment" they meant to prohibit "*any* cooperation between the state and any or all churches," does not stand up under scrutiny either. Madison's own description during the debate in the House on the objective of the part of the amendment dealing with establishment— "that Congress should not establish a religion, and enforce the legal observation of it by law"—indicates an idea of establishment much more narrow than that conceived by those who would interpret the clause to prohibit all forms of nondiscriminatory cooperation between government and religion. Moreover, the same first Congress that passed the First Amendment also readopted, with Madison's approval, the Northwest Ordinance of 1787, the third article of which reads: "Religion, morality, and knowledge, being necessary to good government and the happiness of mankind, schools and the means of learning shall forever be encouraged." It is hardly credible, as Walter Berns has pointed out, that Congress would call on a territorial government set up under its authority "to promote religious and moral education" if it had intended through the First Amendment to forbid all cooperation between the federal government and the churches.[146]

Some ambiguity was no doubt present in the meaning of the establishment clause from the start. But there is nothing in it inconsistent with the virtually unanimous view among the founders that functional separation between church and state should be maintained without threatening the support and guidance received by republican government from religion.

After the French Revolution there was a surge of skepticism and secularism in the United States, particularly among upper-class youth: "Students called each other by such names as Voltaire and Rousseau."[147] By the time of Jefferson's election as president in the last year of the old century, however, religious enthusiasm was again rising. In 1800 a Presbyterian historian wrote, "God was shaking the valley of dry bones on the frontiers." Beginning in Kentucky and western Pennsylvania, the second Great Awakening soon made evangelical Methodists and Baptists by far the largest among Protestant denominations and produced a new church body, the Disciples of Christ, formed from the more evangelical wing of Presbyterianism.[148]

The evangelical tide also spread over the East, entering even the old academic strongholds of rationalism. At Yale, young Lyman Beecher found in 1800 that "infidels were as rare as professing Christians had been," when he entered as a freshman four years before. Benjamin Silliman, the future scientist, was converted in the revival of 1802. "Yale College," he wrote, "is a little temple." At Dartmouth a Students' Religious Society was established in 1801.[149]

As the leaders of the generation of the Revolution passed gradually from the scene, they left a nation that saw no contradiction between the concept of separation of church and state and the concept that the legitimacy of republican government must ultimately be rooted in religion. Alexis de Tocqueville, touring the country early in the nineteenth century, reported, "I do not know whether all Americans have a sincere faith in their religion—for who can search the human heart?—but I am certain that they hold it to be indispensable to the maintenance of republican institutions. This opinion is not peculiar to a class of citizens or to a party, but it belongs to the whole nation and to every rank of society." Tocqueville's traveling companion, Gustave de Beaumont, marvelled at "how a lively and sincere faith can get on with such a perfect toleration; how one can have equal respect for religions whose dogmas differ."[150]

The founders, guided by the constellation of values described in this chapter, sought to construct a charter of fundamental law that would maintain a balance between the dual, and they believed ultimately complementary, goals of a largely secular state and a society shaped by religion. Chapter 4 examines the ways in which this charter has subsequently been applied and sometimes altered through interpretation by the courts.

FOUR

Interpreting the First Amendment

DURING ITS FIRST half century, the Supreme Court devoted little attention to relations between church and state. Except for a few inescapable confrontations between the rights of conscience and the reach of federal authority, the Court either left church-state issues to the jurisdictions of the separate states or regarded them as settled through custom.

In the early years of the nineteenth century, state courts frequently held that "Christianity is a part of the common law that we have inherited from England," whether or not the state maintained an established church. In 1811, for example, Chancellor James Kent of New York upheld the conviction of a freethinker for blasphemy against Christianity on the ground that New York law "assumes we are a christian people, and the morality of the country is deeply engrafted upon christianity." In 1824 the Pennsylvania Supreme Court ruled that "Christianity, general Christianity, is, and always has been, a part of the common law of Pennsylvania." As late as 1838 Abner Kneeland, a popular lecturer against religion, was sent to jail for sixty days in Massachusetts for blasphemy. Kneeland argued unsuccessfully in his own defense that prosecution for blasphemy was in conflict with Massachusetts' Declaration of Rights.[1]

In 1833 in *Barron v Baltimore,* dealing with the right to just compensation for private property taken for public use, the U.S. Supreme Court delivered the landmark decision that the Bill of Rights applied only to the federal government and therefore placed no restrictions on the states. In an 1845 case involving violation by a Roman Catholic priest of a New Orleans ordinance requiring that all funerals be held in a common municipal chapel, this reasoning was applied specifically to the issue of religious freedom. (The ordinance had been passed as a public health measure during a yellow fever epidemic.) "The Constitution," the Court held, "makes no provision for protecting the citizens of the respective states in their religious liberties; this is left to the state constitutions and laws: nor is there any inhibition imposed by the Constitution of the United States in this respect on the states."[2]

A New Doctrine of Rights

One effect of the Civil War was rejection of the extreme states-rights position. The Fourteenth Amendment, approved by Congress in 1866 and ratified by the states in 1868, places three restrictions on the states: that they not "abridge the privileges or immunities of citizens of the United States"; that they not "deprive any person of life, liberty, or property without due process of law"; and that they not "deny any person . . . equal protection of the laws."

The chief immediate objective of the Fourteenth Amendment was to extend full rights of citizenship to the former slaves who had been freed under the Emancipation Proclamation or the Thirteenth Amendment. "Whatever law protects the white man shall afford 'equal' protection to the black man," explained Congressman Thaddeus Stevens of Pennsylvania, chairman of the House delegation to the Joint Committee on Reconstruction, in a speech supporting the amendment. In addition, as its framers repeatedly stated, the amendment was meant to prevent the states from violating civil rights that came with American citizenship, as had sometimes occurred before the Civil War.[3]

Some modern scholars and the Supreme Court itself since 1940 have found in the Fourteenth Amendment the much broader purpose of applying to the states all the restrictions placed on the federal government by the Bill of Rights, including the religion clauses of the First Amendment. Applying this interpretation, the Court has plunged boldly—some would say recklessly—into the thicket of complex relationships involving religion, civil society, and the individual. The result is a tangled body of law, reflecting both traditional standards and contemporary ideological pressures.

The view that the Bill of Rights was extended to the states by the Fourteenth Amendment does not rest wholly on examination of the intentions of the amendment's drafters and enacters. But because all except the most extreme "judicial activists" concede that original intention bears *some* relevance to current interpretation, it is worthwhile to consider what the members of Congress who passed the Fourteenth Amendment and the members of the state legislatures who ratified it seem to have had in mind.

PURPOSE OF THE FOURTEENTH AMENDMENT

The record contains some ambiguities. At times during the debate in Congress, some supporters of the amendment seemed to suggest that it would provide a charter of new rights not only for former slaves but for all citizens. Congressman John Bingham of Ohio, manager of the amendment in the House, asserted that a defect of the Constitution up to that time had been that the federal government lacked the means for enforcing "the immortal bill of rights." The Fourteenth Amendment, he indicated, would correct this shortcoming. Whether by "bill of rights" he meant literally the block of amendments added to the Constitution in 1791 is unclear. Senator Jacob Howard of Michigan, the amendment's chief sponsor in the Senate, was more precise. The new amendment, he said, would give the federal government power to enforce "the personal rights guarantied and secured by the first eight amendments of the Constitution."[4]

Most of the other participants in the debate and Congressman Bingham himself at a later stage, however, seemed to assume that the substantive effect of the amendment would be to prohibit the states from curtailing the inherent rights of American citizenship, which practically no one at that time regarded as including general application of all the personal rights secured against the federal government by the first eight amendments. Senator Luke Poland of Vermont, a supporter of the amendment, said that the privileges or immunities clause "secures nothing beyond what was intended by the original provision of the Constitution, that 'the citizens of each state shall be entitled to all privileges and immunities of citizens in the several states' " (Article IV, Section 2). The due process and equal protection clauses, Poland claimed, would clarify and make permanent the civil rights statute enacted by Congress earlier that year. Congressman Frederick Woodbridge of Vermont, also supporting the amendment, gave a similar interpretation: "It merely gives the power to Congress to enact those laws which will give to a citizen of the United States the natural rights which necessarily pertain to citizenship."[5]

Opponents of the amendment charged that those favoring its passage were in effect conceding that the civil rights act of 1866 was unconstitutional. Congressman James Garfield of Ohio, already a rising star among the Republican majority in the House, responded that the civil rights act was entirely consistent with the Constitution as it stood, but that the amendment would "lift that great and good law above the reach of political strife, beyond the reach of the plots and machinations of any party, and fix it in the serene sky, in the eternal firmament of the Constitution, where no storm of passion can shake it and no cloud obscure it."[6]

Summing up for supporters of the amendment in the House, Congressman Bingham denied that it would "take away from any State any right that belongs to it." No one, he said, now disputed the rights set forth in the amendment. Its opponents, he claimed, were "only opposed to enforcing it by national authority, even by the consent of the loyal people of all the States." The issue then, in Bingham's presumably more considered view, was not the creation of new rights, but the enforcement of rights already established by the Constitution.[7]

On the campaign trail in Ohio later that year, Bingham described what he took to be the essential meaning of the amendment: "It is the spirit of Christianity embodied in your legislation. It is a simple, strong, plain declaration that equal laws and equal and exact justice shall hereafter be served within every State of this union by the combined power of all the people of every State. It takes from no State any right which hitherto did not exist within the letter of your Constitution, and which is essential to the nation's life." So far, Bingham seemed to be talking, as in his summation in the House, of enforcement of existing rights. As his speech continued, however, he offered examples of the "abuses" the amendment would correct: "Hereafter, the American people cannot have peace, if, as in the past, States are permitted to take away freedom of speech, and to condemn men, as felons, to the penitentiary for teaching their fellow men that there is a hereafter, and a reward for those who learn to do well." Precisely which states had condemned men to the penitentiary for teaching that there is a life beyond the grave, Bingham did not say. His examples indicate, however, that he regarded the Fourteenth Amendment as extending at least the free speech and free exercise clauses of the First Amendment to cover the states.[8]

Charles Fairman, in an extensively documented article in the *Stanford Law Review* in 1949, showed that extension of the Bill of Rights to the states was not an issue in the state legislatures that debated ratification of the Fourteenth Amendment. In Tennessee, for example, the governor submitted the amendment to the legislature with the observation, "Practically, this affects mainly the negro, who having been emancipated by the rebellion, and having lost that protection which the interest of the master gave him, became by the very laws of nature, entitled to the civil rights of the citizen, and to the means of enforcing those rights." In Illinois the governor found the issue raised by the amendment embodied in the question, "Are not all persons born or naturalized in the United States and subject to its jurisdiction, rightfully citizens of the United States and of each State, and justly entitled to all the political and civil rights citizenship confers?" In Pennsylvania those opposing the amendment in the legislature argued that it decreed that "negroes are citizens, and no State shall say that they are not the equal of the white man in every sense," while those favoring its ratification held that it was "simply incidental to carrying out" the abolition of slavery.[9]

After the amendment was ratified, the governmental community showed no signs of perceiving that the entire Bill of Rights had been applied to the states. Late in 1868, four months after the Fourteenth Amendment had been ratified, the New Hampshire Supreme Court felt free to rule on a controversy over the doctrinal orthodoxy of a Unitarian minister because, the Court maintained, quoting Justice Joseph Story, "The whole power over the subject of religion is left exclusively to the State governments." A state constitutional convention in Illinois in 1868 debated at great length a proposal for abolishing the grand jury; neither side invoked the provision in the Fifth Amendment that makes the grand jury mandatory for cases involving capital crimes. In 1876 when the Grant administration tried to secure passage of a constitutional amendment that would have prohibited state aid to church-related schools, no one is recorded as having suggested that such aid might already be unconstitutional.[10]

On the basis of the available evidence, it would appear that some of the people most directly involved in drafting and promoting the Fourteenth Amendment had the broad intention of extending the Bill of Rights to the states. Even for these, however, expanding the reach of the first eight amendments was not a primary objective. For most of the governmental community, let alone the nation at large, the idea simply did not exist. The one exception to this conclusion is that the due process clause of the Fourteenth Amendment was clearly intended to apply to the states the same requirement for due process that the Fifth Amendment had placed on the federal government. But specific inclusion of the due process clause in the Fourteenth Amendment provides further evidence that its framers had no definite intention that the amendment should extend the coverage of the entire Bill of Rights.[11]

The due process clause and the privileges or immunities clause might harbor within their meanings certain others among the rights set forth in the first eight amendments. Insofar as a nation can be said to have an intention, however, blanket extension of the Bill of Rights to the states was not part of what was intended by the passage and ratification of the Fourteenth Amendment.

THE MORMON CASES

During the half century of dynamic national growth after the Civil War, the Supreme Court displayed reluctance in applying the prohibitions contained in the religion clauses of the First Amendment to the federal government, let alone to the states. The first significant attempt to invoke the free exercise clause against the federal government came in response to the government's efforts to root out the practice of polygamy by members of the Church of Latter-day Saints. The Mormons, a communitarian sect that grew out of the revivalist enthusiasm that swept upstate New York in the 1820s, had taken up polygamy at the behest of their prophet and founder, Joseph Smith. Though Christian in origin, the Mormon faith turned back toward the idealist core of the archetypal Middle Eastern religion, somewhat as Islam had done in the seventh century. Smith recognized this parallel: "I will be a second Mohammed," he told a gathering of the Mormon faithful in 1838.[12]

Polygamy proved extraordinarily offensive to members of competing evangelical Protestant denominations, who regarded the monogamous family as not only divinely established but also as an institutional check against egoistic chaos in the unstable social atmosphere of the American frontier. Smith, no less concerned than orthodox Protestants with the problem of frontier anarchy, may be said to have offered an alternative solution: consolidation of social power in the hands of a patriarchal elite buttressed by the principle of strict subordination of women.[13]

Hounded ever further west after Smith's murder by a mob in Illinois in 1844, the Mormons settled at last in and around the Great Salt Lake basin in 1847. But as a result of the war with Mexico, the United States soon extended its boundaries to include the projected Mormon homeland, thereby ensuring new confrontation between orthodox Christian mores and the Mormon dispensation.

In 1862, clearly with Mormon practice in mind, Congress outlawed polygamy in the territories. The federal government soon obtained conviction of a Mormon named Reynolds, who freely admitted that he had "married a second time, having a first wife living," but claimed First Amendment immunity on the grounds that he had entered the second marriage "in conformity with what he believed at the time to be a religious duty."[14] (The question of whether the First Amendment applied to the states did not arise; Utah, where Reynolds lived, was a territory under the direct authority of the federal government.)

Reynolds appealed to the Supreme Court, and Chief Justice Morrison Waite delivered the Court's unanimous decision in 1878. "Polygamy," Waite observed, "has always been odious among the northern and western nations of Europe, and, until the establishment of the Mormon Church, was almost exclusively a feature of Asiatic and of African people." Congress, therefore, was operating within the main current of Western moral tradition when it acted to uphold monogamous marriage, upon which "society may be said to be built." Waite dismissed Reynolds' contention that prosecution for polygamy violated his right to free exercise of religion. Under the First Amendment, "Congress was deprived of all legislative power over mere opinion, but was left free to reach actions which were in violation of social duties or subversive of good order." Polygamy was an action, not an opinion and therefore was subject to legal prohibition.[15]

While seeming to limit the reach of the First Amendment, Waite's judgment also created future ammunition for strict separationists by giving official recognition for the first time to Jefferson's view that the religion clauses require "a wall of separation between church and state." Reference to Jefferson's metaphor served Waite's immediate purpose because Jefferson had coupled it with the argument that "the legislative powers of the government reach actions only, and not opinions," a corollary to the distinction Waite was making. But introduction of the "wall" concept into judicial discourse provided support for a line of reasoning that would lead to conclusions far from what the nineteenth century chief justice intended.

In another Mormon case, decided in 1890, the Court made clear that it would approve almost any statutory remedy deemed necessary to stamp out polygamy. Acting under federal authority, the territory of Idaho had passed an election law requiring the voter to swear not only that he was "not a bigamist or polygamist," but also that he was not "a member of any order, organization or association which teaches, advises, counsels or encourages its members, devotees or any other person to commit the crime of bigamy or polygamy." A Mormon named Davis took the oath and was subsequently indicted and convicted for falsely swearing. Davis, who was not himself shown to be a polygamist, appealed to the Supreme Court on the grounds that the requirement that he swear nonmembership in a church violated his right to free exercise of religion.

Justice Stephen Field, speaking for a united Court, rejected Davis's argument. "Bigamy and polygamy," Field wrote, "are crimes by the laws of all civilized and Christian countries" (like many other nineteenth century jurists, Field simply assumed that the designation "Christian country" should be applied to the United States). "Few crimes are more pernicious to the best interests of society. . . . To extend exemption from punishment for such crimes would be to shock the moral judgment of the community." Following the lead given by Chief Justice Waite in *Reynolds,* Field maintained that the First Amendment protects beliefs, not actions. "Laws are made for the government of actions and while they cannot interfere with mere religious belief and opinions, they may with practices. Suppose one believed that human sacrifices were a necessary part of religious worship, would it be contended that civil government under which he lived could not interfere to prevent a sacrifice? . . . Crime is not the less odious because sanctioned by what any particular sect may designate a religion."[16]

Looking back in 1961 at the *Davis* decision, Philip Kurland observed that Field's thesis "would have sustained outlawry of the mass, [and] would have sustained most of the Tudor legislation restricting Catholics and most of the legislation that forced religious dissenters to leave the shores of Europe for haven in the New World. . . ." The distinction between belief and action, Kurland pointed out, breaks down over the fact that the mere meeting of a religious group, surely protected by the First Amendment if anything is, constitutes a form of "action."[17]

However questionable the means, the campaign against polygamy almost wholly succeeded. In 1890, the year of the *Davis* decision, the main body of the Mormon church received a new revelation that plural marriage was after all not required by divine command. The way was thereby opened for the admission of Utah, the principal Mormon stronghold, as a state of the Union in 1896.

JUDICIAL RESTRAINT

The Mormon cases had shown that the Court was not disposed to interpret the free exercise clause as placing much limit on the law enforcement powers of the federal government, at least when these were directed against an unpopular sect. In two cases decided at the turn of the century, the Court appeared equally loath to put a tightly restrictive reading on the establishment clause.

In 1899 the Court rejected a taxpayer's contention that expenditure of federal funds to build an isolation wing for a hospital operated by the Catholic Sisters of Charity in the District of Columbia constituted a "law respecting an establishment of religion." Since the hospital was open to everybody, the Court held, it was not a "religious or sectarian body," and therefore did not offend the establishment clause.[18]

Eight years later the Court similarly decided that payment by the federal government of sums drawn from Indian treaty funds to support schools for Indians operated by the Catholic Church was permissible, because it was the right of the Indians "to choose their own school and to choose it frankly because the education therein is under the influence of the religious faith in which they believe . . . and to have the use of their proportion of tribal funds applied . . . to maintain such schools." Any other construction, the Court argued, would pervert the establishment clause "into a means of prohibiting the free exercise of religion."[19]

Well into the twentieth century the religion clauses had virtually no effect on the numerous practices through which government gave broad acknowledgement to the value of religion: prayer and Bible-reading exercises in the public schools; various forms of financial aid, including exemption from taxation, by government to churches; enforced observance of religious holidays; and many others. But in the 1920s a development occurred that eventually would lead to massive intervention by the federal courts in church-state relations.

CIVIL LIBERTY

The first hints from the Supreme Court that the Bill of Rights might now apply to the states as well as to the federal government had come in 1892 in a case chiefly involving the commerce clause. A subsidiary factor in the case was a claim by the defendant that the state of Vermont had subjected him to "cruel and unusual punishments" in violation of the Eighth Amendment. The agile mind of Justice Field, having rationalized the authority of the federal government to stamp out polygamy, now turned to the question of whether the rights set forth in the first eight amendments might apply to the states.

The Bill of Rights, Field wrote in a dissent from the majority opinion, which had simply ignored the question of cruel and unusual punishments, applies only to the federal government insofar as the amendments represent "limitations on power." But insofar as "they declare or recognize the rights of persons," they must under the privileges or immunities clause of the Fourteenth Amendment apply also to the states. The state, therefore, "cannot apply to [the citizen] any more than the United States, the torture, the rack or thumbscrew, or any cruel and unusual punishment. . . ." Field's interest in extending the Bill of Rights to the states, it should be noted, was motivated not only by passion for judicial logic or humanist concern but also by the practical aim of establishing freedom of contract as a guaranteed constitutional right.[20]

Justice John Harlan, dissenting in the same case, went further: "Since the adoption of the Fourteenth Amendment, no one of the fundamental rights of life, liberty, or property, recognized and guaranteed by the Constitution of the United States, can be denied or abridged by a state in respect to any person within its jurisdiction."[21]

The majority did not agree with Field and Harlan in 1892, but the justices' logic continued to tick away within the collective consciousness of the Court, until the thesis they represented emerged, though not fully developed, as the majority opinion in *Meyer v. Nebraska* in 1922. Expressing nativist sentiments that had grown acute during the First World War, Nebraska had passed a law prohibiting the teaching of any modern language other than English before the ninth grade in the public schools and requiring that all subjects be taught in English. The Courts conceded that "the State may do much, go very far, indeed, in order to improve the quality of its citizens, physically, mentally and morally," but "the individual has certain fundamental rights." These rights now apparently placed restrictions on the states.

Writing for the majority, Justice James McReynolds recalled that Plato had recommended children be raised in common, so that "no parent is to know his own child, nor any child his parent." Sparta had "assembled the males at seven into barracks and entrusted their subsequent education and training to official guardians." Such systems of education had been "deliberately approved by men of great genius," but they were very far from the value system on which the United States was founded. "Their ideas touching the relation between individual and State were wholly different from those upon which our institutions rest." For any state in the United States to impose such requirements would do "violence to both letter and spirit of the Constitution." McReynolds did not specify exactly where in the Constitution the "letter" of the law would be violated if the states were to impose the Platonic or Spartan systems of education, but it must be through some application of the Fourteenth Amendment, as Field and Harlan had argued. Presuming that the Fourteenth Amendment made "certain fundamental rights" inviolable by the states, were they infringed by Nebraska's prohibition against instruction in foreign languages? McReynolds found that they were. "No emergency has arisen which renders knowledge by a child of some language other than English clearly harmful as to justify its inhibition with the consequent infringement of rights long freely enjoyed."[22]

Justice Oliver Wendell Holmes—whose judicial "liberalism," as close commentators have always recognized, was much more subtle and conditional than his popular reputation implies—dissented from the Meyer decision, explaining that he found it not "unreasonable" that the state should require that the child "in his early years . . . shall hear and speak only English at school." But Holmes acknowledged that the issue on which the case turned was whether "the means adopted deprive teachers of the liberty secured to them by the Fourteenth Amendment," thus accepting Justice Field's view that the Fourteenth Amendment protects certain personal rights against violation by the states (though basing this protection on the due process clause rather than on the privileges or immunities clause, as Field had done).

Three years later, Justice McReynolds, again writing for the majority in *Pierce v. Society of Sisters,* extended the logic of the *Meyer* case to establish a right of parents to educate their children in religious schools. Oregon had passed a law through popular referendum requiring that all children between the ages of eight and fifteen attend public schools—in effect outlawing church-operated schools below the college level. An order of Catholic nuns operating a system of parochial schools challenged the law's constitutionality. The Court found for the nuns. "The fundamental theory of liberty upon which all governments in this Union repose excludes any general power of the State to standardize its children by forcing them to accept instruction from public teachers only. The child is not the mere creature of the State; those who nurture him and direct his destiny have the right coupled with the high duty, to recognize and prepare him for additional obligations."[23]

Also in 1925 in the celebrated case of *Gitlow v. New York,* the Court explicitly found that the rights to free speech and freedom of the press established by the First Amendment had been extended to the states by the due process clause of the Fourteenth. As has happened more than once in landmark cases, the Court, having established a historic principle of law, then held that it did not apply in the particular case under consideration. Gitlow, a political radical, had written the *Left Wing Manifesto,* which had been suppressed by the state of New York. The Court decided the book did not qualify for First Amendment immunity because it was an active "incitement" to violence. Justice Holmes, in a dissent more congruent with his reputation for liberalism, drily commented: "Every idea is an incitement."[24]

The Free Exercise Clause

If the clauses of the First Amendment requiring freedom of speech and the press applied to the states, the clause protecting the free exercise of religion must surely do so as well. This finding was made explicit in 1940. Cantwell, a member of Jehovah's Witnesses, a personalist sect sprung from the same pietist branch of Protestantism that had earlier produced the Baptists and the Quakers, had been convicted of breaching the peace. His offense had been to play a record attacking the Catholic religion on a public street in a neighborhood of New Haven where the population was 90 percent Catholic. He had further been found guilty of violating a Connecticut law requiring a religious solicitor to obtain a state license.

The Supreme Court overturned both convictions on the finding that the man's rights under the First and Fourteenth Amendments had been violated. "The First Amendment declares that Congress shall make no law respecting an establishment of religion or prohibiting the free exercise thereof. The Fourteenth Amendment has rendered the legislatures of the states as incompetent as Congress to enact such laws." No matter how offensive Cantwell's utterances might be to Catholics or members of other denominations, he had the right to say (or play) what he pleased about rival faiths, without going through the licensing procedure established by Connecticut.[25]

Besides extending the free exercise clause—and, almost in passing, the establishment clause—to the states, the decision in *Cantwell v. Connecticut* also somewhat modified the distinction that Waite and Field had made between beliefs and actions. Justice Owen Roberts, writing for the Court, first restated the distinction in tempered form: "[The First] Amendment embraces two concepts—freedom to believe and freedom to act. The first is absolute but, in the nature of things, the second cannot be. Conduct remains subject to regulation for the protection of society." This presumably would cover Field's example of a religion requiring human sacrifice. But the state's right to regulate conduct must be balanced in particular cases against the right of the individual or the church to free exercise: "In every case the power to regulate must be so exercised as not, in attempting a permissible end, unduly to infringe the protected freedom."

A few weeks after announcing the *Cantwell* decision, the Court swerved back toward the interest of the state in *Minersville School District v. Gobitis,* another case involving Jehovah's Witnesses, that at the time attracted far more public attention. The Gobitis children had been expelled from public school in Pennsylvania for refusing to salute the American flag in exercises prescribed by state law. According to the Jehovah's Witness faith of the Gobitis family, saluting the flag "of any earthly government" was idolatrous. The children's father, faced with the expense of providing them with a private education, brought suit.

Justice Felix Frankfurter (writing, it should be remembered, during the weeks when Hitler's armies were sweeping across the Low Countries and France, and the very survival of traditional Western civilization seemed threatened) delivered the opinion of the Court. While reaffirming application of the First Amendment to the states and not returning to the narrow distinction between belief and action proposed in the previous century by Chief Justice Waite, Frankfurter found an overwhelming state interest in instilling patriotic loyalty among the nation's youth. "We are dealing with an interest inferior to none in the hierarchy of legal values. National unity is the basis of national security." Frankfurter himself might question whether forced saluting of the flag was a truly effective means for instilling loyalty. "But this courtroom is not the arena for debating issues of educational policy. It is not our province to choose among competing considerations in the subtle process of securing effective loyalty to the traditional ideals of democracy, while respecting at the same time individual idiosyncrasies among a people so diversified in racial origins and religious allegiances."[26]

Three years later, in *West Virginia State Board of Education v. Barnette,* the Court, perhaps influenced by instances of violence and discrimination against Jehovah's Witnesses, including children, that had followed *Gobitis,* reversed itself on the issue of compulsory flag-saluting by vote of six to three. Justice Robert Jackson, writing for the majority, based the reversal on a First Amendment right to freedom of expression, which he maintained included nonparticipation in flag-saluting exercises, rather than on the right to free exercise of religion. "Those who begin coercive elimination of dissent," Jackson wrote, "soon find themselves exterminating dissenters. Compulsory unification of opinion achieves only the unanimity of the graveyard."[27]

Justice Frankfurter, in dissent, suggested that the Court had entered a path heading toward a destination it might not like. "Consider the controversial issue of compulsory Bible-reading in public schools. . . . The requirement of Bible-reading has been justified by various state courts as an appropriate means of inculcating ethical precepts and familiarizing pupils with the most lasting expression of great English literature. Is this Court to overthrow such variant state educational policies by denying states the right to entertain such convictions in regard to their school systems, because of a belief that the King James version is in fact a sectarian text to which parents of the Catholic and Jewish faiths and of some Protestant persuasions may rightly object to having their children exposed?"[28]

By the time of the *Barnette* decision, the Court had further extended the right of free exercise by ruling that Jehovah's Witnesses selling religious tracts door-to-door must be exempted from a local ordinance requiring all itinerant solicitors to pay a small license fee. The case, *Murdock v. Pennsylvania,* went beyond the earlier *Cantwell* decision in that the government of Pennsylvania retained no discretion over whether the license should be issued. "Those who can tax the exercise of this religious practice can make its exercise so costly as to deprive it of the resources necessary for its maintenance."[29]

In 1944 the Court seemed to draw a line, setting a limit beyond which free exercise could not prevail against competing state or humanitarian interests. A woman named Prince, a Jehovah's Witness, had been accustomed to taking her nine-year-old niece and ward, Betty Simmons, along on sidewalk campaigns to sell the Witness publication, *Watch Tower,* in Brockton, Massachusetts. After repeated warnings by the Brockton police that she was breaking the Massachusetts law against using a minor to sell periodicals or other articles of merchandise in a public place, Mrs. Prince was placed under arrest. Betty Simmons, already an ordained Witness minister, testified that she had participated willingly and enthusiastically in the campaigns of sidewalk evangelism. Mrs. Prince, nevertheless, was convicted. Claiming that her right to free exercise of religion had been violated, she carried her appeal to the Supreme Court.

The Court weighed "the obviously earnest claim for freedom of conscience and religious practice" against "the interest of society to protect the welfare of children." The latter interest was held in this case to prevail. "With reference to the public proclaiming of religion, upon the streets and in other similar public places," wrote Justice

Wiley Rutledge for the majority, "the power of the state to control the conduct of children reaches beyond the scope of its authority over adults, as is true in the case of other freedoms. . . ."[30]

During the next three decades, the Court dealt with a large number of free exercise cases, gradually defining both the reach and the limits of the right. In 1961 the Court denied, to the anguish of many civil libertarians, the plea of an Orthodox Jewish merchant, Braunfeld, for exemption from a Pennsylvania law requiring that most retail stores be closed on Sunday. (The question of whether the Sunday-closing law itself violated the establishment clause of the First Amendment had already been decided.) Braunfeld's religion caused him to close his shop on Saturday, which he observed as the Sabbath. He therefore lost two days of business compared to his Gentile competitors' one. Nevertheless, wrote Chief Justice Earl Warren for the majority, "if the State regulates conduct by enacting a general law within its power, the purpose and effect of which is to advance the State's secular goals, the statute is valid despite its indirect burden on religious observance unless the State may accomplish its purpose by means which do not impose a burden."[31]

Two years later, however, the Court, with a somewhat more liberal cast after the retirement of Frankfurter, in a similar case found a valid claim to free exercise. Sherbert, a Seventh Day Adventist, had been fired from her job in a South Carolina textile mill because she refused to work on Saturday, the Adventist's Sabbath. When she applied for unemployment compensation, she was denied benefits under South Carolina law that made a claimant ineligible "if he has failed, without good cause, to accept suitable work when offered him." This requirement, the Court held, violated Sherbert's right to free exercise by forcing her to "choose between following the precepts of her religion and forfeiting benefits, on the one hand, and abandoning one of the precepts of her religion in order to accept work, on the other."[32] (Justice Potter Stewart, in a concurring opinion, argued that the court's liberality toward Sherbert contradicted the "mechanist concept of the Establishment Clause" that it had just applied to Bible reading in the public schools, discussed below.)

THE CONSCIENTIOUS OBJECTOR CASES

Exemption from military service on the basis of "conscientious objection" because of religious belief is a special category among the immunities granted by civil society to honor the free exercise of religion. The first Congress in 1789 debated amending the Constitution to exempt conscientious objectors, then represented mainly by Quakers and Mennonites, but decided against it—not because it rejected the principle, but because it concluded that exemption should be a privilege conferred through statute rather than a constitutional right. Persons objecting to participation in war on religious grounds were exempted from the draft in the Civil War and in both world wars.

In 1918 a legal challenge to the exemption of conscientious objectors based on the establishment clause was dismissed by the Supreme Court with the comment that it was so unsound that it required no discussion (indicating perhaps an underlying intellectual queasiness). In 1934 the Court held that the free exercise clause does not provide an inherent right to exemption from military service for religious pacifists. At the beginning of the Korean War, Congress, aiming to tighten the draft law to exclude from exemption persons objecting to war on secular humanitarian grounds only, specified "religious training and belief in this connection means an individual's belief in a relationship to a Supreme Being involving duties superior to those arising from any human relation, but does not include essentially political, sociological, or philosophical views or a merely personal moral code."[33]

During the Vietnam War, which coincided (perhaps relatedly) with a drift away from traditional religion among many college-educated youth, the requirement that religious exemption be based on a commitment to "duties superior to those arising from any human relation" came under challenge. In 1965 the Supreme Court decided that exemption must be granted to a youth, Seeger, who admitted "skepticism or disbelief in the existence of God" but claimed conscientious objector's status on the basis of his "belief in and devotion to goodness and virtue for their own sakes and religious faith in a purely ethical creed." Congress's use of the term "Supreme Being" rather than "God," the Court held, showed that it intended something broader than traditional theism. "Religious belief" was construed to include any conviction that "is sincere and meaningful and occupies a place in the life of its possessor parallel to that filled by the orthodox belief in God. . . ." In 1970 the Court went further and held that another youth, Welsh, who specifically denied that religion had anything to do with his objection to military service, and based his rejection of war on "readings in fields of history and sociology," must also be granted exemption.[34]

In 1971 the Court set a limit. Exemptions were denied to a "humanist" opponent of American military involvement in Vietnam who said that he would be willing to participate in a war sponsored by the United Nations for a peacekeeping purpose and to a devout Catholic who claimed the right to distinguish between "just" and "unjust" wars. While its definition of religion might be broad, the Court indicated, it was not prepared to allow individuals to make personal distinctions among the wars in which they would serve.[35]

AN INHERENT TENSION

The most definitive opinion so far involving free exercise issues came in *Wisconsin v. Yoder* in 1972. A community of Old Order Amish (a German pietist sect) in Green County, Wisconsin, including Yoder, had defied the state law requiring children to attend public or private school up to the age of sixteen. To send their children to school beyond the eighth grade, Yoder and his coreligionists maintained, would "endanger their own salvation and that of their children."

Through an opinion written by Chief Justice Warren Burger, the Court found religious belief, more strictly defined than in the recent conscientious objector cases, a necessary but not in itself a sufficient condition for approving exemption of the Amish children from the state attendance law. The Amish claim, Burger emphasized, would not be valid if it were based on a merely "philosophical and personal" choice, like that of Henry David Thoreau when he turned away from "the social values of his time" in nineteenth century New England. Even after the claim's religious foundation had been verified, it would still be rejected by the Court if it were found to conflict seriously with the "State's interest in universal education." The actual effects of Amish practice, therefore, must decide.

Examination of the record of the Green County Amish showed that they "had never been known to commit crimes, that none had been known to receive public assistance, and that none were unemployed." Looking beyond the immediate community to the exemplary history of the Amish people over "three centuries and more than 200 years in this country," Burger found that there would be "at best a speculative gain, in terms of meeting the duties of citizenship, from an additional two or three years of compulsory formal education." Exemption of the Amish children from formal schooling beyond the eighth grade, the Court concluded, was therefore justified.[36]

The *Yoder* decision, though approved by all but one participating justice, evidently caused the Court a good deal of soul-searching. Justice Byron White in a concurring opinion worried that some Amish children "may wish to become nuclear physicists, ballet dancers, computer programmers, or historians, and for these occupations, formal training will be necessary." White decided, however, that in this case, "although the question is close," the state had not demonstrated "that Amish children who leave school in the eighth grade will be intellectually stultified or unable to acquire new academic skills later."[37]

Justice William Douglas, the lone dissenter, complained that the majority had given more consideration to the views of the Amish parents than to the interests of their children, which should have been paramount. Douglas also expressed irritation at Burger's reference to the values of Thoreau (as it happened, a particular hero for Douglas) as merely "philosophical and personal." Such narrowness, he claimed, retreated from the broader concept of religion accepted in the conscientious objector cases.[38]

The deeper significance of the *Yoder* case was that it placed beyond question the principle that under some circumstances, otherwise illegal actions as well as beliefs are entitled to protection of the free exercise clause. The Amish were declared a special class, defined by religion, exempt from some laws applying to everybody else. The right to free exercise, then, as long as vital interests of the state are not affected, may endow a particular religious group with unique privileges—moving close, some commentators have argued, to a selective establishment of religion.[39]

DEVELOPING SYNTHESIS

During the 1970s and early 1980s, justices appointed by a series of Republican presidents gradually moved the Court in a more conservative direction. The effects of this shift toward conservatism on interpretation of the free exercise clause have been mixed. Some decisions have reflected the libertarian strain of modern conservatism emphasizing individual rights, while others have represented conservatism's concern for community solidarity.

Several actions of the so-called Burger Court have been consistent with the communitarian side of conservatism. In 1980 the Court declined to hear an appeal from a lower court decision approving the firing of a Jehovah's Witness from her job as a teacher in a Chicago elementary school because she had refused to teach the pledge of allegiance to the flag or the words to patriotic songs. In 1981 the Court upheld the right of the Minnesota State Fair to require that members of the Hare Krishna sect confine their activities to designated places on the fairground rather than solicit money and sell literature freely among the crowd.[40]

The libertarian strain in conservatism, on the other hand, came into play in a 1982 decision involving the Unification church of Reverend Sun Myung Moon. A Minnesota law, clearly aimed at the "Moonies," required that any religious group receiving more than half its financial support from nonmembers must file an annual statement detailing its sources of income. The intimidating effects of this requirement, the Court held, by a five to four majority, violated free exercise.[41]

The evolution, obviously continuing, of the Court's interpretation of free exercise provides an illuminating record of the development of judicial synthesis—swinging back and forth among competing values but proceeding along a discernible trend line. For our purposes the interest of this record lies even more in the Court's gradual discovery of a broad right to pursue one's religion without federal impediment, set forth in the First Amendment, and extended to limit state and local as well as federal authority by the Fourteenth.

"Looking back," Paul Freund has written, "it is hard to see how the Court could have done otherwise, how it could have persisted in accepting freedom of contract as a guaranteed liberty without giving equal status to freedom of press and speech, assembly, and religious observance."[42] Through the process of judicial interpretation, the Court, despite a fair number of missteps, has progressively sharpened the meaning and broadened the application of the concept of religious liberty that was from the start an essential article in the social philosophy on which the United States was founded. This progress has been achieved, moreover, without doing significant violence to the language of the Constitution. The same, unfortunately, cannot be said of the Court's handling of the establishment clause.

The Establishment Clause

In 1940, Justice Owen Roberts extended the establishment clause to the states, without elaboration, in his opinion in *Cantwell v. Connecticut*, although establishment had little or nothing to do with the case's substance. Perhaps Roberts thought that continuing to limit application of the establishment clause to the federal government would be inconsistent with extending free exercise to the states. This view, however, is supported by neither logic nor experience.

Free exercise, like freedom of speech and the press, can be found without extreme semantic ingenuity in the word "liberty" in the due process clause of the Fourteenth Amendment. But discovery of the establishment clause in the same source pushes language beyond reasonable limits. As recently as 1951 Edward Corwin, the most distinguished constitutional scholar of his time, wrote, "So far as the Fourteenth Amendment is concerned, states are entirely free to establish religions, provided they do not deprive anybody of religious liberty." At the present time, religious liberty, in the sense of freedom to practice the religion of one's choice or no religion at all free of government penalty or pressure, coexists comfortably with traditional religious establishments in Britain and the Scandinavian countries and with "multiple establishments," through which the state distributes its support among a number of faiths, in the Federal Republic of Germany and Switzerland.[43]

Whatever Roberts's reason, extending the establishment clause to the states opened questions that were sure to be both difficult and troublesome. Did prohibition of "establishment" make traditional practices of prayer and Bible reading in the public schools unconstitutional? Had state aid to religious education been taken out of the hands of the states altogether and placed under the interdict of the federal Constitution? Did exemption of church property from taxation, provided for in all the states, represent a form of "establishment"? What of such ministerial relationships as the appointment of chaplains by state legislatures? Were laws prohibiting some kinds of commercial activities on Christian days of worship unconstitutional?

EDUCATION FOR SALVATION

The first of these questions actually to be dealt with by the Court after *Cantwell* was the long-disputed issue of state aid to religious education. The men who passed and ratified the First Amendment had no experience with public education of the size or scope that developed in the United States during the nineteenth century. But they seem to have identified education with religion almost as a matter of course, as is shown by their mention of "religion" as one of the values to be promulgated through the schools in the Northwest Territory. Their belief in the impracticality of excluding the churches from the education process was probably one of the reasons they kept the states, which provided most of the public support then given to education, outside the reach of the establishment clause.

Religious instruction had been one of the primary purposes for which schools were founded in the first place in the British colonies of North America, beginning with the Boston Latin School in 1635. School laws in Massachusetts (1647), Connecticut (1650), and New Hampshire (1680) required that every child be given a religious education. "If any children in the neighborhood are under no education," Cotton Mather wrote, "don't allow 'em to continue so. Let care be taken that they may be better educated, and taught to read, and be taught their catechism and the truths and ways of their only savior." A South Carolina statute of 1710 called for "a free school . . . for the instruction of the youth of this province in Grammar, and other arts and sciences and useful learning and also in the principles of the Christian religion." The constitution adopted by North Carolina in 1766 recognized "the great necessity of having a proper school of learning established whereby the rising generation may be brought up and instructed in the principles of the Christian religion. . . ."[44]

After the Revolution, most of the states, including those that did not maintain an established church, continued to support religious education in one form or another. In Massachusetts, where the Congregational church was established, the constitution of 1780 mandated "support and maintenance of public Protestant teachers of piety, religion, and morality, in all cases where such provision shall not be made voluntarily." In New York, which had no established church, the state subsidized church-operated schools from 1795 to 1825. Even Thomas Jefferson, though questioning the value of religious education for children, insisted only that in the public schools of Virginia "no religious reading, instruction or exercise, shall be prescribed or practiced, inconsistent with the tenets of any religious sect or denomination."[45]

During the first half of the nineteenth century, the states, responding to increasing religious pluralism among their populations, gradually reduced their support for religious education. In many states, however, prayer and the reading of a selection from the Bible, almost always the Protestant King James translation, at the beginning of the school day were continued as a means for keeping education within a religious framework. Massachusetts passed the first Bible-reading law in 1825. In Ohio, Alexander Campbell, one of the founders of the Disciples of Christ, led the fight to require Bible reading in the public schools. In most states, prayer and Bible reading were sustained by custom rather than through statute. Horace Mann, often identified as the father of general public education in the United States, favored Bible reading in the schools, though he advocated the practice as a means for instilling moral values and introducing the student to great literature rather than as a devotional exercise.[46]

By the 1840s, growing Catholic populations in several northeastern states were providing the Catholic church with a political base on which to object to the Protestant orientation of the public schools and—not in the church's view inconsistently—to seek public funds for the support of Catholic education. These pressures produced varying responses. Lowell, Massachusetts, where Catholic immigrants were employed in the mills that were bringing the industrial revolution to the United States, subsidized Catholic schools from 1835 to 1852. In Philadelphia the school board voted in 1843 to excuse Catholic children from participating in Bible-reading exercises, contributing to the outbreak of riots by nativist mobs in which several Catholic churches were burned.[47]

In New York the Catholic cause received unexpected support from the state's up-and-coming Whig governor, William H. Seward. Catholics in New York City objected to the use of state funds to finance a Protestant-oriented "public" school system directed by a committee of private citizens, while Catholic schools were left to fend for themselves. Bishop John Hughes, who, according to a historian of New York politics, combined "in his person a priestly sense of mission, the commanding authority of a general, [and] the manipulative skills of a professional politician" proposed that the city's Catholic schools should be given state aid proportionate to the Catholics' share of the population.[48]

New York Catholics were traditionally aligned with the Democratic party. But Seward—perhaps the first but certainly not the last American politician to glimpse what might be accomplished politically by bringing together conservative evangelical Protestants with Roman Catholics—decided to endorse Hughes's position. He favored, Seward said, a system of education "in which the immigrant children may be instructed by teachers speaking the same language with themselves and professing the same faith."

When Democrats in the state assembly, who depended on Protestant as well as Catholic votes, tried to evade the issue, Hughes entered a Catholic slate, composed partly of endorsed Democratic incumbents and partly of Catholic independents, in several city districts in the 1841 legislative elections. The impact of the Catholic slate on the election—endorsed Democrats won while Democrats opposed by Catholic independents were defeated by Whigs—moved the legislature to rush through a compromise bill, which was signed by Seward. While still denying public funds to Catholic schools, the new law prohibited the teaching of "any religious sectarian doctrine" in state-supported schools, thereby dooming the city's old Protestant-oriented semipublic system. Bible reading was continued, but the majority within each neighborhood district was empowered to decide whether the Protestant King James version or the Catholic-approved Douay edition should be used.

None of the participants in the New York controversy got what they wanted. Many Protestants, angered over loss of "our schools," were drawn into the nativist movement that a few years later produced the anti-Catholic Know-Nothing party. Hughes concluded that, for the time at least, state funds would not be forthcoming for Catholic education and set out to build a privately financed independent Catholic school system. Seward, while gaining Hughes's enduring gratitude and perhaps some popularity among Catholic voters, acquired a reputation within his own primary constituency, the evangelical Protestants, for trickiness and unreliability that probably contributed to his loss of the Republican nomination for president in 1860 to the equally open-minded Abraham Lincoln.

NO HELP FOR CATHOLICS

After the Civil War, Catholics resumed their campaign to obtain state funds for church-operated schools. The drive was given new muscle through the support of the Tweed machine in New York and other Democratic city machines with large Catholic constituencies. Its most important immediate political result was to solidify the loyalty of most Protestants, outside the South, to the Republican party.

In 1875 President Grant, who believed that authoritarian tendencies within the Catholic church made Catholicism inherently antidemocratic, called for a constitutional amendment to ensure that "neither state nor nation, nor both combined, shall support institutions of learning other than those sufficient to afford every child growing up in the land of opportunity of a good common school education, unmixed with sectarian, pagan, or atheistical dogmas." The proposed amendment explicitly extended the establishment clause to the states, but specified that it was not to be construed to "prohibit the reading of the Bible in any school or institution."[49]

Grant's amendment was guided to easy passage in the House of Representatives by Speaker James G. Blaine (later identified, perhaps unfairly, with the charge that the Democrats were the party of "rum, Romanism, and Rebellion"), but failed by two votes to achieve the necessary two-thirds majority in the Senate. The Republican platform in every presidential election from 1876 through 1892 contained a plank promising an amendment to forbid "application of any public funds or property for the benefit of any school or institution under sectarian control." But the Republican leadership in Congress did not again press the issue.[50]

Failing to win passage of an amendment to the federal Constitution, opponents of state aid to church schools turned to the states. From 1877 to 1913, thirty-three states amended their constitutions to prohibit financial aid to church-operated schools. The best known of these was that enacted by New York in 1894, prohibiting state aid to "any school or institution of learning wholly or in part under the control or direction of any religious denomination, or in which any denominational tenet or doctrine is taught." Yielding to the drift of the times, New York's Catholic hierarchy accepted the amendment on condition that state subsidies should continue to flow to noneducational Catholic charitable institutions. (The Catholic periodical *America* long after christened the New York amendment the "Blaine amendment," though Blaine, a resident of Maine who died in 1893, had nothing to do with its passage. Campaigning for repeal of the amendment, *America* clearly found it expedient to punch the nerve attached to "rum, Romanism, and rebellion.")[51]

Toward the end of the century, Archbishop John Ireland of St.

Paul, Minnesota, who sought rapprochement between Catholics and Protestants and gave his personal support to the Republican party, proposed a modus vivendi: "I would permeate the regular state school with the religion of the majority of the children of the land, be this religion as Protestant as Protestantism can be, and I would as is done in England, pay for the secular instruction given in denominational schools according to results. . . ."[52]

Part of Ireland's proposal had already been embodied in the so-called Poughkeepsie plan, instituted in 1873, under which the school district of Poughkeepsie, New York, paid nominal rent for parochial school buildings and paid the salaries of nuns serving as teachers. The Poughkeepsie plan was declared unconstitutional under New York's state constitution in 1899. Similar plans were maintained for some time in Minnesota, Illinois, Iowa, and some other midwestern states. Most of these, too, ultimately fell before state constitutional prohibitions.

"A SUPER BOARD OF EDUCATION"

During the early years of the twentieth century, many Protestants, joined by some Catholics and Jews, became concerned that their children were not receiving adequate education in religion. The Sunday school movement launched by Protestant churches in the nineteenth century had been created to help fill this gap, but few believed that instruction given for an hour or two on Sunday mornings by volunteer teachers could match the quality of training in secular subjects being provided by professional educators in the public schools. A program to deal with this problem, under which students were released from the public schools for one or more periods each week to go to the church of their parents' choice for religious instruction, was introduced in Gary, Indiana, in 1914. The so-called released-time plan spread widely among the states. By 1949 a survey conducted by the National Education Association found that only Maryland, New Hampshire, Nevada, and Wyoming had no program for religious education related to the public schools.[53]

Many school districts found released time, which involved students moving back and forth between school and church during the school day, difficult to administer. Students had a tendency to linger in passage, and coordination of school and church schedules was sometimes bothersome. Such administrative problems were largely met through a variation on released time introduced in Champaign, Illinois, in 1940. Under the Champaign plan, religious instruction was provided within the public school itself at a common time by instructors hired and paid by the community's interfaith council, composed of representatives of Protestant, Catholic, and Jewish denominations. Protestant students, who were in the majority, received instruction in their regular classrooms, while Catholics and Jews moved to rooms elsewhere in the building. Students whose parents indicated a preference for nonparticipation in the program were sent to a designated area, theoretically for supervised study. The Jewish program was soon discontinued, and most Jewish parents thereafter enrolled their children in the Protestant classes.[54] The Champaign plan was also widely copied. Fifteen percent of all American school districts were providing religious education in public school buildings during school hours by 1949.

In 1947 the Supreme Court turned its attention to the implications of *Cantwell* for state cooperation with religious education. The first case taken up dealt not with released time or its variations but with the practice of transporting students to and from church-operated schools at public expense. In 1930 the Court had upheld the right of Louisiana to purchase nonsectarian textbooks for pupils attending parochial schools. Chief Justice Charles Evans Hughes, delivering the opinion of the Court, had found no violation of the Fourteenth Amendment. But that was before *Cantwell* had extended the establishment clause to the states.[55]

In the case before the Court in 1947, Everson, a taxpayer in New Jersey, challenged the constitutionality of a state law that permitted local school districts to transport students to private schools "other than private schools operated for profit"—in effect, parochial schools. Justice Hugo Black, writing for the majority, elaborated on *Cantwell:*

> The "establishment of religion" clause of the First Amendment means at least this: Neither a state nor the Federal Government can set up a church. Neither can pass laws which aid one religion, aid all religions, or prefer one religion over another.... No tax in any amount, large or small, can be levied to support any religious activities or institutions, whatever they may be called, or whatever form they may adopt to teach or practice religion.... In the words of Jefferson, the clause against establishment of religion by law was intended to erect "a wall of separation between church and State."

(The bomb planted by Chief Justice Waite six decades before in *Reynolds* had gone off.)[56] Yet, Black continued, the New Jersey law did not transgress the establishment clause because the service provided went to the students rather than to the church-operated schools. "The [First] Amendment requires the state to be a neutral in its relations with groups of religious believers and non-believers; it does not require the state to be their adversary."

Justice Robert Jackson, in dissent, approved the logic of Black's argument but expressed amazement that it should lead to the conclusion that the state might pay for a service clearly of benefit to religion. "The case which irresistibly comes to mind as the most fitting precedent is that of Julia who, according to Byron's report, 'whispering "I will ne'er consent,"—consented.' "[57]

If the Constitution prohibited the states from passing laws that "aid all religions," or from levying taxes that "support any religious activities or institutions . . . whatever form they may adopt to teach or practice religion," the structure of relationships that had developed between churches and local school districts to facilitate religious education was clearly in serious trouble. The ax fell first on the Champaign plan, the most vulnerable of these relationships, in *McCollum v. Board of Education* in 1948. Mrs. McCollum, a resident of Champaign, had indicated preference for nonparticipation in religious education for her son, a student in the fifth grade. During the period set aside for religious education, the boy was sent to a desk in the hall outside his classroom, a place sometimes used for disciplinary purposes, where he was subjected to teasing by passing students. Mrs. McCollum brought suit challenging the constitutionality of the religious instruction program.

Justice Black, again writing for the majority, found that the Champaign plan violated the standard he had set forth in *Everson* for separation of church and state and was therefore unconstitutional. Justice Jackson, while concurring, cautioned that *McCollum* did not mean that "all that some people may reasonably regard as religious instruction" must be "cast out of secular education." Black's position, carried to its logical extreme, Jackson warned, would require the Court "to accept the role of a super board of education for every school district in the nation."[58]

Justice Stanley Reed, the only dissenter in the case, observed that Jefferson's reference to a "wall of separation between church and State" in the Constitution, which Black had invoked, had been a passing remark in a letter and that Jefferson himself had not felt bound by it when he came to outline the role of religious education in connection with the University of Virginia. "A rule of law should not be drawn from a figure of speech."[59]

The *McCollum* decision was almost universally condemned by the nation's churches. Leading figures in the legal and governmental communities were also critical. Anson Phelps Stokes, author of an authoritative history of relations between church and state in the United States, wrote that Black's view that the establishment clause prohibited nondiscriminatory state aid to "all religions" was inconsistent with "the American tradition in interpreting the Constitution." He predicted that "it is not unlikely that the implications of these words will be later overruled." Charles Fairman rebutted the scholarship on which Black had relied to support his argument that the enactors of the Fourteenth Amendment had meant to extend the establishment clause to the states. Edward Corwin thundered that the Court, "by its decision in the *McCollum* case, has itself promulgated a law prohibiting 'the free exercise' of religion, contrary to the express prohibition of the First Amendment!" Eleanor Roosevelt, an oracle of liberal opinion of the time, defended the tradition of Bible reading in the public schools, which Black's line of reasoning obviously threatened.[60]

In *Zorach v. Clausen* in 1952 the Court seemed to draw back. Justice Douglas, who had joined Black in *McCollum,* switched sides along with two other justices and, writing for the majority, found that New York City's released-time program, which made no use of public school buildings, did not violate the First Amendment. Releasing students to attend religious instruction off school premises, Douglas concluded, was no more than an adjustment of school schedules to "accomodate the religious needs of the people." In words that now astonish (he became the Court's most uncompromising separationist) Douglas held that "we are a religious people whose institutions presuppose a Supreme Being. . . . When the state encourages religious instruction or cooperates with religious authorities by adjusting the schedule of events to sectarian needs, it follows the best of our traditions. . . . To hold that it may not would be to find in the Constitution a requirement that government show a callous indifference to religious groups. That would be preferring those who believe in no religion over those who do believe. . . ."[61]

Black, writing in dissent, crossly observed, "It was precisely because

Eighteenth Century Americans were a religious people divided into many fighting sects that we were given the constitutional mandate to keep Church and State completely separate." Jackson, also in dissent, commented, "The wall which the Court was professing to erect between Church and State [in *McCollum*] has become even more warped and twisted than I expected. Today's judgment will be more interesting to students of psychology and the judicial processes than to students of constitutional law."[62]

SECULAR SUNDAY

In the growing shadow of *Cantwell* the Court next turned to the question of whether state laws requiring that Sunday be observed as a day of rest had become unconstitutional. Earlier challenges to Sunday closing laws, on the grounds that they were a burden on interstate commerce or violated the equal protection clause of the Fourteenth Amendment, had been brushed aside when the Court found they had been "enacted in the legitimate exercise of the police powers of the state." The existence of such state laws had indeed been cited in 1872 by Justice David Brewer as evidence that "this is a religious people." Extension of the establishment clause to the states, however, obviously threw into doubt the legitimacy of state regulations that everyone agreed were rooted in religious observance.[63]

In a series of decisions in 1961 the Court held that Sunday closing laws did not violate the establishment clause because Sunday had become so secularized that laws requiring that it be maintained as a day of rest and relaxation for most workers could no longer be said to serve a truly religious purpose. Chief Justice Earl Warren acknowledged that many of the laws in question referred to Sunday as "the Lord's day" or "the Sabbath day." But these titles, he claimed, were forgivable anachronisms. And the fact that a law with a secular purpose happens to coincide with a religious mandate can hardly be said to make it unconstitutional. "Thus, for temporal purposes, murder is illegal. And the fact that this agrees with the dictates of the Judeo-Christian religions while it may disagree with others does not invalidate the regulation."[64]

Justice Douglas, alone in dissent, maintained that the discriminatory effects of Sunday closing laws on persons whose religious convictions required them to abstain from work on some other day could not be doubted. "It is a strange Bill of Rights that makes it possible for the dominant religious group to bring the minority to heel because the minority, in the doing of acts which intrinsically are wholesome and not antisocial, does not defer to the majority's religious beliefs. . . . The Court balances the need of the people for rest, recreation, late sleeping, family visiting and the like against the command of the First Amendment that no one need bow to the religious beliefs of another. There is in this realm no room for balancing."[65]

In an opinion concurring with the Court's decision, Justice Frankfurter rejected Douglas's libertarian view of human rights and expounded the communitarian concept that under some circumstances rights of individuals must be subordinated to rights that depend on general community observance. "One-day-a-week laws [under which each individual would be allowed to choose any day of the week for his day of recreation] do not accomplish all that is accomplished by Sunday laws. They provide only a periodic physical rest, not that atmosphere of entire community repose which Sunday has traditionally brought and which, a legislature might reasonably believe, is necessary to the welfare of those who for many generations have been accustomed to its recuperative effects."[66]

PRAYER IN SCHOOLS

In 1962 the Court at last faced up to the inherent conflict between *Cantwell* and the traditions of prayer and Bible reading in the public schools. At the time, devotional exercises in the public schools, while widely practiced, were by no means universal. A national survey in 1946 showed that Bible reading in the schools was required in thirteen states, and authorized for school districts as a local option in twenty-five more. In 1960 one-third of the nation's schools reportedly began the school day with devotional prayer, and 42 percent required reading the Bible. Beneath these overall national statistics were significant regional differences: a selection from the Bible was read aloud each day in 77 percent of the schools in the South and 67 percent in the Northeast but in only 18 percent in the Midwest and 11 percent in the Far West.[67]

In a few states, courts had found mandated prayer or Bible reading in the schools to be in violation of state constitutions. The Illinois Supreme Court, for example, had decided in 1910, in a case brought by Catholic parents, that reading the King James translation of the Bible and reciting the Protestant version of the Lord's Prayer were forbidden by the Illinois constitution. Most state courts, however, had approved prayer and Bible reading on grounds similar to Douglas's finding in *Zorach:* "We are a religious people."[68]

After *Cantwell* several efforts had been made to bring cases dealing with prayer or Bible reading before the Supreme Court. The Court had dodged, employing considerable judicial ingenuity.

During the 1950s, feeling on both sides of the issue became more intense. Among liberals a consensus gradually developed that state-sponsored prayer and Bible reading in the schools were unconstitutional invasions of civil liberties and should be stopped. Groups particularly concerned with the challenge of international communism or the perceived decline of domestic morality, on the other hand, became more resolute in their support for religious observances in the schools. One important group switched sides: after more than a century of opposition to religious exercises with a Protestant orientation in the public schools, the Catholic church now favored almost any means that would prevent the schools from becoming completely secularized.

Trying to bridge these conflicting points of view, the New York Board of Regents in 1951 composed a prayer for use in the schools that could not be identified with any particular denomination: "Almighty God, we acknowledge our dependence upon thee, and we beg thy blessings upon us, our parents, our teachers, and our country." The Board made provision that children who did not wish to participate in the prayer should be permitted to remain silent or, upon presentation of a written request from parents, could leave the classroom. In 1962 a case brought by parents of five children in the schools of New Hyde Park, New York, who challenged the constitutionality of the Regents' prayer reached the Supreme Court. With *Engel v. Vitale* the Court dodged no longer.[69]

Once more leading the majority, Justice Black found the establishment clause "must at least mean that in this country it is no part of the business of government to compose official prayers for any group of the American people to recite as a part of a religious program carried on by government." Black tried to dispel some of the potential horrors he knew traditionalists would discover in his opinion: "There is of course nothing in the decision reached here that is inconsistent with the fact that school children and others are officially encouraged to express love for our country by reciting historical documents such as the Declaration of Independence which contain reference to the Deity or by singing officially espoused anthems which include the composer's professions of faith in a Supreme Being, or with the fact that there are many manifestations in our public life of belief in God."[70]

Douglas, concurring, was not so cautious. The First Amendment prohibited, he wrote, not only religious exercises in the public schools, but also all other "aids to religion in this country at all levels of government," including, specifically, tax exemptions for churches, religious services at federal hospitals and prisons, use of G.I. Bill benefits to pay tuitions at denominational colleges, the slogan "In God We Trust" on American money, and the recent addition of the words "under God" to the pledge of allegiance to the flag.[71]

Justice Potter Stewart, only recently appointed to the Court, was alone in dissent. "To deny the wish of these children to join in reciting this prayer," he wrote, "is to deny them the opportunity of sharing in the spiritual heritage of our Nation."[72]

The wave of condemnation raised against *Engel* made the criticisms that had been directed at *McCollum* in 1948 seem like a summer squall. Catholic clergy took the lead. Cardinal Francis Spellman of New York was "shocked, and frightened, that the Supreme Court has declared unconstitutional a simple and voluntary declaration of belief in God by public school children." Cardinal Richard Cushing of Boston was sure that "the Communists are enjoying this day." Cardinal James McIntyre of Los Angeles observed that the decision could "only mean that our American heritage of philosophy, of religion, and of freedom, are being abandoned in imitation of Soviet philosophy, of Soviet materialism, and of Soviet regimented liberty." The fury of Catholic spokesmen was matched by many Protestant ministers, particularly, though not only, among evangelicals. Billy Graham, the best known of the new wave of evangelical revivalists attracting national audiences, found the decision "another step towards the secularization of the United States." Episcopal Bishop James Pike of San Francisco announced that "the Supreme Court has just deconsecrated the nation."[73]

Conservative politicians of both parties, whose irritation with the Warren Court had in any case been growing, denounced the decision, sometimes in apocalyptic terms. Former Presidents Hoover and

Eisenhower led the attack for the Republicans. Senator Robert Byrd of West Virginia, a comer among Senate Democrats, charged, "Somebody is tampering with America's soul. I leave it to you who that somebody is." Some Southern politicians found a connection between the prayer decision and the Court's 1954 decision requiring racial desegregation of the public schools. "They put the Negroes in the schools," said Congressman George Andrews of Alabama, "and now they've driven God out." With varying degrees of outrage the decision was criticized by the *Chicago Tribune,* the *Baltimore Sun,* the *Los Angeles Times,* the *Boston Globe,* and *New York News,* and the *Washington Star.*[74]

A factor appeared in the reaction to *Engel,* however, that had generally been absent after *McCollum* fourteen years before: numerous liberal voices were raised to defend the decision or at least to advise compliance. Most, though not all, of the Jewish clergy supported the decision. A substantial number of liberal Protestant ministers agreed with Harold Fey, editor of the *Christian Century*: "The Court's decision protects the integrity of the religious conscience and the proper function of religious and governmental institutions." President Kennedy, who had recently been through an election in which religion had been a significant factor, was cautious. "The Supreme Court has made its judgment. A good many people obviously will disagree with it; others will agree with it. But I think it is important for us, if we're going to maintain our constitutional principle, that we support Supreme Court decisions even when we may not agree with them. . . ." Newspapers defending the decision included the *New York Times,* the *Washington Post,* the *Chicago Sun-Times,* and the *Louisville Courier-Journal.*[75]

If state-sponsored prayer in the schools was unconstitutional, Bible reading could hardly survive. In *Abington School District v. Schempp* a year later the Court struck down the practice of reading ten verses from the Bible and reciting in unison the Lord's Prayer at the beginning of each day in the public schools of Abington, Pennsylvania. Justice Tom Clark, usually identified as a judicial moderate, delivered the majority opinion. "In the relationship between man and religion," Clark wrote, "the state is firmly committed to a position of neutrality. Though the application of that rule requires interpretation of a delicate sort, the rule is clearly and concisely stated in the words of the First Amendment."

Clark provided two tests that a law, state or federal, must pass to avoid violation of the establishment clause: "What are the purpose and the primary effect of the enactment? If either is the advancement or inhibition of religion then the enactment exceeds the scope of legislative power as circumscribed by the Constitution."[76]

In a lengthy concurring opinion, Justice William Brennan argued that findings by scholars that the enactors of the Fourteenth Amendment had never meant to extend the establishment clause to the states were by now irrelevant. "Even if we assume that the draftsmen of the Fourteenth Amendment saw no immediate connection between its protections against state action infringing personal liberty and the guarantees of the First Amendment, it is certainly too late in the day to suggest that their assumed inattention to the question dilutes the force of these constitutional guarantees in their application to the States."[77] Brennan offered chilling reassurance to those who feared that the Court's tests would make unconstitutional the entire array of instances in which civil society acknowledged dependence on religion. The motto "In God We Trust" on currency, Brennan suggested, had "ceased to have religious meaning," and therefore would probably pass muster. The reference to God in the pledge of allegiance "may merely recognize the historical fact that our Nation was believed to have been founded 'under God.' "[78]

Justice Stewart, again alone in dissent, interpreted the Court's latest edict "not as the realization of state neutrality, but rather as the establishment of a religion of secularism, or at least as government support for the beliefs of those who think that religious exercises should be conducted only in private."[79]

There followed more than a decade of attempts by state legislatures to enact some approximation of a religious exercise that would somehow win the Court's approval. Each of these was struck down in turn.

The issue, however, did not go away. National opinion polls have consistently shown that about 75 percent of the public favors return of organized voluntary prayer to the schools. In many rural school districts, teacher-led prayer and Bible reading reportedly have never stopped. They have come to light only when an occasional district has been brought to court. Evangelical Protestants, formerly among the strongest supporters of the public schools, have turned increasingly to church-related private elementary and secondary schools, which by 1983 enrolled more than 1 million students (compared to about 3 million in the long-established Catholic system). The issue helped fuel the rise of the so-called religious new right during the late 1970s and early 1980s, as will be discussed in chapter 6.[80]

Some opponents of the Court's decisions concluded that the only cure was a constitutional amendment specifically authorizing voluntary prayer in the public schools. Numerous proposed amendments were introduced in Congress over the years. Simple majorities approved prayer amendments in the Senate in 1966 and in the House in 1971, but in both cases the vote fell considerably short of the required two-thirds majority. Ronald Reagan was elected president in 1980 on a platform endorsing a constitutional amendment to permit voluntary participation in group prayer in the public schools. In 1982 the Reagan administration sent a proposed prayer amendment to Congress.[81]

Amendment of the Constitution has been an extreme step in the American governmental system, successfully undertaken only sixteen times in the almost two centuries since enactment of the first ten amendments. (Some state constitutions have been amended much more often—218 times in a hundred years in Texas, 417 times in eighty years in South Carolina.) The system has provided substantial political leverage for minorities who have felt threatened by proposed amendments. Many within the minority opposed to restoration of state-approved prayer have regarded the prayer amendment as an affront to their fundamental rights as American citizens—or, more concretely, as a potential source for recurring emotional or physical harassment of their children. The effect of prayer brought back through constitutional fiat, some have argued, would be more coercive than when it was maintained as an ongoing social tradition. The weight of these sentiments in the political system has so far prevented any version of the prayer amendment from winning the required two-thirds majority in either house of Congress.

On March 20, 1984, the Republican-controlled United States Senate produced a fifty-six to forty-four majority for the Reagan administration's prayer amendment—still eleven votes short of the needed two-thirds. In the summer of 1984, after the Democratic national convention at which party leaders had embraced identification with "traditional values," the Democratic-controlled House of Representatives approved a Senate-passed measure permitting religious clubs to use public school facilities outside of regular school hours and amended an omnibus education bill to establish the right of public school students to a "moment of silence" each day for voluntary prayer. The first of these measures was signed into law by President Reagan, but the second died in the waning days of the session.[82]

When the drive for the prayer amendment stalled in the early 1980s, some proponents of school prayer, allied with supporters of the effort to overthrow the Supreme Court's 1973 decision establishing a constitutional right to abortion, advanced the simpler device of cutting off the Court's jurisdiction in these areas. The Judicial Article of the Constitution (Article III) grants the Supreme Court "appellate jurisdiction, both as to law and fact, with such exceptions, and under such regulations as the Congress shall make." This language, promoters of the cutoff approach claimed, gives Congress the power by simple majority vote to declare subjects like school prayer and abortion "exceptions" on which the Supreme Court can no longer hear appeals.

Some opponents of the cutoff argued that because the First and Fourteenth Amendments were passed after the Judicial Article, rights established under these amendments must (or may) lie beyond the power of Congress to designate as exceptions. But several constitutional scholars who testified against the cutoff before the Senate Judiciary Subcommittee on the Constitution in 1982 admitted that the Judicial Article probably does give Congress such power. According to Martin Redish, professor of law at Northwestern: "If Congress truly desires, it can do almost anything it wants to the jurisdiction of the lower federal courts or to the appellate jurisdiction of the Supreme Court."[83]

At the least, enactment of the cutoff would raise the prospect of a constitutional confrontation between Congress and the Supreme Court. Partly for this reason and partly because the cutoff, if successfully enforced, would deeply alter the constitutional foundation of the entire American judicial system, many conservatives as well as liberals, particularly among lawyers, emphatically opposed the maneuver. The most determined effort so far by promoters of the cutoff was turned back in the Senate on September 23, 1982, when a motion to invoke cloture against a filibuster being carried on by opponents was supported by a vote of only fifty-three to forty-five, seven short of the necessary three-fifths.[84]

TAX EXEMPTIONS

Having acted to banish religion from the public schools, the Court could hardly fail to deal with growing subsidization by states of church-related private education. Before ruling definitively on this issue, however, the Court turned to the question of tax exemptions for religious organizations, which some of the opinions in the prayer and Bible-reading cases had hinted might violate the establishment clause.

Exemption of churches from taxation appears to be almost as old as religion itself—partly as a kind of tribute paid by the state to the church's usefulness in maintaining social unity and partly as an expression of the state's recognition, sometimes grudgingly, that the church answers to a higher authority than that represented by the state. Genesis reports an Egyptian edict, attributed to Joseph, directing "that Pharaoh should have the fifth part" of the product of cultivated lands, "except the lands of the priests only, which became not Pharaoh's." The emperor Constantine exempted Christian churches from taxation in the fourth century.[85]

In the United States, all states have always exempted churches from property taxes, and church income has been exempt from the federal income tax since its first enactment. Contributions made to churches may be taken as deductions in figuring the federal personal income tax and most state income taxes. Businesses operated by churches for profit are usually subject to taxation. In many states, parsonages and church parking lots are exempted from property taxes.

It had never been made entirely clear, however, exactly why churches in a pluralist society should be exempt from taxation. The standard justification for granting exemptions to such institutions as private hospitals and libraries is that they perform functions that the state otherwise would have to assume and therefore deserve some encouragement in the form of tax relief. But the churches can hardly maintain that the state in their absence would carry on their religious function, which remains their primary reason for being.

After *Cantwell* and *Murdock* the churches had claimed tax exemption as a protection for free exercise. But some who resented the wealth and privileged positions of the churches read *Cantwell* the other way. Exemption, they argued, was a vestige of the days when particular churches had enjoyed establishment status.

In the 1950s and 1960s several attempts were made to get tax exemption cases before the Supreme Court, always without success. Finally, in 1969 the Court agreed to hear *Walz v. New York*. Walz, a New York lawyer whose sense of indignation on the subject must have been particularly strong, had bought a small piece of land in New York City for the sole purpose of qualifying as a taxpayer to challenge exemption of churches from property taxes. Early in 1970 Chief Justice Burger delivered the opinion of the Court. The "course of constitutional neutrality in this area," he wrote, "cannot be an absolutely straight line; rigidity could well defeat the basic purpose of these provisions, which is to insure that no religion be sponsored or favored, none commanded, and none inhibited." There is room in the First Amendment for "benevolent neutrality" by government toward religion. Perhaps, Burger suggested, "too much weight" had been placed on "a few words or phrases" in Justice Black's *Everson* opinion, which seemed to bar any state assistance to "all religion," without exception. After all, Black himself in that very opinion had found sufficient leeway to countenance New Jersey's transportation of students to parochial schools.[86]

There was nothing in Burger's *Walz* opinion to encourage the argument that churches are entitled to exemption from taxes as a matter of right under the free exercise clause. But if states so desire— as all states have desired from the beginning of American history— they may exempt churches from taxes as a means of rewarding their contribution to "moral or mental improvements." Under the establishment clause, states may not directly subsidize churches. But tax exemptions differ from subsidies because through exemptions government "simply abstains from demanding that the church support the state."

Burger seemed to have sharpened Clark's tests for "purpose and primary effect," set forth in *Schempp*. But then the Chief Justice went on to introduce a new test of his own: to escape the interdict of the establishment clause, a law must not produce "an excessive government entanglement with religion." Exemption of the churches from taxation, Burger found, "occasions some degree of involvement with religion." But "elimination of exemption would tend to expand the involvement of government" by creating the relationship of tax collector to taxpayer. Exemption, therefore, passes the test.[87]

Burger had saved the churches' tax exemptions. Walz, for his pains, had got his name fixed to the decision assuring the legitimacy of that which he deplored. But the new entanglement test would soon be found to have thrown interpretation of the establishment clause into greater confusion than ever.

Since *Walz*, some church representatives, such as Dean Kelley, director of the Commission on Religious Liberty of the National Council of Churches, have continued to argue that "the legislature" cannot "constitutionally tax churches." The Court, however, has indicated that whatever right to tax exemption may rise from the free exercise clause is inferior to some other compelling public interests. In *Bob Jones University v. United States* in 1983 the Court held that the Internal Revenue Service acted properly in denying a tax exemption to Bob Jones University in South Carolina because of the school's policy of prohibiting interracial dating, based on interpretation of biblical injunctions. The public interest in "eradicating racial discrimination in education," Chief Justice Burger wrote, "substantially outweighs whatever burden denial of tax benefits places on petitioners' exercise of their religious beliefs." (The case turned primarily on the question of whether the IRS had exceeded its authority by acting without specific guidelines from Congress. Justice William Rehnquist, the only dissenter, explicitly agreed that Bob Jones did not enjoy an inherent right to tax exemption under the free exercise clause.)[88]

"POTENTIAL FOR DIVISIVENESS"

By the early 1970s, state aid to church-operated schools had become a burning issue toward which the Supreme Court was being irresistibly drawn. In 1968 the Court ruled in *Board of Education v. Allen* that a New York law requiring local school districts to lend textbooks free of charge to students in parochial schools was constitutional. Such indirect assistance, Justice White held for the majority, was justified by "recognition that private education has played and is playing a significant and valuable role in raising national levels of knowledge, competence, and experience."[89]

Encouraged by this opinion as well as by Burger's assertion in *Walz* that government should maintain "benevolent neutrality" toward religion, the Catholic church, under heavy fiscal pressure from the rising costs of maintaining parochial schools, pushed for more significant forms of aid. The legislatures of Rhode Island and Pennsylvania, both states with large Catholic populations, passed laws that, respectively, provided that the state should pay part of the salaries of some teachers in nonpublic schools and authorized payment to private schools for instruction in secular subjects. In 1971 the Court ruled in *Lemon v. Kurtzman* that both state laws were unconstitutional.

Writing for the majority, Burger stated a sweeping conclusion: "Under our system the choice has been made that government is to be entirely excluded from the area of religious instruction and churches excluded from the affairs of government." Taken literally, this dictum could be interpreted to bar the churches from all forms of political action (including anything similar to the decisive role that some of the larger denominations had recently played in the civil rights movement). The Chief Justice elaborated on his recently developed test for "excessive entanglement": a law must not contribute to "political divisions along religious lines," which, he claimed, "was one of the principal evils against which the First Amendment was intended to protect." (The fact that the enactors of the First Amendment had deliberately placed the states, and therefore much of American politics, outside the amendment's authority by now seemed virtually forgotten.)[90]

On the same day the Rhode Island and Pennsylvania laws were overthrown, the Court, perhaps paradoxically, in *Tilton v. Richardson* approved federal grants for the construction of buildings at four Catholic colleges and universities in Connecticut. "Candor compels," Burger wrote, "the ackowledgment that we can only dimly perceive the boundaries of permissible government activity in this sensitive area. . . ." The Chief Justice explained that government aid to church-related elementary and secondary schools, proscribed in *Lemon*, differed measurably from aid to church-related higher education, because "the potential for divisiveness inherent in the essentially local problems of primary and secondary schools is significantly less with respect to a college or university whose student constituency is not local but diverse and widely dispersed."[91] Douglas, in dissent, did not aim directly at this sitting duck. The distinction discovered by the Court between *Lemon* and *Tilton*, he wrote, "is in effect that small violations of the First Amendment over a period of years are unconstitutional . . . while a huge violation occurring only once is *de minimis.*"[92]

The Catholic church, still struggling with growing costs, encouraged sympathetic legislators to continue probing the Court's position. In 1973 the Court seemed to take a decisive stand. New York had set up three state programs to assist nonpublic elementary and secondary schools: a program of direct grants to private schools in low-income areas for maintenance costs; one providing tuition reimbursements for low-income parents of private school students; and one offering tax deductions for parents whose incomes were too high to qualify for the reimbursement. All three, the Court held in *Committee for Public Education v. Nyquist*, were unconstitutional.

Justice Lewis Powell wrote that the New York law had the "impermissible effect of advancing religion" and therefore failed the second of the two tests for establishment set forth by Justice Clark in the *Schempp* decision. Powell discreetly decided that it was unnecessary to "consider whether such aid would result in entanglement of the state with religion."

Chief Justice Burger and Justices White and Rehnquist, each submitting separate opinions, agreed with Powell's majority holding that New York's program of direct grants for maintenance costs was unconstitutional but argued that the tuition reimbursement and tax deduction plans should have been approved. "Under state law," White wrote, "these children have a right to a free public education and it would not appear unreasonable if the state, relieved of the expense of educating a child in the public school, contributed to the expense of his education elsewhere."[93]

During the next decade, the Court approved some minor modifications in the position set forth in *Nyquist*, but the overall trend of decisions indicated firm resolve to deny any but the most trivial aid, direct or indirect, to church-related schools.

JUDICIAL ACTIVISM

In an opinion in one of the lesser school aid cases, Justice White wrote in 1981, "Establishment Clause cases are not easy; they stir deep feelings; and we are divided among ourselves, perhaps reflecting the different views on this subject of the people of this country."[94]

Some of the Court's troubles in this area would, of course, have been avoided if the establishment clause had not been extended to the states—a step, I have argued, that was neither constitutionally necessary nor consistent with American tradition. If application of the establishment clause had been limited to the federal government, the Court need not have become involved with such issues as school prayer, Sunday closing laws, or state aid to nonpublic education. The controversies that grew out of some of these issues would then have been carried on mainly at the state or local levels. This, at the least, would have freed Congress and the executive branch to devote to other purposes the enormous amounts of governmental time and attention these matters have consumed.

This outcome would not, of course, at least in the short run, have pleased persons whose grievances were met by decisions based on the establishment clause. But some of the changes brought about by these decisions would probably have been achieved on a state-by-state basis through actions by state courts or state legislatures, with less accompanying strain on the national social fabric and the governmental system.

There was, it is true, a theoretic possibility that as long as the establishment clause did not apply to the states, some state would try to grant establishment status, requiring direct financial support, to a particular church or group of churches, as five states had done in the early years of the Republic. But the political realities of twentieth century America make this possibility, which would certainly run counter to the American social tradition as it has developed, extremely unlikely. No state had established or seriously considered establishing a particular church or group of churches for more than a century before the *Cantwell* decision in 1940. The practical effect of restricting the reach of the establishment clause to the federal government had been to leave to the states most of the responsibility for regulating relations between religious institutions and civil society.

Limiting jurisdiction of the establishment clause to the federal government clearly is not now in the judicial or political cards. Even if it were, some difficult problems in church-state relations would remain. Proposals for federal actions that would benefit church-related schools and the many symbolic relationships that still exist between government and religion at the national level, for example, obviously fall under federal jurisdiction. The most important question concerning the establishment clause that the Court and therefore the nation now faces is, what does "establishment," whether applied to the state or federal governments, mean within the context of the First Amendment?

Since the 1940s the Court has sometimes seemed to interpret prohibition of establishment to mean not only that there should be no direct tie between government and the organized churches but also that the whole of civil society should be kept insulated against contact with religion. This interpretation has usually been supported by references to the intentions of the founders, particularly Madison or Jefferson. Justice Black, who wrote several of the earlier opinions prescribing almost total detachment of government from religion, maintained throughout his career that he was doing no more than applying the plain language of the Constitution (though in 1968 he found it expedient to switch his basis for extending the first eight amendments to the states from the due process clause to the privileges or immunities clause of the Fourteenth Amendment).[95]

As the account presented in chapter 3 showed, this view of the intentions of the founders is, to say the least, biased. It is mainly derived from a partial reading of Madison's *Memorial and Remonstrance*, coupled with exaggerated emphasis on Jefferson's anticlericalism. In actuality, the founders generally regarded establishment as direct support of religion by government—the kind many of them had experienced in the colonial past and still had before them in several of the states. Prohibition of establishment at the federal level they found entirely compatible with public days of prayer and thanksgiving, appointment of chaplains for the armed forces and both houses of Congress, encouragement of religious values through the schools in the Northwest Territory, and many ceremonial or symbolic relationships between government and religion. Black's contention that the Court was simply carrying out the original purpose of the establishment clause therefore is, on its face, implausible.

A popular modern school of judicial philosophy, increasingly influential with the Court during the 1960s and early 1970s, holds, however, that such questions as what the framers of the First Amendment intended or what the enactors of the Fourteenth Amendment meant by "liberty" are pretty much beside the point. What is now important and relevant is the interplay between current social realities and contemporary standards of social justice (the sources of which are usually left vague). This judicial philosophy is known in the law schools as "noninterpretivism," after its adherents' belief that the courts should not be limited to interpreting the written Constitution. Its more popular title is "judicial activism."[96]

According to judicial activists, the function of the Supreme Court is not to test laws against norms set forth or logically implied by the Constitution but to act as a sort of board of censors, cleansing the social system of abuses or aberrations that do not yield to ordinary political action. Lawrence Friedman, professor of law at Stanford, has set forth the activist position with unusual clarity and candor: "In a pluralist system there are many laws that could not now be passed as an initial matter and yet cannot now be repealed. On some highly controverted subjects, the status quo is frozen; to move up or down, forward or backward, is politically dangerous." Under such circumstances the courts can serve as "brooms" to sweep away the detritus of outmoded attitudes and beliefs. In carrying out this function, the courts draw on a general sense of where society stands. "The measuring rods are very vague, very broad principles. These are attached loosely to phrases in the Constitution. They are connected more organically to the general culture."[97]

The Supreme Court's decision is 1954 declaring racial segregation of the public schools unconstitutional is often offered as an example of how judicial activism works. Racial segregation of the schools, which had been approved by nineteenth century American society, had by the 1950s become intolerable under broadly accepted social norms. Yet the political system was powerless to act. Southern segregationists, through their strategic role in national politics, held a power of veto over legislation dealing with race. Congressional rules permitted the minority supporting segregation to hold out almost indefinitely. Blacks throughout the South were effectively excluded from participation in the political system and therefore were unrepresented. The Court intervened. The system was unfrozen. Desegregation, though at all too slow a pace, followed.

The Court's abortion decision in 1973 is cited as another example of judicial activism cleansing the system. American standards, it is alleged, had shifted by the early 1970s, so that abortion, once regarded as morally wrong except to save the life of the mother, had come to be viewed as acceptable or at least as a subject on which each woman should be permitted to decide for herself. But the political power of the Catholic church, along with vague prejudices among part of the rest of the population, prevented the political system from repealing outmoded laws. Again, the Court acted. A woman's unconditional right to abortion, at least during the first trimester, was secured. No specific constitutional authority was needed, though the Fourteenth Amendment might be quoted for form's sake. The Court was proceeding under its general responsibility to clean up the system.

The assumptions of judicial activism underlay many of the Court's innovative decisions in the 1960s and 1970s that broke traditional or statutory relationships between religion and civil society. Even if the Fourteenth Amendment had not existed, in the activist view, the Court would still have had a responsibility to apply twentieth century norms rather than the anachronistic value systems on which these relationships had been based.

Whatever may be said for or against the substance of judicial activism, one thing can be said with confidence: it does not remotely approximate the idea that most Americans have of what the Supreme Court is supposed to do. Though polling evidence on the subject is sparse, it is probably fair to say that most Americans regard the Supreme Court as a body of legal experts whose function is to decide particular cases according to standards set forth in the Constitution. A somewhat more sophisticated minority would be prepared to agree that the language of the Constitution may grow and develop over time or that interpretation by experts may find meanings that were inherent in the Constitution from the start though they were not perceived in detail by its enactors. The Court's desegregation decision in 1954 thus may be approved, without resorting to noninterpretivism, as an example of the Court's correcting an error in interpretation by one of its predecessors. But the fraction of the population that believes that the justices of the Supreme Court should base their decisions on "vague, very broad principles" that they derive from "the general culture" is almost certainly miniscule.

A Court pursuing a judicial activist approach in a democratic society—or at least in American society as it is now constituted—will always run a substantial risk of losing public confidence. If justices do not reflect the authority of the Constitution, the public must inquire, why should their opinions count for more than those of any other citizen?

When the general culture from which judicial activists claim to get their standards is deeply divided, as occurred in the United States during the 1960s, this risk becomes grave. The fissure in American culture that began in those years was very complex, and its ultimate effects still are not clear. In general, however, it may be said to have pitted a majority within society committed, however vaguely or unreliably, to hybrid versions of traditional theist-humanism against a minority, on the average younger, more affluent, and more exposed to formal education than the overall population, pursuing values derived from civil-humanist or personalist value systems.

Supreme Court justices were hardly in the forefront of the cultural new wave. But civil-humanist and personalist values powerfully influenced the educated upper middle class to which the justices belonged. In varying degrees, therefore, and conditioned by individual temperaments and experiences, they drew on a different "general culture" than that from which the majority of Americans obtained basic values.

Supreme Court justices who reject judicial activism do not, as Lawrence Friedman points out, thereby become value free. Not even the strictest constructionist regards the Constitution as a sort of legal cookbook in which recipes can be looked up to deal with particular cases. The strict constructionist (or "interpretivist") as well as the judicial activist applies values that he brings from his experience and temperament to his understanding of the Constitution. These values unquestionably influence his interpretations, as rays of light played on a gem from different angles bring out different qualities. The strict constructionist claims—or should claim—only that his attention remains focused on the objective reality of the Constitution, while the judicial activist feels to a much greater extent free to apply values taken from the "general culture" without objective constraint.

A CHANGE IN DIRECTION?

In the early 1980s the Burger Court seemed gradually to change direction in deciding cases that involved the establishment clause. The first sign that a shift might be on the way came in the closeness of the vote in a 1980 case in which the Court ruled, by a five-to-four majority, that a Kentucky law ordering the posting of the Ten Commandments in public school rooms is unconstitutional (though the Court itself sits beneath a frieze depicting the development of law in which a tablet containing the Ten Commandments holds the central place).[98]

After that, the majority began tipping the other way. Strict separationists were alarmed in 1980 when the Court refused to hear an appeal from a lower court's decision approving the display of Christmas decorations with clear religious content in the public schools of Sioux Falls, South Dakota. More significantly, the Court ruled in 1981 that the University of Missouri at Kansas City could not deny religious groups the use of school facilities that were made available to secular clubs.[99]

In 1983 the Court came down on the side of "benevolent neutrality" on an issue that had long rankled separationists. The Nebraska state legislature had for many years employed a chaplain—as it happened, the same chaplain, a Presbyterian minister, for the previous eighteen years—who opened each session with prayer. "In light of the unambiguous and unbroken history of more than 200 years," Chief Justice Burger wrote for the six-to-three majority, "there can be no doubt that the practice of opening legislative sessions with prayer has become a part of the fabric of our society." (The "fabric of our society" had not been given much attention in most of the establishment clause decisions of the 1960s and 1970s.) Burger pointed out that only three days before it approved the Bill of Rights, the first Congress authorized the appointment of paid chaplains for both the Senate and the House of Representatives. "Clearly the men who wrote the First Amendment Religion Clause did not view paid legislative chaplains and opening prayers as a violation of that Amendment. . . ."[100]

In an even more significant decision in 1983, the Court seemed to open a large gap in the barrier raised by *Nyquist* against government assistance to church-related schools. Political debate over the issue had continued. In the preceding several Congresses, bills authorizing tax credits to offset tuition payments to private schools at all levels had been introduced by both liberals and conservatives in both houses. Ronald Reagan had entered the presidency in 1981 pledged to support "a system of educational assistance based on tax credits that will in part compensate parents for their financial sacrifices in paying tuition at the elementary, secondary, and post-secondary levels." In the spring of 1982 the Reagan administration sent Congress a proposal to allow credits against personal income taxes for part of tuitions paid to nonprofit elementary and secondary schools.[101]

Simultaneously, arguments that some kinds of government support for church-related education should be regarded as constitutional were coming from experts within the academic community. Philip Kurland's idea, first set forth in 1961, that the free exercise clause and the establishment clause should be read together to produce the conclusion "that government cannot utilize religion as a standard for inaction or action," received new attention. Writing in 1981, Paul Weber and Dennis Gilbert interpreted the Constitution to require "fiscal neutrality," under which parochial schools should be neither advantaged nor penalized in determining eligibility for state aid. Denis Doyle argued that exemption of religious groups from federal and state taxes provides a precedent for approving tax credits or tax deductions to offset tuitions paid to church-related schools.[102]

Nevertheless, the Court's 1983 decision in *Mueller v. Allen* came as something of a bombshell. Minnesota had for many years permitted state taxpayers to claim a deduction from gross income for some expenditures for "tuition, textbooks, and transportation" at either public or private schools. In practice, more than 90 percent of the taxpayers qualifying for such deductions sent their children to religious schools. Justice William Rehnquist, writing for the five-to-four majority, held that because the deductions were available to the parents of students in both public and private schools, the Minnesota law could not be considered a support for religion. Rehnquist also claimed to find significant distinction between the tax deductions permitted under the Minnesota law and the tax credits and tuition reimbursements that had been held unconstitutional in *Nyquist*.[103] Justice Thurgood Marshall, in dissent, protested, "For the first time, the Court has upheld financial support for religious schools without any reason at all to assume that the support will be restricted to the secular functions of those schools and will not be used to support religious instruction."

Opponents of public aid to church-related education took what comfort they could from the fact that most of the bills for federal tax relief so far introduced, including the Reagan administration's proposal, resembled the New York system rejected under *Nyquist* more than the Minnesota program approved under *Mueller*. But the firm line drawn by *Nyquist* clearly had been broken.

In 1984 the Court gave separationists a further jolt through its decision that a display including a nativity scene maintained during the Christmas season by the city government of Pawtucket, Rhode Island, did not violate the establishment clause. Writing for the five-to-four majority, Chief Justice Burger conceded that "the display advances religion in a sense," but such indirect support for religion he maintained, is no more forbidden by the First Amendment than are celebration of Christmas and Thanksgiving as national holidays, displays of religious paintings in public art galleries, or singing by students of "Chistmas hymns and carols in public schools."[104]

A few weeks later, the Court followed up with rulings that programs in New York City and Grand Rapids, Michigan, through which public school teachers were giving remedial instruction to children in parochial schools who had learning problems, violated the establishment clause. "For these children," Justice O'Connor wrote in dissent in the New York case, "the Court's decision is tragic. The Court deprives them of a program that offers a meaningful chance at success in life, and it does so on the untenable theory that public school teachers (most of whom are of different faiths than their students) are likely to start teaching religion merely because they have walked across the threshold of a parochial school."[105]

In June 1985 the Court, appearing at least to pause in its movement toward accommodationism, ruled that a 1981 Alabama statute authorizing a one-minute period of silence in the public schools "for meditation or voluntary prayer" constituted establishment. In a concurring opinion, however, Justice Sandra O'Connor held that state laws calling for moments of silence for meditation without specific mention of prayer might "not necessarily manifest the same infirmity." Such a moment of silence, Justice O'Connor wrote, could not be construed as imposing religion, because "a student who objects to prayer is left to his own thoughts, and is not compelled to listen to the prayers or thoughts of others."[106]

Reasonable Standards

The future direction of Supreme Court decisions on issues involving the establishment clause is difficult to predict. In the middle 1980s the Court appears to be in a state of ferment. While some recent decisions indicate a move toward a more flexible approach to church-state issues, the resistance of liberal justices remains resolute. After the 1984 election, conservatives anticipated that Ronald Reagan would have an opportunity to name several new justices, reinforcing the accommodationist trend. But judicial history has shown that there is no certainty that such expectations will be fulfilled.

Philip Kurland's argument, also advanced by Weber and Gilbert, that reading the free exercise clause and the establishment clause as a unit justifies public aid to nonpublic schools (provided religious institutions are not given special treatment) offers the Court a rationale for approving considerable state assistance to religious schools. The development of a significant number of evangelical Protestant private schools (particularly but not wholly in the South) and the continuing needs of the Catholic system will undoubtedly keep up political pressure for some accommodation of this kind.

One trouble with the Kurland solution, as a number of supporters of public education have pointed out, is that it would make substantial state assistance available to schools with a frankly religious orientation while leaving the public schools, under *Engel* and *Schempp,* insulated against religion. This might satisfy some of the churches that sponsor schools and might be acceptable to some secularists, but it would inevitably have the effect of encouraging parents who wish their children to be educated in an environment that at least symbolically acknowledges dependence on religion to turn increasingly to private schools, thereby further undermining support for public education.

The flaw in the argument of those who wish to remove all sign of religion from civic life, particularly from the public schools, is perhaps that pointed to by Justice Stewart in his dissent from the *Schempp* decision: banishment of religion does not represent neutrality between religion and secularism; conduct of public institutions without any acknowledgment of religion *is* secularism. A secular society should not be thought of as simply operating on a different level from religion, leaving the misty realm of whatever other worlds may be to the churches. Secularism—whether secular humanism, secular egoism, or secular authoritarianism—expresses a broadly consistent view of existence in which religion has no place. A society that excludes religion totally from its public life, that seems to regard religion as something against which public life must be protected, is bound to foster the impression that religion is either irrelevant or harmful.

The founders were determined that the federal government should not become involved with sponsorship or institutional support of any religion. To this end they enacted the establishment clause. But sponsorship or institutional support is not the same thing as acknowledging the dependence of civil society, as of all life, on transcendent direction. The founders' belief in the wisdom of placing civil society within a framework of religious values formed part of their reason for enacting the free exercise clause. The First Amendment is no more neutral on the general value of religion than it is on the general value of the free exchange of ideas or an independent press. The founders' conviction that free institutions derive much of their moral vitality from religion also led them to authorize numerous symbolic expressions of the religious character of the American people.

Where acknowledgment leaves off and sponsorship or institutional support begins is bound to be a difficult question. Most Americans today would probably draw the line more tightly than most of the founders believed was necessary. The two tests set forth by Justice Clark, under which no legislative enactment can have advancement of religion as either its purpose or its primary effect, seem to provide standards that are both reasonable and sufficient as long as a distinction is maintained between advancing religion and facilitating its free exercise by individuals. Under the test for purpose, enactments that confer direct benefits on a religious institution, such as the bill to provide land for construction of a church that Madison vetoed in 1811, are prohibited as clearly partaking of establishment. Under the test for primary effect, enactments under which government subsidies are made available to church-controlled facilities, such as the provisions for public support of teachers' salaries and costs of nonreligious education in parochial schools that were rejected in *Lemon,* also are disallowed.

Chief Justice Burger's added test that a law must not produce "an excessive government entanglement with religion," in contrast, does more harm than good. Philip Kurland, with characteristic bluntness, has described the entanglement test as "either empty or nonsensical." Interpreted literally, it could prohibit state requirements that church-related schools maintain minimum standards of education or forbid all references to God or transcendent values in public discourse. Perhaps the word "excessive" provides an escape hatch; but if so, the test, as Kurland suggests, is almost meaningless.

Burger's related standard that laws must not contribute to "political divisions along religious lines" has proven even less serviceable. Observing events in Northern Ireland, Lebanon, and Iran, as well as large chunks of human history, no one will doubt the potential of religious emotion for causing political disaster. But who can say in advance which issues will produce significant divisions along religious lines? Should all laws that the churches have played an essential role in passing, like the civil rights laws of the 1960s, be declared unconstitutional? Does a potential for even minor division justify silencing the churches in public debate over fundamental values? Faced with these and similar questions, the Court in recent years has tended to abandon the divisiveness test. In a footnote to his decision in *Mueller* in 1983, Justice Rehnquist referred disparagingly to the "rather elusive inquiry" into "divisive political potential."[107]

By limiting itself to the tests for purpose and primary effect, the Court can consistently maintain the constitutional validity of the many practices through which government in the United States traditionally has acknowledged the value of religion without undertaking direct sponsorship, such as exemption of church income from taxation and legal observance of religious holidays. Without undermining the institutional separation between church and state intended by the founders, this approach also should lay a firm constitutional base for measures that primarily facilitate free exercise of religion by individuals, such as authorizing a "moment of silence" that may be used for voluntary prayer in the public schools, making school facilities available for meetings of student religious clubs, and offering tax allowances for fees paid to either public or religious schools.

In its interpretation of the free exercise clause, the Supreme Court has on the whole maintained a balanced course, providing the opportunity for a wide variety of religious expression while protecting the legitimate needs of civil society. In its interpretations of the establishment clause, it has in recent decades been less successful. But this is in part because the complexities of modern life go far beyond those with which the founders had to grapple. Interpretation of the religion clauses remains an unfinished book. As long as most of the American people continue to pursue some combination of the values of religious faith, individual rights, and the security of society as a whole, explication of the establishment clause and the free exercise clause will be among the most challenging of the responsibilities of our judicial system.

FIVE

The Churches and Political Action: 1790 to 1963

THE FIRST AMENDMENT prohibits governmental restraint on religion but does nothing directly to limit participation by organized religion in secular politics. There have always been, however, many Americans who have believed that the churches, for their own sakes as well as in the interest of general social harmony, should stay out of politics. That view has been fed by diverse sources. Anticlericalists like Thomas Jefferson have held that organized religion is inherently authoritarian and therefore potentially subversive to democratic processes. Evangelical Protestants, particularly Baptists, have often regarded politics as a dirty business, distracting the attention of believers from spiritual pursuits. German and Scandinavian Lutherans have espoused the doctrine of the "two kingdoms," prescribing that church and state should each stick to its own affairs. Many Jews, secularists, members of smaller Christian denominations, and practitioners of non-Western religions have feared that political action by the churches would be the prelude to religious persecution.

Yet organized religion has almost continually been deeply involved in American politics. James Otis's "Black Regiment" of dissenting clergy enthusiastically promoted the cause of American independence. Church leaders were in the forefront of political struggles to abolish slavery, prohibit the sale of intoxicating liquor, and win votes for women. Liberal Protestant, Catholic, and Jewish groups campaigned for economic and social reforms during the Progressive Era and under the New Deal. Conservative churches fought for enforcement of Sunday closing laws and suppression of gambling and pornography. By the beginning of the 1960s most of the larger denominations maintained church offices in Washington to represent their views on national issues. The Civil Rights Act of 1964, Hubert Humphrey said, could not have been passed without the backing it received from the churches.

Beyond positions advanced by the churches on particular issues, religion is woven into the underlying texture of American politics. In the 1950s Richard Scammon, then as now the leading national sage on election statistics, used to tell young journalists and political scientists in Washington that the two most important issues in every national election, in terms of the number of votes they determined, were the Reformation and the Civil War—the latter almost as bound up with religion as the former. Since that time, some of the loyalties and animosities arising from those two ancient quarrels have faded or have mixed with sentiments aroused by such newer concerns as the cold war, the civil rights movement, and the growth of the welfare state. But not far from the surface the old passions retain persistent force, and some of the newer concerns have their own religious dimensions.

At an even more fundamental level—beyond the political divisions shaped by religious attachments—the essential unity of American society and American political life is to a great extent based on the religious conception of America's destiny formed by Jonathan Edwards and developed by John Adams, Abraham Lincoln, and Woodrow Wilson, among others. A "nation with the soul of a church"—in Sidney Mead's apt phrase—must of necessity present both exceptional opportunities and exceptional problems for its actual institutional churches.[1]

The question has always been, how far can the churches safely or responsibly go in entering secular politics without imperiling their spiritual and moral responsibilities, which almost everyone agrees remain their primary reasons for being? For many, political involvement seems more a fulfillment of than a distraction from spiritual or moral imperatives. But at some point tension is almost sure to develop between political action and the churches' more purely religious roles, as is shown by some of the controversies over economic and foreign policy issues that have recently erupted within the Catholic church and mainline Protestant denominations and to a lesser degree among evangelical Protestants and within the Jewish community.

In this chapter and the next I will examine some of the roles that churches and other religious groups have played and are playing in American politics. This account will in no way attempt to be an inclusive history of religion in America or of the relationship between religion and politics in the United States. Rather, it will be a kind of tour through history and contemporary practice, aimed at collecting and analyzing ideas and institutional arrangements that shed light on current relationships.

A Pluralist Society

Although George Washington and many of the other founders deplored the development of factions or parties in the young Republic, the nation's political life was soon organized around just such divisions and has usually remained so ever since. Religion was from the beginning an important factor in sorting out the contending political coalitions.

The primary division in early American politics (as perhaps in most modern societies) was between the party of order, emphasizing the need for firm social authority to promote the survival and stable development of the new nation, and the party of equality, emphasizing society's obligation to give each of its members as close as feasible to an equal chance at achieving personal fulfillment. Broadly interpreted, these goals were not incompatible and indeed were to some extent interdependent; but differences in emphasis, reinforced by competing personal ambitions, soon were enough to split the body politic in two. For ideological or strategic reasons, religious groups arrayed themselves on either side of this political fault line.

To understand these alignments, it is first necessary to identify briefly the major religious groups active in the new nation. The relative strengths, in terms of church membership, of the major denominations were undergoing radical shifts during the Republic's first decades. When the Revolution began, Congregationalists, Presbyterians, and Anglicans, each having roughly equal strength, accounted for about 80 percent of church adherents in the former colonies. The Anglican church was identified with the British in the struggle for independence, and during the war some of its members fled or were expelled. Reconstituted as the Episcopal church (with its own bishops at last), the American representative of the Anglican tradition included on its rolls many prominent social and political leaders, most notably General Washington, and offered qualities of liturgical splendor and historical continuity that its Calvinist and evangelical rivals could not match. Nevertheless, the Episcopalians had already slipped to fourth place in membership, behind the Baptists, by the time the Constitution was ratified.[2]

Congregationalists and Presbyterians, both militant supporters of the Revolution, shared the heritage of orthodox Calvinism. The Congregationalists enjoyed official government backing in three of the New England states, and the Presbyterians, besides being numerous in the middle states and Virginia, had developed a presence in the growing West.

It soon became clear, however, that orthodox Calvinism was not well suited to catch the winds of social and individual optimism that were rising in the newly created United States. Belief in predestination and concentration on sin had been socially functional for a beleaguered people clinging to the edge of a continent largely wild or controlled by hostile governments. But by the closing decade of the eighteenth century, prospects for America and Americans had turned favorable—sometimes richly so. The human psyche was entering one of its infrequent encounters with opportunity that was, as Scott Fitzgerald observed, commensurate with its capacity for wonder. Americans knew much of guilt, and a spirit of melancholy continued to pervade much of American art and literature; but hope was now also upon them, hope for personal improvement, for national greatness, for a better world. Orthodox Calvinism, binding men to the inscrutable will of transcendent purpose, could not readily accommodate so much hope.

One conceivable alternative for America was no religion at all, or, at most, acknowledgment of the clockmaker God who had set in motion a world governed by mechanical laws discoverable through human reason. Such rejection of traditional theist-humanism was what a small but articulate minority within the old revolutionary phalanx would have preferred. "We cannot be miserable for the sin of Adam," wrote Ethan Allen, "or happy in the righteousness of Christ, in which transactions we were no ways accessory or assisting as accomplices, or otherwise concerned; and are not at all conscious of these ancient matters. . . ."[3]

During the years immediately after the Revolution, deism and even atheism appeared to be making some headway, particularly among the educated young. Looking back later, Timothy Dwight recalled, "The profanation of the Sabbath, before unusual, profaneness of language, drunkenness, gambling, lewdness, were exceedingly increased. . . . In the meantime, that enormous evil, a depreciating currency, gave birth to a new spirit of fraud, and opened numerous temptations, and a boundless field for its operations; while a new and intimate correspondence with corrupted foreigners introduced a multiplicity of loose doctrines which were greedily embraced by licentious men as the means of palliating and justifying their sins."[4]

The first blows of the French Revolution seemed to American deists the opening strokes of a long awaited age of reason. John Trumbull of Connecticut was shocked when "the National Assembly of France, the elected rulers of a great nation, formed a procession to the metropolitan church of Notre Dame, which had been consecrated during long ages of worship to God, and there in mock bowed their knees before a common courtesan, basely worshiping her as the goddess of reason." Yet, he bemoaned, there were some in America "who threw up their caps, and cried, 'glorious, glorious, sister republic!' " Timothy Dwight could not but ask, "Shall our sons become the disciples of Voltaire, and the dragoons of Marat; or our daughters the concubines of the Illuminati?"[5]

The ultimate answer of American public opinion to Dwight's question was a resounding No! The bloody course of events in France, coupled with the arrogance displayed by some French radical politicians toward the United States, soon shifted popular sentiment against the revolution. In any case, as Adolf Koch noted, "The American liberal, while a republican in politics, was unable to accept republican religion." What remained of deism was swept away by the Second Great Awakening, beginning in 1799. De Witt Clinton, busily constructing the prototype of what was to become New York's Democratic machine, concluded that it would be "wise to disassociate republicanism from deism." Elihu Palmer, who for a time enjoyed considerable renown as a deist publicist in New York City, concluded in 1805, "The world is not yet so enlightened, or so liberal, as to depart in any high degree from its interests and its prejudices. . . . The

philosophers and contemplative men, who have dared to look superstition full in the face, are comparatively speaking, few in number."[6]

Old Tom Paine, returning to the United States in 1802 after
sacrificing his health and almost his life in the service of the French
Revolution, found himself a political outcast. His friend Jefferson
received him, after some delay ("Mr. Paine is not, I believe, a favorite
among the ladies"), at the presidential mansion but was careful to
avoid the topic of religion. Most of the survivors among his old
comrades-in-arms would have nothing to do with him. "His principles
avowed in his *Age of Reason*," wrote Benjamin Rush, "were so offensive
to me that I did not wish to renew my intercourse with him." Hanging
about Deborah Applegate's tavern in Bordentown, New Jersey, Paine
managed to "turn several church members from their faith," but the
time when his views on religion might win a substantial audience in
America had passed—at least for another century.[7]

The Great Awakening of the 1730s, preached by Edwards, Whitefield, and the Tennants, had given some clue to the main direction
that religion would take in the not-yet-created United States. There
was no great market in America for a soft religion or even for a
rationalist religion of the kind promoted by Charles Chauncy and
Jonathan Mayhew. Calvin, most Americans seemed to believe, had
after all been at least partly right: human nature is dominated by an
incorrigible propensity to sin, in the sense that it pursues egoistic
ends in preference to all others. Anyone who believed differently
need only observe the processes of daily life in the commercial marts
on the Atlantic Coast, on the slave-cultivated plantations of the South,
or along the lawless frontier. The only force that could save the
individual from his own natural selfishness was the redeeming love
of an all-powerful God. Where many Americans parted company with
Calvin—not all, of course, for Presbyterianism continued to grow and
Congregationalism remained strong in New England—was in their
belief that the individual human spirit has a part to play, through
repentance, in the experience of salvation.

The expansive nature of life in the growing cities and on the
frontier, as well as the philosophic legacy of John Locke, encouraged
economic and cultural individualism in the United States. Among
many of those drawn to religion, these factors in the surrounding
social atmosphere promoted acceptance of personalist-leaning versions of theist-humanism emphasizing a direct relationship between

individual consciousness and transcendent purpose. In colonial America this tendency was chiefly represented by the Baptists, the Quakers, and several pietist German sects, among which the Mennonites and the Brethren (Dunkers) were the most numerous.

The Quakers' inclination toward personalism seems to have gone beyond the limit within which a system of beliefs can serve as the organizing principle for an enduring total society. Quakerism might survive and even flourish as a dedicated sect within or attached to a more worldly host community. It offered a spiritually attractive alternative way of life and could provide the host community with effective moral criticism and correction—primitive Christianity contained a powerful inclination to play just such a role in relation to the Roman Empire in the centuries before Constantine. But the Quakers' commitment to pacifism, however morally impressive, did not meet the test of political realism in the view of most eighteenth or nineteenth century Americans. The Mennonites and the Brethren were even less prepared to make the political adjustments needed to manage a total society. Brethren, it is said, would vote for Quakers in Pennsylvania but would not hold office themselves; Mennonites would not even vote.

Quakers, Mennonites, and Brethren, it should be recognized, did not generally aspire to dominate the host society in which they lived. The world, they believed, was hopelessly corrupt, and the most a good Christian could do was to pursue a pure life on its fringes. Such rejection of the larger world inevitably limited numerical growth.

Following the tradition of Roger Williams, Baptists also regarded the world as a "wilderness" from which the "garden" of the church must be kept distinct. But most Baptists were fiercely determined that the garden should grow. Responding to Jesus' directive to "go ye therefore, and teach all nations," Baptists plunged into the world, enthusiastically seeking converts to their personalist interpretation of Christianity. Baptist churches, either loosely associated within two major confederations or practically autonomous, sprang up in many parts of the South and West. The intense personal experience of redemption offered at Baptist revivals appealed particularly to the rural poor, who often felt rejected or unserved by the more liturgical churches. By 1850 the Baptists had become the second largest Protestant denomination in the United States, surpassing the Presbyterians and Congregationalists as well as the Episcopalians, who had dropped, respectively, to fourth, fifth, and ninth places among all denominations.[8]

The Baptists' highly decentralized system of church governance was in tune with American individualism, but decentralization also carried with it characteristic administrative weaknesses that allowed local churches to grow lax or spin out of control. During the first half of the nineteenth century, Baptists were outstripped in membership by a denomination that combined religious personalism with a tightly disciplined church structure: the Methodists.

American Methodism, which was an independent denomination in the United States in 1784 before its parent body had departed from the Anglican Church in Britain, marched like a mighty army across the nineteenth century religious landscape. Following John Wesley's lead, as well as that of Whitefield and Edwards in America, the Methodists concentrated on personal experience of salvation rather than on liturgy or dogma. But the institutional means through which this experience was promoted was a hierarchically organized church. "Government of the denomination was in the hands of the clergymen, who seemed as self-sacrificing a band as any Wesley's stern discipline might have asked."[9] The attraction of Methodism extended to all regions and to all social groups: frontier farmers and city millhands, merchants and schoolteachers—and, most important of all, to the formidable ranks of Methodist women.

Together, Methodists, Baptists, the more evangelical branch of Presbyterians, Disciples of Christ (seventh in denominational membership in 1850), and the smaller evangelical sects shared the tradition of personalist religion that descended from the Great Awakening. "The evangelists," according to Timothy Smith, "substituted an existential for the dogmatic concept of original sin, picturing it as a diseased condition of the soul rather than a legal burden of guilt for Adam's fall. More important . . . they spread the faith that divine grace was available here and now to cleanse it all away."[10]

Along the spectrum of religions from individualist personalism to collectivist idealism, all of the evangelical faiths were far toward the personalist side. But within the larger society they were a socializing force, contending against egoistic impulses toward sensual indulgence and commercial exploitation let loose in America by the lack of traditional institutional structures. "The frontier," Ralph Gabriel noted, "was crude, turbulent, and godless. Evangelical Protestantism, more than any other single force, tamed it." William Sweet observed, "A random turning of the pages of any of the old record books of the early frontier churches will soon convince one that the church was a large factor in maintaining order in these raw communities. Discipline was meted out to members for drinking, fighting, harmful gossip, lying, stealing, immoral relation between the sexes, gambling, and horse racing."[11] In the growing cities and small towns, evangelical churches instilled habits of industry, sobriety, honesty, thrift, and family responsibility—the so-called Protestant ethic.

In the second quarter of the nineteenth century, more liturgical churches tending toward the communitarian side of the religious spectrum, like the Catholics and the Lutherans, began to grow as waves of immigrants adhering to their faiths arrived in the United States. While maintaining many inherited characteristics, these churches inevitably experienced change as they adjusted to American life. By 1850, Roman Catholics, a small minority in colonial times, had risen to second or third place in membership among all denominations. In the process the social base of Catholicism had changed greatly from that represented by the Carrolls and a few other landed Maryland families. Massive Irish immigration, spurred on by poverty and famine at home, had transformed American Catholicism into a largely working-class church. Catholics of English or French descent at first tried to maintain control of church administration. As late as 1832 Archbishop James Whitfield of Baltimore wrote privately to another bishop, "I do really think we should guard against having more Irish bishops." The Irish, however, not only predominated in numbers but also gave a larger number of their sons to the priesthood than English, German, or French Catholics. The hierachy, therefore, was soon overwhelmingly Irish. Minority factions of German and French Catholics frequently grumbled against Irish domination but were usually required to submit.[12]

As the church grew in numbers, its bishops moved to consolidate authority over what had developed as a somewhat decentralized ecclesiastical structure. Early in the century, boards of lay trustees at some churches had achieved varying degrees of local autonomy. This tendency was dealt a serious blow in 1822 when a Philadelphia priest who had encouraged lay aspirations was excommunicated. In the 1840s bishops in most dioceses rooted out what was left of "trusteeism" and established tight lines of hierachical control.[13]

Lutherans, at first drawn mainly from Germany, but later from the Scandinavian countries as well, formed the sixth largest demonination at the middle of the century. Unlike members of the German Reformed Church (eighth in numbers), Lutherans did not share a common Calvinst theology with the inheritors of Puritanism. Lutheran culture was hierarchical, ritualistic, communitarian, and relatively open to sensual pleasure—in many ways similar to the cultural tradition of German Catholicism. Lutherans and German Catholics, nevertheless, regarded each other with a good deal of religious animosity.

During the first half of the nineteenth century, Lutheranism was split between Americanizers, who favored moving toward a more evangelical style of religion, and traditionalists, who insisted on maintaining a highly ritualistic form of worship. These competing tendencies led in 1867 to the first of several divisions within the denomination over issues of theology and liturgy. All branches of American Lutheranism remained united, however, on the conviction that the main task of the church was the "bringing of individual members of society to a saving knowledge of Jesus Christ . . . [whose] relation to society is through the individual soul and through the community of saints. . . . The church, Lutherans insisted, was not "a reformer of [society's] evils, or an adjuster of its economic distresses."[14]

The various denominations with substantial followings in the United States during the first half of the nineteenth century pulled socially in somewhat different directions. All had in common, however, shared roots in the theist-humanist convictions that objective moral imperatives apply to human behavior and that each human life possesses unique moral significance. These beliefs provided a body of common values through which individual aspirations were encouraged, shaped, and to some extent limited.

First Alignment

Some of the theological and ecclesiastical differences within and among the denominations corresponded in a general way to the differences in emphasis in the national polity between the party of order and the party of equality. It is not surprising, therefore, that many of the religious factions were attracted to one side or the other

of the primary political division. In some cases, however, denominations or church factions formed alliances with political groups with
which they seemed to share few moral tendencies or even toward
which they might have been expected to be antagonistic. In these
instances the religious group as a rule was resorting to the time-
honored political strategy of seeking friends among the enemies of
one's enemies—as the Quakers had aligned themselves with the British
crown to undermine the power of the Anglican proprietors in
Pennsylvania before the Revolution.

FEDERALIST CHRISTIANS

On the conservative side of the religious spectrum, orthodox
Congregationalists gave strong support to the Federalists, the party
of order in the early years of the Republic. About nine out of ten
Congregationalist ministers were "staunchly Federalist," and many of
them were "energetic politicians."[15] Congregationalists were drawn to
Federalism not only because they regarded the Federalist party as the
special guardian of their establishment status in three New England
states but also because emphasis on social order fitted naturally with
their dour view of human nature.

Particularly after the emergence of Jefferson, whose deist tendencies were well known, as leader of the Republicans, the party of
equality, Congregationalists rallied, sometimes with almost hysterical
vituperation, behind the Federalist cause. Lyman Beecher claimed
that in Connecticut Jefferson's supporters were made up mainly of
"Sabbath-breakers, rum-selling, tippling folk, infidels, and ruff-scruff
generally." After the election of 1796, which made John Adams
president and Jefferson vice-president, a Congregationalist minister
in Connecticut concluded a prayer for the new president with an
added plea: "O Lord! wilt thou bestow upon the Vice President a
double portion of thy grace, *for Thou Knowest he needs it!*" Jefferson's
early sympathy for the French Revolution made him doubly suspect
in the eyes of the Congregationalist clergy. "We cannot," the Congregational ministers of Massachusetts wrote to President Adams,
"but deeply lament and firmly resist those atheistical, licentious, and
disorganizing principles which have been avowed and zealously
propagated by the philosophers of France."[16]

When the Federalist party became less important as a force in national politics, Congregationalist ministers dug in at the state and local levels to resist the expected spread of anarchy. In 1813 Lyman Beecher founded the Connecticut Moral Society to provide a force "distinct from that of government, independent of popular suffrage, superior in potency to individual efforts, and competent to enlist and preserve public opinion on the side of law and order."[17]

Congregationalist adherence to Federalism was not quite unanimous. In the tradition of John Wise a few ministers supported the Republicans as an expression of the equalitarian strain that had always existed as a minor chord within Puritanism. One such, Thomas Allen, sermonized in the late 1790s, "Federalism consists in the love of arbitrary power. . . . It is a leprosy on the body politic, destructive of peace, order, and happiness. Self is its idol. It essentially consists in selfishness." But for every Allen there were a dozen Lyman Beechers and Timothy Dwights.[18]

Theologically conservative divines outside New England were also for the most part ardent Federalists. Martin Van Buren recalled as a youth hearing New York clergymen preach that Jefferson's election would lead to "burning of Bibles, the prostration of religion, and the substitution of some Goddess of Reason."[19] Federalist politicians played the religious card with zest. During the climactic campaign of 1800, Alexander Hamilton did not shrink from describing Jefferson as "an atheist in religion and a fanatic in politics."

Episcopalians, though deprived of the establishment status they had held in several colonies before the Revolution, also generally enlisted on the side of the party of order. Some New England Episcopalians, however, particularly in Connecticut, went over to the Republicans as a means of undermining local Congregationalist establishments. But even in New England most Episcopalians were probably Federalists, "reflecting their generally high status, Anglican tastes, and elitism." In the Middle Atlantic States, Episcopalians were almost all Federalists. After Jefferson's election the Reverend James Abercrombie, an Episcopalian clergyman in Philadelphia, declared himself "very reluctant to read the prayers for the President of the United States, prescribed in the Episcopal ritual; and when informed by his diocesan that it was not a matter in the least discretionary with him, he comforted his federal friends with the assurance that he had not 'prayed,' but only 'read' them."[20] Whether the Episcopalians' support of Federalism expressed much beyond defense of "high status" and "elitism" may be questioned, but emphases in Episcopalian doctrine and practice on hierarchy and social continuity were probably at least reinforcing to conservative political preferences formed by social or economic interests.

Presbyterians, in contrast, usually lined up with the party of equality, partly as a continuation of long-standing struggles against Congregationalist establishments in New England and against socially dominant Anglicans in New York and Pennsylvania. The personalist quality of New School Presbyterianism growing out of the Great Awakening, moreover, was consistent with the political approach of the antiestablishment Republicans. Jefferson, however, was privately critical of his Presbyterian allies, believing that "they pant to re-establish *by law*, that holy inquisition, which they can now only infuse into *public opinion.*" Possibly sensing this distrust, Presbyterians in Virginia's Shenandoah Valley were usually Federalists.[21]

The Quakers' inclination toward religious personalism would seem to have made them likely recruits for the party of equality, and Quakers in New England were indeed as a rule Republicans. But in Pennsylvania and adjacent parts of New Jersey, local political interests supervened. Finding the Republican party dominated by their most formidable local antagonists, the Scotch-Irish Presbyterians, the Quakers threw in their lot with the Federalists (pursuing much the same strategy that had made them allies of the crown in the period just before the Revolution).[22]

EVANGELICALS FOR JEFFERSON

While the older denominations exerted considerable political influence, the overriding question regarding political orientation of religious groups was, which party would attract the rapidly growing mass of evangelicals? For a time the two largest evangelical denominations seemed to be moving in opposite political directions.

Baptists were drawn both by their socioeconomic status and their equalitarian social attitudes to the side of the Republicans. A commentator on church life in Boston observed in 1802, "The Baptists by attaching themselves to the present [Jefferson] administration, have gained greater success in the United States and greater in New England than any sect since the settlement, even beyond comparison." John Leland, the great Baptist leader who had played an important part in the fight for disestablishment in Virginia in 1785, became a fervid Jeffersonian.[23]

The Methodists, following Wesley's example in England, at first tended to be politically conservative.[24] Francis Asbury, the first bishop and virtual founder of Methodism in the United States, supported American independence, but in general, his political instincts were conservative. After the Revolution, he characterized the Baptists' dislike for all kinds of social authority as "republicanism run mad."[25]

As Methodism spread West, however, the circuit-riding preachers, expressing the socioeconomic interests of the region as well as being attracted by common personalist values, generally switched to the Republicans. Peter Cartwright, probably the most famous of the Methodist circuit riders, rivaled even John Leland in the warmth of his support for Jefferson and later Andrew Jackson. The degree of Methodist commitment to the party of equality reached the point that one itinerant preacher was able to claim, "Every convert to Methodism, in those times became a Republican if he was not one before."[26]

The Republican leaders recognized the importance of the evangelical vote. The inclusion of Aaron Burr on their ticket as candidate for vice-president in 1800, which led to a constitutional crisis and almost wrecked the party, was motivated in part by the expectation that Burr's identification as Jonathan Edwards's grandson would win votes from wavering evangelicals. (Another of Edwards's grandsons, Timothy Dwight, was vigorously active on the other side.)

The support the evangelicals gave the Republicans contributed importantly to Jefferson's triumph in 1800 and to the eventual disintegration of the Federalist party, but it also introduced an enduring tension into the party of equality. The evangelicals' loathing for deism and similar expressions of civil humanism was even more pronounced than that felt by conservative Congregationalists or Episcopalians. The humanist elite of the party and its populist evangelical foot soldiers therefore were culturally distant. This difference was to appear again and again throughout the history of the Democratic party that descended from Jefferson's Republicans—most recently in the antagonism between Kennedyites and Carterites in the late 1970s.

Evangelicals differed among themselves on the proper relationship between religion and politics. Some, particularly among the Baptists, believed that the roles of the church and the state should be kept entirely distinct. John Leland, for example, opposed not only the appointment of chaplains by Congress but also church involvement in peace societies, temperance associations, or the drive launched by Presbyterians to stop delivery of the mail on Sundays, "not because he favored infidelity, war, drunkenness, or violation of the Sabbath, but because he opposed making moral principles into laws violating the rights of the individual."[27] Leland supported the Republicans because he agreed with Jefferson that the government that governs least governs best. Other evangelicals, including home-mission Baptists and New School Presbyterians, regarded government as an instrument for the moral reform of society. Charles Finney, the famous free-lance evangelist and president of Oberlin College, for example, taught that "society must be reconstructed through the power of a sanctifying gospel and all the evils of cruelty, slavery, poverty, and greed be done away."

An Immigrant Church

Under what political scientists have called the second party system that began with the election of Andrew Jackson as president in 1828, some of the same alignments that had developed in the early Republic reappeared. The party of equality now became the Democrats and the party of order the Whigs. As before, the party of equality had particular appeal for poor farmers and members of the urban working class, while the party of order had special attraction for the well-to-do and the middle class. There were, however, major crosscutting pressures generated by regional, ethnic, and religious values or identifications. "In the North one can find some occupational and status differences between Whigs and Democrats, and a strong Whiggish bias existed among the super-rich in northern cities. But the major distinctions between the rank and file of Whig and Democratic voters grew from their relation to certain ethnoreligious communities." In the South, "the dominance of Anglo-Protestants, particularly Methodists and Baptists, was so overwhelming that religious or ethnic differences had less impact on politics."[28]

Two factors weighed much more heavily on the second party system than they had on the first: slavery and immigration. Of these, the latter initially had the greater effect on party alignments.

Immigrants with Anglo-Protestant backgrounds continued to arrive in the United States in large numbers during the first half of the nineteenth century. Annual immigration from Britain actually rose from 2,410 in 1820 to 40,669 in 1852. But in the same period annual immigration from Ireland increased from 3,614 to 159,548, and from Germany, 968 to 145,918.[29] A few of the groups arriving from non-British lands, like Irish Protestants and German pietists, were drawn by a spirit of pan-Protestantism to the party of order. But most, being social and economic outsiders, were attracted, at least at first, to the party of equality. The great majority of Irish Catholics, as well as other Catholics and most Germans, Lutherans, and Reformeds became Jacksonian Democrats.

Jackson himself subscribed to John Leland's view that church and state should be kept far apart. He was criticized by conservative church leaders for his participation in a duel in 1817 and later for his ruthless removal of the Cherokee Indians from their homeland in western Georgia. Like Jefferson he refused as president to call for days of prayer. "I am no *sectarian*," he wrote, "tho a lover of the christian religion." When a young political supporter reported the concern of a grandmother over the growth of Catholic power, Jackson replied, "I was brought up a rigid Presbyterian, to which I have always adhered. . . . Let it always be remembered by your Grandmother that no established religion can exist under our glorious constitution."[30]

CATHOLICISM AND DEMOCRACY

The presence of most Catholic voters in the party of equality was to some degree anomalous. The international Catholic church was in one if its more conservative periods. Catholicism had been among the major targets of the Enlightenment and the French Revolution. The church had responded to this attention with unqualified denunciation of liberalism and all its works. Many of the French clergy forced to emigrate by the Revolution had found refuge in Ireland, where they transmitted their hatred of liberalism to the Irish church, which in turn largely shaped Catholicism in the United States. Some European Catholic moderates tried during the 1830s to bridge the chasm that had opened between the church and humanist liberalism, but the Vatican responded that the doctrines of *"liberty of worship* and *liberty of the press* . . . are equally reprehensible in the extreme, and in opposition to the teaching, the maxims, and the practice of the Church." Throughout the nineteenth century, orthodox Catholicism maintained unwavering commitment to the standard that, wherever politically feasible, "the Catholic religion shall be the only religion of the State, to the exclusion of all other forms of worship."[31]

In the United States, of course, the church not only lacked the political resources to make itself supreme but often was hard pressed to avoid being persecuted. State laws and constitutional provisions discriminating against Catholics were gradually repealed. In New York for example, De Witt Clinton in 1806 secured repeal of the state's test oath, enacted in 1788, requiring that all state officers renounce allegiance to every foreign "potentate . . . in all matters ecclesiastical as well as civil," which had effectively barred Catholics from holding elective office. Religious prejudice against Catholics, however, remained a latent force among the nation's Protestant majority. After large-scale immigration from Ireland began in the 1830s, moreover, the church found itself representing some of the most impoverished sections of the national community. The political alliance between Catholicism and the party of equality was thus virtually inevitable.[32]

Many American Catholic leaders nevertheless retained essentially conservative political views. Orestes Brownson, a distinguished New England convert to Catholicism, wrote, "Democracy is a mischievous dream where the Catholic Church does not predominate to inspire the people with reverence and to teach and accustom them to obedience to authority."

On the burning moral issue of slavery, the church took a distinctly moderate position during the first half of the nineteenth century. When Pope Gregory XVI condemned the slave trade in 1838, Bishop John England of Charleston hastened to assure Van Buren's secretary of state that "no pope had ever condemned domestic slavery as it existed in the United States." Early in his career in South Carolina, Bishop England had declared that he was not "friendly to the existence or continuation of slavery," but as the controversy between slave states and free states became more heated, he defended slavery with "arguments from Scripture and Christian tradition." Bishop John Hughes of New York argued that "this condition of slavery is an evil, yet it is not an absolute and unmitigated evil" because it had brought countless Africans to civilization and Christianity. No Catholic bishop called for abolition before the Civil War.[33]

Anti-Catholic feeling among Protestants had seemed to wane during the early decades of the nineteenth century, but as Irish and German Catholic immigrants began to pour into the country after 1830, economic competition served to reinforce doctrinal antipathies. Protestant intellectuals and divines helped whip up latent antagonisms. Samuel F. B. Morse, on his way to inventing the telegraph, issued an anti-Catholic blast titled *Foreign Conspiracy against the Liberties of the United States.* (Morse came of a New England Congregationalist family long noted for hostility toward Catholicism, but his own interest in the subject seems to have been aroused by an incident in which a papal guard knocked off his hat while he was visiting the Vatican.) Lyman Beecher, never far from a good fight, warned in 1834, "The Catholic Church holds now in darkness and bondage nearly half the civilized world. . . . It is the most skilled, powerful, dreadful system of corruption to those who wield it, and of slavery and debasement to those who live under it." Horace Bushnell, who has been called "the father of American theological liberalism," declared, "Our first danger is barbarism [from immigration], Romanism next."[34]

Anti-Catholicism is a recurring theme in American history from earliest colonial times. In part, this sentiment was undoubtedly an expression of simple bigotry: primordial fear and hate of insiders toward outsiders. In part, too, it sprang from economic concern among working-class Protestants over the competition of low-wage immigrant labor.

Some of the doctrinal assumptions of nineteenth century Catholicism did, however, represent a challenge to the pluralist social philosophy on which American democracy had in part been built. Catholics might argue that the prospect of a politically dominant Catholicism in the United States was so remote that the church's theoretic commitment to state-enforced religion had no practical significance for Americans, but the existence of such a commitment was a natural affront to non-Catholics and a weapon made to order for enemies of Catholicism. "Is it credible," Samuel Morse asked, "that the manufacturers of chains for binding liberty in Europe, have suddenly become benevolently concerned for the *religious welfare* of this Republican people?"[35] Besides, some American Catholics were not reassuring in their expressions of Catholic goals. Bishop Hughes saw fit to preach in St. Patrick's Cathedral in New York on "The Decline of Protestantism and its Causes": "Everybody should know that we have for our mission to convert the world—including the

inhabitants of the United States—the people of the cities and the
people of the country, the officers of the navy and marines, com-
manders of the army, the legislators, the cabinet, the President, and
all."[36]

Nativist emotion eventually boiled over into mob violence. In 1834
a Boston mob, excited by lurid tales of alleged mistreatment of
unwilling nuns, burned the Ursuline Convent in Charlestown. Ten
years later Philadelphia Protestants burned several Catholic churches,
after which a pitched battle between armed Protestants and Catholics
resulted in fourteen deaths. When similar tensions developed in New
York, Bishop Hughes issued a terse warning: "If a single Catholic
church is burned in New York, the city will become a second Moscow
[referring to the burning of Moscow by Russian patriots during
Napoleon's occupation in 1812]. . . . We can protect our own." The
Whig mayor (James Harper, of the publishing family), though he
had been elected with nativist support, ordered cancellation of a
planned nativist rally, and the immediate crisis passed.[37]

Anti-Catholicism undoubtedly helped move some of the Protestant
groups that had supported the party of equality under the first party
system to the side of the party of order under the second. Ronald
Formisano has shown that in Michigan, Presbyterians and Baptists,
both descended from groups that had backed Jefferson's Republicans,
heavily supported the Whigs. William Shade reports similar findings
for Illinois Baptists favoring home missions (those more likely to
apply religious values to politics). Economic and regional factors
contributed to these shifts, but the heavy use that some Whig
candidates and newspapers made of anti-Catholic and anti-immigrant
themes indicates that they regarded nativist feeling as one of their
most important political resources.[38]

The Whigs appealed for Protestant support not only through the
negative appeal of nativism but also through positive backing for
much of the program for moral reform promoted by the activist wing
of evangelical Protestantism. The temperance movement, launched
early in the nineteenth century by Lyman Beecher and a few other
New England Congregationalists, became a favorite Whig cause.
Senator Theodore Frelinghuysen of New Jersey, Whig candidate for
vice-president in 1844, was recognized as the national leader of the

drive to reduce consumption of liquor. Horace Greeley, the celebrated New York Whig (later Republican) publicist, observed in 1844, "Upon those Working Men who stick to their business, hope to improve their circumstances by honest industry, and go on Sundays to church rather than to the grog-shop the appeals of Loco-Focoism [the local title of the more radical wing of the Democracy] fell comparatively harmless; while the opposite class were rallied with unprecedented unanimity against us." When the temperance movement began seeking legal prohibition of the manufacture or sale of liquor in the 1840s, many Whig office seekers pledged their support. A rising young Whig politician in Illinois, Abraham Lincoln, guided a prohibition bill to passage in both houses of the state legislature in 1854. (The bill was subsequently rejected in a state referendum.)[39]

Not all the Protestant groups that had given majority support to the Jeffersonian Republicans shifted to the Whigs. German Lutherans, who were put off by temperance and Puritan austerity, generally stuck with the Democrats. Methodists and separatist Baptists also continued to give substantial support to the party of equality. In Michigan, Formisano noted, "Methodists probably had a Democratic tendency and undoubtedly favored the Democrats more than any other major native Protestant group." Peter Cartwright, practically the embodiment of western Methodism, told a Democratic convention in Illinois near the end of his long career that he had "waged incessant warfare against the world, the flesh, and the devil and other enemies of the Democratic party." Larger shares of Methodists and Baptists than of Presbyterians or Congregationalists had economic or regional interests that helped keep them loyal to the Democrats, but it is probably significant that groups that resisted applying religious values directly to politics showed less tendency to shift to the Whigs. In Illinois, for example, separatist Baptists were usually Democrats while mission Baptists became Whigs.[40]

The Whigs, whose leaders aimed to build an inclusive national party, pulled back from giving nativism their full embrace. Few of them followed William Seward in attempting to build Whig-Catholic coalitions, but a fair number of Whig politicians, whether out of political prudence or moral conviction, steered away from religious bigotry. Lincoln, for instance, wrote to a friend that if the nativists got into power, the doctrine, "all men are created equal," which already in practice meant, "all men are created equal, except Negroes," would have to be changed to, "all men are created equal, except

Negroes and foreigners and Catholics." When it came to that, Lincoln said, he would "prefer emigrating to some country where they make no pretense of loving liberty—to Russia, for instance, where despotism can be taken pure, and without the base alloy of hypocrisy."[41]

Leaders of the Know-Nothing movement that burst onto the national electoral scene in the middle years of the 1850s were hampered by no such inhibitions. Organized in the 1840s as a secret society pledged to halt immigration, the Know-Nothings entered electoral politics as the American party in 1854. In some states they seemed for a time to sweep all before them. Their most spectacular triumph was achieved in Massachusetts. In their very first election, Massachusetts Know-Nothings won the governorship and all state offices, every seat in the state senate, and all but 2 out of 378 seats in the state house of representatives. No fewer than 24 of the Know-Nothings elected to the Massachusetts legislature were Protestant ministers—a sharp rise over earlier sessions. Know-Nothing slates also carried Delaware and, through fusion with the Whigs, Pennsylvania. In 1855 the Know-Nothings again won in Massachusetts and added victories in Connecticut, Rhode Island, New Hampshire, Maryland, and Kentucky. Know-Nothing tickets also ran strong races in Virginia, Tennessee, Georgia, Alabama, Mississippi, and Louisiana and won some minor state offices in Texas. More even than the Whigs, the Know-Nothings displayed an ability to reach across class lines to attract working-class Protestants.[42]

The New York *Herald* gloomily predicted that the Know-Nothings would win the presidency in 1856, and even the Boston *Pilot*, a Catholic paper, editorialized that the election of a Know-Nothing president was almost inevitable. As matters turned out, the Know-Nothings' candidate for president in 1856, former President Millard Filmore (who happened to be visiting Pope Pius IX when he was nominated), carried only one state, Maryland, and received only about 20 percent of the national popular vote. By 1860 the party had disintegrated. Nativism had been overtaken by the ultimate cross-cutting issue of American history: abolition of slavery.[43]

The Party of Conscience

Under both the first and second party systems, a major anomaly of American politics had been the prominent role played in the party of equality by southern slaveholders. Though firmly installed as dominant insiders in their own states, many members of the southern planter class regarded themselves as outsiders in relation to the emerging national economy organized around manufacturing and commerce. They therefore allied themselves with representatives of eastern millhands and western farmers to oppose the dynamic political force generated by eastern urban capitalism. The resulting combination, symbolized first by the ticket of Jefferson and Burr, and later by Jackson and Van Buren, constituted the normal majority party in the United States during most of the first half of the nineteenth century. The fact that the party most committed to equality was in the southern states the special protector of radical inequality did not at first cause great ideological strain—in part because many of the planters, following Jefferson's example, held liberal social views on subjects not touched by slavery or race. But by the 1840s, disagreement over slavery had begun to disrupt the internal harmony of the Democratic party.[44]

Seeking to build a winning national party through appeals to economic and cultural interests not strongly represented within the Democratic coalition, the Whigs tried almost as hard as the Democrats to keep slavery off the agenda of national politics. But the Whigs' electoral strategy relied in part on mobilizing evangelical Protestantism as a cohesive political force. They were therefore even more vulnerable than the Democrats to a moral challenge that many evangelical Protestants had come to regard as rising from values inherent to the Christian faith.

THE MOMENT TO DECIDE

From its inception Christianity had coexisted more or less comfortably with various forms of slavery. The apostle Paul, St. Augustine, and St. Thomas Aquinas, among other Christian theorists, taught that slavery was a punishment for original sin (without ever making entirely clear why slaves had been made special targets for divine retribution) and that legal enslavement was a trivial concern when placed in the context of man's larger metaphysical dilemma. ("Beyond question," Augustine wrote, "it is a happier thing to be the slave of a man than of a lust.")[45]

Perhaps there was always a moral contradiction between the

institution of slavery and the emphasis placed by Jesus and some of the Hebrew prophets on the unique value of each human life, a contradiction waiting for a propitious time to be discovered, as the pietists had deduced religious pluralism from the Christian doctrine of human imperfection in the seventeenth century. In any case the Quakers and other pietists began in the eighteenth century—following Francis Pastorius's pioneer protest in Pennsylvania in 1688—to condemn slavery and the slave trade as imcompatible with Christian ethics. Philadelphia's Quaker meeting in 1758 urged all Friends to free their slaves and ruled that any Friend buying or selling slaves should be excluded from participation in the society's business. The first antislavery organization known to history was founded in Philadelphia in 1775, with a largely Quaker membership and with Benjamin Franklin as its president. During the 1770s Jonathan Edwards, Jr., in New Haven, Connecticut, and Samuel Hopkins in Newport, Rhode Island, both leading figures in the mainstream of the evangelical tradition, began preaching against slavery.[46]

In England Lord Chief Justice Mansfield (a conservative Scot who shuddered at the blow he knew he was striking against property rights) in 1772 delivered the momentous judgment that slavery was a relationship "not known to the laws of England" and therefore not entitled to legal protection. In the 1770s the antislavery movement received the powerful endorsement of John Wesley. "Go on," Wesley told William Wilberforce, leader of the drive to end the slave trade in England, "in the name of God, and in the power of his might, till even American slavery (the vilest that ever saw the sun) shall vanish before it."[47]

The year after the Declaration of Independence, Vermont prohibited slavery in its first state constitution. By 1804 slavery had been abolished by all states north of Maryland.[48]

The framers of the federal Constitution considered prohibiting the slave trade, which many believed would lead to the gradual termination of slavery itself, but compromised by giving Congress authority to prohibit "importation of such persons" twenty years after the Constitution went into effect. In 1807 both the United States and Britain outlawed the slave trade, without achieving the predicted result. The Constitution gave legal recognition to slavery by providing that a slave should be counted as three-fifths of a free man in apportionment for the House of Representatives (which later led the abolitionists to call the Constitution "a compact with the devil").

Evangelical Protestants in both North and South early took up the antislavery cause. A conference of Methodists in Baltimore in 1780 condemned slavery as "contrary to the laws of God, man, and nature." Virginia Baptists followed in 1789 with a call for the "use of every legal means to extirpate this horrid evil from the land." The Methodist Conference of 1800 directed the denomination's regional bodies to "draw up addresses for the gradual emancipation of the slaves." In 1818 the Presbyterian General Assembly denounced slavery as "a gross violation of the most precious and sacred rights of human nature . . . utterly inconsistent with the laws of God."[49]

The invention of the cotton gin and the resulting spread of a cotton economy that efficiently employed large battalions of slaves on southern plantations caused some southern Protestants to think again. In 1822 the South Carolina Baptists Association dusted off the old argument that slavery was punishment for original sin. When the Presbyterian church split in 1837 over the perennial division between Old School ecclesiastical conservatives and New School evangelicals, the Old School offshoot, which was strongest in the South, took a moderate position on slavery. A resolution adopted by the Old School's general assembly in 1845 called on slaveholders to regard their slaves as fellow human souls but acknowledged that slavery was biblically sanctioned.

For many northern evangelicals, however, by the 1840s antislavery had joined nativism and temperance in a triad of reform causes that together, they believed, would achieve the moral regeneration of American society. William Lloyd Garrison, until then the unknown editor of a small temperance journal, had in 1831 launched the *Public Liberator*, dedicated to the immediate abolition of slavery: "*I will be* as harsh as truth, and as uncompromising as justice. . . . I am in earnest— I will not equivocate—I will not excuse—I will not retreat a single inch—AND I *WILL* BE HEARD."

The uncompromising position advocated by Garrison and other abolitionists frightened the South but at first attracted little support in the North. The response of most of the mainline churches was so cautious that Garrison castigated them as "a cage of unclean birds and a synagogue of Satan." Garrison was vilified by political conservatives, avoided by most liberals, and threatened with hanging by a mob in Boston in 1835. But he was heard. There was a quality in his style, inherited from the great revivalists, that excited the idealist tendency of evangelical Protestants to regard life as a contest between forces of perfect good and total evil. "Once to every man and nation," wrote James Russell Lowell, a convert to abolitionism, "comes the moment to decide,/ In the strife of truth with falsehood,/ For the good or evil side. . . ."[50]

Somewhat to the dismay of many of their leaders, who foresaw internal division, the evangelical churches in the North were drawn inexorably toward the abolitionist crusade. In 1844 the Methodist General Conference ordered the slaveholding Bishop James Andrews of Georgia to "desist from the exercise of his functions," leading to the immediate secession of fourteen southern regional conferences to form the Methodist Episcopal Church, South. In the same year the Baptist Home Missionary Society turned down the nomination by its Georgia affiliate of a slaveholding clergyman to be a missionary. In retaliation, Baptists representing nine southern states met in 1845 in Augusta, Georgia, to form the Southern Baptist Convention, a considerably more centralized administrative structure, it turned out, than had been characteristic of American Baptism.[51]

In 1852 Harriet Beecher Stowe, Lyman Beecher's daughter, produced *Uncle Tom's Cabin*, a novel that, whatever its ultimate implications for the role of blacks in American society, at the time created a virtual earthquake of antislavery sentiment among northern Protestants. Her brother, Henry Ward Beecher, raised funds to provide rifles ("Beecher's Bibles") for John Brown and fellow insurrectionists seeking to secure Kansas as a free state. Beecher declaimed from the pulpit in 1855, "Let it be settled now. . . . Bring the champions. Let them put their lances in rest for the charge. Sound the trumpet, and God save the right." Wendell Phillips, Garrison's most impassioned lieutenant, went so far in 1858 as to denounce George Washington and Jesus Christ, "the one for giving us the Constitution, the other, the New Testament," both of which he felt had contributed to the legitimization of slavery.[52]

In 1854, more than 3,000 New England clergymen signed a petition opposing passage of the Kansas-Nebraska Bill, which permitted extension of slavery to territories north of the line that formerly had marked its limit: "We protest against it as a great moral wrong . . . as a measure full of danger to the peace and even the existence of our beloved Union, and exposing us to the righteous judgments of the Almighty." Senator James Mason of Virginia responded in the best tradition of Jeffersonian separatism, "Sir, ministers of the Gospel are unknown to this Government, and God forbid the day should ever come when they shall be known to it. . . . Of all others, they are the most encroaching, and, as a body, arrogant class of men."[53] When war finally came, Granville Moody, a leading Methodist publicist, declared, "We are charged with having brought about the present contest. I believe it is true that we did bring it about, and I glory in it, for it is a wreath of glory around our brow."[54]

The abolitionists no doubt exaggerated their role in the events that led to Lincoln's election. Certainly Lincoln himself was no abolitionist. "I do not now, nor ever did," he said during the Lincoln-Douglas debates in 1858, "stand in favor of the unconditional repeal of the Fugitive Slave Law . . . [or] against the admission of any more slave states into the Union . . . [or] pledged to the abolition of slavery in the District of Columbia. . . ." The Republican victory in 1860, won with less than 40 percent of the popular vote against a divided opposition, drew on other issues besides disapproval of slavery. The party supported a protective tariff as the key to economic growth, a stance favored by northern business interests. It also converted nativism into pan-Protestantism, which attracted much of the former Know-Nothing vote while drawing in many German Lutherans and Reformeds who had felt threatened by Know-Nothingism in its rawer form. Probably a sizable majority of even Republican voters in 1860 opposed immediate abolition of slavery in the states where it was then established.[55]

Yet the drive to abolish slavery, largely inspired by religion, was indeed the issue primarily responsible for wrecking the second party system, submerging the appeal of nativism as a polarizing issue, and electing Lincoln. When slavery came to be viewed among large numbers of northern evangelical Protestants as incompatible with the value system of Christianity, it slashed at previous party attachments. In 1860 many northern evangelicals who had identified with the Democrats as the party that best served their economic interests or came closest to representing their broadly equalitarian ideology shifted to the Republican party because they thought it more prepared to take a stand against the moral evil of slavery. Hope of holding the loyalty of wavering evangelicals and the pangs of their own consciences caused northern Democratic politicians, led by Stephen Douglas, to refuse at last to accommodate further the demands of proslavery southern Democrats. As a result the Democratic party divided, virtually assuring Republican victory.[56]

If the issue of slavery had not existed, the Whigs or even the Know-

Nothings might have used nativism and the tariff to establish at least a temporary national majority for a fairly conventional conservative party. But the question of slavery pushed the party system into a new mold, one in which it remained for the next seventy years. The party of equality was morally discredited through identification with what most Americans came to believe was the worst moral evil ever to afflict American society. The party of order took into its ranks the nation's most progressive and in some ways most radical political forces, drawn not only from the rigorous tradition of New England Congregationalism but also from the more utopian and more millennial traditions of Methodism and the evangelical sects.

Lincoln said that by the time of the Civil War it was as though the two great parties of American history had stolen each other's clothes. The metaphor was apt—and more significant than may at first appear. The two parties had indeed exchanged vestments of rhetoric and even of some programs. But their bodies, their essential beings, retained many of their original characteristics. Beneath the shabby clothes of racism and municipal corruption that were their principal public attributes for several decades, the Democrats, when all was said and done, remained the party of outsiders—urban Catholics, new waves of immigrants organized by Democratic city machines, out-of-luck farmers, and above all the tattered legions of the South, which after the Civil War gave the party their almost unbroken loyalty for close to a century. And the Republicans, along with their program for progressive social change, remained the party of order. Preserving the Union, which they accomplished at whatever cost in human suffering, was after all the most emphatic expression of a fundamentally conservative outlook in American history. And the Republicans were from the start attached to the engine of industrial capitalism through which they, and those like them in the other industrial democracies, were to redefine the nature of modern conservatism.

"JUDGMENTS OF THE LORD"

It was the commanding genius of Lincoln to wed the goal of order to the goals of social justice and progress beyond even what the founders had achieved. Preservation of the Union, regarded as an indissoluble nation founded on an irrevocable social covenant, was always Lincoln's highest priority. He spoke highly of Jefferson and said he had "never had a feeling politically that did not spring from the sentiments embodied" in Jefferson's Declaration of Independence. But as Garry Wills has pointed out, Lincoln departed radically from Jefferson's concept of the nation as a voluntary association formed to facilitate its members' "pursuit of happiness." Lincoln actually belonged to the nationalist tradition of Hamilton, as is suggested by his alignment with the party of order under the second party system. But he went beyond Hamilton, and indeed returned to Jefferson as well as to Edwards, in his insistence that the nation existed not simply as an end in itself but to serve some higher purpose: that it had been "conceived in liberty and dedicated to the proposition that all men are created equal."[57]

To accomplish this fusion of organic union with transcendent purpose, Lincoln drew again and again on religious symbolism that he found around him in the evangelical tradition. Though never a member of a particular denomination, and sometimes given to religious skepticism, he had concluded by the time he became president that nationhood requires the bond of religious faith. If the United States were to be "one nation," he believed, it must be "under God." In his first inaugural, Lincoln invoked "intelligence, patriotism, Christianity, and a firm reliance on Him, who has never yet forsaken this favored land" as means for solving the crisis of secession. When war came, he expressed confidence, quoting Washington, that every member of the Union army would "live and act as becomes a Christian soldier." In 1862 he ordered observance of the Sabbath by members of the armed forces: "The discipline and character of the national forces should not suffer, nor the cause they defend be imperilled, by the profanation of the day or name of the Most High." In 1864 the motto "In God We Trust" was for the first time placed on the nation's coinage.[58]

As the war's carnage grew, Lincoln, who had inclined in his youth toward rationalism, turned back to the inscrutable Calvinist God whose will is directed toward purposes that human reason can never fully comprehend. "The will of God prevails," he wrote in a private meditation, probably after the Second Battle of Bull Run. "In great contests each party claims to act in accordance with the will of God. Both *may* be and one *must* be wrong. God cannot be *for* and *against* the same thing at the same time. In the present civil war it is quite possible that God's purpose is something different from the purpose of either party—and yet the human instrumentalities, working just as they do, are of the best adaptation to effect his purpose. I am almost ready to say this is probably true—that God wills this contest, and wills that it shall not end yet."[59]

In his second inaugural address, delivered as the Confederate army fell back on Richmond and little more than a month before his own death, Lincoln articulated his final understanding of the war's meaning:

> If we shall suppose that American slavery is one of those offenses which, in the providence of God, must needs come, but which having continued through His appointed time, He now wills to remove, and that He gives to both North and South this terrible war as the woe due to those by whom the offense came, shall we discern therein any departure from those divine attributes which the believers in a living God always ascribe to Him? Fondly do we hope, fervently do we pray, that this mighty scourge of war may speedily pass away.
>
> Yet, if God wills that it continue until all the wealth piled by the bondsman's 250 years of unrequited toil shall be sunk, and until every drop of blood drawn with the lash shall be paid by another drawn with the sword, as was said 3,000 years ago, so still it must be said, "The judgments of the Lord are true and righteous altogether."
>
> With malice toward none, with charity for all, with firmness in the right as God gives us to see the right, let us strive on to finish the work we are in, to bind up the nation's wounds, to care for him who shall have borne the battle and for his widow and his orphan—to do all which may achieve and cherish a just and lasting peace among ourselves and with all nations.[60]

The clergy of the North heartily endorsed Lincoln's view of the war as divinely ordained, though usually without his distinction between God's will and the war aims of the Union. "It is a holy and righteous cause in which you enlist," Thomas March Clark, the Episcopal bishop of Rhode Island, told the state militia in 1861. "God is with us. . . . the Lord of hosts is on our side." After three years of war, the *Methodist Magazine* seemed almost impatient that God had not yet asserted himself decisively on the side of the North: "We must take the moral, the sacred, the holy right of our struggle up before the throne of God. We must accustom ourselves to dwell before the throne, clothed in the smoke of our battles. . . ." When Richmond fell at last, the Reverend Phillips Brooks of Massachusetts gave thanks to God "for the triumph of right over wrong . . . for the loyal soldiers planted in the streets of wickedness . . . for the wisdom and bravery and devotion which Thou has annointed for Thy work and crowned with glorious victory."[61]

The South, though its religious roots in evangelical Protestantism were very close to those that animated the antislavery cause, of course viewed the war in quite a different light. Unable or unwilling to give up slavery, which it regarded as both economically necessary and politically indispensable as a bulwark against black domination in deep southern states, the South sought positive sanction in its religious tradition for the course it had taken. Leonidas Polk, Episcopal bishop of Louisiana, argued in 1861 that the South fought "for constitutional liberty, which seems to have fled to us for refuge, for our hearth-stones, and our altars." As good as his word, Polk laid aside his ecclesiastical duties and became a general in the Confederate army. The Southern Presbyterian church, split off in 1861 from the Old School Presbyterians, announced that its "peculiar mission" would be "to conserve the institution of slavery, and to make it a blessing both to master and slave." Repairing the federal Constitution's omission, the constitution adopted in 1861 by the Confederate States of America called in its preamble on "the favor and guidance of Almighty God."[62]

A nondenominational "army church," intensely revivalistic, was formed among Confederate soldiers and was an important source, according to Timothy Smith, for the "revivalistic, missionary Christianity" that has remained dominant in much of the South to the present day. Military defeat did not lead southerners to lose faith in religion but rather forced them to find justification and reassurance in a faith that claimed to transcend the ebb and flow of secular politics. This particularly benefited the Baptists, who now seemed confirmed in John Leland's warning that the church should stay clear of entanglement with worldly causes. From 1860 to 1876 the number of Southern Baptists more than doubled, while the number of Methodists increased less than 40 percent.[63]

Was religion, then, no more than a cloak for economic or political interests, as Marx would claim? Religion did not persuade the South to give up slavery, and it did not deter the North from imposing its will through military force. Very similar religious value systems were used to justify diametrically opposed social conclusions. Shared roots in the Great Awakening and evangelical Protestantism did not prevent the two sections from settling their differences at a cost of almost 500,000 human lives. What religion did do was to instill the conviction, widely held in both North and South, that human experience is fundamentally moral, requiring choice "for the good or evil side" and possessing significance beyond individual "pursuit of happiness" or collective material security. It thereby probably contributed to the stubbornness with which both sides resisted compromise in 1861. But when the war was over and the question of slavery settled, religion also provided a shared cultural outlook on which national reunion and reconciliation could eventually be built. It caused, moreover, a determination that the war should not have been fought for nothing, that the forthcoming national society should be qualitatively better than what had gone before in either North or South.

WHY NORTHERN PROTESTANTS BECAME REPUBLICANS

The Republican party led by Lincoln not only ended slavery and preserved the Union but also enacted an unprecedented program of social and economic reforms that included opening up public lands for free settlement by homesteaders, establishing state land-grant colleges, chartering the first transcontinental railroad, creating a national banking system, establishing the immigration bureau, and sharply increasing the protective tariff. After Lincoln's death the record of Republican-sponsored reforms continued, though at a slower pace: the Civil Rights Act and the Fourteenth Amendment in 1866, the Fifteenth Amendment prohibiting racial qualifications for voting in 1869, and legislation for forest and land conservation in 1873 and 1877.

Many items in the Republican program—the tariff, the banking system, the transcontinental railroad, and even the immigration bureau—were designed to facilitate the expansion of American capitalism. Republican publicists and politicians, including "radicals" like Greeley and Thaddeus Stevens as well as moderates like Lincoln and conservatives like Seward, did not regard this as inconsistent with their view of themselves as friends of the common man. Economic growth, they argued, would benefit laborers and their families as well as capitalists. The protective tariff, for instance, was "a prerequisite for social harmony and for the preservation of a citizen body capable of taking part in democratic government." Republican Congressman William Kelley of Pennsylvania claimed that in England free trade had led to the "concentration of land and machinery in the hands of a constantly diminishing number of persons," and to the "rapidly increasing destitution . . . and despair of her laboring class."[64]

The Republicans' stance favoring business naturally won them support from businessmen and from the laborers and farmers who accepted the business argument that what was good for business would over the long run be good for the entire nation. Republican politicians also became skilled at "waving the bloody shirt"—persuading veterans of the Union army that the Republican party was the party of the Union and that they therefore should "vote as you shot." The most important key, however, to the Republicans' extended record of electoral success (victories in eleven of the thirteen presidential elections from 1860 through 1908 and majorities in both houses in seventeen of the twenty-five Congresses elected during the same period, with majorities in at least one house in all but two) was that the Republicans were identified in the North as the party of Protestantism.

The Republicans were able to unite native and immigrant orthodox Calvinists and evangelicals into a "single though often uneasy coalition." The tendency of northern Protestants to gravitate toward the party of order, already substantial under the second party system, became overwhelming under the third. Northern Methodists, who had leaned toward the Democrats before the Civil War, now shifted heavily to the Republicans, a realignment that was particularly important because of their numerical strength and because they voted in greater proportions than any other denomination. Northern Baptists, too, became predominantly Republican. Scandinavian Lutherans, who had tended to support the Democrats before the Civil War as a defense against Yankee nativism, also swung to the Republicans.[65]

On the basis of extensive analyses of election returns, Paul Kleppner estimates that between the Civil War and the election of 1896, "northern stock" Methodists were about 75 percent Republican; various kinds of northern Baptists, between 65 and 80 percent Republican; Norwegian Lutherans, 80 percent; and Swedish Lutherans, 85 percent. These groups joined politically with Congregationalists, Presbyterians, Episcopalians, and Quakers, who had already been strongly aligned with the party of order under the second party system. The resulting coalition made the Republicans the normal majority party in most northern states. (Among the twenty northern states when the Civil War ended, Republican candidates carried all but five in at least seven of the eight presidential elections from 1864 through 1892.)[66]

German Lutherans in the Midwest seem to have been the major holdout against the Republican tendency among northern Protestant groups. In the East, German Lutherans usually joined the general Protestant alignment within the Republican party; in the Midwest many of them preserved their pre-Civil War preference for the Democrats. Kleppner argues that this difference in electoral behavior was in part related to the distinction between "ritualistic" Lutherans, who strongly resisted, both in Germany and the United States, the introduction of Calvinist ideas and forms of worship, and "pietist" Lutherans, who were more receptive to Calvinist influence. The ritualistic Lutherans, who had generally emigrated to America first, were, in Kleppner's view, inclined to stick with the Democrats, because the party provided a kind of ritualistic front for liturgical Lutherans and Catholics. The pietist Lutherans were naturally more at home with the Congregationalists, Presbyterians, and Methodists, all with strong Calvinist strains, in the Republican party.[67]

Perhaps a more important cause for the political division among German Lutherans was the difference in ethnopolitical contexts in which they found themselves. In states or localities that were heavily Protestant, Yankee Protestants who dominated the Republican party could indulge nativist impulses. But where Catholics, about 70 percent of whom continued to support the Democrats (80 percent among Irish Catholics), were a significant political force, as in New York, New Jersey, and Pennsylvania, German Lutherans tended to become Republicans as an expression of common Protestantism. William Gudelmas and William Shade have shown that in Schuylkill County, Pennsylvania, a coal-mining county that also includes part of the Pennsylvania Dutch (German) region, many German Lutherans who had been Jacksonian Democrats under the second party system shifted in the late 1850s to join their former Anglo-Protestant Whig antagonists in the Republican party when the local Democratic party came under the control of Irish Catholics. Where Catholics were numerous, the bond of ritualism seems to have exerted less influence on German Lutherans than did pan-Protestantism.[68]

Kleppner also suggests that Episcopalians, who clearly belonged on the ritualist side of the ritualist-pietist scale, were less heavily Republican than such other northern Protestant denominations as the "pietist" Presbyterians, Congregationalists, or Methodists. He offers little evidence, however, for this addition to the ritualist front. Upper-class Episcopalians in northeastern cities no doubt viewed both Calvinists and evangelicals with condescension and rejected parts of the pietists' program for moral reform, like the drive for prohibition. Episcopalian clergymen, moreover, moved more quickly than most Calvinists to support the right of industrial workers to organize into trade unions. But such differences with the more moralistic Protestants do not seem to have blunted the instinct of most Episcopalians to align themselves with the party of order, which in England caused their Anglican cousins to be regarded as "the Tory party at prayer."[69]

Why did northern Methodists, Baptists, and other Protestant groups swing heavily to the Republicans under the third party system? Identification of the Republicans with the Union cause in the Civil War and support for the party's economic policies probably attracted many northern Protestants. But these factors cannot have been the whole story, because they had so little effect on northern Catholics, who remained overwhelmingly Democratic.

Kleppner's general argument that under the third party system "the Republican party was above all else the party of morality," appears basically sound. Despite some modifications to meet local or regional distributions of political forces and some pragmatic accommodations at the national level, the Republican party strove to promote the Protestant concept of "right behavior." The party did not move fast enough for the more ardent prohibitionists, who in 1869 formed their own political party, but it did cooperate closely with the temperance movement. In 1888 and thereafter, the Republican platform promised to support "all wise and well-directed efforts for the promotion of temperance and morality." Republicans led the fight to enact a constitutional amendment prohibiting use of state funds to support parochial schools, but with the specific provision that the amendment should not be construed to "prohibit the reading of the Bible in any school or institution." The party continued to provide most of the support that was available at the national level to advance the rights of blacks, though with less diligence after the overthrow of the last of the Republican state administrations in the South in the middle of the 1870s. When the evangelicals added women's rights to their agenda of causes, the Republicans were at least rhetorically supportive long before the Democrats. The 1896 Republican platform endorsed "equal opportunities, [and] equal pay for equal work" for women, and favored "admission of women to wider spheres of influence."[70]

Northern Protestant leaders largely reciprocated the Republicans' attention by marshalling their congregations in support of Republican candidates. The Republican party, a New England Congregationalist minister declared early in its existence, was "the *party* of God, the *party* of Jesus Christ," standing "*against* the party of iniquity." His sentiment was repeated from many Protestant pulpits throughout the rest of the century. A Republican Baptist minister in Illinois called on his congregation to "vote as we pray."[71]

The nineteenth century Republican party, as several commentators have pointed out, acquired many of the characteristics of a "political church." Republican campaigns came to resemble revival meetings, attracting participation not only by political jobholders and ideological activists but also by great masses of the party faithful. In 1896, 756,000 enthusiasts, more than 10 percent of the total Republican vote in November, traveled by rail to Canton, Ohio, to march before the front porch of William McKinley.[72]

There is probably a natural affinity between the Protestant virtues of industry, sobriety, and family responsibility and political support for the party of order. In the first half of the nineteenth century this affinity for order had been in tension with the claim of the party of equality to stand for social justice for the downtrodden, presumably attractive to persons professing the Judeo-Christian ethic. But the slavery issue and the Civil War discredited the Democrats' claim to represent social justice, thereby releasing the evangelicals to pursue the part of their value system emphasizing moral discipline.

James G. Blaine's failure to disavow the Reverend Samuel Burchard's labeling of the Democrats as the party of "rum, Romanism, and rebellion" may have cost the Republicans victory in the close election of 1884. But Protestant antagonism toward this triad of perceived threats to right behavior made a large contribution to Republican successes in many other elections.

Why then did not southern Protestants join their northern brethren within the Republican ranks? In part, of course, because the reference to rebellion in Burchard's triad of evils represented antagonism toward the South. The Republicans were identified among southerners as the party of the North in the Civil War and perhaps even more damagingly as the party of the hated carpetbag administrations during Reconstruction. In part, too, the somewhat more personalist nature of southern evangelicalism, particularly after the Civil War, discouraged enlistment in the moral crusades that in the North tied the evangelicals to the Republicans. Not until after 1900, for example, did the Southern Baptist Convention take a position in favor of Prohibition. Even the southern Methodists did not join the Prohibitionist cause until late in the 1880s. But the most important factor that kept the South, and therefore southern evangelicals, overwhelmingly Democratic was the issue of race.[73]

After resurgent Democrats succeeded in excluding blacks from political participation in most southern states, most white southerners became committed to the belief that preservation of white supremacy depended on maintenance of a one-party system. If a viable Republican party came into existence in the South, both parties would inevitably begin to compete for black support, leading to concessions to black interests. This prospect was so frightening to most white voters that it decisively inhibited any move among evangelicals toward political alliance with northerners sharing their religious orientation. The overwhelming supremacy of evangelicals in the South in any case made religion less a factor in determining party alignment. Like German Lutherans in areas where Catholics were scarce, southern evangelicals felt little pressure to join a national Protestant coalition.

Religion and the Industrial Age

Developments within both the Republican party and American Protestantism strained the bond between northern Protestantism and Republicanism as the nineteenth century approached conclusion. In the years following Ulysses Grant's election as president in 1868, the Republicans became increasingly committed to the free-market philosophy that the best thing government can do for the economy is to leave it alone. When depression struck in 1874, Grant's first instinct was to launch a program of public works to help the unemployed, but he was dissuaded by the Treasury Department and the brilliant chairman of the House Ways and Means Committee, James A. Garfield. "It is not part of the functions of the national government," Garfield told the president, "to find employment for the people."[74]

Democratic leaders of the period also generally approved the noninterventionist policy. Grover Cleveland responded to the depression of 1893 with the observation that "while the people should patriotically and cheerfully support the Government, its functions do not include the support of the people." Through their opposition to the tariff the Democrats were indeed more consistent free-marketeers than their opposition. But the Republicans, who usually controlled the federal executive and were supported by most of the business community, became more closely identified in the public mind with the doctrine of laissez-faire.[75]

At the national level over the long run, the Republican program was fantastically successful: the gross national product of the United States more than quadrupled from the Civil War to the turn of the century—probably the most rapid rate of economic growth achieved to that time in world history. But by the 1890s it had become apparent that a market system unmitigated by government-sponsored redistribution or cushioning produced extreme economic inequality and avoidable human suffering.

AWAITING THE MILLENNIUM

Protestantism, meanwhile, had been affected by two frequently antagonistic forces: millennialism and religious liberalism. Millennialism, the belief that Christ is about to return to earth to institute a thousand years of peace that will be followed by the final end of the created universe, has always figured in Christian theology, particularly during the church's first century and again at the time of the Reformation. It was brought to America by the Puritans, among others, and Jonathan Edwards related it to the concept that America is destined to play a special role in human history.

Amid the revivalist excitement of the 1830s (which also helped produce the Church of Latter-day Saints and a number of exotic evangelical sects), William Miller, a Baptist minister from Vermont, prophesied that the millennium would begin in 1843. According to one scholarly estimate, "hundreds of thousands" of people began to prepare for the Lord's coming.[76] On the appointed date (shifted to October 22, 1844, after a series of recalculations), crowds of believers, among whom were many who had disposed of all their worldly goods, assembled on hillsides to await the promised deliverance. When nothing happened—at least nothing visible—millennialism suffered a setback. The Millerites, through a complicated series of further revelations and reinterpretations, issued finally into the Seventh-Day Adventists, a small but vigorous sect that ever since has confidently awaited Christ's imminent return. But for a time the millennial idea lost some of its attraction.

Responding perhaps in part to the enormous grief and suffering caused by the Civil War or in part to the severe social dislocations that were being produced by industrialization, interest in millennialism revived in the 1860s and 1870s. Millennialists, found mainly among evangelical Protestants, divided into two camps: premillennialists, who expected that "a warrior Christ" would soon "usher in with the sword the millennial period of peace," pretty much as Miller had predicted, and postmillennialists, who believed that perhaps the millennium had already begun or, if it had not, that it would "be announced quietly, attained gradually, and marked by steady progress in religion, science, and the arts." Because both camps crossed denominational lines, there is no way to measure accurately their numbers. Postmillennialists seem to have been more numerous among Methodists and Presbyterians and premillennialists more numerous among Baptists and the independent sects.[77]

Premillennialism gave support to the highly personalist version of evangelicalism that regarded secular politics as essentially irrelevant to the deeper concerns of human life. The only truly important question, the premillennialists were convinced, was who would be chosen for salvation when Christ came? Fervid revivalist preachers like Dwight L. Moody assured their audiences that secular society was a sinking ship from which Christians could do no more than "save as many as we can." The economic depression of the mid-1870s, Moody acknowledged, caused "great misery." But what was the chief cause of this misery? "Why the sufferers have become lost from the Shepherd's care. When they are close to him, under his protection, they are always provided for."[78] The revivalists, it should be noted, provided inspiration and solace for many who could find no other.

Most premillennialists insisted on the literal "inerrancy" of the Bible, which was coming under challenge from humanist scholars (many of whom remained devout Christians). Following the pietist tradition, premillennialists rejected the authority of any institutional church as an original source for religious doctrine. Natural reason and observation, too, they held, were inadequate providers of meta-physical knowledge: "man, because of sin, has been so blinded that he cannot read the divine script in nature." The Bible, therefore, was the only reliable source for knowledge of God's will and man's part in the unfolding universal drama. So God, through miraculous intervention, guaranteed the literal truth of "every sentence, every word, every syllable, every letter" in the Bible. According to a modern premillennialist, "God has preserved the Scriptures for us so that they have remained unadulterated, by which we mean free from error."[79]

Belief in inerrancy gave rise to a school of evangelical theologians who in the early years of the twentieth century set forth their views in a series of volumes that began appearing in 1910 under the title, *The Fundamentals*. The term "fundamentalists" was quickly applied by both supporters and critics to the right wing, made up largely of premillennialists, of evangelical Protestantism. Fundamentalists generally scorned proposals for social change. Trying to save the world through political or economic reform, wrote I. M. Haldeman, a popular fundamentalist theologian, was "like cleaning and decorating the staterooms of a sinking ship."[80]

Postmillennialism, in contrast, through the application of its doctrine that humankind was evolving toward moral perfection, could encourage social action. Though they shared many cultural and social values with the premillennialists—as was shown by their later participation in the fight to forbid the teaching of evolution in the public schools—postmillennialists did not regard the secular world as spiritually or morally irrelevant. If they entered politics, they usually concentrated on such traditional evangelical social concerns as temperance and opposition to gambling. But some extended their political interests to include broader social and economic issues. When a cycle of bad weather devastated the agricultural economies of the South and West in the late 1880s, postmillennialism provided a religious sanction for those among its believers, like William Jennings Bryan of Nebraska, who favored government action to bail out the desperate farmers.

RISE OF THE SOCIAL GOSPEL

At this point, postmillennialism intersected with religious liberalism, a force descended from a very different strand of American Protestantism. In the early nineteenth century, the deism of Jefferson, Tom Paine, and Ethan Allen had mixed with New England Unitarianism to produce liberal Protestantism, exemplified by such dynamos of moral self-confidence as Ralph Waldo Emerson and Horace Bushnell. Far from denying the relevance of politics to religion, the liberals regarded social reform as the essence of the Christian message. "The Christian church," said Theodore Parker, one of Emerson's associates, "should be the means of reforming the world." As a first step, this humanist-leaning segment of Protestantism provided vigorous support for abolition. After the Civil War, the liberals backed radical reconstruction in the South, combated the thick layer of corruption that soon settled over all levels of government, and encouraged the "higher criticism" of the Bible, which deepened their division with the conservative evangelicals.

Postmillennialism and liberal Protestantism, despite their cultural and theological differences, came together in the 1890s to produce the body of ideas and political initiatives that became known as the Social Gospel. The themes of the Social Gospel were developed and popularized by a number of articulate Protestant ministers, including Washington Gladden, Josiah Strong, and, above all, Walter Rauschenbusch. Drawing on his experience as a German Baptist minister, Rauschenbusch set forth the definitive formulation of the Social Gospel in a series of articles and books, culminating in *A Theology for the Social Gospel*, published in 1917 (after the movement had passed its first peak).

Rauschenbusch combined qualities derived from both the postmillennial and liberal traditions. In many of his social attitudes he was fairly conservative. He regarded drunkenness as "like profanity and tatooing . . . one of the universal marks of barbarism." His idealization of the family led him to oppose women's neglecting housekeeping to take up a profession and to express alarm that contraceptives were debasing "womanly purity" and making "sin easy and safe." As much as Cotton Mather, he admired worldly enterprise and hard work. "Idleness is active selfishness; it is not only unethical but a sin against the Kingdom of God."[81] Rauschenbush, however, rejected the tendency of conservative evangelicals to identify sin mainly with such matters of personal behavior as "drinking, dancing, card playing, and going to the movies." While serving as pastor of a church near the Hell's Kitchen section of New York in the 1880s, he had been in frequent contact with men "out of work, out of clothes, out of shoes, and out of hope." Capitalism, he concluded, "tempts, defeats, drains, and degrades, and leaves men stunted, cowed, and shamed in their manhood." The most important source of sin lay not in personal moral weakness but in an economic system that had "turned the patrimony of a nation into the private property of a small class."[82]

The objective of true Christianity must be the coming of the Kingdom of God, defined as both "the realm of love" and "the commonwealth of labor." For believers in the Social Gospel, pursuit of the Kingdom is the key concept, as "the incarnation was to Athanasius, justification by faith alone to Martin Luther, and the sovereignty of God to Jonathan Edwards." The Kingdom could be attained by altering man's social environment, because "the permanent vices and crimes of adults are not transmitted by heredity, but by being socialized."[83]

Like many other prophets, Rauschenbusch was a good deal clearer about what he was against than about the kind of society he sought. At times he sounded like Karl Marx: "A divinely ordered community . . . would offer all the opportunities of education and enjoyment, and expect from all their contribution of labor." But he offered no political or economic blueprints for how the Kingdom was to be achieved. And unlike Marx he did not believe that a "commonwealth of labour" could be established without the inspiration of transcendent purpose. "We shall understand the Kingdom so far as we understand God, and we shall understand God so far as we understand His Kingdom."[84] Some proponents of the Social Gospel, including Rauschenbusch, subscribed to a vague kind of socialism, but their tactics were reformist rather than revolutionary. They concentrated on eliminating specific social evils—sweatshops, rotting tenements, business monopolies, international wars—rather than pressing for immediate liquidation of the capitalist system.

It is easy to exaggerate the direct impact of the Social Gospel on the religious community. The established social and economic order did not want for defenders among the clergy. Henry F. May concluded that "in 1876 Protestantism presented a massive, almost unbroken front in its defense of the social status quo." This situation did not change much during the next two decades. Some ministers became virtual cheerleaders for capitalism. Russell Conwell, the celebrated evangelist and founder of Temple University, told audiences, "I say that you ought to get rich, and it is your duty to get rich." Bishop William Lawrence of Massachusetts observed, "Material prosperity is helping to make the national character sweeter, more joyous, more unselfish, more Christlike."[85]

Yet, the Social Gospel unquestionably won converts among some of the brightest and most active minds in American Protestantism. Its appeal was based in part on authentic reflection of some of the values of theist-humanism, in part on natural sympathy for the socially downtrodden, and in part on the attraction of a doctrine that seemed to return the church to the role of social umpire that it had largely lost since disestablishment. Major Protestant seminaries became seedbeds of the Social Gospel, spreading its influence among succeeding generations of ministers and leading in time to what Martin Marty has called the "two-party system" of American Protestantism, with a conservative majority, particularly strong among the laity, and a liberal minority, increasingly numerous among the clergy.[86]

THE DECISION OF 1896

The religious tendencies that produced the Social Gospel were to some degree enlisted by the populist movement of the 1890s, which reached its climax and apogee in William Jennings Bryan's campaign for the presidency in 1896. Populism expressed the protest of western and southern farmers, who regarded themselves as victimized by existing economic structures and felt they were not being effectively represented by either of the two major parties. In the 1892 election a separately organized People's party received more than a million votes, almost 10 percent of the national total, and carried four western states.

The populist movement championed many of the concerns and aspirations that traditionally had been represented by the party of equality. It thereby won support from some postmillennial evangelicals and liberal Protestants who considered advance toward equalization of wealth one of Christianity's inherent goals. Populism also, however, had roots in nativism, which caused moral uneasiness among some liberals. Some liberal Protestants, moreover, believed that the populists' support for inflation of the currency through free and unlimited coinage of silver at a ratio of 16 to 1 with gold was economically crackpotted. In 1896 populism captured control of the Democratic party and, with Bryan as its candidate for president, waged serious assault on national power.

The 1896 campaign became a struggle for the conscience of American Protestantism. Bryan wrapped himself in religious imagery and strove to bring back to the Democratic party the evangelical groups that had shifted to the Republicans at the time of the Civil War. The famous peroration to his speech to the Democratic national convention—"You shall not press down upon the brow of labor this crown of thorns, you shall not crucify mankind upon a cross of gold"—identified the most sacred passage of Christian experience with the populists' monetary program. Some commentators have suggested that it also carried a nativist touch of anti-Semitism.

A few evangelical clerics responded positively to Bryan's appeal. "He is undoubtedly the Moses," said one, "to lead [us] out of the sin-cursed land of gold-bugs. . . ." The most prominent Methodist magazine in the Midwest expressed doubts about the populists' demand for free coinage of silver but nevertheless found it "wonderful to witness their grim and determined will to take the reins out of the hands of the syndicated powers which have had their way for so many decades."[87]

The overwhelming majority of Protestant clergyman, however, rallied behind the candidate of the party of order, William McKinley. Bryan, they held, inflamed class antagonism, thereby threatening to bring on social chaos. Free coinage of silver, moreover, would undermine the value of dollars earned not only by capitalists but also by all industrial workers—a form of theft. A prominent Baptist minister said simply of the Democratic program, "That platform was made in hell." A Chicago evangelist deplored Bryan's use of "the Crown of Thorns and the Cross of the Nazarene" to support "the unholy spectres of dishonor and revolution." The leading Episcopalian magazine warned that Bryan's election would cause the "ruin of national fiscal morality and reputation for honesty." Try as they might, Bryan's managers could find in all the United States only four prominent clergymen willing to endorse the Democratic candidate. On the Sunday before election, many Protestant pastors preached sermons on the text, "Thou Shalt Not Steal."[88]

The most direct effect of Bryan's effort to bring the evangelicals back to the Democratic fold was to release large numbers of Catholics to vote Republican. The Catholic church, its ranks increased by continued migration from Ireland and the beginning of mass influxes from southern and eastern Europe, had by 1896 become the nation's largest single denomination, with almost as many members as Methodists and Baptists combined (though still less than half the Protestant total). Most Catholics had remained Democrats, held to their traditional loyalty by working-class economic status, by clientship to Democratic city machines, and out of response to identification of the Republicans as the party of Protestantism.

The church hierarchy had pursued Catholic interests in seeking government aid for church schools and charities but had usually maintained a low political profile. The "Americanist" movement within the church, which aimed at adapting Catholicism to the pluralist spirit of American society, was sharply rebuked in 1895 by an encyclical letter from Pope Leo XIII. While praising the absence of persecution of religion in the United States, the encyclical maintained that the American church "would bring forth more abundant fruit if, in addition to liberty, she enjoyed the favor of the law and the patronage of public authority." Archbishop John Ireland of St. Paul, a leading Americanist, lamented, "The unfortunate allusion to Church and State cannot be explained to Americans."[89]

The Catholic hierarchy, for the most part, had relied on contacts within the Democratic party to advance the church's political interests. Bryan's nomination and campaign, however, seemed to signal that social forces hostile to Catholicism were taking command of the party. Moreover, as governor of Ohio, McKinley had appointed Catholics to major state offices and had combated forces of nativism within the Republican party. Openly supporting McKinley's election, Archbishop Ireland warned that the populists were "lighting torches which, borne in hands of reckless men, may light up in our country the lurid fires of a commune." Whether or not they were motivated by fear of communards, many urban Catholics on election day cast their first Republican ballots.[90]

In cities with large blocs of Catholic voters, the Democrats' share of the vote fell dramatically from what it had been in 1892: by one-third in Baltimore, more than one-third in Philadelphia, and almost 30 percent in New York City. Only Irish Catholics were relatively unaffected by the swing to McKinley: they regarded loyalty to the Democratic party as a kind of tribal obligation and were mindful that the desertion of other groups would make their control of local Democratic organizations even more secure.[91]

Bryan's attempt to sway the evangelicals, meanwhile, largely failed. He held the South and carried ten western states, mainly in the silver-producing Rocky Mountains region, but in the East he was simply wiped out, carrying not a single county in all New England, and only a few in the Middle Atlantic states. In the evangelical heartland of the Middle West, which both sides regarded as crucial, Bryan was soundly beaten. As James Sundquist has pointed out, his share of the vote fell below the combined percentages cast for the Democratic and People's tickets in 1892 in every county of Illinois, Indiana, Iowa, and Wisconsin, all states with large evangelical constituencies. These Democratic losses were no doubt in part due to defections by Catholics or German Lutherans, but such defections could not have counteracted to this extent a substantial swing by evangelicals to Bryan. The Democratic candidate carried only 3 counties out of 70 in Wisconsin, 15 out of 83 in Michigan, 39 out of 102 in Illinois, and 17 out of 99 in Iowa. In some heavily evangelical rural counties he ran relatively well for a Democrat. Kleppner found a positive correlation in counties of Michigan and Ohio between the vote for Bryan in 1896 and support for Prohibition, a favorite postmillennialist cause, on referenda in other years. But even in the 5 "pietist" Ohio counties cited by Kleppner, Bryan could do no better than 45.5 percent of the vote, compared to 45.2 percent given to Cleveland in 1892.[92]

The expensive Republican campaign and attempts at economic intimidation by some conservative businessmen no doubt contributed to the size of McKinley's victory, but business support alone probably would not have brought success. It had not done so in 1892, though admittedly the stakes then were not so high. Cultural and moral factors at least reinforced economic interests. Given a clear choice, northern Protestants, with strong encouragement from their clergy, came down heavily on the side of the party of order. At least for 1896, the spirit of Cotton Mather had prevailed over the spirit of John Wise (who, like Bryan, had found sanction in the Bible for a program designed to bring on economic inflation).

After 1896 urban Catholics, still finding the Protestant culture dominant in the Republican party inhospitable, largely returned to the Democrats. But northern Protestants had become so overwhelmingly Republican that such states as Pennsylvania, Illinois, Michigan, Iowa, Wisconsin, and Minnesota, which, while leaning Republican, had maintained a measure of competition between the two parties from the end of reconstruction to 1896, became virtually one-party Republican domains. They were soon joined in this status by some of the western states that had been carried by Bryan on the silver issue.

The 1896 election thus turned out to be not so much realigning as reinforcing, a dynamic second wave of the Republican era launched by Lincoln in 1860. It resembled the election of 1828 in which Jackson renewed the trend begun by Jefferson in 1800, and that of 1960 in which John Kennedy revived the Democratic hegemony initiated by Franklin Roosevelt. "Those who did change their party loyalty [in 1896] . . . were for the most part voters whose shift in attachment was in the direction of conformity with the regional party system established before and during the Civil War. So that system, rather than being weakened by the new upheaval, was reinforced."[93]

"WE STAND AT ARMAGEDDON"

Protestant support for social reform did not sink in the wake of Bryan's defeat. In 1901 both Episcopalian and Congregational churches established commissions to deal with labor issues. The northern Presbyterians followed in 1903 with a "special mission to workingmen." In 1908 the northern Methodists set up their Federation for Social Service to coordinate the church's social welfare activities and adopted a progressive "social creed." Most significantly of all, in 1908 several Protestant denominations formed the Federal Council of Churches as an ecumenical structure to broaden church impact on social and economic problems.

Protestant reformers who had distrusted populist economics or felt uncomfortable cooperating with largely Catholic Democratic city machines welcomed the development in the Republican party of a vigorous progressive movement in the tradition of Lincoln, a movement committed to capitalism but proposing government action to ameliorate the harsher effects of the market system. When Theodore Roosevelt became president following McKinley's assassination in 1901, the reformers had one of their own breed in the White House. Though more conservative as president than his later reputation has suggested, Roosevelt drew on ideas inspired at least in part by the Social Gospel in his efforts to expand social services provided by government and to bring about a more even distribution of the wealth being produced by industrial capitalism.

When standpat conservatives regained dominance in the Republican party during the administration of Roosevelt's personally selected successor, William Howard Taft, Republican progressives rose in revolt. Assuming leadership of the progressive insurgency in 1912, Roosevelt took an explicitly millennial theme from the book of Revelation: "We stand at Armageddon and we battle for the Lord." The Progressive party convention that assembled in Chicago to nominate Roosevelt for the presidency after the Republicans had renominated Taft had strong religious overtones. Evangelistic excitement filled the convention hall. Delegates marched through the aisles singing "Onward Christian Soldiers," and "The Battle Hymn of the Republic." An irreverent flier circulated in the press gallery announcing that Theodore Roosevelt would walk on the waters of Lake Michigan at three o'clock the following afternoon.

While conceding at the behest of Roosevelt's Wall Street allies that "concentration of modern business, in some degree, is both inevitable and necessary," the Progressive platform pledged support to much of the Social Gospel's agenda, including women's suffrage, prohibition of child labor, and "the adoption of a system of social insurance adapted to American use." Jane Addams, the pioneer urban social reformer, said the new party's platform contained "all I have been fighting for for a decade."[94]

The split in the Republican party produced the election of Woodrow Wilson with 42 percent of the popular vote. Wilson, who earlier had appeared to be a conservative Democrat of the Cleveland mold, had bitingly criticized Roosevelt's progressivism while Roosevelt was president. But after he entered active politics in 1910, Wilson, too, announced support for many of the proposed reforms identified with the Social Gospel. The son of a Presbyterian minister, Wilson brought to the presidency a sternly moral attitude toward politics and social problems. "Sometimes," he said, "people call me an idealist. Well, that is the way I know I'm an American: America is the most idealistic nation in the world."[95]

Wilson pushed a substantial body of progressive economic legislation to enactment during his first term. He is, however, best remembered for trying to introduce democratic moral values into the conduct of international relations. Americans had long believed that their nation had been chosen by God to play a special role in human history. But once the conquest of the continent was completed, most had assumed that this mission would be carried out mainly through example—by creating the Puritans' "city on a hill," which would serve as a model of democratic virtue that other nations in time would come to emulate. Roosevelt had pursued a vigorous and sometimes interventionist foreign policy but chiefly in support of goals discovered in the national interest.

For Wilson, the national interest, though important, was not enough. With Bryan as his secretary of state, Wilson concluded treaties requiring arbitration of political differences with nations all over the world during his first two years in office. When he tilted toward Britain and France in the war that broke out in Europe in 1914, Bryan, a pacifist, resigned. Reluctantly leading the United States into the World War in 1917, Wilson insisted that American participation be interpreted as part of an international crusade for democratic values. (Framing the conflict in these terms may have contributed to the unbridled ferocity with which most American clergymen, Protestant, Catholic, and Jewish, supported the war effort. The satisfaction expressed by one prominent Protestant minister in contemplating "Jesus himself sighting down a gun barrel and running a bayonet through an enemy's body," was not untypical.)[96]

Wilson's effort to form a postwar concert of democratic nations dedicated to maintaining world peace was largely defeated because of the resurgence of isolationism in the United States, because most European political leaders had narrower objectives, and because of his own stubborn refusal to compromise with his opponents. He left, however, the conceptual framework for one of the possible courses that America might pursue in world affairs: internationalist, to some extent altruistic, concerned with values as well as interests—often derided, hardly ever consistently applied, but never thereafter wholly erased from public consciousness.

WHISKEY AND DARWIN

Holding fast to John Leland's view that the church should steer clear of entanglement with social causes, premillennialist evangelicals remained largely aloof from both populism and the Progressive movement. But on one social objective premillennialists and postmillennialists were generally in agreement: enactment of prohibition of the manufacture or sale of liquor. Even Dwight Moody had excepted the drive for prohibition from his general rule that religion and politics should not mix.

Why did evangelicals concentrate such uniform and unrelenting attention on the effort to outlaw the sale of liquor? Perhaps the destructive effects of alcohol on personal health and social tranquility provided reason enough. But liquor, along with its attendant institutions, the saloon and beer hall, seem also to have summed up and symbolized many of the cultural and social tendencies that appeared to be challenging the evangelicals' view of life: the increased openness to sensual pleasure, the growing intellectual authority of scientific rationalism, the decline of the work ethic, the concentration of population in large cities, and the increasing presence in eastern and midwestern cities of non–English-speaking immigrants, mostly Catholics or Jews from southern and eastern Europe.[97]

The temperance movement, Sydney Ahlstrom has observed, "hit America in three major waves."[98] The first wave, set off by Lyman Beecher and his associates in the early years of the nineteenth century, produced the Maine Law, the first state law imposing Prohibition, in 1846. During the next decade, thirteen states followed Maine's example. Most of these, however, quickly backslid, and by the end of the Civil War only two states remained dry.

The second wave, identified with the Prohibition party founded in 1869 and led by Frances Willard, the charismatic president of the Women's Christian Temperance Union, attempted to link the campaign for temperance to a number of other social causes, particularly women's rights and populist economics. Prohibitionist rhetoric of the second wave identified "grog shops and monopolies" as enemies of total abstinence. Frances Willard made the familiar point that alcoholism leads to poverty but added the less fashionable charge that poverty is a major cause of heavy drinking.[99]

The third wave, dating from establishment of the Anti-Saloon League in 1893, concentrated exclusively on Prohibition, thereby avoiding friction with conservative evangelicals who wanted no part of populism or the Social Gospel. The "narrow gauge" strategy, instituted by the league in collaboration with the Methodist church and other evangelical denominations, worked. Providing a model for all later believers in the idea that a single-issue approach is a more effective way to promote a particular cause than participation in a broad political coalition, the Anti-Saloon League tested candidates for Congress or state legislature by one standard only: wet or dry? The fight, said Wayne Wheeler, superintendent of the league, was one of "the churches organized against the saloon." Methodist Bishop James Cannon of Virginia, the so-called Dry Messiah, became a powerful figure in national politics, courted by leaders of both major parties. From 1906 to 1917 twenty-six states enacted some form of Prohibition. In 1914 the House of Representatives voted to make Prohibition part of the Constitution. With ratification of the Eighteenth Amendment in 1919, Prohibition of the "manufacture, sale, or transportation of intoxicating liquors" entered the nation's fundamental legal charter. It was, Ahlstrom noted, "the last great corporate work in America of legalistic evangelism."[100]

Triumphant evangelicals at the time did not see it that way. With Prohibition anchored to the Constitution, leaders of the fundamentalist wing of evangelicalism looked about for other worldly evils to conquer. The one on which they fastened could not have been more likely to bring them to grief: the teaching of Charles Darwin's theory of biological evolution in the public schools. In the nineteenth century many Christian leaders of all denominations had attacked the Darwinian theory as inconsistent with the biblical account of creation. For fundamentalists, who regarded the literally interpreted Bible as the only reliable source for spiritual or moral direction, this apparent contradiction was particularly disturbing and offensive. By the 1920s the more rationalistic or liturgical branches of Christianity, which had never cut themselves off from practical reason or church tradition as additional sources of guidance, had begun to accommodate evolution within their doctrines (though not without a good deal of theological strain). For the fundamentalists, however, evolution and Christianity seemed mutually exclusive. They therefore proposed legislation to forbid teaching of this dangerous heresy to their children, or any other children, in the public schools.

Religious and civil humanists reacted with outrage. Banning the teaching of evolution would infringe on "science," which most humanists and many other citizens with mixed value commitments had come to regard as authoritative for at least some levels of experience.

Endorsement by government of a church-inspired version of truth, moreover, would implement an absolutist view of the relationship between church and state that religious and civil humanists had devoted centuries to combating.

The drive to prohibit liquor had already raised fears among many nonfundamentalists of a tendency toward absolutist idealism within the fundamentalists' social outlook. That campaign, however, while motivated by religious values, could be defended through medical and social arguments that did not depend on religion. But banning the teaching of evolution rested squarely on the belief that a religious doctrine applied by government should be the primary criterion for public truth. The position taken by the fundamentalists thus placed them outside the American tradition of pluralism represented by the First Amendment and state constitutional guarantees of religious liberty.

During the early 1920s, fundamentalists won enactment of laws against teaching the theory of evolution in several southern states. William Jennings Bryan, venerable champion of populism and post-millennialism, was called on to lead the new crusade. The issue came to a head in the 1925 trial of John Scopes, a Tennessee high-school biology teacher who had been indicted for violating the state's law against teaching the Darwinian theory. Bryan appeared for the prosecution and Clarence Darrow, the famous liberal trial lawyer, for the defense. Scopes was convicted (the decision was later reversed by the state supreme court on a technicality), but Darrow succeeded— where Wall Street bankers, conservative politicians, and liberal publicists had previously failed—in making Bryan a national laughing-stock.

The fundamentalists' campaign against teaching evolution won a few more legislative victories but generally receded, and such laws as remained on the books were usually not enforced. (The effort by fundamentalists in the early 1980s to mandate teaching of "creationist" science in the public schools has had the more modest objective of requiring that the account of special creation set forth in the Bible be given equal time, or at least mentioned, along with evolution. In 1982, creationist laws passed by two southern states were overturned by federal courts.)

Prohibition, meanwhile, had gone badly. Though total consumption of alcohol seems to have dropped, and heavy drinking declined substantially according to a 1947 study of alcoholism from 1920 to 1945, violation of the law in many parts of the country soon became widespread and flagrant. By the end of the 1920s, critics of the Eighteenth Amendment were able to argue persuasively that its chief effects were to turn normally law-abiding citizens into habitual lawbreakers and to increase corruption of government at all levels. In addition, revenues raised through the illegal traffic in liquor were funding the beginnings of a national crime empire.[101] In 1932 Franklin Roosevelt was elected president on a platform promising repeal. Within less than a year after his inauguration, Prohibition was swept out of the Constitution.

Defeated on the issues of evolution and Prohibition and lacking a politically relevant response to the national economic crisis of the 1930s, religious fundamentalism moved back toward its earlier posture of detachment from politics. Members of fundamentalist churches voted their economic or regional interests or became politically inactive. Fundamentalist preachers continued to rail against rationalist science and sensual self-indulgence, but they appeared baffled as to how these manifestations of modernism could be stopped.

The New Deal Coalition

The election of Franklin Roosevelt of course grew out of far stronger political trends and more potent issues than public dissatisfaction with Prohibition. The most important foundations of Roosevelt's 1932 victory, in terms of where most Democratic votes came from, were the same two pillars that had usually supported the party since the Civil War: Catholics and southern whites. To these were added enough northern Protestants and Jews to give Roosevelt a comfortable margin of victory—57 percent of the popular vote. Blacks, later an important group in the New Deal coalition, remained largely Republican in 1932, actually supporting Hoover more heavily than they had in 1928.

CATHOLICS FOR ROOSEVELT

The Catholic segment of Roosevelt's support was motivated not only by loyalty to the Democratic party and reaction to the economic crisis but also by response to progressive tendencies gathering strength within the Catholic church. During the First World War, the nation's Catholic bishops, who until then had shown little interest in concerted national action, authorized formation of the National Catholic War Council to facilitate the church's relationship to the war effort. After the war the bishops, meeting for the first time as a national body in September 1919, voted to transform the War Council into the National Catholic Welfare Council (NCWC), charged with coordinating church activities that were national in scope.[102]

Though socially conservative, the Catholic church in both Europe and the United States had never displayed warm regard for free-enterprise capitalism, which Catholic leaders and theorists considered the progeny of Protestantism or rationalist individualism. Socialism, when it developed, seemed to express communitarian values in some ways similar to those espoused by Catholicism. But the emphasis placed by socialists on class conflict ran counter to the church's traditional commitment to the organic view of society. Besides, most socialists were radical anticlericalists, in the line descended from the French Revolution. Catholicism, Catholic theorists liked to claim, offered a "third way," neither capitalist nor socialist, that was set forth in a series of papal encyclicals beginning with Leo XIII's *Rerum Novarum* in 1891 and based on values that both of the modern ideologies had abandoned.[103]

Catholic social thought in the United States was strongly influenced by Monsignor John A. Ryan, director of the NCWC's social action department from 1919 to his death in 1945. Early in 1919 he issued a pamphlet titled *Social Reconstruction: A General Review of the Problems and Survey of Remedies* in which he applied the traditional Catholic concept of society as a corporate union to the problems of modern industrial society. Among other things, Ryan called for abolition of child labor, publicly provided insurance for unemployment and retirement, legal enforcement of the right of workers to organize, and a national housing program. Women, he recommended, should be freed from "any occupation that is harmful to health or morals," but where they were "engaged at the same tasks as men," they "should receive equal pay for equal amounts and qualities of work."[104]

Ryan denounced collectivist socialism as leading to "bureaucracy, political tyranny, the helplessness of the individual as a factor in the ordering of his own life, and in general social ineffeciency and decadence." But he proposed worker participation in the governance of industry, perhaps through shop committees or cooperatives. Above all, he suggested, "a reform in the spirit of both labor and capital" was needed.[105]

Ryan's pamphlet was attacked by the president of the National Association of Manufacturers as "partisan, pro-labor union, socialistic propaganda," but the bishops constituting the administrative committee of the NCWC nevertheless gave it their endorsement, and it came to be known as the Bishops' Program of Social Reconstruction.[106]

In its early years the NCWC came under criticism both from some of the American bishops, who feared that it might limit their administrative autonomy, and from some officials in the Roman Curia, who suspected it would encourage development of a "national church" in the United States. Pope Benedict XV, who originally had approved formation of the council, acceded to these criticisms and ordered its dissolution in 1922, shortly before his dealth. The next pope, Pius XI, initially directed that Benedict's decree be carried out, but responding to an urgent appeal from a majority of the American bishops, he soon reinstated the NCWC, requiring only that the word "conference" be substituted for "council," a term with connotations of substantive authority in Catholic canon law.[107]

The title of the organization was later changed to the United States Catholic Conference, under which name it has continued to function as the "highest authoritative body within the American Church." Operating out of its Washington headquarters, the conference seeks to advance the policies adopted by the bishops at their annual meetings, such as the widely discussed 1983 pastoral letter on nuclear arms. The relationship of the conference to individual bishops, however, remains essentially advisory. Each bishop, according to John Tracy Ellis, the leading historian of American Catholicism, maintains full "canonical authority" within his own diocese.[108]

During the early decades of the twentieth century, most Catholics voted Democratic, but the Democrats gained fewer benefits from this support than they might have because many Catholic immigrants from central and eastern Europe failed to participate in elections. Reforms sponsored in voting laws by progressives had undermined the electoral efficiency of political machines in eastern and midwestern cities where most of the immigrants lived. Some of the machine bosses, moreover, apparently were not eager to encourage political activity among groups of whose future loyalty they were unsure. Besides, southern and western Democrats, who usually dominated Democratic national conventions, did not hold much attraction for urban Catholics.[109]

This situation was dramatically changed when the Democrats nominated Al Smith, the Catholic governor of New York, for president in 1928. Smith was overwhelmingly defeated in the general election by Herbert Hoover, losing five southern states that had regularly supported the Democrats since the end of Reconstruction and running poorly in northern cities that were predominantly Protestant, like Minneapolis and Seattle. But in most of the cities of the East and Middle West, where Catholic voters were concentrated, Smith hugely increased the Democratic vote. In New York City, his vote was 63 percent greater than the combined vote for the Democratic and Progressive candidates for president (John W. Davis and Robert LaFollette) in 1924. In Suffolk County, Massachusetts, which includes Boston, he ran 75 percent above the combined Democratic-Progressive vote four years earlier; in Philadelphia, 178 percent; in Cook County, Illinois (Chicago), 68 percent; in Wayne County, Michigan (Detroit), 141 percent.[110]

The increased Democratic vote in the cities enabled Smith to carry Massachusetts and Rhode Island, both Republican strongholds since the Civil War but including large Catholic populations. In the other industrial states the rise in the Democratic vote in the cities was more than offset by Protestant support for Hoover in rural hinterlands. But the most significant result of the 1928 election, as several commentators have pointed out, was not the Republican gains in the South, which proved to be ephemeral, but the mobilization of Catholic voters in northern cities, which would help produce a new Democratic majority in the 1930s.

In the years that followed Roosevelt's election in 1932, Catholic politicians and labor leaders played important roles in promoting economic and social reforms. They were supported not only by John A. Ryan at the NCWC but also by progressive leaders of the hierarchy like Cardinal George Mundelein in Chicago and Archbishop (later Cardinal) Edward Mooney in Detroit.[111]

The Catholic Worker movement, begun by Dorothy Day in 1933, sought to go beyond the New Deal and beyond what most of the hierarchy thought was feasible. Day called on the church to end its connivance with the "oppression" of "the poor, the worker, the Negro, the Mexican, the Filipino" by "our industrial capitalist order." The Worker movement rejected Marxist socialism as firmly as did Monsignor White or the hierarchy but laid the groundwork for the development of tendencies toward radical political activism in one segment of American Catholicism in the 1960s.[112]

Moving in a contrary direction, Father Charles Coughlin, the famous radio priest of the Shrine of the Little Flower in Royal Oak, Michigan, preached a combination of populist economics and absolutist values. At the peak of his popularity in the 1930s, Coughlin's Sunday afternoon radio programs reached an audience of 10 million. Coughlin was not, in the American context, a conservative. He blamed the depression impartially on "godless capitalists, the Jews, Communists, international bankers, and plutocrats." His proposal for establishment of a "corporate state" had some roots in traditional Catholic social theory but found models nearer at hand in contemporary fascist dictatorships in Europe. Coughlin gained some following among fundamentalist Protestants, who shared his hatred for all things modern, but his primary constituency was among Catholics. A Gallup poll in 1938 found 42 percent of Catholics approving him and 25 percent disapproving, while responses from Protestants were 19 percent approving and 25 percent disapproving (the remainder of both groups had no opinion).[113]

In 1936 in collaboration with Dr. Francis Townsend, author of the renowned Townsend plan for universal old-age pensions, and some former henchmen of Huey Long, the late Louisiana demagogue, Coughlin launched the Union party. With William Lemke, an oldtime agrarian populist, as its presidential candidate and Coughlin as its chief publicist, the Union party won about 2 percent of the national popular vote.

The tacit approval that Coughlin had at first enjoyed from the bishop of his diocese was withdrawn when Archbishop Mooney arrived in Detroit in 1937. Coughlin's scorn for democracy and the virulence of his attacks on Jews, set against the background of fascist repression in Europe, ultimately caused him to lose most of his public following and to be forced off the air, but not before, as James Hennessey has written, he had touched "fears, prejudices, and insecurities" that formed "an important if dark side" of "the American Catholic subconscious."[114]

Growing affluence and migration to the suburbs in the 1940s and 1950s produced some movement among Catholics toward political conservatism. America's participation in the Second World War and the identification during the postwar years of international communism as a dangerous adversary of both Christian and democratic values contributed to the development of a mood within American Catholicism of intense nationalism, symbolized by the aggressively patriotic and anticommunist Cardinal Francis Spellman of New York. Having long suffered charges by nativists that their loyalty to Rome made them not quite American, Catholics were understandably pleased to find themselves among the most dedicated defenders of "the American way of life," at a time when some Yankee patrician types such as Alger Hiss were turning up on the other side. Catholics gave disproportionate support to the campaign of intimidation and vilification waged during the early 1950s by Senator Joseph McCarthy, himself a Catholic, in the name of anticommunism. In December 1953 the Gallup poll found 58 percent of Catholics viewing McCarthy favorably and 23 percent unfavorably. Protestant reactions were 49 percent favorable and 28 percent unfavorable and Jewish were 15 percent favorable and 71 percent unfavorable. Expressing support for a more moderate form of conservatism, 44 percent of Catholics voted for Dwight Eisenhower for president in 1952 and 49 percent in 1956.[115]

Still, most Catholics in the 1950s continued to think of themselves as Democrats. John Petrocik's analysis of survey data compiled from 1952 through 1960 shows that the average party identification among Irish and Polish Catholics was 60 percent Democratic, compared to 28 percent independent, and only 12 percent Republican. The Democratic lead among other Catholic groups was less overwhelming but still large.[116]

John Kennedy's election as president in 1960 was both a triumph and vindication for many Catholics. In all parts of the country, Catholics voted for Kennedy by huge majorities: 77 percent in the East, 81 percent in the Middle West, 75 percent in the South, and 74 percent in the Far West. Kennedy's share of the national Catholic vote was more than 50 percent greater than that which had been given to Adlai Stevenson, the Democratic candidate in 1956. Protestants in some parts of the country voted almost as heavily for Richard Nixon: 72 percent in the East, 62 percent in the Middle West, and

63 percent in the Far West, but only 53 percent in the South. Nixon received support from popular Protestant clergymen like Norman Vincent Peale and Daniel A. Poling, who based their endorsements explicitly on Kennedy's Catholicism. Nevertheless, Nixon's national support among Protestants was 1 percentage point less than that which had been given to Eisenhower four years before.[117]

Kennedy's victory, according to James Hennesey, "lessened the psychological defensiveness that had historically marked the Catholic American."[118] Established at last as full participants in American society, Catholics felt, perhaps paradoxically, a degree of release from loyalty to the Democratic party. Although they were still much more likely to be Democrats than Republicans, in the 1970s, as new issues developed and party configurations somewhat changed, many appeared willing to consider fresh political options.

NIEBUHRIAN REALISM

Northern Protestants who were normally Republicans voted in substantial numbers for Franklin Roosevelt in 1932 and 1936. In thirty predominantly Protestant rural counties in New York, Michigan, and Illinois surveyed by James Sundquist, Roosevelt's 1932 share of the vote was just under 50 percent, compared to 30 percent given to Al Smith in 1928. In the five most heavily Protestant northern counties containing cities with populations over 100,000—including the cities of Indianapolis, Columbus, Akron, Seattle, and Minneapolis (all of which also of course contained many non-Protestants)—Sundquist found that Roosevelt won 53 percent of the vote compared to 37 percent given to Smith. In 1936, the year of Roosevelt's greatest landslide, Sundquist's thirty rural counties actually moved back part way toward the Republicans, giving Roosevelt only 41 percent of their vote; but in Sundquist's five heavily Protestant northern urban counties the Democratic vote soared to 61 percent (partly because of the continuing mobilization of Catholic and Jewish voters and the shift in allegiance among blacks).[119]

This swing to the Democrats among some northern Protestants received encouragement from the liberal minority among Protestant ministers and lay activists who carried on the tradition of the Social Gospel. The 1932 northern Presbyterian General Assembly resolved that "nothing is more obvious than that the present economic order is now on probation and its continued existence and justification must be found not in the wealth produced or the power gained, but in its contribution to social service and social justice." Benson Landis, a leading Congregationalist social activist, praised the New Deal for "applying most of the policies which the churches have advocated for two decades."[120] Some Protestant activists felt that even more radical medicine was needed. In 1934 the National Council of Methodist Youth, for instance, endorsed socialism "as being at present the most workable political expression of Christian social ideals," and called upon its members to "renounce the Capitalistic system."[121]

The majority of church leaders, both clerical and lay, however, remained conservative. In 1932 most Protestant periodicals, while avoiding outright endorsements, indicated a preference for Hoover. Four years later, a survey of more than 21,000 Protestant clergymen found 70 percent of them opposed to the New Deal. The Layman's Religious Movement was formed within the Methodist church in 1936 to combat social liberalism. In 1938 the Southern Baptist Convention resolved, "There ought to be no room for radical Socialism and for atheistic Communism in the United States of America, and the widespread propaganda now carried on in their interest should be as speedily as possible and in every way possible prevented and counteracted." John C. Bennett, then a young liberal Protestant theologian, lamented in 1939 that "one of the hardest facts to face is that the success of the most promising political forces in American life [the New Deal] must be in spite of the opposition of the majority of the members of the Protestant churches."[122]

In terms of enduring impact the most effective criticism of the Social Gospel tradition came not from conservatives but from a new school of "realists" that developed on Protestantism's left wing. Reinhold Niebuhr, son of a minister in the German Evangelical church (an American offshoot of German Calvinism with Wesleyan overtones), was himself in many ways a product of the Social Gospel movement. Throughout his long career, first as a German Evangelical pastor in Detroit and then as a professor at Union Theological Seminary in New York, Niebuhr gave leadership or support to liberal social causes. But in his theological and historical writing, he pounded at the optimistic assumptions on which much of the Social Gospel was based.

Niebuhr rejected the belief, which he attributed to "both secular and Christian modern liberalism," that "the bias toward evil" in human nature resides "not in man's will but in some sloth of nature which man has inherited from his relation to brute creation." Evil, he maintained, is the consequence of man's "inevitable though not necessary unwillingness to acknowledge his dependence, to accept his finiteness, and admit his insecurity." Man can be freed from this vicious circle of evasion by accepting God's redeeming love, but the experience of divine love can never fully be translated into politics or other finite human relationships, which are indelibly marked by humanity's propensity to sin and error. Human history, therefore, "is permanently suspended between the flux of nature and finiteness and its eternal source and end."[123]

The church exists to give human beings access to life's "eternal source and end." When the church turns to concrete problems that grow out of "the flux of nature and its finiteness," as Niebuhr believed it must, it inevitably partakes of human imperfection. "Wherever religion is mixed with power and wherever the religious man achieves power, whether inside or outside the church, he is in danger of claiming divine sanction for the very human and frequently sinful actions, which he takes and must take." The medieval Catholic church made the momentous error of "identifying the church with the Kingdom of God and of making unqualified claims of divinity for this human, historical, and relative institution." Lutheranism, toward which Niebuhr felt strong affinities, made the equally serious mistake of splitting human experience into "the realm of heaven" where "nothing is known except forgiveness and brotherly love," and "the realm of earth" where "nothing is known except the law, the sword, the courts, and chains," with the church assigned exclusive responsibility for the former and the state for the latter.[124]

Modern religious liberalism of the kind represented by the Social Gospel holds that the church, through the reform of civil institutions, can make the realm of earth subject to "the law of love." Such optimism, Niebuhr insisted, stands in "obvious contradiction to the tragic facts of human history, particularly contemporary history." Christianity, he pointed out, has never guaranteed "the historical success of the 'strategy' of the Cross." Jesus advised his disciples: "In this rejoice not, that the spirits are subject unto you; but rather rejoice because your names are written in heaven."[125]

Recognition of the limits imposed by the finite human condition does not excuse the church or the religious individual from pursuing social justice. Both the Old and the New Testaments hold human beings responsible for doing what they can to improve the human lot. Moreover, "there are possibilities of success because history cannot be at complete variance with its foundation." It is a good thing, Niebuhr maintained, "to seek for the Kingdom of God on earth," though "it is very dubious to claim to have found it."[126]

Niebuhrian realism provided many Protestant progressives with a welcome alternative to the goals and strategies of utopian liberalism. The "danger of the Social Gospel," wrote Richard Niebuhr, Reinhold's more severely Calvinist brother, was "its idealism and its tendency to deny the [religious] presuppositions on which it was based."[127] Reinhold Niebuhr's formulation of the inherent bias toward sin in human nature not only seemed to match the facts of contemporary history but also offered a means for confronting the evils of totalitarianism, both fascism and communism, within the context of Christian and progressive values. At the same time, his vision countered the familiar American temptation to identify the national interest of the United States with divine purpose.

Most Protestants emerged from the New Deal years neither enthusiasts for the Social Gospel nor Niebuhrians. They remained social conservatives or moderates, either practicing a largely personalist religion or finding the existing social order, while no doubt improvable, on the whole the best available means for promoting moral as well as material progress. In the South where the one-party system had been firmly reestablished after the aberration of 1928, most of these Protestant conservatives and moderates were Democrats. Elsewhere they tended to be Republicans, adhering to the decision of 1896 (of which of course many of them had never heard). By 1948, Sundquist's thirty northern rural Protestant counties were 65 percent Republican—almost where they had been in 1928. The five most Protestant counties including major cities (Indianapolis, Columbus, Akron, Seattle, and Minneapolis), on the other hand, were about evenly divided between the two major parties. But since these metropolitan counties included substantial Catholic, Jewish, and black populations, all strongly Democratic, their white Protestant residents must have been predominantly Republican.[128]

The Great Depression and the New Deal caused northern Protestants to divide politically to some extent along class lines. But even working-class white Protestants were still more likely to be Republicans than Democrats. Gerhard Lenski's famous study of the influence of religious practice on political behavior in Detroit in the 1950s found that both middle-class and working-class Protestants were more than twice as likely as white Catholics of the same class to be Republicans. More active church members (among Catholics as well as Protestants, however) were significantly more likely to be Republicans than those less active.[129]

Why did northern Protestants continue to identify disproportionately with the Republican party? In part they remained suspicious of the Democrats as the "Catholic party," citing Catholic efforts to obtain government aid for parochial schools. The momentum of family tradition was also a factor, even if the tradition was by now tied only vaguely to the issues over which denominational partisan alignments had originally been formed. Many Protestants also probably continued to regard the Republicans as more responsive than the Democrats to traditional Protestant values (hard work, sobriety, family responsibility, and the like). Lenski found that in Detroit 52 percent of white Protestants, a share 18 percent larger than among white Catholics though only 8 percent larger than among Jews, gave the sense that "the work is important and gives a feeling of accomplishment," a higher priority than pay, job security, working hours, or chance for advancement in evaluating a job. White Protestants were also much more likely than white Catholics or Jews to oppose drinking or gambling. It is reasonable to conjecture that such attitudes found some translation into politics.[130]

WHY JEWS ARE LIBERAL

Although relatively few in number before the mass migration from eastern Europe that began in the 1880s, Jews have always been disproportionately active and influential in American politics. In 1774 Francis Salvador, Jr., a member of Charleston's Sephardic Jewish community, was elected to represent South Carolina in the first Continental Congress—"the first Jew in American history and probably the first Jew in the modern world to serve in an elective office." In New York in the 1790s Jews played an important part in forming the Tammany Society, a political club dedicated to the promotion of equalitarian values, and a Jew, Solomon Simson, was one of Tammany's first grand sachems.[131]

In the early years of the Republic, Jews concentrated on removing constitutional or legal obstacles to their full participation in public life. This interest naturally drew them to the party of equality and particularly to Jefferson, the nation's leading proponent of religious freedom. Under the second party system, most Jews supported the Democrats, both because they approved the relatively liberal policies of Jackson and Van Buren, and because they regarded the Whigs as conveyors of nativism, which could phase into anti-Semitism. By the 1850s, however, some successful Jewish merchants were being attracted by economic interest toward the party of order. Besides, the Democrats were increasingly identified with the Catholic church. In Europe Jews viewed Catholicism as an implacable enemy. Many American Jews, according to Lawrence Fuchs, "probably opposed a Catholic 'church militant' even more than they feared nativism."[132]

In the realignment that began with the election of 1860, Jews swung heavily to the Republicans. Identification of the Democrats with slavery and disunion released Jews to follow their economic and cultural interests into the new progressive conservative coalition that set the course of the Republican party. Presidents Lincoln and Grant took pains to get on good terms with successful Jewish businessmen like the Seligman brothers, Joseph and Jessie, of New York. Efforts by Grant and James G. Blaine to prohibit public aid to Catholic schools were warmly supported by Jews, and Jewish politicians became key figures in Republican city machines in New York, Philadelphia, and Chicago.

The capture of the Democratic party by populism in the 1890s confirmed the loyalty of most Jews to the Republicans. Bryan's style was as abrasive to Jews as it was to Catholics, and many among his populist supporters made no secret of their anti-Semitism. An Associated Press dispatch from St. Louis during the Populist convention held in 1896 to endorse Bryan reported "extraordinary hatred of the Jewish race" among the delegates. "It is not possible to go into any hotel in the city without hearing the most bitter denunciation of the Jews as a class and of particular Jews who happen to have prospered in the world."[133]

Within the Republican party, Jews consistently supported the progressive wing. Theodore Roosevelt was a special favorite because they liked his style and supported his program for domestic reform and because they appreciated his outspoken protests against persecution of Jews by czarist Russia and other eastern European governments. (Some Republican leaders seem to have viewed their efforts on behalf of Jewish rights with a measure of cynicism. "The Hebrews—poor dears!" John Hay, Roosevelt's secretary of state, privately noted. "All over the country they think we are bully boys.")[134]

Religious and cultural forces at work within Judaism during the nineteenth and early twentieth centuries had important political effects. Early Jewish settlers from England and Holland had been Sephardic Jews (the strain of Judaism that had entered western Europe through Spain and Portugal after long migration across northern Africa). By 1850 these were outnumbered by more recently arrived German Ashkenazic Jews (part of the Yiddish-speaking strain that had entered Europe from the east). The Sephardic communities had maintained "placid orthodoxy" in their religious attitudes. But the Ashkenazim brought with them the ferment of discord between orthodoxy and reform that was dividing central European Judaism.[135]

The Reform movement had begun in Germany early in the nineteenth century as an effort to adapt Judaism to modern conditions and to redefine the nature of the Jewish people. Orthodox Judaism regarded the Jews as a people in exile from their homeland in Palestine who were held together by strict observance of Talmudic law, which was based not only on the Bible but also on a great quantity of interpretation "elaborated by rabbis over the course of a thousand and more years." The reformers, in contrast, emphasized the contemporary role of Judaism. Claiming the authority of Isaiah, they taught that the Jews "had been sent out into the world by divine providence, not as a punishment, but to teach the true faith to the unenlightened."[136] Jews, then, were above all else a people with a mission, a view in many ways similar to that which the early Puritans had brought to New England.

The "extreme congregationalism" of American Judaism created a situation in which "each synagogue and each group that wished to form one, was a law completely to itself." Such institutional openness provided a fertile environment for reform. Led by Rabbi Isaac Mayer Wise, the Reform movement for a time seemed to carry all before it. In 1875 Hebrew Union College, the first American school to train rabbis, was founded in Cincinnati under Reform auspices. Ten years later Reform leaders meeting in Pittsburgh adopted a statement of principles. This Pittsburgh Platform proposed among other things the abandonment of portions of Talmudic law "not adapted to the views and habits of modern civilization," rejection of a return to Palestine as a Jewish goal, and participation by Jews in "the great task of modern times, to solve, on the basis of justice and righteousness, the problems presented by the contrasts and evils of the present organization of society."[137]

A degree of reaction shortly set in. Even among those who welcomed release from the strict confines of Orthodox Judaism, many felt that some parts of the Pittsburgh Platform pointed toward dissolution of Judaism as a distinct faith. A banquet sponsored by Hebrew Union College at which one of the forbidden foods, shrimp (*terefa*), was served as the opening course caused a particular uproar. During the final decade of the nineteenth century, moderates who had grown dissatisfied with Reform Judaism but did not wish to go the whole way back to Orthodoxy set in motion steps that led to Conservatism, a denomination of modern Judaism indigenous to the United States. Because Hebrew Union College was the central institution of Reform, the newly founded Jewish Theological Seminary in New York became the flagship of Conservatism. While restoring traditional elements of Jewish liturgy and affirming hopes for restoration of Israel as a Jewish homeland, Conservatism did not deviate from the commitment of Reform to progressive social action.[138]

While Reform and Conservatism were contending for the allegiance of Sephardic and German Ashkenazic Jews, a new wave of migration from eastern Europe, particularly from Russia, was contributing to a vigorous revival of Orthodox Judaism. The number of synagogues in the United States rose from 270 in 1880 to 1,901 in 1916, and most of the new synagogues were founded by and for eastern European Jews. Also Ashkenazic, these Jews came from lands that had been little touched by the liberal enlightenment of the eighteenth and early nineteenth centuries. They were "attached to a religion that completely enveloped their lives and dictated a large part of their behavior. . . . Everything about the law became holy; even the fact that Yiddish was used to expound the Talmud gave the language a kind of holy character, and it became unthinkable that the Talmud might be expounded in Russian or German or English."[139]

Before 1880 Jews had been distributed more or less evenly across the United States, actually forming a slightly larger share of the population in the rural West than in the industrial East, but the new immigrants were concentrated heavily in a few major cities of the East and Midwest. Partly as a result of the increase in migration and the nature and distribution of the new immigrants, discrimination against Jews, which had been minimal during most of the nineteenth century in the United States, began to rise. "Private schools began to be closed to Jewish children," recalled Richard Gottheil, the son of a famous New York rabbi of the period. "Advertisements of summer hotels, refusing admittance to Jewish guests, commenced to appear in the newspapers. . . . In 1893, the Union League Club of New York . . . refused to admit Jews to membership."[140]

The cultural traditionalism of the eastern European Jews was not as a rule accompanied by commitment to political conservatism. Jews in eastern Europe had been treated more harshly than those in Germany, England, or Holland. Desire for change that in Germany had found outlet through support for social liberalism and religious reform was directed in Russia and other eastern European countries toward political radicalism.

The very strength of Orthodox Judaism among the eastern Europeans may have fed the trend among American Jews to break with religion altogether. Children or grandchildren who found the requirements of orthodoxy too heavy a burden were more likely to move to outright secularism than to accept what seemed the compromises of Reform or Conservative denominations. In 1937 the *American Jewish Year Book* estimated that only about one-third of the approximately 4 million Jews in the United States were "associated with religious organizations and activity." (Only heads of family were usually listed as synagogue members.) Among observant Jews, about two-thirds were Orthodox, about one-fifth Conservative, and the rest Reform. Yet many nonobservant Jews continued to think of themselves as Jews—members, that is, of the Jewish people though no longer practitioners of the religion of Judaism. In place of religion many secular Jews turned to humanist values, pursued through science and the arts as well as through social service, which already were emphasized by the Reform tradition.[141]

Particularly among secularized eastern European Jews, socialism attracted numerous supporters in the early decades of the twentieth century. Stephen Isaacs has estimated that in the 1920 presidential election, 38 percent of Jewish voters cast ballots for the Socialist party candidate, Eugene Debs (compared to 43 percent for the Republican, Warren Harding, and 19 percent for the Democrat, James Cox). In the United States, as in Europe, Jews were disproportionately represented among the leaderships of left-wing causes. Several explanations have been advanced for the appeal of socialism for Jews. Some have traced a passion for equalitarian collectivism to ethical precepts set forth by the Hebrew prophets. Others have found in Jewish experience of persecution the roots of sympathy for all downtrodden groups. Still others have suggested that some Jews found in the industrial proletariat a substitute for the Hebrew nation as a group specially chosen to play a decisive role in history.[142]

While some Jews were drawn to socialism, and a narrow majority of Jewish voters apparently supported Woodrow Wilson for president in 1916, most Jews during the first quarter of the twentieth century continued to think of themselves as Republicans. In the Sixty-seventh Congress elected in 1920, for example, there were eleven Jews, among whom ten were Republicans, and one (Meyer London of New York) a Socialist.[143]

In New York City, which contained by far the largest concentration of Jewish voters in the United States, the swing to enduring alignment with the Democrats began with the gubernatorial election of 1924. The ebullient personality and liberal views of Al Smith struck a sympathetic chord with Jewish voters. Smith ran well ahead of both his Republican and Socialist opponents (respectively, Theodore Roosevelt, Jr., and Norman Thomas, both of whom had some appeal for Jews) in heavily Jewish assembly districts. When the Democrats nominated Smith for president in 1928, he again carried Jewish sections of New York by large majorities, and outpolled Herbert Hoover in Jewish strongholds in other cities as well. In Chicago's Twenty-fourth Ward, which the Democratic candidate for president in 1924 had lost, Smith won 75 percent of the vote. In Boston's Fourteenth Ward, previously dominated by a Jewish Republican machine, Smith won 61 percent of the vote. Nationwide, about 70 percent of Jewish voters in 1928 supported Smith.[144]

The onset of the Great Depression and the unpopularity of Prohibition, both of which Jews identified with the Republicans, accelerated the shift to the Democrats. In 1930 six of the eight Jews elected to Congress were Democrats. Two years later more than 80 percent of the nation's Jews voted for Franklin Roosevelt, who had already excited enthusiasm among them as governor of New York. In the next three presidential elections, Jewish support for Roosevelt continued to rise, peaking at over 90 percent in 1944. Even in 1948, after Roosevelt's death and with Henry Wallace running as the presidential candidate of the Progressive party, an agglomeration of liberal and left-wing ideologues, Harry Truman still won about 75 percent of the Jewish vote. During the 1950s, Dwight Eisenhower had some success at reducing Democratic majorities among Jews, but Jewish voters still gave Adlai Stevenson more than 60 percent of their vote in both 1952 and 1956.[145]

From the 1930s onward, Jews were far more likely to be Democrats than were members of other religious groups enjoying high educational and economic status. A study by Wesley and Beverly Allinsmith in the 1940s found Jews ranked third among religious groups in educational status, behind Congregationalists and Episcopalians, and fourth in economic status, behind Congregationalists, Presbyterians, and Episcopalians. In the 1944 presidential election, the Allinsmiths reported, 92 percent of Jews voted for Roosevelt, while he was backed by only 45 percent of his fellow Episcopalians, 40 percent of Presbyterians, and 31 percent of Congregationalists. Even in elections in which the Republican candidate was Jewish, most Jews usually voted for the Democrat. In the 1956 senatorial election in New York, Jacob Javits, the Republican candidate and a Jew, was outpolled in Jewish districts by his Democratic opponent, Robert Wagner, a Catholic. (Javits won anyhow.)[146]

Attitudinal surveys showed Jews to be more liberal in their social and economic views than members of other groups at parallel social or economic levels and often more liberal than most members of other groups at lower socioeconomic levels. The Allinsmiths found 58 percent of Jews agreeing that "everybody would be happier, more secure, and more prosperous if working people were given more power and influence in government," while only 31 percent of Congregationalists, 37 percent of Presbyterians, and 34 percent of Episcopalians indicated agreement with this statement. Gerhard Lenski's study of religious groups in Detroit in the 1950s showed middle-class Jews more supportive of expanding the welfare state than working-class white Protestants or Catholics. V. O. Key found that Jews identifying closely with the Jewish community were more liberal than those who identified less closely. Data gathered by the University of Michigan Survey Research Center in 1956 showed 85 percent of the Jews who identified closely with the Jewish community favored federal job guarantees, compared with 59 percent of those identifying less closely, and 52 percent of non-Jews. Federal support for medical services was favored by 78 percent of more identifying Jews, compared with 65 percent of less identifying, and 59 percent of non-Jews.[147]

The tendencies of Jews to be more Democratic and more liberal than non-Jews with parallel economic or social status have been explained as rising from some of the same factors that are said to attract Jews to socialism: Jewish ethical values derived from religion and Jewish experience of persecution. A more immediate cause was Roosevelt's inclusion of Jews—Henry Morgenthau, Jr., Felix Franfurter, Benjamin Cohen, David Lilienthal—among the principal designers and administrators of the New Deal. Jews came to feel "at home" with Democratic administrations in the White House. Even more important, Roosevelt's leadership of the wartime alliance against Nazi Germany made him a hero of unprecedented stature to the Jewish people. ("The synagogues were more crowded after Franklin Roosevelt's death," Lawrence Fuchs wrote, "than they had been for a long time.")[148] Support by subsequent Democratic administrations and party leaders for Israel further solidified this relationship (although Republican leaders were hardly less outspoken in their backing for the new Jewish state). Beyond all of this, liberalism, in the sense of support for socially active but morally neutral government, appeared to many Jews to be the political expression and guardian of humanist values, which they specially prized and which they believed to be continually threatened by forces of nativism or absolutist idealism that they suspected lurked behind the various kinds of political conservatism.

Whatever the reasons for their support, Jews brought to the liberal wing of the Democractic party enormously valuable political gifts and resources. Jewish skills at conceptualization and articulation helped design liberal programs and publicize liberal causes. Jewish affluence and fund-raising abilities provided vital financial support for Democratic campaigns. Jews usually turned out to register and vote in larger proportions than any other major group and could be crucial in deciding outcomes in states where they were numerous and the two major parties competitive. In the 1968 presidential election the reported turnout among Jews was 76 percent, compared with 69 percent among Catholics, 67 percent among white Protestants, and 55 percent among black Protestants. A study of 1960 election returns by state showed that Jewish voters gave John Kennedy his margin of victory in New York, Pennsylvania, Illinois, New Jersey, and Missouri—and therefore triumph in the electoral college.[149]

Partly because of the congregational nature of Judaism and partly to accommodate the high degree of secularization among ethnic Jews, Jewish efforts to influence public policy have been carried out more through Jewish social action agencies than through overtly religious bodies. The most important of these social agencies are the American Jewish Committee, formed in 1906 in response to a particularly horrendous Russian pogrom to defend Jewish rights both in the United States and throughout the world; the Anti-Defamation League, organized in 1913 as an affiliate of B'nai B'rith, the Jewish service society, to identify and combat instances of anti-Semitism; and the American Jewish Congress, founded in 1918 to promote establishment of a Jewish homeland in Palestine.

These organizations appealed of necessity to the same potential supporters and inevitably became competitors. They often differed on both strategy and tactics. The American Jewish Congress regarded resort to the courts as the most effective means for promoting Jewish interests; the Anti-Defamation League and the American Jewish Committee were more inclined to proceed through negotiation and conciliation. All, however, pursued essentially the same goals, derived from Jewish progressivism, and were united in seeking American support for the establishment and defense of Israel.[150]

In the 1960s, Jewish allegiance to the Democratic party seemed among the most enduring constants of American politics. In 1960 Jews gave Kennedy more than 80 percent of their vote, despite misgivings among some over the closeness of the Democratic candidate's relationship to his father, Joseph Kennedy, an isolationist in the 1930s and later a backer of Senator Joseph McCarthy. In 1964 Jewish support for Lyndon Johnson rose to 90 percent, close to Roosevelt's highest level, although Barry Goldwater, the Republican candidate, was of partly Jewish descent.

Yet the inevitability of Jewish alignment with liberalism or with causes to the left of liberalism remained unproven. The communitarian strain in Jewish tradition, which has always been much stronger in Judaism than religious personalism, could form the basis for political conservatism and had in fact done so at various times and places in Jewish history. The prophet of modern equalitarian collectivism, Karl Marx, was an ethnic Jew, but so was the leading architect of modern progressive conservatism, Benjamin Disraeli. Hitler's holocaust produced profound skepticism among Jews toward the efficacy of nonviolent resistance to social repression, a course increasingly attractive to many non-Jewish liberals during the 1960s. Support for Israel had its own political logic, leading toward alignments that were not necessarily congruent with the traditional liberal coalition. And of course the economic interests of many Jews were in at least short-run tension with liberal policies on taxation and government spending. In the early 1960s Jewish loyalty to the liberal wing of the Democratic party appeared secure, but, as with Protestants and Catholics, forces were at work that would soon call old allegiances and long-standing commitments into question.

BLACK PROTEST

Among blacks, the other major group participating in the New Deal coalition after 1936, the churches had always exerted enormous social authority. Offering one of the few routes open to success for American blacks, separately organized black churches, formed in the eighteenth and nineteenth centuries as seceding offshoots from Protestant denominations practicing racial discrimination, regularly recruited many of the most gifted among black youth for the ministry. "The Preacher," W. E. B. DuBois wrote, "is the most unique personality developed by the Negro on American soil. A leader, a politician, a 'boss,' an intriguer, an idealist—all of these he is, and ever, too, the center of a group of men, now twenty, now a thousand."[151]

Blacks were attracted to evangelical Protestantism, partly because these denominations were dominant in the South where most of them continued to live up to the Second World War, but probably also because intensely personalist religion brought experiences of release and triumph in the midst of life situations to which no worldly remedies seemed relevant. The 1936 *Census of Religious Bodies* found that about two-thirds of churched blacks were Baptists, about 20 percent belonged to three separately organized black Methodist denominations, 3 percent were members of predominantly black local churches within the Methodist Episcopal church (the main body at that time of northern Methodism), and 2 percent were Roman Catholics in predominantly black parishes. Black Baptists were assembled in largely autonomous local churches, usually built around a charismatic minister. The three black Methodist denominations (African Methodist Episcopal, African Methodist Episcopal Zion, and Colored Methodist Episcopal) were organized, like their predominantly white counterparts, through tightly structured hierarchies.[152]

Some common Protestant social attitudes were maintained among black Baptists and Methodists. Lenski's study of Detroit in the late 1950s showed that black Protestants were even more opposed than white Protestants to drinking and gambling and much more opposed than white Catholics or Jews. In response to the question on qualities sought in a job, however, only 24 percent of black Protestants placed "feeling of accomplishment" first—in large part, no doubt, because they had more cause than whites to feel acute concern over pay and job security. Probably for similar reasons, blacks did not share the traditional Protestant distrust of big government. Survey data gathered by the University of Michigan Survey Research Center in the 1950s showed blacks 21 percent more likely than the general population to favor government taking responsibility for "things like electric power and housing" and 66 percent more likely to favor a federal role in providing job security, education, and medical services.[153]

In their social leadership roles, many black clergymen organized their congregations as voting blocs and carried on negotiations with local white power structures. "Churches were meeting places," James Deotis Roberts notes. "Ministers were often the only persons in a community sufficiently well developed to lead the people. They, therefore, had to devote themselves not just to church work, but to every matter of concern to the race."[154] When blacks began winning important elective offices, some of the most visible among them were ministers, including Adam Clayton Powell and later Andrew Young, Walter Fauntroy, and William Grey, Jr. The two most effective national black political leaders to date, Martin Luther King, Jr., and Jesse Jackson, have come from the ministry.

Well into the 1960s, however, most politically active black clergymen continued to concentrate on local problems and generally avoided taking stands on controversial national or international issues other than civil rights. As Walter Fauntroy has said, "It was almost inevitable in those days that the black churches should concentrate on problems directly affecting the black community, and anyhow blacks were shut out of the larger political process."[155]

Before the 1930s blacks who were able to vote had usually been overwhelmingly Republican. Identification of the Democrats with white supremacy in the South, which most northern Democrats made little effort to disavow, was by itself almost enough to keep blacks loyal to the "party of Lincoln." Republican politicians distributed some minor patronage among their black supporters and occasionally made halfhearted efforts on behalf of civil rights. Whatever leanings blacks may have felt toward the Democrats during the Progressive Era were crushed when Woodrow Wilson, who had grown up in the South and held conventional white southern attitudes on racial matters, ordered racial segregation of the federal civil service, which had been unsegregated under Republican administrations. Blacks, like Jews, applauded Al Smith's struggle against the Ku Klux Klan within the Democratic party and gave the pugnacious New York governor a sizable share of their vote in the 1928 presidential election. But in 1932 blacks were once more firmly Republican, voting heavily for Hoover.[156]

The New Deal gave a low priority to racial issues. Whatever Franklin Roosevelt's personal inclinations may have been, he was careful to avoid antagonizing powerful white southerners in the Democratic party leadership, including Vice-President John Garner and the majority leaders of both houses of Congress, on whose support he depended for passage of his economic recovery program. Eleanor Roosevelt was a determined advocate for black rights within the administration, and some New Deal officials made symbolic gestures supporting black aspirations. But on the key legislative objective sought by black leaders in the 1930s, enactment of a federal anti-lynching law, the president and the administration remained aloof.[157]

Nevertheless, by 1936 blacks had swung strongly to Roosevelt. In his race for a second term, he improved on his 1932 showing in black districts by 132 percent in Chicago, 250 percent in Cleveland, 157 percent in Philadelphia, and 60 percent in New York (where he had already won about half the black vote in 1932). New Deal programs, though often rigged to discriminate against blacks, brought direct economic relief to the poor, and most blacks were among the poorest of the poor. "The key to black electoral behavior," according to Nancy

Weiss, "lay in economics rather than race." Rayford Logan noted, "Negroes had been so depressed, so frustrated, almost having given up hope, that nearly anything could have created substantial support."[158]

Many older blacks, particularly in the South where white supremacy remained official Democratic doctrine, continued to think of themselves as Republicans. But in presidential elections they became overwhelmingly Democratic. In 1952 blacks were the only major group to vote more Democratic for president than they had in 1948 giving Adlai Stevenson almost 80 percent of their vote. Four years later some black church and political leaders supported Eisenhower and the Democratic share of the black vote fell to about 60 percent.[159]

In the late 1950s some black clergymen decided that the time had come to launch a concerted drive to end legally enforced segregation in the South and to improve economic opportunities for blacks throughout the nation. In 1957 Martin Luther King, Jr., like his father a Baptist minister, became president of the newly formed Southern Christian Leadership Conference. King urged nonviolent resistance to laws imposing segregation. Blacks, he said, should meet "physical force with an even stronger force, namely, soul force."

As the 1960 presidential campaign approached, Richard Nixon, who as vice-president had compiled a strong record on civil rights, at first seemed disposed to make a determined effort to better or at least equal Eisenhower's 1956 showing among black voters. After the Democrats nominated John Kennedy, whose Catholicism was expected to give him problems with southern white Protestants, however, Nixon decided to play down identification with civil rights. Two weeks before the November election, Martin Luther King was arrested in Atlanta for refusing to leave a department store restaurant reserved for white customers. Nixon did nothing. Kennedy intervened to help secure King's release on bail. King's father, the leading black Baptist minister in Atlanta, who several weeks before had endorsed Nixon, announced, "I've got a suitcase of votes, and I'm going to take them to Mr. Kennedy and dump them in his lap."[160] Even so, Nixon won 32 percent of the black vote—a good showing for a Republican but not quite enough to bring victory in the crucial states of Pennsylvania, Illinois, and Michigan. On the other side of the political balance, Nixon, despite his caution on the race issue, won only three of the eleven southern states.

In the spring of 1963, King went to Birmingham, Alabama, to lead an economic boycott aimed at desegregating public facilities. On Good Friday he was jailed for organizing an unlicensed parade. A group of Birmingham clergymen charged that he was in their city as an "outside agitator." King replied from prison,

> I am in Birminghham because injustice exists here. Just as the prophets of the eighth century B.C. left their villages and carried their 'thus saith the Lord' far afield, and just as the apostle Paul left his village of Tarsus and carried the gospel of Jesus Christ to the far corners of the Greco-Roman world, so am I compelled to carry the gospel of freedom beyond my own hometown. . . .
>
> When I was suddenly catapulted into the leadership of the bus protest in Montgomery, Alabama, a few years ago, I felt we would be supported by the white church. I felt that the white ministers, priests, and rabbis of the South would be among our strongest allies.
>
> Instead, some have been outright opponents, refusing to understand the freedom movement and misrepresenting its leaders; all too many others have been more cautious than courageous and have remained silent and secure behind stained glass windows. . . .
>
> If today's church does not recapture the sacrificial spirit of the early church, it will lose its authenticity, forfeit the loyalty of millions, and be dismissed as an irrelevant social club with no meaning for the twentieth century. . . .[161]

After the Birmingham boycott achieved its objectives, King carried the demand for "jobs and freedom" for blacks across the nation. His challenge, delivered from pulpits and lecture platforms, and finally in August 1963 from the steps of the Lincoln Memorial in Washington, mightily reshaped the social agendas not only of the black churches but also of all organized religion in the United States, and ultimately of national politics.

King's dream, with which he concluded his speech at the Lincoln Memorial, of "that day when all of God's children, black men and white men, Jews and Gentiles, Protestants and Catholics" will join hands and sing "in the words of the old Negro spirituals, 'Free at last! Free at last! Thank God Almighty, we are free at last!'" nobly expressed the essentially religious aspiration that from the time of Jonathan Edwards on has, more than political theory or economic appetite, driven American democracy.[162]

SIX

Time of Turmoil: 1964 to 1985

FOR THE CHURCHES, as for American society in general, the decade of the 1960s turned out to be a time of extraordinary ferment. The civil rights struggle and the Vietnam War, the two most visible public issues of the period, caused intense controversy and soul-searching within most denominations. The apparently uncheckable advance of modernity, a complex phenomenon shaped by industrialization, urbanization, social liberalism, science, and other forces, produced varied responses from churches—rebuke, accommodation, or withdrawal from confrontation. The assassinations of John Kennedy, Martin Luther King, and Robert Kennedy, coupled in the public consciousness with widespread urban rioting and student disorders, created a sense that the social fabric was coming unstuck, or, as the novelist John Updike wrote, that "God had taken away his blessing from the United States."

Along with these common experiences, there were singular events with special significance for particular denominations or groups. For Catholics the Second Vatican Council, concluded in 1965, brought major departures from traditions and attitudes that had endured without essential change since the Middle Ages. For Jews the Israeli occupation of east Jerusalem after a brief but intense war in which the very survival of Israel had seemed threatened caused a surge of ethnic and even religious identification among many who had considered themselves wholly secularized.

Some religious groups met these developments and challenges with renewed emphasis on personal salvation. But the more general response among the churches was to become more deeply involved, in one way or another, in secular politics. Growing political involvement produced conflict or collaboration with secular ideologues and power brokers and impassioned controversy within the churches over the role of religion in the modern world that has continued to the present.

The Churches Come to Washington

By the time the National Catholic Welfare Council was established in Washington on a permanent basis in 1919, the Methodists had already had a Washington office for three years, mostly to help promote the temperance crusade. The stately Methodist Building on Capitol Hill, national nerve center for Prohibition forces, was completed in 1923. Most denominations, however, had no regular representation in Washington on public issues before the Second World War.

In 1943 the Quakers, whose religious objection to military service caused frequent collisions with the federal government, launched the first full-time Protestant lobby devoted to a wide range of public issues. Through their Washington office, the Friends Committee on National Legislation resolved, they would "contribute as best we may to the shaping of wise and right legislation in those areas in which our principles and the causes we believe in are most closely affected."[1]

Other Protestant denominations soon followed. In 1946 the northern Presbyterians assigned a part-time representative to Washington, mainly "for the purpose of securing information rather than for the purpose of influencing legislation." Later that same year the Baptist Joint Conference Committee, representing the conservative Southern Baptists, the more liberal Northern Baptists, the black National Baptists, and several smaller denominational offshoots, appointed a Washington lobbyist whose chief initial responsibility, according to one Baptist commentator, was "to watch the Catholics." In 1948 the Lutheran Council, representing eight separate Lutheran bodies, created the post of "Washington secretary." The Lutheran minister selected for this role did not, however, register as a lobbyist, because "in accordance with the traditional position of the Lutheran Church, the activities which might be classified as lobbying are excluded from the function of the Washington secretary." Also in 1948 the Methodist Women's Division of Christian Service appointed a full-time Washington representative to deal with issues that went beyond the Methodists' traditional support for temperance. Significantly, the office opened by the Methodist Women was not at first located in the Methodist Building.[2]

The establishment in 1950 of the National Council of Churches (NCC) as successor to the old Federal Council of Churches and several other ecumenical bodies provided an instrument for coordinating the public policy activities of the so-called mainline Protestant churches. (Exactly what these denominations are in the "mainline" of has never been entirely clear. The term seems to designate churches that are more inclined at their leadership levels toward political liberalism and are less evangelical in devotional practice, though several denominations with rich evangelical traditions, like the Methodists and some of the Baptists, are included.) At the founding meeting in Cleveland, representatives of twenty-nine Protestant and Orthodox Christian denominations gathered under a huge banner proclaiming "This Nation Under God."[3]

The NCC sought to promote functional cooperation among all churches that "confess Jesus, the incarnate Son of God, as Savior and Lord." (This credal stipulation required exclusion of the Unitarian-Universalists, who on social issues have usually participated in the mainline coalition.) Several large Protestant denominations, including the Southern Baptists and the Missouri Synod Lutherans as well as the Catholic church and the independent Protestant fundamentalists, have never joined the NCC. Within the ecumenical structure the Orthodox churches have on some issues acted as a conservative check on the liberal proclivities of the mainline Protestant leaderships. The NCC's Washington office was originally directed "not to engage in efforts to influence legislation," a limitation that was dropped when the NCC decided to play a leadership role in the fight for enactment of the Civil Rights Bill of 1964.[4]

In his 1951 study, *Church Lobbying in the Nation's Capital*, Ray Ebersole found sixteen church offices operating in Washington and a degree of cooperation maintained through a recently formed Joint Washington Staff of Church Legislative Representatives. Ebersole made an observation that was to become a common complaint among critics of the churches' Washington lobbies: "In many cases . . . church lobbyists promote the causes in which groups of church leaders are interested rather than the views of church members in general."[5]

During the Eisenhower years the churches' Washington offices operated at relatively low levels of activity, each concentrating on its own special preoccupations: the Catholics pursuing aid to parochial schools, the Methodists keeping up the fight for temperance, the Baptists maintaining a watchful eye for encroachments by the Catholics, and so forth. With the election of John Kennedy as president and the quickened social atmosphere of the 1960s, church involvement with public policy issues began to pick up. Several additional denominations sent representatives to Washington, and the Union of American Hebrew Congregations, representing Reform Judaism, opened a Washington office, joining the long-established bureaus maintained by the Jewish social agencies. The drive for racial equality initiated by the black churches in the late 1950s provided the perfect moral catalyst for joint political action among Protestants, Catholics, and Jews.

"VIOLATIONS OF THE LAW OF GOD"

During the 1950s a sense had gradually developed among the churches that the persistence of legally enforced racial segregation in the South and racial discrimination throughout the country were morally unacceptable blots on American society. On a visit to Europe in the summer of 1957, Father John Cronin, assistant director of the social action department of the National Catholic Welfare Council, was appalled by pictures he saw in French and Italian newspapers showing mobs assaulting black children who were attempting to attend white schools in the South. Returning to the United States in the fall, he urged the Catholic bishops to denounce racial discrimination at their annual November meeting. Leaders of the church hierarchy demurred on procedural grounds. The next year, however, under Cronin's continued prodding, the bishops resolved that "the heart of the race question is moral and religious. . . . Discrimination based on the accidental fact of race or color, and as such injurious to human rights, regardless of personal qualities or achievements, cannot be reconciled with the truth that God has created all men with equal rights and equal dignity."[6]

In 1959 the General Synod of the United Church of Christ (formed in 1957 from a merger of the Congregational church and the Evangelical and Reformed church, of German Calvinist origin) called for work and prayer for "the end of racial segregation and discrimination in our communities." The much larger Methodist church for a time hung back, anxious not to disturb the delicate balance maintained since the 1939 reunion of northern and southern Methodism. In 1958, however, the Methodists did agree to phase out over a ten-year period the Central Jurisdiction, which included all black Methodist churches regardless of geographic location (white Methodists were organized through five regional divisions). In 1960 northern Presbyterians, separated from the southern Presbyterian church since the Civil War, forcefully asserted that "some laws and customs requiring racial discrimination are . . . such serious violations of the law of God as to justify peaceable and orderly disobedience or disregard of these laws."[7]

When Martin Luther King began mass demonstrations in Birmingham in April 1963, hundreds of white churchpeople flew to Alabama to walk shoulder to shoulder with black protesters. In June the National Council of Churches created a Commission on Religion and Race, and authorized a crash program to support the fight against segregation. Eugene Carson Blake, a former president of the NCC and stated clerk of the northern Presbyterian church, was named chairman of the commission.[8]

In May 1963 the House Judiciary Committee opened hearings on the Civil Rights Bill sponsored by the Kennedy administration. Joe Rauh, longtime civil rights activist, later recalled, "Standing outside the Committee Room was the most beautiful sight I had ever seen— twenty Episcopalian priests, fully garbed, all young beautiful WASPS. I used to think that the only two people out in front for civil rights were a Negro and a Jew—[Clarence] Mitchell [Washington lobbyist for the National Association for the Advancement of the Colored People] and myself. But this was something we had never seen before. I knew then we really were in business."[9]

On July 24 Eugene Carson Blake, accompanied by Father Cronin and Rabbi Irving Blank, representing the Synagogue Council of America, testified before the Judiciary Committee. "The religious conscience of America," Blake said, "condemns racism as blasphemy against God. It recognizes that the racial segregation and discrimination that flow from it are a denial of the worth which God has given to all persons. . . . As churches, synagogues, and religious leaders, our concern is with the purpose of civil rights legislation and with the moral principles that indicate the necessity of enacting such legislation."[10]

During the year that followed, as the civil rights bill slowly made its way through House and Senate, churchpeople contributed significantly to the struggle for enactment. "They marched in Washington, led political workshops across the nation, buttonholed Congressmen and Senators, urged church members to deluge their elected representatives with mail backing the bill, participated in around-the-clock vigils at the Lincoln Memorial, and printed and distributed literature explaining the purpose of the bill and why it should be enacted into law."[11]

Protestant and Catholic leaders differed on tactics. Protestant clergy prowled the halls of the Capitol; Catholics preferred to bring pressure through their parish constituencies. But the two approaches were complementary rather than divisive. More than 5,000 churchpeople, including Stated Clerk Blake, were arrested at one time or another for staging demonstrations in support of the bill. "It is tragic," Blake said of the publicity given his arrest, "that the secular press finds so much news when a Christian does what he says."[12]

Southern opponents of the bill counterattacked. Representative Arthur Winstead of Mississippi complained that "a great number of liberal church people have flooded Congressmen with letters urging passage of the Civil Rights Bill—probably more than the Negroes themselves—yet they are thinking only in terms of what they believe the Congress should do to right some wrongs which they consider have been placed upon the Negro race." Looking up from the House floor, Congressman John Bell Williams of Mississippi found clergy in the gallery "peering from their perch . . . the political parasites of our day." Senator Richard Russell of Georgia, dean of Senate Democrats, declaimed, "I have observed with profound sorrow the role that many religious leaders have played in urging passage of this bill, because I cannot make their activities jibe with my concept of the proper place of religious leaders in our national life. . . . This is not, and cannot be, a moral question. However it may be considered, it is a political question. . . . This is the second time in my lifetime that an effort has been made by the clergy to make a moral question of a political issue. The other was Prohibition. We know something of that."[13]

At the 1964 meeting of the northern Presbyterian General Assembly, the Presbytery of West Tennessee (which had remained within the northern wing of Presbyterianism) presented a motion to censure Blake. The assembly voted instead to commend the stated clerk.[14]

The key to passage of the bill, it became apparent, was held by Senate Minority Leader Everett Dirksen of Illinois. If Dirksen supported cloture to break the filibuster through which the southerners were stalling the bill in the Senate, enough Republicans would follow his lead to end debate, and the bill would be sure to pass. In January 1964 Father Cronin and several other church leaders visited Dirksen in his Capitol office. "Obviously in January," Cronin recalled, "Senator Dirksen was not going to promise us anything, but he was signalling. We went out of there feeling we had a bill. He received us very cordially."[15]

Five months later at the crucial moment, Dirksen rose on the Senate floor. "The time has come," he said "for equality of opportunity in sharing in government, in education, and in employment. It will not be stayed or denied. It is here. . . . We are confronted with a moral issue. Today let us not be found wanting in whatever it takes by way of moral and spiritual substance to face up to the issue and vote cloture."[16]

Besides providing support that both sides agreed was essential to passage of the bill, the churches' involvement in the civil rights struggle produced a sense of moral exhilaration among church leaders. Almost twenty years later, Paul Kittlaus, director of the Washington office of the United Church of Christ, looked back: "Every surfboard rider knows the ninth ninth wave. Every ninth wave is big, but the ninth ninth is the one which gives the biggest challenge of them all. The civil rights movement in the 1960s was like that."[17] Participation in the civil rights movement taught church leaders something about political tactics and aroused feelings of social responsibility that could be carried over to other causes. It also may have given some misleading signals.

Despite Senator Russell's denial, civil rights *was* primarily a moral issue. Though it also included questions of technical and political application, as do all public issues, the basic question to be decided was whether legal segregation by race was right or wrong. Once this question was answered, American society could not indefinitely duck responsibility for solving secondary problems of application, debatable and troublesome though these might be. On the moral issue that lay at the heart of the civil rights struggle, the churches by their very nature were able to speak with unique authority and expertise.

Once the fundamental question in civil rights was politically settled, some church leaders were eager to shift the churches' moral energies to resolving thorny problems in economic and foreign policy. But these issues were in some important ways essentially different from civil rights. The central dispute in the civil rights struggle was over social goals, not over means for achieving those goals. On most foreign policy and economic issues, in contrast, differences of opinion do not usually extend to fundamental goals. Virtually everybody wants international peace; almost everybody aims at a growing economy and the highest feasible level of employment. But the means for achieving these commonly held foreign policy or economic goals are questions that turn to a great extent on issues of fact or practicality. The technical and empirical sides of these questions normally lie in areas in which the churches can claim no special expertise.

This does not mean that economic or foreign policy issues are without moral content or that the churches cannot make useful contributions on these matters. Distribution of wealth and use of military force, for instance, pose some of the most profound moral challenges facing any society. But by 1970 it was already apparent that some of the analytic approaches and some of the methods for building consensus that the churches had used effectively on civil rights would not work as well for some other issues. On the other great political issue of the 1960s, the Vietnam War, the churches had found themselves deeply divided over both the substance of American policy and their own political strategies.

VIETNAM

Under the Eisenhower and Kennedy administrations, the churches raised few objections about American military involvement in Southeast Asia. The Catholic hierarchy indeed strongly supported efforts to prop up the beleaguered anticommunist South Vietnamese regime, which maintained close ties with the Vietnamese Catholic church.

By 1965, however, several Protestant denominations, troubled by President Johnson's decision to escalate the bombing of North Vietnam, were calling for a change in course. The Methodists, who had been slow to enter the civil rights action, took the lead. In February

1965 the Methodist General Board of Christian Social Concerns proposed that the Johnson administration turn over responsibility for settling the Vietnam War to the United Nations. Nine representatives of the Interreligious Conference on Vietnam, including three Methodist bishops, met with Secretary of Defense Robert McNamara to urge a negotiated peace.[18]

Within the Catholic church, protest against American participation in the war gathered around the leadership of Father Daniel Berrigan, a Jesuit. A handful of activists resorted to civil disobedience. In November 1965 Roger LaPorte, a member of Dorothy Day's Catholic Worker movement, apparently inspired by the examples of Buddhist monks in Vietnam, burned himself to death in the United Nations Plaza in New York. Berrigan compared LaPorte's suicide to the death of Christ. Members of the "action community," including Protestants and Jews as well as Catholics, undertook raids on draft board offices and other government installations, inflicting property damage but avoiding violence to persons. Berrigan's brother, Phillip, a Josephite, specialized in the tactic of pouring blood or homemade napalm over draft records.[19]

Most Protestant, Catholic, and Jewish leaders, however, stopped short of condemning America's role in the war. In 1966 the Catholic bishops found that "in balance, the United States presence in Vietnam" was "useful and justified." Monsignor George Higgins, director of social action for the United States Catholic Conference (successor to the old NCWC), criticized the "almost irresistible compulsion to stage clerical rallies and demonstrations at the drop of a hat just to prove that the church is relevant." Rabbi Arthur Hertsberg warned, "The relevance of religion in the modern world cannot mean that there is a direct and clear mandate from God either to get into South Vietnam further or to get out entirely. . . ."[20]

The assembly of the National Council of Churches in 1966 passed a resolution questioning "whether U.S.A. policy does not rely too heavily upon a massive military intervention." But the NCC, like the Catholic bishops, concluded that "precipitate and unconditional U.S.A. withdrawal would open the road to even greater danger and suffering for people whose rights of self-determination, justice, and peace the U.S.A. seeks to set forward." James Hamilton, secretary of the NCC's Washington office, who had been a leader in the fight for the civil rights bill, acknowledged that "the activists say we are pussyfooting on Vietnam," but he rejected such criticism. "We don't see it as our major responsibility. Rather than issuing statements saying it was wrong for us to be in Vietnam, we have tried to raise some basic questions rather than rendering judgments."[21]

With no end to the carnage in sight, opinion among church leaders began to swing decisively against the war. In April 1967 the Methodist Board of Christian Concerns adopted a resolution urging withdrawal of American forces from Vietnam. In 1968 Rodney Shaw, a spokesman for the United Methodist church (formed that year through a merger of the Methodists and the Evangelical and United Brethren church, itself the product of an earlier merger of two small German Wesleyan denominations) announced that the church had appropriated $100,000 to force the American government to face the fact that "we have been defeated" in Vietnam. "I believe," Shaw said, "this is the first time a church has sought to directly influence foreign policy."[22]

Polling evidence in 1968 indicated, however, that Protestant church *members* generally continued to support pursuit of victory in Vietnam. Majorities within all denominations polled disapproved of the Johnson administration's conduct of the war. But among southern Presbyterians, 72 percent favored using "all strength needed for victory." This view was also held by 61 percent of Disciples of Christ, 60 percent of northern Presbyterians, and 58 percent of Lutherans. Only among members of the United Church of Christ was this position approved by less than a majority—36 percent. Continued bombing of North Vietnam was favored by 74 percent of southern Presbyterians, 62 percent of Lutherans, and 55 percent of Episcopalians. Even within the United Church of Christ, only a narrow majority, 53 percent, wanted the bombing stopped.[23]

A split had clearly developed between Protestant clergy and laity. A poll by the *Lutheran Magazine* found that 85 percent of Lutheran clergy believed that the church should defend protests against the war, but that 58 percent of lay Lutherans took the opposed position. The *Lutheran* concluded, "Officially the churches may coo like a dove but the majority of their members are flying with the hawks."[24]

In 1969 a conclave assembled by the National Council of Churches issued a detailed list of recommendations to the newly installed Nixon administration, calling for a coalition government, including the communists, in South Vietnam with "specific authority to (1) require the withdrawal of external military forces from South Vietnam, and

(2) determine its future relationship with North Vietnam. . . ." By 1971 even the Catholic bishops favored giving up the struggle: "At this point in history, it seems clear to us that whatever good we hope to achieve through continued involvement in this war is now out-weighed by the destruction of human life and of moral values which it inflicts. It is our firm conviction, therefore, that the speedy end of this war is a moral imperative of the highest priority."[25]

The ultimate fall of South Vietnam to the communists in 1975 was regarded by most church leaders as evidence that their only mistake had been in not opposing the war sooner. Some clergy and lay observers, however, took other lessons from the experience. Richard John Neuhaus, a young Lutheran minister who had helped lead Clergy and Laymen Concerned About Vietnam, became convinced that the churches were undermining their effectiveness by making recommendations on details of policy. Political leaders, Neuhaus observed, responded to the specific recommendations but "neglected the main points, which were moral." (Neuhaus had begun a journey that was to carry him to quite a different role in the politics of the 1980s.) Carl Henry, editor of *Christianity Today* and the leading evangelical theologian of his generation, worried that the churches were going beyond their area of competence; the churches, he wrote, "should either say the war is just or it's unjust and then leave the rest to military experts." Paul Ramsay, a Methodist theologian in the Niebuhr tradition, expressed a similar concern: "The religious com-munities as such should be concerned with *perspectives* upon politics, with political doctrine, with the direction and structures of the common life, not with specific directives."[26]

From another angle, James Adams, in a searching 1970 examination of *The Growing Church Lobby in Washington*, warned that the churches would not be taken seriously by the public or the government if they appeared not to be speaking for their members. In the civil rights struggle, Adams argued, the churches had represented the considered moral judgments of most of their members. But "the plethora of pronouncements released opposing the Administration's Vietnam position in 1965–66" had shown the "futility of issuing church statements which do not have the backing of the majority of the members in the pew."[27]

Elliott Corbett, chief Washington lobbyist for the United Methodist church, replied to Adams's criticism. Although he admitted that church members did not support their leadership on the Vietnam issue in 1965, he claimed that by 1970 a majority of them favored withdrawal from the war. If the church leadership had waited until then to protest, Corbett asked, "what, in the meantime, would have happened to the prophetic voice of the church?" His point was that the church is answerable not only to its own constituency, like economic interest groups such as business or labor, but also in some sense to objective moral truth. "Where deep moral issues are involved, the church cannot afford to wait for most of its members to agree before it exercises leadership."[28]

Yet within Protestant tradition at least, Adams's objection had force. Protestants have regarded the church as an imperfect human institution conveying the ripened moral judgments of its members. In theory the view of the humblest church member must be included in the balance, though not necessarily assigned an equal weight, with those of church leaders and theologians. Even Corbett conceded that church officials should "be ahead but not too far ahead on the issues."[29]

Adams argued that the churches' representatives in Washington spoke mainly for themselves. "Church lobbyists," he reported, "form a kind of self-perpetuating religious curia operating in a free-wheeling fashion with no accounting to the people they supposedly represent and who incidentally pay their salaries." Defenders of the church lobbies pointed to the array of assemblies and boards, to some extent democratically chosen, through which church policies were set. But the issue would continue to rankle.[30]

"A SWORD OF DAMOCLES"

One constraint on the activities of the churches' Washington representatives, Elliott Corbett observed, was their concern "that they not endanger the tax-exempt and tax-deductible status of their respective church bodies."[31]

The status of the churches with regard to the federal income tax is governed by the Internal Revenue Code of 1954. Under section 501(c)(3) of the code, corporate groups "organized and operated exclusively for religious, charitable . . . or educational purposes" are tax exempt. To maintain this exemption, a religious organization must not devote a "substantial part" of its activities to "carrying on propaganda, or otherwise attempting, to influence legislation," and must not participate or intervene in "any political campaign on behalf of any candidate for public office." Under section 170, contributions by individual taxpayers to a "church or a convention or association of churches" may be deducted from gross income for income tax purposes—a provision essential, most church fund-raisers believe, to maintain church revenues.[32]

In the early 1960s the Internal Revenue Service revoked the tax-exempt status of Christian Echoes National Ministry, an Oklahoma organization whose main function was to sponsor radio broadcasts by Billy James Hargis, a right-wing fundamentalist preacher. A large part of Hargis's airtime had been devoted to attacks on the legislative program of the Kennedy administration. Hargis took the IRS to court.[33] In 1971 the district court found in Hargis's favor, holding that Christian Echoes was indeed a church, and that neither the IRS nor the courts had any business scrutinizing its "work product" to determine how much was religious and how much was political. On appeal, however, the Tenth Circuit Court reversed, agreeing with the government's contention that Hargis's tirades against liberal legislation and his organization's later endorsement of Barry Goldwater for president in 1964 violated the provisions of the tax code restricting legislative or political activity. Hargis appealed to the Supreme Court.[34]

The National Council of Churches (one of Hargis's favorite targets) entered the case on his behalf. The ruling of the circuit court, the NCC maintained, was inconsistent with the Supreme Court's recent *Walz* decision (discussed in chapter 4). Dean Kelley, director of the NCC's Commission on Religious Liberty, challenged the constitutionality of forcing churches to "keep silent on public issues" to qualify for tax-exempt status—and by implication for their even more precious right to the tax deductibility of their contributions. The Supreme Court, perhaps resting after its labors over *Walz*, declined to hear the case.[35]

The courts have usually been liberal in interpreting how much time or effort churches may devote to action on public issues before overstepping the "substantial part" limitation set by 501(c)(3). Many church leaders nevertheless felt that the *Hargis* decision raised a "sword of Damocles" over their efforts to influence government behavior. In the early 1970s the IRS seemed to make this anxiety concrete by warning the Episcopal church that a planned solicitation for a student political education program would jeopardize the church's tax-exempt status.[36]

The Religious New Left

Neither signs of disaffection among some conservative church members nor threatened loss of tax privileges did much to dampen the enthusiasm for political involvement that religious liberal activists carried into the 1970s. The vital contribution by the churches to passage of the Civil Rights Act was acknowledged by both supporters and opponents. Many church leaders were able to persuade themselves that the churches' opposition to the Vietnam War had helped push Lyndon Johnson out of the presidency and forced Nixon to withdraw American forces from Southeast Asia. The churches, some believed, should be on the cutting edge of all sorts of ongoing "revolutions"— economic, racial, social, and sexual.

The tradition of the Social Gospel still provided inspiration and intellectual direction for some of the liberal activists, but many regarded it as hopelessly bound to old-fashioned ideas about work and the family that buttressed oppressive social structures. For a more dynamic analysis they turned to a new kind of theology rising from the experience of the Catholic church in Latin America.[37]

A THEOLOGY OF POLITICS

Historically, Latin American Catholicism had generally lined up closely with authoritarian social oligarchies. "The overwhelming sentiment of Church leaders was that true social harmony and welfare were identical with Catholic influence and power."[38] In some Latin American countries, Catholicism had largely divorced itself from the social and economic needs and even from the spiritual lives of the great masses of ordinary people.

There had always been a minority within the church hierarchy that regarded this situation as morally scandalous. In the reform atmosphere created within international Catholicism by the Second Vatican Council, the social conscience represented by this minority suddenly became dominant. In the summer of 1968 the Catholic bishops of

Latin America gathered in Medellin, Colombia, to discuss "the Church in the Present Day Transformation of Latin America in the Light of the [Second Vatican] Council."[39]

The documents issued by the Medellin conference proposed that Catholic social policy in Latin America be fundamentally changed. Social and economic conditions, the bishops found, had caused "almost universal frustration of legitimate aspirations" and had produced a "climate of collective anguish in which we are already living." The church could no longer ignore its social responsibilities. "The Christian quest for justice is a demand arising from biblical teachings. . . . In the search for salvation we must avoid the dualism which separates temporal tasks from the work of sanctification."[40]

The bishops had relatively little to say about the authoritarian political structures that had characterized many Latin American societies for several centuries. The real source of the trouble, they decided, was a relative newcomer: "liberal capitalism . . . an erroneous conception concerning ownership of the means of production and the very goals of the economy." The effects of capitalism on Latin America were particularly baneful because the capitalist system operated to make "the value of raw materials . . . increasingly less in relation to the cost of manufactured products." As a result, "the countries which produce raw materials—especially if they are dependent upon one major export—always remain poor, while the industrialized countries enrich themselves."[41]

This argument might seem to lead toward Marxist conclusions, but the bishops were by no means prepared to embrace "the temptations of the Marxist system." While capitalism erred in assuming "the primacy of capital," Marxism, "although it ideologically supports a kind of humanism, is more concerned with collective man, and in practice becomes a totalitarian concentration of state power." The true solution, the bishops concluded, was the "third way," which liberal Catholics had been promoting since Pope Leo XIII's *Rerum Novarum* of 1891 and which also had underlain the writings of Monsignor John Ryan in the United States. "In the economy of salvation the divine work is an action of integral human development and liberation, which has love for its sole motive."[42]

The Medellin conference, according to one commentator, offered "theoretical analyses of Marxism." A conference of Christians for socialism held four years later in Santiago, Chile, involving Latin

American Protestants as well as Catholics, went much further and called on Christians to "form a strategic alliance with Marxists." Where the Medellin conference had remained essentially reformist, the Santiago conference foresaw "no solution without revolution, not necessarily violent." For the delegates assembled in Chile, which was then experiencing the Allende government's attempt to build a socialist society, the "third way" no longer held appeal. Christians, they declared, must "be involved in the liberation process in socialist terms."[43]

The themes announced at Santiago have been carried forward by the works of several Latin American theologians. The most important are Gustavo Gutiérrez and Juan Luis Segundo, both Catholics, and José Miguez-Bonino, an Argentine Methodist.

Gutiérrez's *A Theology of Liberation*, based on a lecture first given in Peru in 1968, set the direction for the entire school. For Gutiérrez, liberation theology is "not so much a new theme for reflection as a *new way* to do theology . . . a theology which does not stop with reflecting on the world, but rather tries to be part of the process through which the world is transformed."   Like the preachers of the Social Gospel, Gutiérrez finds the heart of Christianity in the pursuit of social justice. But he goes much further than the Social Gospel in identifying justice with "liberation from all that limits or keeps man from self-fulfillment, liberation from all impediments to the exercise of his freedom." This goal, Gutiérrez acknowledges, is utopian in the sense that it expresses an "effort to create a new type of person in a different society." The "utopia of liberation," he argues, requires "a new social consciousness and . . . a social appropriation not only of the means of production but also of the political process. . . ."[44]

The strategy of liberation is to supersede the strategy of "developmentalism," which Gutiérrez finds "synonymous with *reformism* and modernization, that is to say, synonymous with timid measures, really ineffective in the long run and counterproductive to achieving a real transformation." Poor countries must grasp that "their underdevelopment is only the by-product of the development of other countries, because of the kind of relationship that exists between rich and poor countries." Among "more alert groups" there will be growing awareness that "authentic development for Latin America [can come] only if there is liberation from the domination exercised by the great capitalist countries, and especially by the most powerful, the United States of America."[45]

Gutiérrez foresees that the liberation strategy will remind some readers of the approach taken by the New Testament's revolutionary Zealots, which Jesus rejected. He ruminates over the possibility that some of Jesus' disciples "were Zealots or had some connection with them. . . . One of the Twelve—Simon the Zealot—*certainly* belonged to the Zealots; others *probably* did, like Judas Iscariot, Peter, and *possibly* the sons of Zebedee." But Jesus himself, Gutiérrez admits, "kept his distance from the Zealot movement." In part, this was because Jesus felt that "the universality of his mission did not conform with the somewhat narrow nationalism of the Zealots." But also, Gutiérrez concedes, "Jesus is opposed to all politico-religious messianism which does not respect either the depth of the religious realm or the autonomy of political action."[46]

Juan Luis Segundo, smoother and intellectually more sophisticated than Gutiérrez, makes no bones about extracting much of his theology from current politics. In *Liberation of Theology* he acknowledges that "Jesus himself seems to focus his message on liberation at the level of interpersonal relationships, forgetting almost completely, if not actually ruling out, liberation vis-à-vis political oppression. The same would seem to apply to Paul and almost all the other writings in the New Testament." It is for this reason that "liberation theology prefers the Old Testament and, in particular, the Exodus account . . . [in which] God the liberator reveals himself in such close connection with the political plane of human existence." But the "admonitions and examples" of both the Old and New Testaments establish only a very broad moral perspective, which depends for its content on the actual situations of contemporary life. Jesus' "commandment of love" must be "translated to an era in which real-life love has taken a political focus." So applied, Christianity must "break that conservative, oppressive, undifferentiated unity of Christians" that helps perpetuate social injustice and "establish an open dialogue with all those, be they Christians or not, who are committed to . . . historical liberation."[47]

In *Christians and Marxists: The Mutual Challenge to Revolution*, José Miguez-Bonino squarely confronts the question of how "liberated" Christians should relate to Marxists, who, while offering a revolutionary social perspective, explicitly reject many Christian values. Bonino does not deny that difficulties exist. "The country with the longest 'socialist history,' the USSR, leaves a very painful impression. It is not only—and perhaps not mainly—the absence of some forms of liberty after more than half a century. The most serious sign is the apparent inability to move in the direction of a real communist society. . . ." Some parts of Marx's analysis now seem dubious. "The proletariat of the industrial countries, in which Marx saw the agent of revolution, seem to have no sense of revolutionary vocation but rather to have been totally integrated into the capitalist system." Marxists in power have often trampled on the rights of the oppressed they promised to free. "Stalinism has emerged as the very negation of humanism."[48]

But no matter. Marxism is invaluable as an intellectual tool to liberated Christians because it alone among modern ideologies provides a system of social analysis based on the "recognition that 'man' is not the single individual but a communal unity in the form of a concrete social formation. . . ." Moreover, liberated Christianity and Marxism share a common enemy: market capitalism. "The basic ethos of capitalism is definitely anti-Christian: it is the maximizing of economic gain, the raising of man's grasping impulse, the idolizing of the strong, the subordination of man to the economic production." Christianity, therefore, "must criticize capitalism radically, in its fundamental intention, while it must criticize socialism functionally, in its failure to fulfill its purpose." The upshot, according to Bonino, is that "it should be inconceivable for progressive Christians" to undertake political action "without the orientating contribution of Marxism-Leninism or without the protagonist activity of the working class."[49]

As developed by Gutiérrez, Segundo, Bonino, and other writers, liberation theology is, in the terminology of this book, a form of utopian idealism. Casting political action as a direct route to religious salvation ("liberation") rather than as a means for making life somewhat better in an inherently imperfect natural world, utopian idealism encourages political leaders and parties pursuing its goals to regard themselves as agents of transcendent moral purpose. If politics brings salvation, there is no moral basis for limiting its reach. The results of this attitude are more than theoretic. After the overthrow of the Somoza dictatorship in 1979, religiously inspired participants in the Sandinista regime in Nicaragua resorted without apparent qualm to repressive measures that would have seemed natural to the Inquisition. Liberation turned out to require conformity after all. "Party discipline," according to Bonino, "is not, for the militant, an external imposition: it is the core of his spirituality."[50]

DOMESTIC LIBERATION

Liberation theology quickly acquired a significant following among religious social activists in the United States. Its claim to provide a bridge between political radicalism and Christianity appealed to those who, while feeling called to revolution (not necessarily violent), retained a need for religious faith. Its origin in the third world, free of taint by either capitalism or the kind of mechanistic socialism practiced in the Soviet Union, seemed to enhance its authenticity.

Robert McAfee Brown, already an experienced social activist and Protestant theologian, became the leading exponent of liberation theology in the United States. In *Theology in a New Key: Responding to Liberation Themes*, Brown announced the "discovery" that "the structures of our democratic society that benefit me here at home (the vote, the capitalist system, the police) often destroy others both at home and abroad." Traditional Christianity, Brown claims, has tended "to interpret evil in individualistic terms: a few bad people create the trouble, and if they can just be converted (or removed), all will be well." The great insight of liberation theology is that "*evil is systemic*—it has an uncanny way of becoming embodied in the structures of society in ways that almost give it an independent existence of its own." From this insight comes a new revelation: "It does not seem possible to reread the Bible (as liberation theologians have helped us to do) without entertaining the possibility of some sort of socialism (whether we call it that or not) and speculating about how it could be achieved."[51]

Brown draws the conclusion that contemporary America is badly in need of "radical social change," but his operational recommendations are surprisingly mild: liberated Christians should practice "relinquishment" in "personal life-styles" and "find adroit and clever ways of challenging a system that allows a few in the world to have so much at the expense of so many . . . which in our modern idiom means being politically savvy."[52]

Liberation theology in the United States mingled with other sources to produce two additional strains of radical religious thought: "black theology" and "feminist theology."

By the time of Martin Luther King's death in 1968, many black militants were questioning whether the civil rights movement would ever achieve much real improvement in objective conditions for American blacks. The Black Power movement was an attempt somehow to strike through structures of discrimination that seemed impervious to legal change.

In *Black Theology and Black Power*, published in 1968, James Cone argued that adherence to Black Power tests the authenticity of contemporary Christianity. "Jesus is not safely confined in the first century. He is our contemporary, proclaiming release to the captives and rebelling against all who silently accept the structures of injustice. If he is not in the ghetto, if he is not where our men are living at the brink of existence, but is rather in the easy life of the suburbs, then the gospel is a lie. . . . Christianity is not alien to the Black Power; it is Black Power."[53]

Though he admired Martin Luther King, Cone doubted that King's strategy of nonviolence would succeed. King's acceptance among white liberals came largely "because his approach was the least threatening to the white power structure." There is, Cone charged, "an ugly contrast between the sweet, nonviolent language of white Christians and their participation in a violently unjust system." Black people "must be taught not to be disturbed about revolution or civil disobedience if the law violates God's purpose for man." Yet Cone recognized that violent revolution would have its own costs in sin and suffering. The choice between violence and nonviolence is a decision "between the less and the greater evil." To choose nonviolence is to decide "that revolutionary violence is more detrimental in the long run than systemic violence." But "if the system is evil, the revolutionary violence is both justified and necessary."[54]

In the end, perhaps reflecting on the prospects for black revolution in a country almost 90 percent white, Cone preached a kind of racial ecumenicism after all. "Being black in America has very little to do with skin color. To be black means that your heart, your soul, your mind, and your body are where the dispossessed are."[55]

Just as proponents of black theology find the key to contemporary Christianity in Black Power, some feminists have located it in radical feminism. Advocates of feminist theology divide into two groups: those finding "elements of liberation in the Jewish and Christian traditions" and those believing that "the religious traditions are irreduceably agents of oppression, constructed to sustain male supremacy."[56]

Rosemary Ruether holds that through association with liberation theology feminism can find a bridge to the Judeo-Christian tradition. Prerequisite to this relationship, however, is a thorough purging from Judeo-Christianity of the dualism between spirit and matter that was imposed on it during the classical period by Greco-Roman philosophy. "We have entered the era of the 'demise of heaven' and the death of the 'spiritual,' and of the God who was defined in terms of one side of these dualisms." After this purge is carried out, liberated Christians will discover that "anger and pride, two qualities viewed negatively in traditional Christian spirituality, are the vital 'virtues' in the salvation of the oppressed community."[57]

Rosemary Ruether seems not to notice that discarding dualism leads either to no religion at all (secularism) or to a religious attitude that regularly has opened the way to social repression (utopian idealism). But such finicky analytical objections she would no doubt regard as melting before her apocalyptic vision: "Mankind will either conquer necessity in a non-oppressive form, or else the revolutionary tension bred in mankind by its Jewish-Christian roots will end in a final explosion."[58]

For Mary Daly, Judeo-Christianity has lost even latent spiritual authority. In *Beyond God the Father: Toward a Philosophy of Women's Liberation*, published in 1973, she finds the Judeo-Christian concept of the deity fatally flawed: "The divine patriarch castrates women as long as he is allowed to live on in the human imagination." There can be only one solution: "I propose that Christianity itself be castrated by cutting away the products of supermale arrogance: the myths of sin and salvation that are simply two diverse symptoms of the same disease." After Christianity is gone, it may be possible to achieve a new kind of spirituality, based on "androgynous existence." The way to this "breakthrough" is clear: "Only radical feminism can act as the 'final cause,' because of all revolutionary causes it opens up human consciousness adequately to the desire for nonhierarchical, nonoppressive society, revealing sexism as the basic model and source of oppression."[59]

"ALL OF US, REALLY, ARE HOSTAGES"

The extent to which most leaders or clergy of mainline Protestant churches read deeply in the writers of liberation theology or its attendant theories is conjectural. But after 1970 liberation themes and ideas became popular in mainline discourse. Words and deeds closely paralleling the themes of liberation theology issued from the upper levels of many mainline establishments:

—A guide for Methodist study groups, published in 1975 by the Division of Education of the United Methodist church, and authored by Else Adjali and Carolyn McIntyre, both key figures on the Methodist church's national staff, traced most of the troubles of the world's poorer nations to the United States and Western captalism: "Officially the United States condemns both colonialism and the policies of apartheid. However, more and more people suggest that the United States is colonizing Puerto Rico and has been doing so since 1898. . . . Profit, military might, and alliances with power interests in the world have made our nation the hub of a vast network of 'economic plunder.' . . . Development as we know it in the West—an industrialized, highly technological society—was achieved at the detriment of others. Development in the West is in a large measure the cause of the underdevelopment of nations in the Third World. . . ."[60]

—The Reverend William Howard, president of the National Council of Churches, embarked on a program of visiting "political prisoners" in American prisons. "One of our favorite beliefs in this country," Howard explained, "is that we have no political prisoners," but in fact "much of our prison population is comprised of people who are victims of the social, economic, and political structures of our society." A 1979 NCC task force concluded that the American legal system is designed "to suppress non-violent political dissent, to cope with social problems, and to provide cheap labor."[61]

—In 1971 the United Presbyterian church donated $10,000 to aid the defense of Angela Davis, a highly publicized black communist on trial for murder in connection with an attempted prison break. Davis, who was ultimately acquitted, attracted a large outpouring of financial support from liberal and leftist groups, so the purpose of the donation must have been to a great extent symbolic. (Conservative Presbyterians as well as liberals apparently grasped the symbolism: six years after

the event a poll of Presbyterian laity found "Angela Davis" more remembered than any other social issue, including civil rights and the
Vietnam War, dealt with by the Presbyterian church in recent years.)[62]

—A delegation of seven churchmen, including Robert McAfee
Brown and Methodist Bishop James Armstrong, later president of
the NCC, returned from a visit to Cuba in 1977 with the recommendation that "a political revolution that is in the process of creating a
society without beggars, starvation, or illiteracy is a revolution that
deserves our respect and support." Responding to charges that the
Castro government denied civil liberties, the delegation commented,
"The limit appears to be that there is freedom to be critical *within* the
revolution but not be critical *of* the process of revolution itself." The
churchmen found "a significant difference between situations where
people are imprisoned for opposing regimes designed to perpetuate
inequities (as in Chile and Brazil, for example) and situations where
people are imprisoned for opposing regimes designed to remove
inequities (as in Cuba)."[63]

—In 1978 the Committee on Justice and Service of the World
Council of Churches, chaired by Robert C. Campbell, executive
secretary of the American Baptist church (the former Northern
Baptists), approved a grant of $85,000 to be spent for humanitarian
purposes among guerrilla forces fighting to overthrow the government
of Rhodesia (later Zimbabwe). The government was at that time
headed by Bishop Abel Muzorewa, a black Methodist, and supported
by the socially dominant white minority. The WCC defended the
grant on the ground that it had been made on the condition that
none of the money would be used to pay for weapons or munitions.
But no accounting was required; and, as Campbell conceded, even if
the money were used for food and hospital supplies, it would release
other funds to be spent on arms.[64]

—Methodist Bishop Dale White responded to the seizure of
American hostages in Iran in 1979 with the observation that "all of
us, really, are hostages, those in the developed countries as well as
the developing nations. Hostages to a vast political economic system
of the cruelty structures which are preordaining that the rich get
richer and the poor get poorer. . . ."[65]

—A pamphlet issued by the American Friends Service Committee
suggested that "before we deplore 'terrorism,' it is essential to recognize
clearly whose terrorism came first." According to the author of the

pamphlet, James Bristol, to much of the world "the United States is an outlaw nation." Russell Johnson, an AFSC official, wrote in the *Fellowship of Reconciliation* magazine that "our nation today is the very fount of violence in many places in the Third World."[66]

There were both external and internal causes for the popularity of liberation themes within mainline establishments. The trauma of Vietnam was even more rending among some church activists than it was for American society as a whole. For the first time in American history, a substantial portion of the clergy disowned involvement by the United States in a foreign war. Some activists disaffected over Vietnam extended their rebukes to the whole course of American foreign policy. "What my nation did in Vietnam," Robert McAfee Brown wrote, "was not an exception to U.S. foreign policy, but an example of it. We do the same destructive things (more subtly) in many other countries." The revelations of Watergate were taken as further evidence of the corruption of the entire American system.[67]

The contrast between the wealth of the industrialized countries and the poverty of much of the third world weighed heavily on religious consciences. At its Nairobi assembly in 1975 the World Council of Churches, in which most of the mainline denominations are active, traced "the ever-widening gap between rich and poor nations and between rich and poor within many nations" to such factors as "the present international economic structures, [which] are dominated by a few rich countries" and "transnational corporations, often in league with oppressive regimes, [that] distort and exploit the economies of poor nations."[68]

In the late 1960s and early 1970s, just at the time when disaffection from national policy in the mainline seminaries was at its most acute, the number of youth deciding to take up careers in the ministry markedly increased. From 1964 to 1973 attendance at Harvard Divinity School rose 33 percent; at Andover-Newton School of Theology (United Church of Christ and American Baptist), 37 percent; at Princeton Seminary (Presbyterian), 24 percent; at Wesley Seminary (Methodist), 30 percent. There were several reasons for these increases, some of which, such as reaction against secular materialism, were not directly related to the Vietnam War. It seems fair, however, to postulate that many of the new ministers who began pouring out of the mainline seminaries in the early 1970s had begun their theological studies in moods of estrangement toward the American governmental and economic systems.[69]

The popularity of liberation themes also resulted in part from persistent uncertainty about the role of the church under religious pluralism. Ministers, priests, and rabbis on the cutting edge of political change would at least be "socially relevant." The almost complete secularization of religion recommended by the most fashionable theology of the 1960s, typified by Harvey Cox's *The Secular City*, had left a spiritual void. Whatever else might be said of the God of liberation theology, he certainly was not dead.[70]

Mainline Protestants in Crisis

Political changes of the kind called for by the more radical formulations of liberation theology have never had enough practical political support in the United States to get anywhere near the Washington agenda. But since the early 1970s the Washington offices of most mainline denominations have consistently supported the most liberal option available (liberal in the sense of favoring an expanded role for the federal government in dealing with domestic problems and a more conciliatory approach in world affairs) on a wide range of economic, social, and foreign policy issues. Mainline Protestant laities, in contrast, opinion surveys and voting behavior show, have remained predominantly moderate or conservative in their political inclinations.

THE MAINLINE LOBBY

Some of the legislative causes championed by the church lobbies, such as the successful drive in 1977 to eliminate the purchase requirement from the food stamp program, were uncomplicated efforts to make more resources available to the poor. But others, like the campaign for the Humphrey-Hawkins Full Employment Bill, which in its early versions required the federal government to act as "employer of last resort" whenever adult unemployment exceeded 3 percent, or like extension of the agricultural price-support program as a means for saving the family farm, have reflected dubious ideological assumptions about how the economy works or how society functions. On issues of national defense, the mainline church lobbies have generally seemed to proceed on the assumption that almost any measure undertaken to strengthen military capabilities should be resisted, as in their vigorous opposition to President Carter's call for reinstatement of draft registration in response to the Soviet Union's invasion of Afghanistan at the end of 1979.

Early in 1978 the Washington office of the United Church of Christ, following the example of ideological and economic interest groups, issued a report on twenty "representative" votes in Congress during the year, ten each in the House and Senate. For each vote, members were marked "to indicate whether he or she supported ($+$) or opposed ($-$)" the position recommended by the church's Washington staff. Among positions for which members were awarded pluses were votes against the B-1 bomber, for confirmation of Paul Warnke as chief negotiator for the United States in the SALT II talks, for the farm price-support program, against placing statutory limits on the use of busing to achieve racial integration of public schools, against barring direct or indirect allocation of foreign aid funds to the governments of Vietnam, Laos, Cambodia, or Uganda, and against prohibiting use of federal funds to finance or encourage abortions. The report's introduction allowed that members voting against the positions favored by the church office might "see compelling reasons other than lack of concern for justice or peace for casting their votes as they did."[71]

Since 1969 the major mainline church lobbies have participated in IMPACT, "an interreligious project to locate and organize grassroots support in selected Congressional districts for legislation to meet the crisis in the nation." According to a memorandum prepared at the beginning of 1980 by George Chauncey, chief Washington lobbyist for the southern Presbyterian church, IMPACT is "a *coalition* of 15 or so denominational/faith group (D/FG) agencies plus some ecumenical state IMPACT coalitions, who have joined together and provided funds (a) to enlist their constituents in a common grassroots political action network; and (b) to provide communications to their constituents in the network." Church offices belonging to IMPACT have access to a common mailing list, maintained on computers, which in the early 1980s contained about 14,000 names (small in comparison to the lists kept by major economic or ideological interest groups).[72]

Largely coinciding with IMPACT in its purpose, though including more church offices and interest groups, is WISC (the Washington Interreligious Staff Council). At first, "IMPACT and WISC were often described as two sides of the same coin. One side [WISC] faced the Congress and the other [IMPACT] faced the grassroots constituency." Over the years, however, WISC has evolved into a planning body primarily devoted to coordination and discussion, while IMPACT is an action agency. According to Chauncey, WISC is "a greatly needed *association of staff* . . . who [join] together to share information, work on common tasks, and mutually encourage and support each other." Both WISC and IMPACT include representation from liberal Catholic and Jewish groups as well as from the mainline Protestant denominations.[73]

The mainline lobbies, most of which are housed in the United Methodist Building on Capitol Hill, also participate in broader coalitions formed among Washington representatives of liberal interest groups and staffs of liberal members of Congress to promote particular causes. As their contribution to these joint efforts, the church lobbies perform three main functions: researching issues, giving testimony before congressional committees, and stimulating grassroots support among church constituencies. The church offices do little direct lobbying with members of Congress—partly out of concern over potential challenges to their parent bodies' tax exemptions and partly because, as Elliott Corbett observed, "when a church bureaucrat . . . makes a call on a Congressman's office, the Congressman knows good and well that he does not represent ten million members (nor does the visitor pretend to)." Far more effective than direct approaches by "our man in Washington" are "representations that are made by persons 'out there'" in response to stimulation by the Washington offices.[74]

LIBERAL ESTABLISHMENTS, MODERATE LAITY

Do most church members "out there" favor the liberal positions their churches' Washington lobbies have been advocating? Available survey evidence indicates that majorities within most mainline Protestant denominations remain fairly conservative on social and economic issues. Ministers in local churches also tend to be somewhat more conservative than their churches' national bureaucracies or Washington representatives.

A survey conducted by the research division of the northern Presbyterian church in 1974 found that 60 percent of Presbyterian laypersons were Republican, 17 percent were Democrats, and 4 percent were independents (the rest did not answer the question). A national Harris poll taken about the same time found the electorate as a whole dividing 47 percent Democratic, 25 percent Republican, and 38 percent independent.[75] As Lenski found in Detroit in the 1950s, the more active church members were somewhat more likely to be Republicans than the less active. Among Presbyterian pastors of local churches, Republicans also outnumbered Democrats, but only by a narrow margin: 41 percent to 39 percent, with 6 percent independent. An enormous generation gap existed among pastors: 60 percent of those under thirty were Democrats; but among those over sixty-five, less than 1 percent expressed a Democratic allegiance.

The same 1974 poll of Presbyterians found pastors much more inclined than their congregations to believe that local churches should take stands on a variety of social issues. Among the laity, church elders were even less inclined than average to have their churches take social stands. Asked whether a number of topics were "appropriate social concerns" for "your local congregation," the following percentages of the three groups answered "yes":

Issue	Pastors	Members	Elders
Abortion	69	38	37
Civil liberties	54	31	27
Employment	58	25	23
Military spending	47	13	13
Peace	65	50	47
Racism	68	37	37

Another survey, carried out by the northern Presbyterian church in 1976, found that 69 percent of the church's national staff believed that the church should be "concerned" about the effect of "business activities" on "environmental issues," compared with 28 percent of the laity and 55 percent of local pastors; 67 percent of the national staff believed that the church should be concerned about the "effect of multinational corporations on undeveloped countries," compared with 17 percent of the laity and 44 percent of local pastors. Interestingly, only 37 percent of the national staff believed the church should be concerned with the "marketing of drugs" (presumably legal drugs), compared with 34 percent of the laity and 35 percent of local pastors.[76]

A survey of Lutherans in the early 1980s also found the laity significantly more resistant than the clergy to involving the church in political or social controversies. Fully 75 percent of Lutheran laity believed that the church should maintain a policy of "no involvement" with "elections and candidates," compared with 50 percent among the clergy. On "business-government relationships," 73 percent of the laity and 38 percent of the clergy favored no involvement, and on "medical care issues" 53 percent of the laity and 20 percent of the clergy favored no involvement. On the question of rights of minorities, on the other hand, only 38 percent of the laity and 11 percent of the clergy favored no involvement.[77]

A 1980 survey sponsored by the United Methodist church measured social attitudes of bishops, national staff, local clergy, and "chairpersons of local church councils," among other categories, but included no sample of "rank-and-file laypersons." Omission of the general laity, the authors of the study admitted, was "a weakness of the survey method." Nevertheless, significant differences emerged among the responses of the groups that were tested. Agreement with statements on a variety of social issues (selected for pertinence from twenty-five presented) is shown in table 6-1. On every one of these questions the most conservative responses were given by lay chairpersons; local ministers were more conservative on every question than either bishops or national staff. Lay chairpersons were predominantly "liberal" on questions of national defense, racial equality, and women's rights, and were liberal by smaller majorities on abortion and public health insurance. They were substantially "conservative," and in disagreement with official church policies, on racial or ethnic quotas, guaranteed annual income, and school prayer, and conservative by smaller majorities on environmental protection and capital punishment.

Though disagreeing with some of the positions taken by their church, Methodist lay chairpersons generally approved an active role by the church on social issues. Fully 90 percent of lay chairpersons as well as 94 percent of local clergy and 100 percent of bishops agreed that it is appropriate for the church to "lobby local, state, and national officials regarding public policies of concern to the Christian faith," a position perhaps reflecting Methodism's longstanding commitment to social involvement as well as more recent liberal activism. A much smaller but still impressive portion of lay chairpersons, 24 percent, said they would be willing to "practice civil disobedience in the social

Table 6-1.   *Attitudes among Methodists on Public Issues, 1980*

Issue	Lay chairpersons	Local clergy	National staff	Bishops
Favor funding of health insurance for those who cannot afford to pay	56.5	71.1	94.2	81.5
Support quotas for racial and ethnic minorities in church and society in order to redress previous wrongs	34.9	49.7	65.4	81.5
Favor a guaranteed annual income that permits each person to live with dignity	30.7	47.6	63.5	63.0
Admit that policies designed to protect the environment have gone too far[a]	55.4	39.0	25.0	3.7
Support the legal option of abortion under proper medical care	56.7	58.0	96.2	92.6
Support the Strategic Arms Limitation Talks (SALT)	67.3	79.4	92.3	92.6
Favor equal rights in housing for persons of racial and ethnic minority groups	84.6	94.8	100.0	96.3
Favor the return of prayer to public schools[a]	74.8	49.5	28.8	15.4
Reject war as an instrument of national policy	63.1	74.4	82.0	92.6
Oppose the equal rights amendment[a]	36.9	30.7	13.7	3.8
Oppose capital punishment	45.9	68.3	78.8	76.9

Source: James Foyle Miller, *A Study of United Methodists and Social Issues* (General Council on Ministries, United Methodist Church, 1983), pp. 8–9.
a. Contrary to official position taken by the United Methodist church.

witness of the Christian faith," a degree of commitment that was expressed by 53 percent of local clergy, 75 percent of national staff, and 77 percent of bishops.[78]

The 1982 Gallup poll of religious attitudes included a question on "increasing the amount of government spending for social programs." Among members of Protestant denominations regarded by Gallup as mainline, 59 percent said they were opposed to such increases and only 38 percent in favor. Mainline Protestants were considerably more conservative in their responses to this question than were either Gallup's category of evangelical Protestants (49 percent favorable, 47 percent opposed), or Catholics (56 percent favorable, 43 percent opposed).[79]

Surveys on electoral choices in the 1980 and 1984 presidential elections bear out the impression that mainline Protestants are politically somewhat more conservative than the national average. The CBS/*New York Times* survey[80] of voters as they left the polls in 1980 found the following percentages:

Voters	Reagan	Carter	Anderson
White Protestants	63	31	6
Catholics	49	42	7
Jews	39	44	15
Black Protestants	11	85	3

The University of Michigan's 1980 National Election Survey[81] found the following divisions within the major mainline Protestant denominations:

Voters	Reagan	Carter	Anderson
Episcopalians	69	25	6
Lutherans	56	31	12
Methodists	53	40	5
Presbyterians	67	24	7
United Church of Christ	57	39	4

The relatively small majority for Reagan among Methodists was probably the result of the high numbers of black Methodists, most of whom are organized in three independently organized black Methodist denominations, and the large proportion of Methodists in the South, where Carter retained some of his regional favorite-son popularity. Among northern members of the predominantly white United Methodist church, the vote for Reagan was probably at least as high as among members of the United Church of Christ.

Economic, regional, and secular ideological interests, and inherited loyalties to the Republican party, of course, were important factors in moving substantial majorities of white Episcopalians, Presbyterians,

Lutherans, Methodists, and members of the United Church of Christ
to vote for Ronald Reagan in 1980. But traditional Protestant values
probably also played a part. The theme words of the 1980 Republican
platform, "Family, Neighborhood, Work, Peace, Freedom," were
practically a summary of the Protestant ethic. When Reagan called
for the return of "voluntary, nondenominational prayer" to the public
schools, and promised that under a Reagan administration "traditional
moral values" would be "reflected in public policy," he appealed not
only to fundamentalists but also to many members of mainline
denominations who remained loyal to conservative moral values they
had learned in Protestant Sunday schools.[82]

THE MAINLINE CHURCHES MEET RONALD REAGAN

During the four years of Reagan's first term the national leaderships
of most of the mainline denominations and their Washington offices
directed a steady barrage of opposition and criticism at most aspects
of the administration's program. In May 1981 the governing board
of the NCC issued a manifesto charging that the administration's policies represented "a reversal of direction for this country as a whole,
and [threatened] the vision of America as the model and embodiment of a just and humane society." The administration's philosophy,
the NCC maintained, was "not just to cut back on human services,
but to deny that people are entitled to them." In foreign policy the
administration "would shore up repressive regimes around the world
by military assistance." Reagan, the NCC said, aimed to make the
United States "number one in military dominance, in the ability to
impose our will on others or to kill multitudes in the attempt." The
administration's tax program would produce "a substantial redistribution of wealth to those already wealthy." In the NCC's view the
Reagan administration was the embodiment of "an old and seductive
vision of what America is all about," a vision of "America as private
opportunity and empire." The NCC urged an alternative vision of
"America as public responsibility and compassionate neighbor."[83]

As the 1980s proceeded, some mainline leaders proposed that the
churches go beyond combating the Reagan administration and promote the restructuring of American society in line with collectivist
and equalitarian values—in effect, supply the missing noncommunist
left wing of American politics. Peggy Billings, director of the Christian

Social Involvement section of the Methodist Women's Division, for example, wrote in the Methodist magazine *Engage/Social Action* that the existing American social system reflects "the heavy emphasis that Western traditions place on individualism," which "is alien to Hebrew thought as developed in early biblical texts." The resulting inequality separates "people into the categories of 'ruler' and 'ruled,' 'leaders' and 'followers,' 'managers' and 'workers,' ending up with a world in which the former always seems to have and the latter always seems to have not, or at least to have less." In such a world the obligation of the church is clear: "It is not our message; it is God's message." The energies of Christians "must be given over to working in the midst of our society for the specific conditions that promote equality, and not those that will perpetuate privilege." She made clear the kind of privilege she had in mind: "God does not feel at home in the corporate board rooms of multinational corporations."[84]

Exit polls on election day 1984 indicated that the political distance between the mainline leaderships and their laities had if anything widened since 1980. The CBS/*New York Times* exit poll found that support for Reagan among all white Protestants had risen to 73 percent, and among nonevangelical white Protestants to 69 percent. A national exit poll taken for the *Los Angeles Times* found voting for Reagan by Episcopalians was somewhat lower than had been shown by the University of Michigan survey in 1980. Among Presbyterians, Reagan's support stayed about the same, though some 1980 voters for John Anderson apparently swung in 1984 to Walter Mondale. But among Methodists and Lutherans, backing for Reagan in 1984 substantially increased.[85]

Voters	Reagan	Mondale
Episcopalians	60	40
Lutherans	66	34
Methodists	65	35
Presbyterians	68	32

A MANAGERIAL REVOLUTION

How did the gap develop between the positions advocated by mainline church offices in Washington and the political approach actually supported by majorities of mainline Protestants in the polling booths? Most mainline church lobbyists personally hold liberal political and social views that they derive from their own interpretations of Christianity, whether shaped by the Social Gospel, liberation theology, or some other source. Among the seventeen Washington mainline church representatives who responded to a brief questionnaire sent in 1983 to twenty-seven key staff members, twelve said they were registered Democrats, five were independents, and none were Republicans. On an "ideological scale of 1 to 5, on which Ronald Reagan is a 4, Edward Kennedy a 2, someone to the right of Reagan a 5, someone to the left of Kennedy a 1, and someone between Reagan and Kennedy a 3," four placed themselves at 1 (left of Kennedy), six at 2 (Kennedy), four at 3 (somewhere between Kennedy and Reagan), and the other three skipped the question. Of the four who had indicated on the party identification question they were independents, two placed themselves to the left of Kennedy on the ideological question. On a question asking if government in the United States is spending too much, too little, or about right for various purposes, fifteen indicated too little for welfare; thirteen too little for environmental protection; and all seventeen too much for military defense. On a question as to whether the United States should "rely more on market forces to make economic decisions, more on government, or about the same as now," twelve indicated they would rely more on government, one preferred more on the market, one about the same as now, and the other three gave qualified replies or did not answer.

Some of the churches' Washington representatives argue that their personal views are not relevant because in their public activities they are expressing not their own preferences but the views of their churches as set forth in various "social principles," "social statements," or "resolutions on social policy" adopted at church conventions, general conferences, general synods, or general assemblies.[86]

These resolutions and policy statements do indeed give at least general support to liberal approaches on a wide range of national and international issues. In 1980 the General Conference of the United Methodist church, for example, passed resolutions on fifty-one separate topics, endorsing causes ranging from national health insurance to sovereignty for the Lakota Indians, from nuclear disarmament to boycotting J. P. Stevens. The 1983 General Assembly of the reconstituted United Presbyterian church (rejoining at last the long-divided branches of northern and southern Presbyterianism) passed resolutions expressing generally liberal views on political, social, and economic issues under forty-six topic headings. (Sometimes, though, the jump from resolution to application is fairly broad. In 1981 the Methodists' Washington office opposed the Reagan administration's proposal for returning responsibility for social programs to the states on the ground that such a change would go against the General Conference's resolution calling for a government "guarantee of the right to adequate food, clothing, shelter, education, and health care.")[87]

Why do churches with at least moderately conservative majorities among their memberships approve, through their governing bodies, liberal policy statements? Part of the reason may be that church activists, even at the local level, tend to be more liberal than church memberships as a whole, though evidence on this is mixed. It may also be that as part of a kind of moral check-and-balance system some conservatives are willing to have their church take more liberal positions than they themselves favor. In addition, churches are not (and do not pretend to be) pure democracies. Clergy are represented far out of proportion to their share of church membership in church legislative bodies. In the Methodist General Conference, for example, one-half of the delegates are clergy elected by clergy; in the General Synod of the United Church of Christ, one-third ("a pretty fair dose of affirmative action," Paul Kittlaus admitted); in the Presbyterian General Assembly, one-half; in the Episcopal House of Deputies (which shares authority with the House of Bishops), one-half. Even lay delegates in most denominations are selected through procedures that strongly favor established leaderships.

But perhaps the most significant reason for the disparity is an organizational change within the mainline churches, described by Richard Hutcheson, a Presbyterian minister with long experience in his church's national bureaucracy. In the late 1960s and early 1970s a "wave of reorganizational restructuring swept through the mainline denominations," leaving the "church agency organizations made to order for managers." Almost always these managers were drawn from the ranks of what Hutcheson calls "the liberal-ecumenical faction in the mainline churches." There was, he observes, "nothing sinister about it . . . but the liberal ecumenicals—perhaps because they are by inclination more alert to the new, open to the secular world, and inclined to respect science in any form—have become the skilled process managers, strategy planners, and agents of change."[88]

A major result of this "managerial revolution" in the mainline churches "was to place control of the denominational representative bodies in the hands of the church bureaucracies." From his own experience, Hutcheson concludes, "In this managerial age, if you can control the agenda, control the form in which business is presented, control the source of expert advice on the basis of which decisions are made, and control the way decisions are implemented once they are made, you may lose a few, and you may give up a few, for window dressing, but I guarantee you can control most of the outcome of the representative body."[89]

Debate at church conferences, assemblies, or conventions is often heated, and recommendations of established leaderships, particularly on issues with high emotional content like the ordination of homosexual clergy, are sometimes overruled. But on most subjects, resolutions prepared in advance by leaders and staff are voted through with little dissent. Delegates brought together for a few days from all over the country—in some cases from all over the world—are presented with huge agendas, covering a multiplicity of topics on most of which most of the delegates cannot possibly be particularly knowledgeable. Not surprisingly, they usually follow the guidance of established leaders.

The National Council of Churches, which has often shaped the direction taken by the mainline denominations on social issues, has not been even nominally accountable to the memberships of participating churches. Its policies have been set by a governing board composed mainly of staff members appointed by other staff members in denominational headquarters. An extensive investigation of NCC governance by the *United Methodist Reporter* in 1983 concluded that "by giving denominational agency staff so much authority over NCC actions, it is readily possible for these persons to use the NCC to advance their pet projects. . . . In their own agencies, these same staff persons have to get approval for their actions from their agency board. But on the NCC oversight committee, they are the board."[90]

MEMBERSHIP DRAIN

From 1970 to 1980 all of the larger mainline denominations suffered significant membership losses: the United Presbyterian church (northern) lost 21 percent; the Episcopal church, 15 percent; the Presbyterian church in the United States (southern), 12 percent; the United Church of Christ, 11 percent; the United Methodist church, 10 percent; and the Lutheran Church of America, 8 percent. During the same period, important evangelical and fundamentalist Protestant denominations achieved spectacular membership increases: Assemblies of God up 70 percent, Jehovah's Witnesses up 45 percent, Seventh-Day Adventists up 36 percent, and the Southern Baptist Convention (which in 1970 supplanted the United Methodist church as the largest single Protestant denomination) up 16 percent. The Mormons grew by 36 percent during the decade to become the nation's seventh-largest denomination. The Catholic church grew 5 percent—largely as a result of heavy immigration by Catholic Hispanics.[91]

Sociological studies commissioned by some of the mainline denominations during the 1970s generally pointed to causes other than the churches' political involvements as the major reasons for losses of membership. Declining numbers, these studies concluded, were largely traceable to demographic or socioeconomic factors. Birth rates were falling more rapidly among members of mainline denominations. Migration within the United States was away from the Northeast and North Central regions, where the mainline churches have traditionally been strong, and toward the West and Southwest, where evangelical churches have always been popular. (For the United Methodist church, at least, this argument does not seem consistent with the discovery at the end of the decade that the church's loss was greatest, 19 percent, in the West, which led in general population increase.) Mainline church members were disproportionately represented at higher socioeconomic levels, where the trend away from formal religion had been most pronounced (a finding that seems to indicate the presence of factors beyond narrowly socioeconomic causes). Some studies also placed part of the blame on internal church causes, such as the not-surprising finding that churches with less competent pastors are more likely to lose members.[92]

A strikingly different explanation for the churches' membership losses was offered by Dean Kelley, a liberal Methodist minister on the staff of the NCC. Kelley agreed with the sociologists that the social and political stands taken by the mainline denominations were not in themselves driving away many members. But the trouble, he maintained, went deeper than socioeconomic factors or personnel problems. Changes in church membership, Kelley argued in *Why Conservative Churches are Growing,* are closely related to the extent to which churches meet the needs that draw most people to religion. He cited survey evidence supporting his contention that most church members look to their churches primarily to find "purpose, promise, and possibility" in "the human predicament." This does not mean that most of the laity oppose efforts by the churches to help deal with material or social problems: "Men still need food, shelter, clothing, jobs, education, medical care." But liberal churches that allow commitments to social action to crowd out "their unique and essential contribution to healing the world's wounds: *meaning*" will lose members to more conservative or evangelical denominations that concentrate on religion's "distinctive and indispensable service: making sense of life."[93]

Part of the reason that political stands taken by the mainline denominations at the national level did not cause much immediate controversy in local churches during the 1970s was that, except in a few highly publicized instances like the Angela Davis case, most church members were hardly aware of the political activities being carried on in their churches' names. Among those who were aware, many regarded the church lobbies as ineffective. "Everyone knows," said Martin Marty, the leading historian of American Protestantism, "that when the mainline churches take a position, it is only six people in a room on Riverside Drive [the headquarters in New York of the NCC and several mainline denominations]."[94]

In the early 1980s, however, charges, sometimes overstated or unbalanced, by national media and conservative church groups that, as the headline on one magazine article put it, "your church offerings . . . may be supporting revolution instead of religion," brought the whole question of political action by the churches to the attention of local congregations.[95]

Under fire, national staffs of mainline churches responded for the most part with vitriol and cries of "McCarthyism." Some of their leaders acknowledged, however, that a substantial gap had opened between some of the social positions advanced by the churches and the views of majorities among their members. Paul Kittlaus said in an interview, "The United Church of Christ is most liberal at the general synod level, and most conservative at the local church level." Charles Bergstrom, chief Washington spokesman for the Lutherans, commented that "church activists tend to be liberal, and, since these are the people who go to church conventions, their views are represented beyond their numbers in the church." Joyce Hamlin, director of the Washington office of the Methodists' Women's Division, said that "probably about seventy percent of Methodists are fairly conservative. Methodists, after all, are middle America."[96]

Church leaders who acknowledged that the churches' social positions differ to some degree from the views of majorities among their members did not necessarily draw the conclusion that these positions should be modified. James Hamilton, assistant general secretary of the NCC (the same who twenty years before had helped lead the civil rights fight), said that "the church has a responsibility to be both representative and prophetic. The trick is to prevent too large a gap from opening between the two." For Joyce Hamlin, "the leadership of the church tries to be in tune with its constituencies. But it is much more important to be in tune with Jesus Christ than with the person in the pew."[97]

Some, however, suggested that the social role of the churches should be more carefully defined. Randolph Nugent, director of the Methodist Board of Global Ministries, which has been a particular target for conservative critics, said that the church should not shrink from dealing with social problems but should concentrate on areas in which it has particular expertise. "The church does not know how to produce steel, or how to make cars, but it does have something to say about the impact of industrialization on people. . . . Economic analysis is important, but economic analysis does not take into consideration human costs, which is where the church should put its first attention." Nugent said that the church can interact beneficially with capitalism. "Capitalism keeps things moving in the economy. The church, through its investments, utilizes capitalism. But ours is a moderated capitalism. . . . Protestantism helped encourage the rise of capitalism, through its emphasis on the Biblical teaching that God gave man dominion over the earth. So Protestantism has a special responsibility to see to it that the dominion is exercised wisely and justly."[98]

Black Activism

While leaderships and laities in most mainline Protestant denominations seemed to be moving politically in opposite directions, their counterparts in the black Protestant churches remained closely united. The 1964 Goldwater campaign, in which the national Republican leadership was perceived to oppose further federal action to promote racial equality, had virtually wiped out what remained of Republican support among blacks. Lyndon Johnson won a majority of 94 percent among blacks in 1964—a Democratic advantage only marginally reduced in later elections. After passage of the Civil Rights Act of 1964 and the Voting Rights Act of 1965, black registration and voting began to rise, though still lagging well behind the percentages of most white groups.

The black churches, mostly evangelical or mainline Protestant, continued to function as centers of black political activity. Many black ministers regularly endorsed favored candidates in Democratic primaries and urged support for the Democratic ticket in general elections. In order to protect their churches' tax exemptions, ministers usually designated these endorsements as "personal." But most of them did not hesitate to put the moral prestige of their church offices behind their political recommendations. "You would be surprised at the awesome power that a Baptist minister has," said the Reverend T. J. Jemison, president of the National Baptist Convention, the nation's largest black denomination, when he endorsed Jesse Jackson, himself a Baptist minister, for president in 1983.[99]

During the 1970s many black leaders, including both ministers and politicians, became increasingly restive over the black community's relationship to the Democratic party. Black support for the Democrats had become so overwhelming and apparently unshakable that most Republicans did not make serious efforts to attract blacks and most white Democratic politicians, in the view of blacks at least, tended to take the black vote for granted. Jesse Jackson, creator and guiding spirit of Operation PUSH (People United to Save Humanity), an organization dedicated to promoting black economic progress, for one, suggested that blacks consider establishing a political third force that could hold the balance of power between the two major parties in close elections. In some state and local races Jackson endorsed progressive Republicans. The rise of Ronald Reagan, perceived as Goldwater's political heir, to leadership of the national Republican party at the end of the 1970s, however, seemed to limit opportunities for this kind of strategic collaboration.[100]

In the third year of Reagan's presidency, Jackson announced that he would seek the Democratic nomination for president in 1984 as the leader of a "religious crusade" to "save the soul" of America. (Representative Shirley Chisholm, a black congresswoman from Brooklyn, had run for president in 1972 but had made little headway.) Jackson, who in his youth had been a sometimes impetuous aide to Martin Luther King, regularly linked his political involvements to his sense of religious mission. "I'm blessed, you see," he once told the *Los Angeles Times*. "I am a conduit . . . [and] many ideas flow through and from me from the Lord. . . . I stand at the very center of moral power." Most members of the secular black political establishment, who resented Jackson's skill at capturing the limelight and his occasional support for Republican candidates in states like Illinois and Pennsylvania, backed the presidential candidacy of Walter Mondale. But black church groups for the most part rallied enthusiastically behind Jackson. The Jackson for President Campaign Committee sent a memorandum to thousands of black ministers "detailing how they could raise funds for the candidate without violating federal election law." In some churches, Sunday morning plate collections were taken to aid the Jackson campaign. Blacks voted overwhelmingly for Jackson in most presidential primaries. But outside the black community Jackson had little success at putting together a multiracial "rainbow coalition" of disadvantaged groups.[101]

Early in the primaries Jackson became embroiled in controversy over the support he was receiving from Minister Louis Farrakhan, leader of a sect of Black Muslims (descended from the Nation of Islam, a communitarian religious group founded by Elijah Muhammad, a black prophet, in Detroit in the 1930s). Farrakhan made slurring references to Israel and Judaism and described Adolf Hitler as a "very great man," though "wickedly great." At one point Farrakhan appeared to threaten the life of a black journalist who had reported that Jackson sometimes called New York City "Hymie town." Jackson's resistance to repudiating Farrakhan reinforced the hostility that many Jews and other white liberals already felt toward the campaign because of Jackson's sympathetic attitude toward Palestinian irredentism. Though Farrakhan occasionally supplied Jackson with bodyguards and other assistance, his faction of the Black Muslims, numbering no more than 10,000 members, played only a minor role in the campaign, compared for instance to the 7-million-member National Baptists with their 29,000 ministers.[102]

Jackson entered the Democratic convention in July with the support of about one-tenth of the delegates, most of them blacks, but he failed to win major concessions from Mondale, who by then was ducking identification with so-called special interest groups.

During the fall campaign, drives by black churches to increase black registration produced impressive results, though apparently the gains were smaller than those achieved by conservative white evangelicals. Black ministers supporting Mondale in the general election were even more direct in their political appeals than were their white evangelical counterparts backing Reagan. In Alabama, for example, an election day poll by CBS found that 29 percent of all Mondale voters, more than half of whom were black, had been urged by their preachers to support the Democratic candidate, compared to only 9 percent of Reagan backers who reported direct appeals by their preachers to vote for the Republican. (Such figures understate actual political activity by the clergy because most ministers act with some degree of circumspection to protect tax exemptions.) On election day, blacks cast 90 percent of their vote for Mondale and were the one group in the former New Deal coalition that maintained historic levels of support for the Democratic ticket.[103]

After the election the black leadership in general and Jesse Jackson in particular entered a period of reflection on the future role of the black community in politics. Overtures by the Reagan administration to win a significant minority of blacks to the Republicans seemed to have little immediate effect. Most black politicians continued to believe that the Democratic party, despite its faults, remained the best political vehicle for black interests. The elevation of Congressman William Gray, a black clergyman from Philadelphia, to the chairmanship of the powerful House Budget Committee early in 1985 gave blacks an influential spokesman within the Democratic national leadership. But among the younger generation of blacks who had supported Jackson in the presidential primaries, there was renewed talk, encouraged by Jackson, about the option of organizing blacks as a political third force.[104]

Future party alignment apart, the politically active black churches appeared to take from their 1984 experience a renewed zest for politics and a conviction that the churches should if anything extend their political involvements. Though many of the churches have approached or passed the limits on political action set by the Internal

Revenue code, none of the other major political combatants seemed anxious to challenge them on the tax-exemption issue—partly because conservatives, too, have in recent campaigns been benefiting from clerical support.

The historical development of the black community has virtually required that black churches offer political leadership, which in the middle years of the 1980s still seems to a great extent justified. But as blacks move more fully into the mainstream of American life, their churches are bound to come under increasing public pressure to reassess the scope of their political roles and ultimately to bring their practices more into line with the norms expected for other churches. (The whole question of the extent to which all churches should participate directly in politics will be discussed more fully in chapter 7.)

Catholics in Ferment

During the post-Vietnam years, the Roman Catholic church, the nation's largest single denomination, faced its own internal crisis, partly growing out of differences over the church's social role.

The Catholic doctrine that the state in a Catholic society has a responsibility to uphold the church, based on the idealist medieval doctrine that the "temporal sword" of the state should be "available at the will and command of the priest for the protection of the religious unity of Christendom and for the extermination of heresy," had seemed unalterable and unbending. A series of nineteenth and twentieth century popes, beginning with Gregory XVI, had consistently condemned "modern liberties, especially freedom of religion." Pius XII, entering the papacy in 1939, had reaffirmed the traditional view: "That which does not correspond to the truth and the norm of morality has, objectively, no right either to existence or to propaganda or to action." In countries where Catholicism was not politically dominant, Pius XII found room for tolerance: "Not to inhibit [error] by means of public laws and coercive methods can nevertheless be justified in the interests of a higher and greater good." But such tolerance was entirely tactical. As a moral objective the idealist view that the state should on matters of religion and morals be the dutiful instrument of the church remained fully in force.[105]

In the United States, so progressive and "modern" a churchman as Monsignor John A. Ryan wrote, with Frances Boland, "If the state is under moral compulsion to profess and promote religion it is obviously obliged to promote and profess only the religion that is true; for no individual, no group of individuals, no society, no state is justified in supporting error or in according to error the same recognition as to truth." Monsignor Ryan and his coauthor argued that non-Catholic Americans should not find the church's position disturbing or offensive, because "the danger of religious intolerance towards non-Catholics in the United States is so improbable and so far in the future that it should not occupy their time and attention."[106]

GOODBYE TO CONSTANTINE

There had always been some within the American Catholic hierarchy who recognized that the church's commitment to state-imposed religion, even if only theoretic, raised a difficult barrier against full participation by Catholicism in American society. When the Second Vatican Council convened in Rome in 1962, delegates from the United States, particularly Cardinal Francis Spellman of New York, who carried on the Americanist tendency launched by John Ireland and others in the 1890s, were determined to win enactment of a Declaration of Religious Freedom. To advance this objective, in April 1963 Spellman persuaded Pope John XXIII to name as one of the council's theological advisors an erudite Jesuit who had sometimes seemed a thorn in Spellman's own side: John Courtney Murray, America's leading Catholic theologian. Murray had been silenced during the 1950s when he dared to differ on the church-state question with the Vatican's powerful and traditionalist Cardinal Alfredo Ottaviani. That very spring of 1963 he had been banned from lecturing at Catholic University in Washington, D.C.[107]

Murray was far from being a humanist libertarian. "By divine ordinance," he wrote, "this world is to be ruled by a dyarchy of authorities, within which the temporal is subordinate to the spiritual." He warmly rebuked the Supreme Court for its 1948 *McCollum* decision prohibiting the use of public schools for voluntary religious instruction. The Court, he complained, had replaced the "constitutional formula no 'establishment of religion,'" with the "more accordian-like slogan, 'separation of church and state.' " Though enjoying a newsmagazine reputation as an ecumenicist, Murray was not above getting off occasional whacks at the church's departed Protestant brethren: Connecticut's law against the sale of contraceptives, he wrote, "reveals a characteristic Comstockian-Protestant ignorance of the rules of traditional jurisprudence" (the effective approach, Murray suggested, would be to go after the *manufacturers* of contraceptives); and the "American pragmatist mind" does "not hearken to discourse of the morality of war" because "it bears beneath its pragmatism the American-Protestant taint of pacifism."[108]

Murray doubted no more than Cardinal Ottaviani or Monsignor Ryan that "religious pluralism is against the will of God." But pluralism, he had decided, "is the human condition; it is written into the script of history." For the very reason of human imperfection, no government should be entrusted with responsibility for imposing a religion— a view that he identified with the American founding fathers.[109]

Murray distinguished between "the public profession of religion by society" and "the care of religion by the public power." The first is proper and, in fact, obligatory. Efforts to root out public acknowledgment of religion stem from the "Jacobin revolutionary principle which abolishes all social institutions intermediate between the individual and the state," rather than from the American tradition of religious liberty. But attempts at care of religion by the state improperly extend the authority of government into the spiritual realm. Government "is not the judge or the representative of transcendent truth with regard to man's eternal destiny; it is not man's guide to heaven." Failure to differentiate between these two entirely distinct concepts of church and society had led to the church's misguided endorsement of state-imposed religion.[110]

When Murray arrived in Rome after his appointment as advisor to the Vatican Council, he found that the subject of religious liberty had been dropped from the council's agenda. Working with Spellman, he rallied the American delegates to insist on its restoration. During the next two years, the American delegation fought off repeated efforts by traditionalists to sidetrack the proposed Declaration on Religious Liberty. On September 21, just before the council's end, the declaration, holding that "the right to religious freedom has its foundation in the very dignity of the human person," largely written by Murray, was approved. "A very ancient order of things," wrote Robert Cushman, an American delegate-observer, "at least in principle—passed away. In principle, the era of Constantine—sixteen hundred years of it—passed away."[111]

In an address to the world's governments at the end of 1965 the new pope, Paul VI, declared, "What does the Church ask of you today? Nothing but freedom." Murray, writing the following year, observed, "The notion of the sacral society is dismissed into history, beyond recall. The free society of today is recognized to be secular."[112]

The Vatican Council's Declaration of Religious Liberty sprang from a changed view of the role of the state rather than from any abandonment by the Catholic church of its claim to unique spiritual authority. The church had accepted the inevitability of social pluralism in a fallen world, but it had not accepted religious pluralism in the sense of acknowledging that all human institutions, including religious institutions, are finite and relative. Richard McBrien of Notre Dame, who has perhaps succeeded Murray as America's best known Catholic theologian and is in many ways a social and cultural progressive, has written, "There are many churches, but one Body of Christ. Within the community of churches, however, there is one Church that alone embodies and manifests all the institutional elements that are necessary for the whole Body. In Catholic doctrine and theology, that one Church is the Catholic Church."[113]

Catholicism's enduring claim to be the one true church, while perhaps inevitably irritating to some non-Catholics, is not inconsistent with social pluralism. Indeed, if the Catholic church were to give up its claim to *religious* primacy, American pluralism would be poorer rather than richer, because the option of choosing an institution claiming unique spiritual authority and designation by the founder of the Christian religion would no longer be available. (Some of the fundamentalist faiths make somewhat similar claims, but not for their churches as institutions in history.)

THE CATHOLIC LOBBY

The Declaration on Religious Liberty may well have been, as Murray maintained, the most important single product of the Second Vatican Council. But the more general relaxation of traditional discipline and the openness to modernizing change, which the council symbolized even if it did not in all cases authorize, were more immediately wrenching to the institutional life of American Catholicism. According to James Hitchcock, a Catholic traditionalist, relaxation of discipline contributed to a moral and cultural atmosphere in which "nuns seek to become priests, priests get married, and married people get divorced in ever greater numbers." Taking advantage of the liturgical flexibility approved by the council, Catholic modernizers were "devising liturgies which have almost no organic connection with those of the Church, or else are abandoning liturgy altogether."[114]

American Catholic advocates of liberation theology, itself in part derived from the spirit of innovation and reform unleashed by the council, called for even more rapid change. The time had come, Rosemary Reuther wrote, for "gathering the children of light and repelling the children of darkness," and for moving to correct "the irony . . . that the local churches are generally in the possession of the hard-hearted who bar the doors in the meeting places against the agape community. . . ."[115]

In the short run at least, the sense of upheaval generated by the council, along with other forces at work in the common social environment, were severely traumatic for American Catholicism. "American Catholics," James Hennessey wrote, "had now to cope with the staggering reality of dissent, change, and diversity at the highest levels of the Church they had grown up believing was 'the same all over the world.'" A perplexed Jesuit, Walter Burghardt, asked, "How much discontinuity is compatible with Catholic continuity?"[116]

Whether as a result of the changes issuing from the council or because the reforms embodying them had been too long delayed or, as seems probable, because of some combination of these causes and other social forces, American Catholicism began to suffer institutional reverses. The portion of Catholics regularly attending mass dropped, according to Gallup surveys, from 75 percent in 1957 to 54 percent in 1975. The number of Catholic seminarians fell from almost 50,000 in 1964 to just over 13,000 in 1980. A 1979 survey found that "16.1 percent of Americans who were raised as Catholics profess another or no religion when they reach adulthood." Total membership increased slightly, but only because of the large influx of Catholic Hispanics.[117]

Moves instituted by the council to broaden participation in church governance had the effect of reducing the authority of bishops over their dioceses, though the administrative structure of Catholicism still remained considerably more hierarchic than those of most Protestant denominations. Perhaps reacting in part to this diminution of their local authority, American bishops began acting together more as a national body. Their annual November meetings in Washington, D.C., became forums for issuing pronouncements on social and governmental as well as ecclesiastical matters. Rather than spreading these pronouncements over a wide range of topics, as some of the Protestant churches were doing, the Catholic bishops generally concentrated on a few major issues. Some of these became subjects of pastoral letters, such as those on the world food crisis (1974), race relations (1979), the role of the United States in Central America (1981), and nuclear arms (1983).[118]

The pronouncements of the bishops on domestic policy reflected an approach broadly favorable to an extensive welfare state, an attitude often linked to the concept of the "third way" between free-enterprise capitalism and socialism that had been set forth and elaborated in numerous papal encyclicals. In 1974 the bishops quoted with approval a warning by Paul VI that, "like the ideology of Marxism, the liberal (capitalist) ideology likewise calls for careful discernment." In foreign policy the bishops gradually moved from enthusiastic support for American preeminence in the world as a bulwark against communism, a position represented by figures like Cardinal Spellman, to a position sternly critical of the backing given by American administrations to right-wing military dictatorships in third world countries.[119]

Like the mainline Protestant churches the national structure of Catholicism went through a "managerial revolution" in the early 1970s. One result was a stronger role for the Washington bureaucracy attached to the National Council of Catholic Bishops and the United States Catholic Conference—"two bodies," in the unadmiring view of James Hitchcock, "which house innumerable committees, special offices, and designated experts in every conceivable area of both ecclesiastical and social life."[120] The Catholic policy experts tended, like their mainline Protestant counterparts, to be liberals, though often of a somewhat more cautious variety. But on some social issues, particularly those dealing with sex and the family, the Catholic activists parted company with their usual allies in Washington's liberal coalition.

DEFENDING THE UNBORN

During the 1960s the Catholic hierarchy carried on a vigorous resistance against contraception. Many predicted that the church, recognizing that large numbers of otherwise observant Catholics were already practicing artificial birth control, would soon modify its position. Instead, in July 1968, acting against the majority recommendation of a special commission created by his predecessor, Pope Paul issued a papal encyclical reaffirming the church's prohibition. "The encyclical," wrote Andrew Greeley, a Chicago priest and sociologist (and later best-selling novelist), "was ignored in practice by both the clergy and the laity in the United States. Almost four-fifths of both groups agreed that birth control was not sinful." At their November meeting in 1968 the bishops nevertheless issued a pastoral letter firmly supporting the pope's position. Resentment over the church's policy on birth control, Greeley claimed, rather than feelings of dislocation stemming from the changes instituted by the Vatican Council, was the chief cause of American Catholicism's subsequent internal troubles.[121]

The apparatus set up by the bishops within the national Catholic bureaucracy to combat contraception was soon turned to an even more contentious issue: abortion. Before the middle of the 1960s, abortion had not been much of an issue in the United States. State laws against it apparently were violated fairly frequently but were strongly supported by both the religious and medical communities and were rarely challenged openly. But during the 1960s, improved medical techniques, increasing preference for small families, and the emerging feminist movement contributed to a gradual change in public attitudes. In 1967 Colorado and California reformed their laws to permit abortions under a wide range of circumstances (including rape, incest, and danger of impairment of the physical or mental health of the mother). By the end of 1972 eighteen states had either modified or repealed their abortion laws. Statewide referenda on repeal in Michigan and North Dakota in 1972, however, were defeated.

In January 1973 this normal political process of debate and search for consensus was abruptly terminated. The Supreme Court's decision in *Roe v. Wade* established a constitutional right to abortion during the first six months of pregnancy, absolute in the first trimester and limited in the second trimester only by the state's right to enact procedural regulations "reasonably related to maternal health."[122]

Roe v. Wade represented a new high-water mark for the judicial activist tendency. Justice Harry Blackmun, writing for the majority, based the right to abortion on a "right to personal privacy," which he somehow found in "the Fourteenth Amendment's concept of personal liberty." But the Court seemed to be acting on the conviction that it possessed what Lawrence Friedman later called a "cleanup function," requiring it to serve as a sort of super legislature with responsibility for cleansing the system of outmoded laws that for some reason do not yield to ordinary politics. "What is frightening about *Roe*," John Ely wrote in the *Yale Law Journal* a few months after the decision, "is that this super-protected right [to privacy] is not inferable from the language of the Constitution, the framers' thinking respecting the specific problems in issue, any general value from the provisions they included, or the nation's governmental structure."[123]

The sweeping nature of the Court's decision practically guaranteed that opponents of abortion would fight back in a similarly draconian spirit. Many lay Catholics who had stopped listening to their bishops over contraception and had been prepared to accept some modification of absolutist laws against abortion were startled and outraged by the Court's contention that for the first six months of gestation, unborn life has no rights whatever. They agreed with the bishops that the Court's ruling violated the fundamental value attached to individual human life not only by Catholicism but by the entire Judeo-Christian tradition, and indeed by most forms of Western humanism. Catholic opponents of abortion, Raymond Tatolovich and Byron Daunes wrote in *Commonweal*, were "psychologically prepared to accept defeat in those states which enacted abortion reform, though they clearly did not relish the prospect." But "deciding this question in the courts . . . was steadfastly opposed by the anti-abortion forces because it undermined the process of negotiation and compromise and denied effective representation to the unborn."[124]

Opponents of abortion organized politically, not simply to restore the states' authority over the issue as it had existed before *Roe*, but to enact a constitutional amendment that would make outright prohibition of abortion part of the permanent law of the land. The Office for Pro-life Activities of the United States Catholic Conference, originally set up by the bishops in the 1960s to coordinate the campaign against contraception, became the national nerve center for Catholic participation in the drive for a constitutional amendment. Though kept at arm's length by the USCC's Department for Social Development and World Peace, which felt uncomfortable with some of the political associations that came with the abortion issue, the Office for Pro-life Activities quickly became a significant force in national politics.

In 1976 the bishops expressed disappointment over Jimmy Carter's ambiguous responses to their questions on abortion but stopped short of indicating a preference for President Ford (who favored returning jurisdiction over the issue to the states). In 1978 the defeat of a number of candidates who had been targeted by the antiabortion forces, notably Senator Dick Clark in Iowa, was widely attributed to a block of single-issue voters, mainly Catholics, who cast their ballots on the abortion issue alone. Though small in numbers (providing a net advantage of about 3 percentage points for opponents of abortion, one poll indicated), this group was perceived as holding the balance of power in close elections.[125]

Politicians viewed the abortion issue as particularly important because it seemed to be a "conversion" issue, one that actually could move voters from one side of the partisan fence to the other. Of course, there were also some voters supporting the right to abortion (pro-choicers) who cast their ballots on the basis of that preference. But through the 1980 election at least, the political community generally agreed that single-issue pro-lifers outnumbered single-issue pro-choicers by several percentage points. Although polling evidence was inconclusive, several surveys did agree that "pro-life supporters seem more single-minded and determined than their pro-choice counterparts."[126]

Liberals within the hierarchy agreed with the church's opposition to abortion but were disturbed by the extent to which the issue seemed to be crowding out all others for growing numbers of Catholic voters. Monsignor Francis Lally, director of the Department for Social Development and World Peace, said in 1982, "There are many of us who are concerned about the phenomenon of single-issue voting. We are making a strong effort to emphasize that Catholic teaching is concerned with the whole span of life, not just with conception." At Lally's suggestion, the bishops issued a statement before the 1980 election urging "that voters . . . examine the positions of candidates on the full range of issues as well as the person's integrity, philosophy, and performance."[127]

THE BISHOPS WRITE A LETTER

Some Catholic liberals, particularly Bryan Hehir, Lally's deputy for international policy (Lally tended to concentrate on domestic issues), used the church's concern for human life, at first focused on issues of reproduction, as a means for turning the bishops' attention to questions of war and peace. "Until rather recently," Father Hehir said in 1981, "the church in the United States was not very active on foreign policy issues. Traditionally, the Vatican did not encourage the various national churches to become involved in foreign policy because it was the Vatican's feeling that the Holy See has a unique responsibility to establish the church's position on international issues. But after the Vatican Council, the church began to encourage the bishops to take positions on foreign policy, and in 1968 the American bishops laid out a foreign policy agenda."[128]

During the 1940s and the 1950s, Hehir said, the church's approach to international issues was largely shaped by its opposition to communism. "More recently, the church has become to understand the complexity of the communism issue. There is still recognition that communism is a danger, but also that it is not the only danger. The church does not now subscribe so much to the sharp dichotomy between East and West. The church's awareness of the enormous danger of nuclear weapons has intensified, and this has contributed to the church's change in attitude. The arms race has become the primary focus of the church's concern."[129]

At least since the Vatican Council, there had been a potential for discord between Catholic doctrine and American nuclear strategy. The council had condemned "any act of war aimed indiscriminately at the destruction of entire cities or of extensive areas along with their populations." This pronouncement could be interpreted as reprehending American deterrence doctrine, which is based on the assumption that neither the United States nor the Soviet Union will resort to a nuclear attack if each side knows the other will respond with a strike against the attacker's cities.[130]

A 1979 statement issued by the American bishops made the criticism explicit: "not only is it wrong to attack civilian populations, it is also wrong to threaten to attack them as a part of a strategy of deterrence." Testifying on behalf of the bishops before the Senate Foreign Relations Committee in September 1979, Cardinal John Krol of Philadelphia, generally regarded as a conservative within the hierarchy and a close personal associate of the new pope, John Paul II, seemed to go further. "Deterrence can be tolerated as a lesser evil than use, as long as serious negotiations are pursued, aimed at phasing out nuclear deterrence. If the pursuit of that goal is foresaken, the moral attitude of the Catholic Church would almost certainly have to shift to one of uncompromising condemnation of both use and possession of nuclear weapons."[131]

Cardinal Krol's testimony was interpreted by some Catholic liberals and doves to mean that if disarmament negotiations failed, the church would feel compelled to call on the United States to give up unilaterally its arsenal of nuclear weapons. Monsignor Vincent Yzermans wrote excitedly in the *New York Times* that the Catholic church was moving "dramatically and swiftly from the company of mainline Protestant and Evangelical churches into the quiet meeting place of the Society of Friends"—in other words, to outright pacifism.[132]

Some of the hierarchy disagreed. Cardinal Terrence Cooke of New York, whose charge included Catholic chaplains in the armed forces, wrote that the Catholic doctrine of just wars continued to hold that "a government has both the right and the duty to protect its people against unjust aggression," and that Catholics "who produce or who are assigned to handle" nuclear weapons systems could "do so in good conscience," as long as the United States was "sincerely trying to come up with a rational alternative" to deterrence. Bishop John J. O'Connor, a former navy chaplain and Cooke's auxiliary in the military vicarate, attacked a suggestion by a fellow bishop that Catholics should refrain from association "with the use or production of nuclear weapons." There was nothing, Bishop O'Connor said, "in official church teaching that suggests that our military people are engaging in immoral activity in carrying out their military responsibilities."[133]

At the 1980 meeting of the bishops in Washington just after Reagan's election as president, Bishop Thomas Gumbleton of Detroit, a founder of the American chapter of Pax Christi, a Catholic pacifist movement, called for a discussion of the morality of nuclear war. Though the subject was not on the agenda, Gumbleton was granted one hour, in the course of which, with help from other bishops, he built a persuasive case that a time of crisis was at hand. The following year a committee of five bishops was named to draft a pastoral letter on war and peace, with particular concentration on nuclear weapons. The committee, which included Bishops O'Connor and Gumbleton, was chaired by Archbishop Joseph Bernardin of Cincinnati, former president of the NCCB and widely identified as a rising star within the hierarchy.

For two years the Bernardin committee deliberated, hearing testimony from moral theologians, peace activists, and defense experts, non-Catholic as well as Catholic, and drawing on discussions that reached down to the parish level. While the committee worked, several bishops acted on their own—"we read about it in the newspapers," Bryan Hehir said—to oppose the Reagan administration's military buildup. In June 1981 Archbishop Raymond Hunthausen of Seattle called for unilateral disarmament and suggested that Catholics refuse to pay 50 percent of their federal income taxes—the share he calculated went for military spending. Three months later, Bishop Leroy Matthiesen of Amarillo, Texas, recommended that Catholics working at a nuclear warhead assembly plant in his diocese "seek new jobs or something that they could do which would contribute to life rather than destroy it." Neither appeal produced much noticeable response among lay Catholics, but the atmosphere seemed to be forming for a possible confrontation between the nation's government and its largest church.[134]

In November 1982 Bernardin—by then made cardinal and given charge of the Chicago diocese, a prize jewel in the crown of American Catholicism—presented a draft of the proposed pastoral letter at the bishops' annual meeting. The draft was, in a favored term of the time, heavily "nuanced," but its conclusion was clear: nuclear deterrence is a "key element" in a "sinful situation," barely tolerable as a means to prevent the use of nuclear weapons by others, and justifiable even in the short run only as "a step on the way toward progressive disarmament."[135]

Though some expressed disappointment that the draft did not condemn deterrence outright, liberals and doves were generally pleased. Conservatives, led by Cardinal Cooke, objected that the draft did not make sufficiently clear that the evils being deterred by the American nuclear force include not only nuclear war but also the danger of Soviet aggression and that it dealt with issues of war and peace in a context that was "almost secular." Archbishop Oscar Lipscomb of Mobile, Alabama, called upon his fellow bishops to emphasize that "we seek not survival but resurrection," a formulation that some in the press section found bizarre. Bernardin promised to have a revised draft ready for a special assembly of the bishops scheduled to meet in Chicago the following spring.

During the winter of 1983 the Reagan administration, which included several lay Catholics in its upper echelons, decided to head off what it at last recognized as a significant moral challenge to the nation's nuclear defense policy. On the drafting committee, Bishop O'Connor dug in against calling for a unilateral freeze in the deployment of nuclear weapons. The French and German Catholic bishops implored their American counterparts not to strike a pose that would undermine the credibility of the American deterrent and thereby increase the likelihood of war. Most influentially of all, the Vatican expressed concern that the committee's draft seemed to present political choices as moral judgments.[136]

In January, Bernardin and several associates were called to Rome. At a meeting with Cardinal Agostino Casaroli, the Vatican secretary of state, and with spokesmen for the European bishops, the Americans were advised that among other things the draft seemed to imply a parity within Catholic doctrine between the just-war theory and a tradition of pacifism like that of the Quakers, where in fact "there is only one Catholic tradition: the just-war theory." A more general criticism was that the draft did not distinguish sufficiently between moral imperatives, including protection of free societies as well as avoidance of war, and the practical steps through which these goals might be pursued. Proposals by the bishops on the latter, Cardinal Casaroli recommended, should be offered "in such a manner that it helps those [governmental] authorities to get a correct orientation according to the basic principles of human and Christian morals and not to create even greater difficulties for them in an area so enormously difficult and so full of responsibility."[137]

The new draft presented by Bernardin to the bishops in Chicago in May included modifications that made it more compatible with existing American policy but preserved much of the essential thrust of the earlier version. The revised draft unequivocally affirmed the just-war theory that nations have a "right to lawful self-defense," but it went on to emphasize the church's teaching that even in a just war civilian populations must not be purposely attacked. More attention was given to the political setting in which democratic values are threatened by the "Soviet imperial drive for hegemony." At Bishop O'Connor's insistence, "curb" was substituted for "halt" in a section calling for a check on "testing, production, and deployment of nuclear weapons systems"—a change that the White House imprudently hailed as a move toward sensible moderation. The new draft stressed "the distinction between our statement of moral principles . . . and our application of these to concrete issues." It specifically acknowledged that individual Catholics, particularly those in the armed forces and working in defense industries, may consider the application of these views differently. But the letter's conclusion remained that nuclear deterrence is acceptable only as a temporary expedient on the way to "nuclear arms control, reductions, and disarmament," and that even on this basis deterrence must be limited to "the specific objective of preventing the use of nuclear weapons or other actions which would lead directly to a nuclear exchange."[138]

The assembled bishops approved a move by the liberals to change "curb" back to "halt"—clearly glad for an opportunity to shake off the embrace of the Reagan administration. A motion by Archbishop John Quinn of San Francisco, a leader among the doves, that the letter's expression of "profound skepticism" over the moral acceptability of using nuclear weapons under any circumstance be changed to "opposition on moral grounds" at first carried. But after Bernardin took the microphone to relate that just such a change had been discussed with "Rome" and had been found objectionable, the bishops smoothly reversed themselves. At the end of two days of debate and discussion the bishops gave final approval to the letter, little changed in its main points from the committee's previous draft, by vote of 238 to 9.[139]

Almost as remarkable as the final 150-page document itself was the process, shepherded mainly by Cardinal Bernardin and Father Hehir, through which it was developed. In a real sense almost the entire church had been involved in producing a detailed, scholarly, carefully reasoned, theologically rich pronouncement on what is surely the most important moral issue as well as one of the most politically and technically complex problems of our time. Many Catholic and non-Catholic Americans have disagreed with some or all of the bishops' concrete recommendations. Some have argued that by encouraging intransigence among the rulers of the Soviet Union the bishops' letter, even as modified, has made the danger of nuclear war greater. But few would dispute that the bishops have at least helped cast the debate in moral terms, have reminded the American people and the world that the issue of nuclear arms turns finally, beyond all the terribly important arguments over military technology and political feasibility, on choice "for the good or evil side."

THE CATHOLIC VOTER

While the bishops were taking on the issues of abortion and the nuclear arms race and in 1984 and 1985 were exploring once more the relationship between Christian values and market capitalism, many lay Catholics were moving toward a new political alignment. Catholics had traditionally supported the Democratic party. This allegiance was not ideologically anomalous, as it was for much of the white South, because Catholics have tended to be more liberal than the national average on most economic and social issues. Catholics generally shared the fierce anticommunism espoused by leaders like Cardinal Spellman, but through the middle of the 1960s this, too, placed them in the mainstream of the Democracy.[140]

In the 1970s as the hierarchy moved left, particularly on foreign policy issues, many Catholic laypersons, influenced by improvements in their economic situations and angered or disturbed by challenges to traditional morality, began to move right. The Republican party, which as recently as 1960 could fairly be described as in some sense anti-Catholic, began to court Catholic support through its positions on such issues as abortion and state aid to nonpublic schools. In 1972 Catholics voted by a narrow margin for Richard Nixon (the Catholic bête noire of 1960) over George McGovern. Four years later, troubled by Watergate and economic recession, a majority of Catholics were back in the Democratic fold, despite misgivings about Jimmy Carter, who seemed in the line of Democratic leaders descended from Bryan.

Since at least 1964 conservative strategists had regarded working-class Catholics as one of the two major blocks of voters (white southerners being the other) who would have to be attracted to the conservative side in order to achieve a realignment of American politics. Mobilizing blue-collar Catholics around abortion and other social issues, said Paul Weyrich, a founder of the "new right" in the late 1970s, could be "the Achilles heel of the liberal Democrats." Conservatives controlling the Republican national convention in 1980 included in the party platform promises of support for "a constitutional amendment to restore protection of the right to life for unborn children" and tax credits to aid parents of students attending parochial schools. The platform of the Democratic party, the historical home of most American Catholics, endorsed legalized abortion and was carefully ambiguous on aid to nonpublic education. In November Ronald Reagan ran 7 percentage points ahead of Jimmy Carter among Catholic voters—the largest plurality in history won among Catholics by the Republican candidate for president.[141]

During the early 1980s the gradual shift among Catholics toward Republicanism continued. The National Opinion Research Center at the University of Chicago found that the average share of Catholics identifying themselves as Republicans rose from 15 percent in surveys taken in 1976–1978 to 20 percent in surveys taken in 1980–1983; the share of Catholics calling themselves Democrats fell from 50 to 44 percent. Among Irish Catholics the Republican gain was particularly pronounced, rising from 17 percent in 1976–78 to 25 percent in 1980–83. The increase in Republican strength among Irish Catholics, however, came almost entirely from former independents; Democratic identification declined only from 41.4 percent to 40.6 percent.[142]

The most recent wave of Catholic immigrants, Hispanics, showed the lowest level of Republican identification among Catholic ethnic groups in 1980–83, 7 percent, up from 5 percent in 1976–78. But Democratic alignment among Hispanics was dropping precipitously, from 84 percent in 1972–74, to 63 percent in 1976–78, to 51 percent in 1980–83. About one-third of Hispanics voted for Reagan in 1980. Hispanics were internally divided, the relatively small segment of Cubans leaning Republican, the Puerto Ricans and Mexicans remaining predominantly Democratic. But polls showed shifts toward the Republicans among all Hispanic groups. A 1984 study by the nonpartisan Committee for the Study of the American Electorate found that 49 percent of new registrants among Hispanics identified themselves as Republicans and 32 percent as Democrats.[143]

In 1984 Catholics once more voted for Reagan, this time by a margin of 55 to 44 percent. In congressional elections the pattern was reversed—55 percent cast ballots for House Democratic candidates and 45 percent for Republicans—but the result was far below historic levels of Democratic support.[144]

While most Catholics clearly have not become Republicans, automatic landslide majorities among them for Democratic candidates seem a thing of the past. In industrial states of the Northeast and Midwest, where the Democrats traditionally have relied on solid support from Catholics in big cities to offset similar backing for Republicans in suburbs and rural areas, the effects of this change may be profound.[145]

As a group, survey evidence shows, Catholics are still somewhat more liberal than Protestants (though more conservative than Jews) on many economic and social issues, mainly those involving social services provided by government. Whether growing conservatism on some issues, economic and foreign policy as well as social, and general annoyance over the permissive moral attitudes represented by a segment of the Democratic national leadership will produce enduring conversion of a sizable block of Catholics to the more conservative party remains, therefore, in doubt. A party receiving the support of moderate-to-conservative Protestants, Catholics, and Jews (some of whom also have been moving in a more conservative direction) could reasonably expect to dominate national politics for many years to come. But if the Republican party should swing hard to the right, as some among its leadership appear to prefer, it would probably lose attraction for independent or weakly Democratic Catholics and Jews as well as for a substantial share of its own traditional constituency among Protestants.[146]

Many within the American Catholic hierarchy, some of whom have served in Latin America as missionaries, have indicated sympathy for the social approach recommended for Latin American and other third world countries by liberation theology. Some also find it applicable to the internal problems of the United States. On the whole, however, liberation theology seems to have exerted less influence in the upper reaches of American Catholicism than among the leadership cadres of mainline Protestantism. A highly institutionalized church, which Catholicism remains, with a mass membership will probably be drawn toward political moderation, at least in a society maintaining the levels of freedom and stability that currently exist in the United States. Moreover, the Catholic doctrine of "subsidiarity," calling for decentralization of social authority and maintenance of many institutional buffers between the individual and the state, runs counter to collectivization of society through central government controls.[147]

John Paul II's theological conservatism and staunch anticommunism have encouraged social conservatives within the American church. When Cardinal Cooke died at the end of 1983, the pope appointed as his successor Bishop O'Connor, the most conservative member of the committee on war and peace, thereby maintaining a kind of balance between the moderately liberal Bernardin in Chicago and the moderately conservative O'Connor in New York. During the 1984 presidential campaign O'Connor and Archbishop William Law of Boston, also recently appointed by the pope, took the lead among a number of bishops who criticized Representative Geraldine Ferraro, the Democratic candidate for vice-president and herself a Catholic, for allegedly misrepresenting the Catholic position on abortion. In the spring of 1985 the pope raised both O'Connor and Law to the office of cardinal.[148]

Some within the hierarchy and the staff of the USCC have predicted that the bishops' letter on nuclear arms will ultimately draw lay Catholics back toward liberalism. Whether this in fact occurs will depend on the extent to which the church tries to make arms control a central political issue and on the degree to which the Reagan administration, or any successor, attempts and is able to achieve the nuclear arms reductions and the progress toward disarmament called for by the bishops.

Post-Liberal Jews

The 1967 Six-Day War in the Middle East, Jewish commentators have observed, was crucial to the experience of modern Jews. Faced with the declared intention of Arab leaders to destroy Israel and "drive its Jewish inhabitants into the sea," Norman Podhoretz wrote, "Jews everywhere trembled." When war broke out, they "rose up to declare that they would do everything in their power to insure the survival of the state of Israel . . . not in a philanthropic spirit or even in a spirit of fraternal concern, but rather out of conviction that their *own* survival as Jews was linked to the survival of Israel." Given such stakes, it is not surprising that the quick and decisive Israeli victory that returned the site of Solomon's temple to Jewish control for the first time in more than two thousand years produced what can fairly be called a spiritual reaction. "Even many who did not openly and consciously credit God with the victory of 1967 experienced intimations of the miraculous in the deliverance."[149]

The content of Judaism for most American Jews, according to Nathan Glazer, had come to consist of an amalgam of ethnic loyalty and political liberalism. The 1967 war led most to conclude that the ethnic element was the more basic of the two. "There are unconscious depths," wrote Rabbi Richard Rubenstein, "to the phenomenon of Jewishness which even those of us who have spent our lives in its study cannot fathom. No Jewish theology will be adequate which fails to take account of the response of the world's Jews to Israel's recent struggle."[150]

For a long time, liberalism, in the American sense, and ethnic Judaism had seemed mutually reinforcing. Liberalism represented the principles of fairness and nondiscrimination that had helped open the way for Jews to achieve not only political freedom but also the highest levels of economic affluence, social celebrity, and professional distinction. Liberalism had been in the forefront of the struggle against Nazi Germany. The equalitarian strain of liberalism was congruent with, and indeed partly traceable to, the tradition of social justice inherited from biblical Judaism. The internationalist branch of liberalism, with which most Jews were associated, was both supportive toward Israel and committed to applying this same tradition of social justice on a global scale.

In the middle of the 1960s, significant tensions for the first time began to appear between Judaism and liberalism. Jews had been among the strongest supporters of the drive for civil rights, but when some liberals went beyond the goal of equality of opportunity to call for equality of result, many Jews began to develop reservations. Most supported some form of "affirmative action" to advance blacks and Hispanics along the educational and economic ladders (though many noted that Jews had made their own way without benefit of any affirmative action by the older Gentile establishment—quite the reverse). But when some liberals moved on to advocating quotas for disadvantaged minorities—*quotas,* the very device through which the older establishment had long limited access by Jews to economic and professional opportunity—Jewish resistance hardened.[151]

Although some Jews, generally the wealthier and better educated, continued to follow the straight liberal line, others, particularly those living in the older neighborhoods of large cities, began to break with liberalism on some issues. "Those wealthier Jews," Nathan Glazer has written, "who lived in all-white or largely white suburbs could still support integration. Less properous Jews in the central cities who would bear the brunt of integration resisted it. They were often denounced as 'racists' (even by fellow Jews), but in their own minds their motivation was concern for the education of their children and the maintenance of a Jewish community." Jewish teachers and principals in city schools, who had earned their positions through a merit system, feared and opposed liberal proposals for "community control" of schools, which they believed would result in their jobs being turned over to blacks. Jews living in poorer city neighborhoods, where the crime rate was high, had little patience with liberal efforts to set up civilian review boards to curb police brutality. "Jews began to ask themselves for the first time whether they were still liberal."[152]

THE ISRAELI CONNECTION

To all of this was added a changing attitude toward Israel among segments of the liberal community. In part this change reflected troubled consciences among Western liberals over the plight of homeless Palestinian Arabs. But it also resulted from shifts in world political alignments. Impoverished third world nations found maligning Israel at the United Nations and in other international forums a costless and in some cases agreeable means for strengthening their ties with oil-rich Arab states. American liberals who gave uncritical support to third world aspirations, particularly religious liberals after the advent of liberation theology, were drawn first to understand, then to tolerate, and finally in some cases to endorse the third world view of Israel as an "outlaw nation." Meanwhile, besides oppressing its internal Jewish population, the Soviet Union also found baiting Israel an effective tactic for winning third world favor. American Jews who may have once felt a certain sympathy toward the Russian experiment with socialism came to regard the Soviet Union not only as hostile to the United States and democratic values but also as a principal antagonist of Israel. American liberals anxious for better relations with the Soviet Union as the key to world peace were further moved to distance themselves from Israel and from Zionist Jews. "To be 'liberal' in 1967," Glazer wrote, "might mean . . . to support leftists who wished to see Israel destroyed, to oppose American aid to Israel."[153]

A new school of Jewish intellectuals, labeled neoconservatives, discovered that all along there had been a conservative strain in Jewish tradition, or at least a strain on which conservatism could be built. Jewish concepts of family, community, nationhood, professional excellence, and law all could be read as pointing in a conservative direction. Most Jews would never feel at home with the kind of restrictive authoritarianism with which right-wing conservatism has often been identified, particularly in Europe but also to some extent in the United States. "To the Jewish mind," Ernest van den Haag has written, "the *Gestalt* of the rightist requires anti-Semitism . . . no matter whether they are: they ought to be."[154] But a broader, more inclusive, more progressive conservatism of the kind represented by Disraeli and Theodore Roosevelt was fully compatible with Jewish culture. Churchill and Eisenhower, as well as Franklin Roosevelt, after all, had fought Hitler. By the 1970s left-wing collectivism on the world scene was at least as threatening as right-wing authoritarianism to Jewish interests and values.[154]

The neoconservative school, communicating its views through *The Public Interest* and *Commentary*, has included such notable non-Jews as Daniel Patrick Moynihan, Jeane Kirkpatrick, Michael Novak, and James Q. Wilson. But the core group of intellectuals who have defined the school's orthodoxy—Norman Podhoretz, Nathan Glazer, Irvin Kristol, Midge Decter, and Daniel Bell—are all Jewish, as are many of its more visible outriders, such as Ben Wattenberg and Seymour Martin Lipset. Many share common origins in New York radical politics of the middle third of the twentieth century. Their turns toward conservatism have been variously explained, but concern for Israel is at least a mutual bond. Together they have constructed a formidable critique not only of social radicalism but also of many aspects of welfare-state liberalism. Even more important, they have provided American conservatism with what it has almost never had: a reasoned and more or less systematic body of social ideology.[155]

The mass of Jewish voters moved more slowly. In 1972 Richard Nixon, hardly a favorite among Jews, won about 35 percent of the Jewish vote in his race against George McGovern—not exactly an electoral tidal wave but almost twice the share he had received against

Hubert Humphrey four years before. After Watergate, which many Jews felt confirmed their (almost) worst fears about Republicans, most who had defected to Nixon returned to the Democrats, giving Jimmy Carter 82 percent of the Jewish vote in 1976. The Carter administration, through association with economic hard times and its efforts to establish a balance in the relationships of the United States with Israel and the Arab nations, managed to reignite Jewish doubts about liberalism. In 1980 John Anderson's independent candidacy provided many Jews with a means for voting against Carter without going the whole way to the Republicans. But Ronald Reagan was supported by almost 40 percent of Jewish voters—the largest share of their vote that had gone to a Republican candidate for president since Warren Harding in 1920. Carter was favored by only 44 percent of Jews, the first time since 1928 that a majority had not voted Democratic for president. "It was a real experience for many Jews," Nathan Perlmutter, director of the Anti-Defamation League, said, "to find that they could vote Republican without their hands freezing to the lever. Up until 1980, many Jews would have been more likely to become Christian Scientists than to become Republicans."[156]

The movement toward conservatism proceeded at different rates among different subgroups. The most ritually observant Jews were significantly more likely to be drawn toward political conservatism. As observance and identification with the Jewish community declined, fealty to liberalism increased, up to the point of minimal attachment to Judaism. But once the line to complete secularization was crossed, conservatism again increased. Two processes seemed to be at work: cultural conservatism and concern for Israel among the most observant Jews increasingly found outlet in political conservatism; general trends toward economic and social conservatism in the larger society affected ethnic Jews who had separated themselves from religious attachments. (In the early 1980s about 36 percent of the nation's 5.7 million ethnic Jews identified themselves as Conservative, 26 percent as Reform, 6 percent as Orthodox, and 32 percent as unaffiliated.)[157]

Neither the foreign nor domestic policies of the Reagan administration in its first term did much to reinforce the trend of Jewish voters toward the Republicans. The administration's somewhat inchoate policies in the Middle East led many Jews to conclude, as one leader put it, that "Reagan is doing to Israel what Jews were afraid Carter would do." The administration's cuts in federal welfare programs troubled Jewish consciences; its positions on social issues like school prayer and abortion revived fears of absolutist tendencies on the political right. Beyond specific complaints, many leaders of national Jewish groups felt less comfortable dealing with Republicans in the White House. The Reagan administration, one said, did not "look Jewish."

THE JEWISH LOBBY

In the early 1980s a survey of the nation's Jews found 77 percent predicting a rise in anti-Semitism. This anxiety was in part a response to a significant increase in vandalism against synagogues and similar acts of anti-Semitic hoodlumism. Yet by historical measures, overt anti-Semitism remained very low. Most Jewish leaders acknowledged there had been a change in national social attitudes. "When I was a young man [in the 1940s]," Nathan Perlmutter said, "anti-Semitism was accepted behavior among the majority. Today, it is deviant."[158]

More disturbing than occasional attacks on property were suggestions by some political leaders, including some generally identified as liberals, and in parts of the media, that American Jews harbored "dual loyalty between the United States and Israel" and excessively influenced American policy in the Middle East. During the debate over the Reagan administration's proposal to sell high-technology surveillance planes (AWACS) to Saudi Arabia in 1981, several senators cautioned that Jewish agencies should not press too hard on the issue for fear of stirring up latent anti-Semitism. Washington representatives of Jewish organizations reacted with shock. "These suggestions may have been benignly motivated," Hyman Bookbinder, director of the Washington office of the American Jewish Committee and informal chairman of the board for the entire Jewish lobby, said soon after the debate was over (and the AWACS approved), "but their effect was to threaten the right of Jews to participate in the democratic process. I said to those senators, 'argue with me on the merits, but do not tell me not to raise the issue for fear of causing anti-Semitism.' "

Bookbinder maintains that the size and influence of the Jewish lobby has been greatly exaggerated. "All Jewish groups [in Washington] together employ from fifteen to eighteen professionals—about the same as a medium-size oil company."[159]

Although the Jewish lobby is small compared to those operated by major economic interest groups, Washington observers regard it as the capital's most effective religion-oriented interest group, except possibly that of the Catholic church. (Whether most of the Jewish agencies and groups active in Washington *are* religion-oriented is open to question. Most have no direct affiliation with any Jewish denomination. Almost all, however, maintain close ties with Jewish religious establishments and regard themselves as representing not only Jewish interests, but also "values and attitudes . . . ultimately based on Jewish religion and philosophy.") More than half of a randomly selected sample of twenty-six congressional offices reported regular contacts by Jewish agencies, a bit less than by Catholic groups but much more than by groups related to any Protestant church.

Meeting on the first Tuesday of each month, with Bookbinder in the chair, Washington representatives of Jewish organizations coordinate their efforts and divide assignments. A major part of their work is to stay in close touch with their organizations' local chapters or affiliates. "The strength of the Jewish lobby is not with professional lobbyists in Washington," Bookbinder has said, "but with the Jewish community all over the country. It is the ability of these groups to mobilize influence within their local constituencies that makes the Jews an effective force in Washington."[160]

There is no doubt that defense of Israel is a primary concern of most Jewish groups. The overwhelming majority of Jews, however, find no tension between support for Israel and loyalty to American interests. Survey evidence shows that more than 90 percent believe that defense of Israel serves the national interest of the United States. But they do not give uncritical support to the policies of a particular Israeli government. A poll in the early 1980s, for example, found that 60 percent of American Jews favored returning some Israeli-occupied territories to Arab control in return for genuine peace.[161]

As liberal Protestant and Catholic groups drifted away from support of Israel—or, as they would say, devoted more attention to the plight of Palestinian Arabs—the collaboration that had existed among the Washington representatives of the three major divisions of religion in America during the 1960s and early 1970s began to decline. The groups still came together to fight for such causes as elimination of the purchase requirement from the food stamp program in 1977 and a human rights amendment to the foreign aid bill in 1978, but as anger within the Jewish community grew over what was regarded as insensitivity by the other two religious groups to the needs of Israel, much of the former closeness was lost. (The abortion issue somewhat similarly drew Catholics away from mainline Protestant and Jewish groups.)

Support for Israel and distrust of the Soviet Union also led some of the Jewish groups to differ with liberal Protestants and Catholics on defense issues. "More and more," Bookbinder said, "Jews have come to recognize that we cannot show indifference to the whole question of defense of the West if we expect the defense of Israel to be supported by the United States. Traditionally, Jews have believed in spending more on social services and less on defense. But this attitude is changing, which causes the Methodists and the Unitarians and some of the other religious groups to become upset over the new attitude of the Jewish community. Some are saying that the Jewish community is copping out on liberalism. The strange thing is that some liberals are now saying the same things that Nazis and other kooks have said in suggesting that Jews are disloyal to America."[162]

Disagreement over Middle Eastern and defense issues inevitably affected collaboration on other issues. "We still participate in WISC," said Warren Eisenberg, director of the International Council of B'nai B'rith, "but we find they spend a lot of time on issues that are of no particular interest to the Jewish community. The law of the sea, for instance, has consumed a great deal of time at WISC meetings in recent years."[163]

While moving away from liberal Protestant and Catholic groups, Jews have found a new and unexpected, and for some alarming, ally in some fundamentalist Christian groups, notably Jerry Falwell's Moral Majority. There are several reasons for the backing recently given by fundamentalists to Israel, but the fundamentalists' expectation, based on biblical prediction, that the Jews will return to Israel just before the millennium provides a linkage that understandably bemuses some Jews. As Martin Marty has said: "Some knowledgeable Jews feel at least ambivalent about the role given to them in the first act of a drama, the second act of which they will not be in at all."[164]

Beyond theological or cultural qualms, many Jews have felt uncomfortable accepting support from a group that historically has not been famous for religious tolerance and that on many economic and social issues takes positions diametrically opposed to traditional Jewish liberalism. Hyman Bookbinder, for example, expressed strong skepticism over the feasibility of Jewish collaboration with the so-called religious new right, composed largely, though not exclusively, of fundamentalists. "A few voices have been raised in the Jewish community suggesting that we should mute our criticism of the new right. But that would be intellectually dishonest. Of course we would prefer that the evangelicals be pro-Israel. But we must continue to make clear that we differ with the religious right on a large number of issues."[165]

Rabbi David Saperstein, director of the Washington office of the Union of American Hebrew Congregations, set forth some of the grounds on which Jews are critical of the religious right: "First, the religious right believes that government should regulate private morality, while we feel that on issues of private morality, the religious groups must convince their own members. Second, the religious right does not believe that government should act to help the poor. Their literature says almost nothing about the poor. And third, and most important, the religious right takes the position that the whole shebang of their program is mandated directly by God. What they really want is a Christian America, though they do not quite say it."[166]

Despite these misgivings, many American Jewish leaders have felt obliged to take tactical assistance where they can find it. When the National Council of Churches in 1981 condemned Israel's bombing of a nuclear reactor in Iraq, Jerry Falwell, at the request of the Israeli government, issued a rebuttal. Jews were understandably grateful. "They [the fundamentalists] strongly support a lot of things I think are dreadful for the country," said Howard Squadron, chairman of the Conference of Presidents of Major American Jewish Organizations, "but I'm not going to turn away their support of Israel for that."[167]

As with Catholic voters, the extent and duration of the shift of Jewish voters in the direction of conservatism remains uncertain. Polls continue to show Jews well to the left of the national average on most social and economic issues. During the 1970s many of them lost some of their former confidence in government as a regulator of the economy, but most still support an extensive welfare state. Most liberal politicans, particularly those with ambitions for national office, still strive to outdo each other in the extravagance of their promises of support for Israel. Wealthy and middle-class Jews remain far more likely to be Democrats than their counterparts in other religious groups.

Early in 1984, concern among Jews over the role that Jesse Jackson was playing in the Democratic party and over the support Jackson was receiving from some openly anti-Semitic firebrands, caused many once more to reassess their alignment with the Democrats. For a time it seemed that Jewish backing for Reagan might exceed that which he had received in 1980, perhaps even reaching 50 percent. But Reagan's determined courting of the religious right during the summer caused alarm among Jews, who continue to associate right-wing fundamentalism with religious repression. Jews were the one group with whom Walter Mondale's charge that Reagan was under-mining traditional separation between church and state appeared to have significant effect. In the end, as was often observed, most decided that they were more frightened by Jerry Falwell than they were angered by Jesse Jackson. They gave Mondale about two-thirds of their vote, a solid majority, though well below the 82 percent cast for Jimmy Carter as recently as 1976.[168]

In a report prepared for the American Jewish Congress in 1984, Donald Feldstein observed that, while Jews "still stand to the left of where Americans as a whole are now standing," tension between liberalism and support for Israel could lead to one of two develop-ments: "liberalism could be identified as unfriendly to Israel and become rejected by Jews" or "pro-Israelism itself could diminish" among the next generation. "Either of these developments," Feldstein wrote, "would be a major change for American Jewry."[169]

Revolt of the Evangelicals

After the fiasco of the Scopes trial and the repeal of Prohibition, evangelical Protestants largely withdrew from the public arena and even to a great extent from national public consciousness (except in novels and plays like *Elmer Gantry* and *Tobacco Road*, in which they were treated with contempt). Evangelical churches continued to hold their own, particularly in the rural South and Midwest, but evangelical preachers for the most part returned to the earlier view of John Leland and Dwight L. Moody that the churches should devote themselves to promoting individual salvation and had no business mixing religion with politics.

In 1941 a number of fundamentalist churches, increasingly alarmed by the continuing advance of modernism, or modernity as it came to be called, joined to form the American Council of Christian Churches. The ACCC promised to bear witness to "the historic faith of the church," which, it charged, was being abandoned "in the darkening days of apostasy" by the mainline denominations. Errors attributed to the mainline denominations included doubting the literal truth ("inerrancy") of the Bible, accommodating "impurity" in personal conduct (from divorce to going to the movies), and suggesting that salvation might be achieved through good works alone. The ACCC also had no truck with the Social Gospel, which it regarded as derived from the humanist heresy that man through his own resources can become master of his fate.[170]

The following year a somewhat larger body of evangelicals, also disturbed over apostasy among the mainliners but uncomfortable with the negative tone of the ACCC, formed the National Association of Evangelicals. The NAE aimed to combat modernism without resorting to "dog-in-the-manger, reactionary, negative, or destructive type" tactics. Mindful of the absolutist tendencies associated with fundamentalism, the association promised to "shun all forms of bigotry, intolerance, misrepresentation, hate, jealousy, false judgment, and hypocrisy."[171]

The distinction between evangelicalism and fundamentalism was, and has remained, somewhat hazy. Evangelicalism is best defined as a branch of Christianity, descended from the pietist movement of the Reformation by way of the Great Awakening, that emphasizes direct experience by the individual of the Holy Spirit (being "born again") and that regards the Bible as an infallible source of religious and moral authority. Fundamentalism is an extreme form of evangelicalism. All fundamentalists are evangelicals, but not all evangelicals are fundamentalists.

Evangelicalism's emphasis on individual spiritual experience places it on the personalist side of the religious spectrum. But its view of the Bible as infallibly authoritative partly offsets the socially centrifugal tendency of religious personalism. Fundamentalism carries insistence on biblical inerrancy to the point of absolutist reaction, not an uncommon tendency at the extremes of personalism. Fundamentalism fosters not only the spiritual enthusiasm bred by personalism but also the dogmatism and social rigidity associated with absolutist idealism.

Evangelicals as a whole, including most Baptists and Disciples of

Christ, many Methodists, Presbyterians, and Lutherans, and members of independent local evangelical churches, now make up about one-fourth of the total population of the United States and about two-fifths of all Protestants. Demographic studies show that evangelicals tend to be more rural, more southern, less affluent, and less well educated than the general population. Fundamentalists, concentrated in the independent churches but found also among some of the organized denominations, particularly the Southern Baptists, Missouri Synod Lutherans, and Disciples of Christ, constitute about one-third of all evangelicals. No part of the one-fifth of evangelicals who are black are usually designated as fundamentalists, though many of the independent black churches are theologically close to the doctrinal views of white fundamentalists.[172]

In its early years the National Association of Evangelicals steered clear of politics. But the American Council of Christian Churches, led by Carl McIntire, an eloquent preacher and skilled organizer, displayed a pronounced taste for political involvement. Drawing on the strand of evangelical tradition, traceable to Jonathan Edwards and the Puritans, that holds that America has been specially chosen by God to launch the world's redemption, McIntire directed the ACCC into the anticommunist crusade of the 1950s. Communism, seen as the principal adversary of God's chosen people, was identified with Satan.[173]

From the 1940s onward, conservative politicians recognized that evangelicals battling modernism offered a potential source of electoral support. But the affinity of many fundamentalists for anti-Catholicism, anti-Semitism, and racism caused most mainstream conservatives to play the evangelical card with caution. Robert Taft, Dwight Eisenhower, and Barry Goldwater were separated by substantial political and ideological differences, but all held in common the belief that the future health of the Republican party depended on its ability to attract supporters from outside its northern white Protestant base. Prudence as well as social responsibility therefore required that they keep their distance from right-wing preachers who could be depended upon to insult major groups from which recruits for the conservative coalition must be drawn.

Billy Graham, representing the main body of less extreme evangelicals, was another matter. Early in his career Graham could invoke the red peril with the best of them. "Communism," he said in 1949, "is inspired, directed, and motivated by the Devil himself. America is at a crossroads. Will we turn to the left-wingers and atheists, or will we turn to the right and embrace the cross?"[174] He also confidently predicted the imminent arrival of the millennium. During the 1950s, however, it was Graham's great social achievement—apart from his more directly religious role—to move most evangelicals back into the mainstream of American life. Building on the platform established by the NAE, he shaped evangelicalism as a positive force. In the process he gradually came to terms with some aspects of modernity, for which he was eventually criticized by some purists on the fundamentalist far right. But Graham's prestige among the mass of evangelicals was such that efforts at detraction never had much effect.

Association with Graham was avidly sought by political leaders of both major parties, liberals as well as conservatives. He hobnobbed with them all, particularly Eisenhower, Lyndon Johnson, and Richard Nixon. In 1960 he skirted the anti-Catholic enthusiasm that galvanized most evangelicals against John Kennedy. Graham's closest political association was with Nixon. (On the morning after Nixon's election in 1968, he arrived at the successful candidate's hotel suite and announced, "We did it!" leaving unclear exactly what he meant by "we.")[175] After Nixon's fall he was more wary in his contacts with politicians. In the 1980s, once gain proving his capacity to surprise, Graham spoke out forcefully against the arms race (while avoiding close identification with the organized peace movement) and set out to evangelize the Devil's own bailiwick, the Soviet Union.

THE ELECTRONIC CHURCH

Neither Graham nor the right-wing preachers had much success during the 1950s or 1960s in stirring the evangelicals to political action. Several studies during the period showed "without exception . . . that evangelicals were less inclined toward political participation than were their less evangelical counterparts." One scholar concluded in 1971, "Evangelicals concentrate on conversion, and except for occasional efforts to outlaw what they deem to be personal vices, evangelical Protestant groups largely ignore social and political efforts for reform."[176]

Yet studies in the late 1970s and early 1980s just as uniformly have shown evangelicals to be the religious group *most* favorable to political action by the churches. A Gallup survey in 1980 discovered that they were more likely to be registered to vote than nonevangelicals, despite being overrepresented in demographic groups that historically have been relatively low in political participation.[177]

What happened? The evangelicals in part were responding to the urgings of a few highly visible television preachers, proprietors of the so-called electronic church. The Federal Communications Commission has always required television stations to devote a fixed amount of their airtime to religious programming. In the early years most stations met this requirement by making time available free to local churches or to well-known evangelists with national followings, like Graham, Oral Roberts, and Rex Humbard. But in the early 1970s, many stations, with FCC approval, began charging for the time they set aside for religion. Most mainline churches declined to enter this market. Religious time therefore became available, usually at bargain rates, to enterprising preachers, almost all fundamentalists or evangelicals, who financed their programs through fund-raising appeals made in the course of their broadcasts. Some of these programs were linked to elaborate feedback systems, utilizing telephone banks and computerized files, through which individual viewers could obtain personalized counseling.[178]

Under the new arrangement the audience for religious programs greatly expanded. A study in 1963 showed that only 12 percent of all Protestants regularly watched or listened to religious broadcasts. Gallup polls taken in the late 1970s showed that this figure had more than doubled, and a poll in 1981 found that 27 percent of the national public claimed to have watched more than one religious program in the preceding month. A study in 1984 by Gallup and the Annenberg School of Communications placed the regular audience for religious broadcasts at about 13.3 million.[179]

The older evangelists who maintained regularly scheduled broadcasts, like Oral Roberts and Rex Humbard, for the most part remained apolitical. But some of the younger preachers who were buying time on stations wherever they could attract an audience, including Jerry Falwell, James Robison, Pat Robertson, and Jim Bakker, began offering comments on political and social issues as part of their broadcasts.

In the 1960s Falwell, an independent Baptist, had been resolute in his commitment to the tradition of political noninvolvement. "We have few ties to this earth," he said in 1965. "We pay our taxes, cast our votes as a responsibility of citizenship, obey the laws of the land, and other things demanded of us by the society in which we live. But, at the same time, we are cognizant that our only purpose on this earth is to know Christ and to make Him known."[180]

Events of the late 1960s and early 1970s led Falwell and many others to change their minds. The Supreme Court's 1961 decision prohibiting organized prayer in the public schools caused outrage in the evangelical community (though many evangelicals in the Baptist tradition had previously been critical of state-sponsored prayer). The 1973 abortion decision intensified the impression that the Court had set out to achieve a completely secularized society. Partly in response to the prayer decision and other perceived challenges to traditional morality in public education—though also in part to evade the Court's 1954 decision requiring racial desegregation of the public schools— many evangelical churches, mainly in the South, began establishing "Christian academies" in which the children of believers could be educated in "creationist" science and traditional values. Though the federal Internal Revenue Service at first routinely granted most of these schools tax-exempt status, their existence gave the churches a concrete interest in protecting themselves against governmental intrusion or regulation. The financial needs of the schools also weakened the evangelicals' longstanding opposition to government aid for church-sponsored education.

More important than specific court decisions or concrete institutional interests was a general sense among evangelicals in the 1970s that the moral foundations of American society were crumbling. Earlier many evangelicals and even fundamentalists seem to have begun to believe that modernism, much as it jarred their sensibilities, must after all represent the wave of the future. Modernism was associated with rising national prosperity, with burgeoning government programs to help the sick and the elderly and the poor, with increased personal freedom and opportunities for travel and awareness of a wider world. Were not most of these developments, despite their disruptive effects on traditional ways, on the whole good things? But the Vietnam War and Watergate and the violent social disorders of the late 1960s shook the aura of moral prestige that modernism had begun to acquire for some evangelicals—somewhat as these phenomena startled those at the other end of the ideological spectrum who were drawn to liberation theology. Even more damaging was the growth of what appeared to be pervasive social sickness. During the 1970s, divorce increased 67 percent. Families headed by unwed mothers rose 356 percent. By the end of the decade, 21 percent of families with children under eighteen were headed by single parents. In 1979, 17 percent of all children and 55 percent of black children were born out of wedlock. Recreational drugs and pornography were readily available to all who could pay. Violent crime rose to an all-time high in 1980. A Gallup poll found one-third of Americans reporting a problem with alcoholism in their own families. If this be modernity, how much more could the nation take and survive?[181]

Most people agreed that these were alarming trends. But many secular social scientists, and many leaders of mainline Protestant and Jewish denominations and even of the Catholic church, argued either that their main cause was economic injustice, correctible through redistribution of wealth, or that they were so intertwined with progressive developments (like increased autonomy for women and youth) that the only fair way to deal with most of them was through expansion of welfare programs that would make their effects less painful or destructive. Most evangelicals and fundamentalists, on the other hand, as well as many Americans of other religious persuasions, were convinced that these social afflictions had best be met, at least in part, by some restoration of traditional morality.[182]

Fundamentalists believed they had identified the prime source of moral decline: "secular humanism," a philosophy which Tim LaHaye, a leading fundamentalist publicist, characterized as based on "amorality, evolution, and atheism." Francis Schaeffer, the best-known fundamentalist theologian, charged that secular humanism is itself a religion "which the government and courts in the United States favor over all others!" Because it was being imposed by government, the only way to overcome its pernicious effects was to get control of government into different hands. To do this evangelicals would have to set aside their inhibitions against involvement in politics.[183]

By 1976 Jerry Falwell had moved so far from his earlier aversion for politics that he organized a series of "I Love America" rallies on the steps of state capitols all across the United States. But the spotlight of media attention that year was moving toward another evangelical who applied the values of "born-again" Christianity to national problems: Jimmy Carter. In my own observation along the campaign trail in 1975 and 1976, Carter was not retiring about stating his religious beliefs, but he did not exploit them. Everywhere he went, reporters asked him about his religion. In reply he would describe his conversion and explain why he believed religious faith is a valuable moral asset for a political leader but would also state his adherence to the Baptist tradition of separation between church and state. Many reporters then went to their typewriters and wrote stories that Jimmy Carter insisted on parading his religion.

Without making much public effort, Carter attracted widespread support from evangelicals and fundamentalists, who regarded him somewhat as Catholics had regarded John Kennedy in 1960. Pat Robertson, one of the most popular of the television preachers, gave him an outright endorsement. In November Carter outpolled Ford among white Baptists by 56 percent to 43 percent. Evangelicals gave him his margin of victory not only in the South (where he also was helped by regional pride) but also in such key northern states as Pennsylvania and Ohio with large rural populations that usually voted Republican. Because his national advantage in the popular vote was only 2 percent, Carter may fairly be said to have owed his election to the evangelicals (though also, of course, to blacks, Jews, and other groups that favored him by wide margins).

Once in office Carter was perceived by evangelicals to have turned his back on them. The administration made no effort to press for action on social issues like school prayer and abortion that had high priorities for evangelicals. "It was a tremendous letdown," said one evangelical activist, "if not a betrayal, to have Carter stumping for [the Equal Rights Amendment], for not stopping federally funded abortions, for advocating homosexual rights." Not incidentally, evangelical activists were not given federal jobs. "Carter promised in 1976 that if he were elected, he would appoint qualified evangelical Christians to positions in the federal government," an evangelical spokesman said in 1980. "He did not follow through."[184]

Despite their disappointment with Carter, many evangelicals had found their experience with national politics exhilarating. "Evangelicals entered politics in the first place to defend their way of life," one said, "but before long they found that politics can be fun." A more faithful champion was soon available.[185]

FUNDAMENTALISTS FOR REAGAN

Some political conservatives had tried in 1976 to organize religious fundamentalists behind the presidential candidacy of Ronald Reagan on the ground that his social views were congruent with fundamentalist principles. Fundamentalist support apparently contributed to his breakthrough victory in the North Carolina primary, when his campaign seemed about to expire, and to his later successes in the South. After Reagan narrowly lost the Republican nomination to Ford, most of his fundamentalist backers either switched to Carter or sat out the election.

Organizers of what was at that time coming to be known as the new right had, however, spotted a political potential. "The New Right is looking for issues that people care about," observed Paul Weyrich, director of the right-wing Committee for the Survival of a Free Congress. "Social issues, at least for the present, fill the bill." Weyrich's view was shared by the other two principal new right strategists, Richard Viguerie, who had practically invented mass direct-mail fundraising for conservative candidates, and Howard Phillips, founder of the Conservative Caucus, a national organization of grassroots activists. Concentration on social issues was said to be a major difference between the new right and the old (identified with leaders like Goldwater and Reagan). The old right, according to *Conservative Digest,* published by Viguerie, had "stressed almost exclusively economic and foreign policy" issues. The new right, while not abandoning these issues, would emphasize concerns like "busing, abortion, pornography, education, traditional biblical moral values, and quotas," which specially motivated "ethnic and blue-collar Americans, bornagain Christians, pro-life Catholics, and Jews."[186]

Because none of the triumvirate of new right strategists had roots in evangelicalism (Weyrich and Viguerie are Catholics, and Phillips is a Jew), they needed outside help to make contact with the fundamentalist part of their projected coalition. Weyrich cultivated the friendship of Robert Billings, a fundamentalist educator whom he had met when Billings ran unsuccessfully for Congress in Indiana in 1976. Phillips recruited Edward E. McAteer, a former sales promoter for Colgate Palmolive with wide contacts among evangelical preachers and their financial backers, as a field director for the Conservative Caucus.[187]

In 1978 the Carter administration tightened standards for tax-exempt status for church-operated schools, requiring that the percentage of their student bodies drawn from racial minorities be at least one-fifth of the percentage in the local community. The new right strategists saw the opening for which they had been waiting. With Weyrich's encouragement and counsel, Billings formed a national organization to represent the political interests of the Christian academies. Through Billings, Weyrich got to know Jerry Falwell.

The 1978 election turned out to be a trial run for the planned alliance bringing together the political new right, Protestant fundamentalists, and Catholic right-to-lifers. Opposition to abortion (which formerly had not been much of an issue among fundamentalists) became the unifying cause. Conservatives made gains in the congressional elections. Fundamentalist leaders began speaking of a religious new right that would be the dominant partner in a new conservative coalition. Pat Robertson, conductor of a religious talk show emanating from Virginia Beach, said bluntly, "We have enough votes to run the country." Jim Bakker, a former protégé of Robertson's, now hosting his own talk show in North Carolina, agreed. "Our goal is to influence all viable candidates on issues important to the church. We want answers. We want appointments in government." New right leaders decided that Billings's lobby for the Christian academies should be broadened to become a more comprehensive organization that would work for the entire conservative agenda.[188]

Members of the new right's inner circle firmly believe that their moral attitudes are shared by the great majority of Americans but that the preferences of this majority are being systematically thwarted by a liberal elite (the secular humanists) controlling the federal government, the national media, and the great universities (and probably also most of Wall Street). During a strategy session of new right leaders in the spring of 1979, Weyrich, making this point, used the expression "moral majority." Falwell, it is said, instantly recognized the phrase as summing up the theme of the new national political organization they were about to launch. The Moral Majority, Inc., with Falwell as its president and Billings as its executive director, came into existence in June 1979.[189]

Falwell sought to maintain the Moral Majority as an ecumenical body of political activists, composed of "Catholics, Jews, Protestants, Mormons, Fundmentalists" united by the common goal of returning the United States to "moral sanity." In practice, most of the chairmen of the state chapters, all appointed by Falwell, were fundamentalists. At least twenty-five of the state chairmen were affiliated with churches that sponsored Christian academies.[190]

Using the mailing list of 250,000 prime donors to Falwell's "Old Time Gospel Hour," the Moral Majority raised one-third of its projected $3 million first-year budget in one month. By the middle of 1980 the organization claimed a membership of 300,000, including 70,000 ministers.[191]

During its first year the Moral Majority concentrated on getting its name well known and on registering voters for the 1980 election. At the first of these objectives it was spectacularly successful. A Gallup poll in December 1980 found that 40 percent of a national sample had heard of the Moral Majority. Surveys taken in the South and Southwest found levels of recognition almost twice the national figure. Part of the Moral Majority's fame stemmed from the use of its name by national media and liberal publicists to designate the entire religious new right. Many of the people who had heard of the Moral Majority did not like it.[192]

The results of the Moral Majority's drive have been much debated. In his own church in Lynchburg, Virginia, Falwell instituted an effective Sunday morning exercise. Following the regular worship service, he asked the entire congregation to stand. After telling the registered voters to sit down, he lectured those who remained standing on their duty to get on the election rolls and warned that he would repeat the same procedure every Sunday until election day. This routine was copied in other fundamentalist churches. In some churches, voter registration booths were set up after services. At the the end of the campaign the Moral Majority claimed to have registered from 4 million to 8 million new voters (the kind of spread that automatically induces skepticism). Outside observers estimated that the entire religious right had registered about 2 million—still impressive. Voter turnout rose in the South, the evangelical stronghold, in 1980, while it declined in all other regions.[193]

Other organizations claiming to represent evangelicals in politics took the field. Christian Voice, gathering most of its support from the West and Southwest, sponsored its own political action committee, which raised about $500,000 for conservative candidates in 1980. Religious Roundtable, founded by Ed McAteer and Jim Robison, a Texas evangelist, set out to attract evangelicals in the mainline denominations put off by the Moral Majority. Christian Voice achieved notoriety by issuing report cards, on which congressman were given "moral ratings" on the basis of their votes not only on such issues as school prayer and abortion but also on economic sanctions against Rhodesia, the American defense treaty with Taiwan, and the creation of the Department of Education. The media gleefully pointed out that while a number of liberal congressmen who were active church members received zero ratings, a conservative Florida congressman convicted of accepting a bribe in the Abscam investigation was given a moral rating of 100 percent.[194]

Ronald Reagan, still identified with the old right, was not the first choice for president of most religious right leaders in 1980. Some followed Richard Viguerie in supporting Congressman Phillip Crane, a full-blooded new rightist. Others preferred John Connally. But Reagan seems from the start to have been the favorite among rank-and-file fundamentalists. When the campaigns for Crane and Connally fizzled, religious right leaders rushed to get behind Reagan's candidacy. Christian Voice was the first to move. Falwell soon followed, promising that the Moral Majority would mobilize voters for Reagan "even if he has the devil running with him."[195]

After the Republican convention the religious right's political operations were closely meshed with the Reagan campaign. Robert Billings left the Moral Majority to become coordinator of church groups supporting Reagan. Evangelical leaders were urged to submerge their theological differences in the common effort to restore conservative moral principles. "Knowing pastors as we did," Tim LaHaye said, "we all recognized that the only way to organize them was to make it clear that our basis of cooperation was moral, not theological. . . . " At a conclave of evangelicals in Dallas organized by McAteer and Robison, Reagan announced, "Religious America is awakening, perhaps just in time for our country's sake. . . . If *you* do not speak your mind and cast your ballots, then who will speak and work for the ideals we cherish?" A bemused evangelical observing the scene reported, "Thousands of people were cheering for all they were worth—cheering away the eschatalogical doctrines of a lifetime, cheering away the theological pessimism of a lifetime."[196]

Midway through the campaign, the news media discovered—and at first wildly exaggerated—the impact of the religious right. The *Washington Star* placed Falwell's weekly television audience at 25 million, making him the "second most watched TV personality in the country, surpassed only by Johnny Carson." *Newsweek* guessed that his televised appeals were reaching 18 million every week. (The actual figure, according to Nielson and Arbitron ratings, was about 1.4 million.) The *New York Times* surmised that Falwell had "created something very similar to a political party." *U.S. News and World Report* found "a political holy war without precedent . . . in full swing in this country."[197]

Some of the leading evangelists apparently developed misgivings about the extent of their political involvements. Pat Robertson and Jim Bakker, who had earlier gone even further than Falwell in taking political positions, distanced themselves from the campaign. To a remarkable degree, however, most of the fundamentalist leaders, normally a highly individualistic lot, held together in support of Reagan.

In the immediate aftermath of the election the media attributed a large share of the cause for Reagan's victory and the Republicans' surprise capture of control of the Senate to the religious right. *Time* speculated that as much as two-thirds of Reagan's margin had come from a shift in political attitudes among white fundamentalists. Some liberals drew the conclusion that a wave of religious repression was about to sweep the country. "I am beginning to fear," said Patricia Harris, secretary of health and human services under Carter, "that we could have an Ayatollah Khomeini in this country, but he will not have a beard . . . he will have a television program."[198]

A second round of analysis produced indications that the initial appraisals had greatly exaggerated the impact of the religious right. In a widely read article in *Commentary* Seymour Martin Lipset and Earl Raab pointed out that while Reagan had won the votes of 61 percent of born-again white Protestants, he had also been supported by an even larger share, 63 percent, of other white Protestants. (This finding, however, was not necessarily inconsistent with the view that the religious right had played an important part in the election:

mainline Protestants outside the South have always constituted the most important element in the Republican base, but votes won by Reagan among evangelicals often came from persons who formerly either had voted Democratic or had not been politically active.) Case studies by political scientists on individual state chapters of the Moral Majority showed that many were little more than letterhead organizations composed of a few right-wing preachers and a mailing list. Polls revealed that even in states like Virginia and Texas, where the religious right was presumably strong, voters with unfavorable impressions of the Moral Majority greatly outnumbered those with favorable impressions. (Such polls, however, did not measure how much favorable or unfavorable impressions had actually influenced voting behavior.) An NBC/Associated Press poll found that only 3 percent of the public said they would be "more likely to vote for a candidate if asked by a member of the clergy." (But the effects of less direct political recommendations by the clergy were not measured.) Recovering from their earlier fright, some sophisticated liberals decided that the new religious right was little more than a phantasm. The Moral Majority, Andrew Greeley commented, was "a ghost, a spook, a bogey man . . . a fiction of the paranoia of some segments of the liberal media elite. . . ."[199]

A third round of analysis, carried out over an extended period, again shifted the balance of interpretation. Analyzing data gathered by the University of Michigan's 1980 National Election Survey, Arthur Miller and Martin Wattenberg found that while only 6 percent of the public indicated they felt "close to evangelical groups active in politics such as the Moral Majority," members of this core group had voted as a cohesive electoral block in 1980. Moreover, 26 percent regarded themselves as born-again Christians, and 27 perecent said they felt general sympathy for "evangelical groups such as the Moral Majority," suggesting a pool of voters among whom the religious right might grow. "The conservative Christians," the analysis concluded, "represent an emerging political force in U.S. electoral politics. . . . The cohesiveness evident in their political attitudes and voter behavior suggests a unique impact attributable to shared religious interests and the mobilizing influence of the new Christian right leadership."[200]

As president, Ronald Reagan did not copy Jimmy Carter's performance in dealing with supporters among the religious right. He spoke out frequently in favor of constitutional amendments to restore school prayer and prohibit abortion. Though he clearly did not give so-called social issues the same amount of attention or political muscle he devoted to major economic or defense policies, he appeared to make good-faith efforts when bills embodying such issues were before Congress. The administration at first moved to drop the Internal Revenue Service ban against tax-exempt status for church schools that appear to discriminate against racial minorities (the issue that had been the immediate grievance triggering formation of the religious new right in 1978). Following an uproar among civil rights groups, it restored the ban but then supported the appeal of Bob Jones University against it before the Supreme Court, where the ban was upheld.[201]

Some leaders of the religious right complained that Reagan did not do enough to promote their causes and that powerful members of the White House staff were indifferent if not hostile to their interests. But rank-and-file fundamentalists appeared satisfied that the president was on their side. Reagan spoke often before gatherings of evangelicals and expressed solidarity with their religious beliefs (the Bible, he said, contains "all the answers to all the problems that face us today"). His administration, moreover, awarded federal appointments to a few key individuals in the leadership of the religious right. Robert Billings, who had helped get the religious right started in 1978, was named director of regional offices in the Department of Education. Morton Blackwell, who had performed liaison duties between the evangelicals and the Reagan campaign, became a coordinator of political strategy on the White House staff.[202]

For its part the religious right supported not only the administration's initiatives on moral and social issues but also many of Reagan's positions on economic and foreign policy. While mainline Protestant denominations, Jewish welfare agencies, and the Catholic church protested against the administration's proposed cuts in domestic social programs, the religious right praised the president's efforts to give freer rein to the private sector. Falwell found the free-enterprise system "clearly outlined in the Book of Proverbs in the Bible." Others quoted the advice of the apostle Paul to the Thessalonians: "If any would not work, neither should he eat." (When Falwell was asked why he had not included "helping the poor" among the objectives of the Moral Majority, he replied: "We could never bring the issue of the poor into Moral Majority because the argument would be, Who is going to decide what will reach those people? Mormons, Catholics? No, we won't get into that.")[203]

The religious right supported the administration's drive to strengthen national defense, arguing that only a strong America will be able to play its assigned role in the drama preceding the final days. The Moral Majority took full-page ads in major newspapers warning, "We cannot afford to be number two in defense! But, sadly enough, that's where we are today. Number two. And fading!" Falwell declared it a "sad fact" that in an all-out nuclear exchange the Soviet Union "would kill 135 million to 160 million Americans, and the United States would kill only 3 to 5 percent of the Soviets. . . ." Yet with no apparent sense of inconsistency, Falwell sometimes returned to the optimistic fatalism characteristic of some forms of religious idealism: "If God is on our side, no matter how militarily superior the Soviet Union is, they could never touch us. God would miraculously protect America," a statement that if interpreted literally would seem to require no military defense at all and would place Falwell in agreement with the most extreme branch of Christian pacifists.[204]

The future political durability of the religious new right remains uncertain. Economic recession in 1982 drew many evangelicals with Democratic roots who had voted for Reagan in 1980 back to their former attachments. Some commentators suggested that the new religious right as a political force had passed its peak and probably would have little impact on future elections.

In 1984, however, the religious right was more active and apparently more effective than ever. Through much of the South, white evangelical churches conducted drives to get more of their members registered as voters. In the competition between conservative white evangelical church groups seeking to increase registration among their constituents and black churches working to register supporters of first Jesse Jackson and then Walter Mondale, the white evangelicals were the clear winners in terms of total voters registered, partly because white evangelicals greatly outnumber blacks. In North Carolina, for example, black registration increased by 179,373, but this impressive gain was more than offset by the huge increase of 307,852 among whites, many of them evangelicals. Registration drives by evangelical churches apparently contributed to sharp rises in Republican strength in Florida and Texas.

On election day 81 percent of white evangelicals voted for Reagan, up almost one-third over 1980. Perhaps even more important, 77 percent of white evangelicals voting in congressional elections supported Republican candidates for the House of Representatives. If anything approaching this level of support is maintained in future elections and if it eventually is translated into voting for Republicans for state and local offices, without offsetting losses among economic conservatives with more liberal social views, the Republican party will be well on its way to regaining the majority party status it lost in the 1930s.[205]

THE CONSERVATIVE COALITION

One reason evangelicalism declined as a social force during the first half of the twentieth century was that it allowed itself to become isolated from social conservatives in other religious groups. Jerry Falwell, in particular, has been determined that this shall not happen to the religious new right. He has, for instance, emphasized the tie of fundamentalists to Jews as the chosen nation of the Old Testament: "Every nation that has ever stood with the Jews has felt the hand of God's blessing on them. I firmly believe that God has blessed America because America has blessed the Jew." There is no reason to question the sincerity of such statements. But it cannot have escaped the attention of leaders of the religious right that a positive relationship with the Jewish community is politically and socially advantageous.[206]

Much more sensational is the friendly relationship that has developed between Falwell's camp and conservative Catholics, Catholicism having traditionally been viewed among right-wing Protestants as at least as reprehensible as secular humanism. This change represents a broad conclusion among most conservative religious groups (also including Mormons, another historical antagonist of both evangelicals and Catholics) that the forces of secular humanism have grown so strong that all forms of theistic religion must band together if they are to have any hope of standing off the common foe. The issue immediately uniting them is the drive to overthrow the Supreme Court's decision establishing a constitutional right to abortion.

Although it has become a major concern among fundamentalists only recently (partly because it did not enter public debate until the 1960s), the abortion issue has acquired extraordinary emotional

intensity for the religious right. Francis Schaeffer suggested that if
the federal government should resume financing abortions, Christians
at some point must consider refusing "to pay some portion of their
tax money." Cal Thomas, director of public relations for the Moral
Majority, said in 1982 that "if the abortion problem is not solved
through legal means, it will be necessary to take some form of radical
action."[207]

The possibility of martyrdom in the struggle to stop abortion seems
to fire the imaginations of some fundamentalists—in part, it appears,
because on this issue they are certain they are on the side of the
angels. Many fundamentalists, including Falwell, at one time supported racial segregation and most have never given strong backing
to civil rights. At least some fundamentalists recognize that the
conservative defense and economic policies that they endorse involve
moral ambiguities. But on the issue of abortion, they believe it is the
liberals who are countenancing mass destruction of potential life,
while fundamentalists, in alliance with Catholics, stand up for the
rights of the most vulnerable of all forms of human life, the unborn.
"The strength of Martin Luther King," Cal Thomas has said, "came
through his willingness to go to jail. By dramatizing his belief in black
equality, he went to work on the conscience of the nation. Those who
regard abortion as infanticide have got to show that this is not just a
bunch of philosophic beliefs they are holding—that they are prepared
to suffer in order to stop the killing."[208]

Not all evangelicals have been swept up by the religious new right.
Many fundamentalist preachers in the separatist tradition continue
to rail against the blasphemy of mingling religion with politics. During
the 1980 campaign Bob Jones II described Falwell as "the most
dangerous man in America so far as Biblical Christianity is concerned."
(Falwell replied that he was "dangerous to liberals, feminists, abor-
tionists, and homosexuals, but certainly not to Bible-believing Christians.")[209]

More moderate evangelicals, while not faulting the religious right
for entering politics, have criticized the stridency of expression
sometimes employed by groups like the Moral Majority and the
willingness of the political preachers to take positions on all kinds of
economic and foreign policy issues (following the example of some
of the mainline denominations). Carl Henry, the most respected
evangelical theologian, has spoken out against efforts to impose

"goose step morality." Billy Graham told an interviewer, "It would disturb me if there was a wedding between the religious fundamentalists and the political right. The hard right has no interest in religion except to manipulate it." Senator Mark Hatfield of Oregon, an active Baptist layman and moderate Republican, questioned the religious right's choice of issues: "Many evangelicals share my concern that the grievous sins of our society are militarism and materialism, rather than the Taiwan treaty, the Equal Rights Amendment, or the Panama Canal." In the early 1980s the National Association of Evangelicals, following the course set by its Washington director, Robert Dugan, edged cautiously toward the political arena, while avoiding identification with what Graham called the "hard right."[210]

On the left, a small segment of evangelicals, centered on the Sojourners community in Washington, D.C., has been in the vanguard of the movement to stop American participation in the nuclear arms race, through civil disobedience if necessary. The Sojourners group, however, has maintained solidarity with more conservative evangelicals on social issues like abortion.[211]

Social scientists have described the rise of the religious right as an example of "status politics," the struggle of a declining social group to recapture some of its lost prestige and power. Status anxieties have no doubt helped motivate fundamentalists and evangelicals to participate in politics—as they also have entered, though less remarked, the bundle of motives carrying mainline Protestant, Catholic, and Jewish establishments into political involvements. But as with mainline Protestants, Catholics, and Jews, evangelicals have also been propelled by substantive concerns over objective conditions in social reality. The central concern that has motivated most of those drawn to politics is the decline of moral standards, particularly those relating to the family.

It may be that the remedies proposed by the evangelicals to reverse this decline would not work, or that the measures they propose would cause inequities outweighing whatever good they might do, or that, in any case, current social and political limits ensure that such remedies will never be tried. ("Everyone can 'affirm' family values, of course," Phillip Hammond has noted, "but divorce rates are not likely to decrease, birth rates are not likely to increase, women's participation in more and more arenas outside of the house is not likely to be reversed, and children are not likely to find home an adequate substitute for the technical training required to live in this modern world. Traditional family values can be affirmed, therefore, but they are doomed to be elusive in reality.")[212]

Survey evidence indicates, nevertheless, that the moral concerns expressed by the evangelicals are shared far beyond the ranks of the organized religious right. A nationwide survey by the National Opinion Research Center in the late 1970s that included a series of questions on such social issues as homosexuality, school prayer, the role of women, and abortion, found that predominantly conservative answers were given by 82 percent of Baptists, 77 percent of Methodists, 75 percent of Lutherans, 72 percent of Presbyterians, and 70 percent of Catholics—though only 48 percent of Episcopalians and 37 percent of Jews.[213]

Even some dedicated political opponents of the religious right have welcomed its appearance as a counterforce to the atomizing effects of egoism and materialism. Dean Kelley, far from a right-wing fundamentalist, has asserted, "I disagree strenuously with many of the objectives of the 'moral majority' and will do my best to oppose them on those objectives. But I think their influence can be salutary for the nation as a whole. . . . A period of regularizing rigor may be distressing and even destructive to some persons and groups, but the continued atomization and deterioration of this culture is the way of social destruction and death, not for one or a few, but for all."[214]

Why then do national polls consistently show that a majority of the public regards the religious new right as threatening? The cause of this concern does not appear to lie primarily in objection to the moral attitudes that the right claims to represent but rather in the widely held impression that conservative religious groups aim to impose narrowly conceived formulations of these attitudes through official coercion. The public suspects, in short, that the religious right is not fully committed to democratic pluralism.

The shrewder or perhaps more enlightened among the managers of the religious right have tried to dispel this impression. The first item in the platform of the Moral Majority reads, "We believe in the separation of church and state." When Ronald Godwin, vice-president of the Moral Majority and director of its Washington office, was asked if the group aims to make the United States a Christian nation, he replied, "No, no, no, that is the furthest thing from our minds. . . . If America were Christian today, it could be Moslem tomorrow. What we need is a pluralist society. The Moral Majority is not trying to impose its values on others. The last thing we want is a theocracy."[215]

Yet many pronouncements by leaders of the religious right *do* have an absolutist ring. "People want leadership," Robert Billings has said. "They don't know what to think for themselves. They want to be told what to think by some of us here close to the front." Tim LaHaye looks forward to the time when "the real American People will regain their country and culture." LaHaye has also expressed the view that "no humanist is qualified to hold any governmental office in America— United States senator, congressman, cabinet member, State Department employee, or any other position that requires him to think in the best interest of America" (an opinion that would appear to run counter to the constitutional provision that "no religious test shall ever be required as a qualification to any office of public trust under the United States"). In 1981 Ed McAteer said with regard to the controversy over the teaching of evolution that he would, if it were possible, "go to the extreme and prohibit the teaching of evolution altogether, since it is contrary to the word of God, but since that is not now practical, all we are asking is that creationism and evolution be presented as alternatives." Falwell has likened the church to "a disciplined, charging army. . . . Christians, like slaves and soldiers, ask no question." Paul Weyrich has said flatly: "We're radicals working to overturn the present structure in this country—we're talking about Christianizing America."[216]

There has always been a strain of absolutist idealism in American fundamentalism and in the Puritan tradition from which it is partly descended. This tendency clearly influences the religious new right. The heartening thing from the standpoint of democratic pluralism, however, is that some of the ablest leaders of the religious right feel obliged, whether by a sense of social responsibility or political prudence, to struggle to prevent this absolutist tendency from becoming dominant.

A New Center?

Neither the liberal establishments of the mainline churches nor their right-wing opponents appear to represent the views of most church-going Protestants. Polls and general observation indicate that most Protestants feel dissatisfied with some aspects of modernity and are strongly anticommunist but remain committed to pluralism and are convinced that the churches should play some role in promoting peace and social justice. It is therefore not surprising that efforts have been made to move the churches toward the ideological, or nonideological, area vaguely identified as the center.

The first major attempt to act against destructive aspects of modernity without rejecting pluralism or social responsibility was launched by a group of reformers, mostly liberals, who gathered in Hartford, Connecticut, in January 1975. Two of them, Richard John Neuhaus, a Lutheran theologian, and William Sloane Coffin, chaplain at Yale, had been leaders in the religious protest movement against the Vietnam War in the 1960s. Another of the moving spirits, Peter Berger, a Lutheran layman, is a sociologist specializing in the study of modernity. The "Hartford appeal" as it was called was signed by seventeen churchmen and one churchwoman, mostly mainline Protestants but also including a few Catholics, evangelicals, and Orthodox Christians.

The appeal criticized both the secularist tendency within the contemporary church to argue that "the world must set the agenda for the Church" and the idealist tendency to assume that "the struggle for a better humanity will bring about the Kingdom of God." On the secularist tendency, the appeal commented, "The Church must denounce oppressors, help liberate the oppressed, and seek to heal human misery. . . . But the norms for the Church's activity derive from its own perception of God's will for the world." And on the idealist tendency, it held, "The struggle for a better humanity is essential to Christian faith. . . . But imperfect human beings cannot create a perfect society. The Kingdom of God surpasses any conceivable utopia. . . ."[217]

The following year, eight of the signers of the Harford appeal published a book of essays elaborating some of its principles. Modernity, Peter Berger observed, tends to replace the traditional Judeo-Christian world view, under which social value is tied to transcendent purpose, with a world view that regards "the reality of ordinary life . . . [as] the only reality." One difficulty with this change, Berger claimed, is that without "transcendent referrents," social authority loses its main source of "legitimation."[218]

Picking up this point, Richard Neuhaus argued that rejection of a transcendent level of reality imperils all of humanist social ethics: without a religious referrent there is no compelling motive for human solidarity. "By what standard are [the poor], or my next door neighbor for that matter, worth loving for themselves?" Neuhaus acknowledged that some secularists claim a sense of moral responsibility may be deduced from the terms of the human condition, "but the average businessman and church elder is not likely, if he is the unsentimental sort, to be activated by the proposition that the things he values—his marriage, his second car, his spiritual well being—are threatened by the death of another starving child in Colombia." The economically fortunate are inclined by nature to regard suffering among unrelated others as irrelevant to their own situations. "There is no compelling argument to the contrary—unless it is God." If the church subordinates revelation of transcendence to social action, therefore, it ultimately chokes off the source from which the motivation for social action comes.[219]

Even worse than subordination of the church's spiritual function, in Neuhaus's view, is identification of transcendent purpose with a particular political point of view. The church, he suggested, needs a dose of Niebuhrian, or Lutheran, realism: "Politics, far from being the singular path to the kingdom, is under the sign of the Whore of Babylon. It is the vocation of some to take the risks of wrestling good from an evil process. . . . If their vocation is built upon the belief that their cause is God's cause, it is built upon sand, and it is likely to be very bloody sand at that. . . ."[220]

The coalition of Hartford reformers did not hold. Coffin, who soon left Yale to become paster of the Riverside Church in New York, one of the great shrines of American Protestantism, became an effective gadfly for liberal causes. Berger and Neuhaus were drawn toward the circle of neoconservative intellectuals gathering around Irving Kristol. Other signers of the Hartford appeal, such as Randolph Nugent, advanced to positions of leadership within their separate denominations.[221]

Under the auspices of the American Enterprise Institute, a neo-conservative stronghold in Washington, D.C., Berger and Neuhaus undertook a study of the role that private institutions, including the church, may play as "mediating structures . . . standing between the individual in his private life and the large institutions of public life." Public policy, they concluded in a paper published in 1977, "is presently biased toward what might be called the symbolic nakedness of the town square," and the public interest would be better served if the churches were "unfettered" to carry out many social services currently being performed by government.²²²

At the American Enterprise Institute Berger and Neuhaus met members of the intellectual cadre attached to what was then known as the Jackson wing of the Democratic party—domestic liberals or even socialists who shared the hawkish views on foreign and defense policies of Senator Henry Jackson of Washington. Jackson's position, based on the assumption that the Soviet Union is inherently expansionist, had dominated the Democratic party from the time of Harry Truman through the administration of Lyndon Johnson but was decisively rejected by the Democratic National Convention of 1972 that nominated George McGovern for president. Though still supported by much of organized labor, it now represented a minority view within the party. Some Jackson Democrats were concerned over the support being given by mainline Protestant denominations to groups allegedly promoting communist regimes or communist-controlled insurgencies in third world countries. This concern was shared by Berger, Neuhaus, and some of the other neoconservative reformers.

In the spring of 1980 David Jessup, a young political organizer for the AFL-CIO, distributed among selected delegates to that year's quadrennial general conference of the United Methodist church a paper, thereafter known as the "Jessup report," charging that Methodist funds were being "siphoned off" to support "totalitarian" causes or governments. Jessup listed specific grants by Methodist agencies to twelve organizations that were, he claimed, linked in one way or another to the "totalitarian left."²²³

Jessup has said that his interest in the political orientation of the United Methodist church first became aroused when his children brought home appeals for what he regarded as Marxist causes from the Sunday School of the Methodist church he and his wife had joined in Silver Spring, Maryland. He was at first, he says, troubled by this literature, "but not persuaded that these projects represented anything more than minor aberrations from a more consistent tradition of Methodist support for democratic values." But after "several months of research on the political orientation of groups receiving church funds," he was "no longer so certain."²²⁴

Jessup had only become a Methodist after moving to the Washington area in 1977. But he was, as the national staff of the United Methodist church later pointed out, no newcomer to political controversy. Since his student years at the University of Colorado in the early 1960s, he had been active in various socialist causes, and since 1972 he had been a member of the Social Democratic party, an anticommunist offshoot of the Socialist party with close ties to the Jackson Democrats. (In the Byzantine history of the socialist movement in the United States, the Social Democrats represent a faction, particularly strong in organized labor, which holds that extirpation of communism should be the first order of business for the American left.) With his wife, Jessup had also served in the Peace Corps in Peru and participated in the civil rights movement on the West Coast. In his work with organized labor, first in the San Francisco Bay area and then on the staff of the AFL-CIO's political action arm in Washington, he had vigorously supported the anticommunist and anti-Soviet stances of the union federation's national leadership. In 1980 he was given responsibility for maintaining liaison between the AFL-CIO and President Carter's campaign for reelection.

Penn Kemble, Jessup's closest friend at the University of Colorado and a regular political associate ever since, was even more active as a promoter of militant anticommunism on the left. Kemble had helped organize Frontlash, a labor-sponsored anticommunist youth organization. In 1972 he was a founding member of the Coalition for a Democratic Majority, an organization of Jackson Democrats formed to combat the rise of McGovernism in the Democratic party.[225]

Jessup's report sparked considerable debate at the 1980 Methodist General Conference. At Jessup's suggestion a delegate moved the creation of a committee on accountability to examine the church's grant procedures; the motion did not pass, but the conference did vote to make financial records of the denomination's boards and agencies more readily available. Jessup's position was supported by some of the delegates associated with the Good News movement, an evangelical caucus within the United Methodist church that for some years had been trying to move the denomination toward a more conservative theological orientation. After the conference, Jessup continued to consult with Edmund Robb, a Methodist evangelist from Texas who was a leader of Good News.[226]

During the early months of 1981, while the newly elected Reagan administration was taking hold in Washington, Jessup, Kemble, Robb,

Neuhaus, Berger, and other leaders of the Coalition for a Democratic Majority and the Good News movement discussed means for dealing with the tilt to the "totalitarian left" that they perceived in some of the operations of the mainline churches. These talks were sometimes joined by Carl Henry, the evangelical theologian, and by two Catholics, Michael Novak, a theologian and social commentator at the American Enterprise Institute who had moved from being a speechwriter for McGovern in 1972 to composing an ardent defense of free-enterprise capitalism in the 1980s, and James Schall, a Jesuit political scientist at Georgetown University who had been a persistent critic of what he regarded as the leftward drift of American Catholicism since the Second Vatican Council. Several participants in these discussions later said they were concerned not only by the direction being taken by the mainline churches but also by the possibility that the religious new right, which had just appeared on the scene and which they regarded as both theologically and socially flawed, might come to be regarded as the chief religious alternative to current mainline policies.[227]

Though most of these individuals had their political roots in the Democratic party (or in one of the socialist factions pursuing its goals through the party), several were at that time establishing close ties to the Reagan administration, whose hard-line foreign policy they found congenial. Berger and Novak, for example, accepted temporary diplomatic assignments from the administration.

The upshot of the talks among assorted neoconservatives, members of the Coalition for a Democratic Majority, and moderate evangelicals was the formation in April 1981 of the Institute on Religion and Democracy, with Robb as its chairman. The purpose of the new organization, its prospectus announced, would be "to illuminate the relationship between Christian faith and democratic governance . . . [and] to oppose policies and programs in the churches which ignore or deny that relationship."[228]

A statement of principles, written by Neuhaus, set forth the organization's operating assumptions: "The first political task of the Church is to be the Church . . . a sustaining community of faith and discipline under the Lordship of Christ." While the church's primary responsibility is to "proclaim and demonstrate the Gospel," this does not mean that Christians should "withdraw from participation in other communities." To the contrary, "we are called to be leaven and light in movements of cultural, political, and economic change." Christian principles can be applied through "a variety of social, political, or economic systems." But Christianity is totally incompatible with modern totalitarianism, whether of the communist or fascist varieties. Since the defeat of Nazi Germany, "the only global ideology that is committed to the monistic denial of freedom is Marxist-Leninism." Christians, therefore, "must be unapologetically anti-Communist."[229]

There is, Neuhaus argued, "a necessary linkage between Christian faith and human freedom." Democracy, "in this moment of history . . . is the necessary product and protector of freedom." Neuhaus rejected the distinction popular within the Reagan administration between communist "totalitarian" regimes and right-wing "authoritarian" governments friendly to the United States. "The churches should reflect an unwavering adherence to a single standard in the judgment of human rights . . . whether the regime in question is repressive only to maintain itself in power or whether it aspires to totalitarian control over its people . . . whether it is friend or foe or neutral toward whatever great power. . . ." Nevertheless, the churches should not affect neutrality between the two superpowers. In the world today "the United States . . . is the primary bearer of the democratic possibility [and] . . . the Soviet Union is the primary bearer of the totalitarian alternative." The United States, therefore, "is, on balance and considering the alternatives, a force for good in the world."[230]

Unfortunately, Neuhaus claimed, some persons holding positions of authority in the churches do not share this "understanding of democracy and America's role in the world." Some, motivated by the goal "of a new and, it is claimed, more equitable social order," have indeed become "apologists for oppression."[231]

Many mainline leaders, and particularly members of the denominational bureaucracies, reacted to the formation of the Institute on Religion and Democracy like medieval clerics scenting the rise of a particularly foul brand of heresy. Charges of McCarthyism were hurled like anathemas. A report commissioned by agencies of the United Methodist church and the United Church of Christ suggested that there was something underhanded in the fact that the IRD founders had known each other through previous associations with the Social Democrats, the Coalition for a Democratic Majority, or the

Good News movement—an odd objection from church groups that have made networking almost a way of life. Some mainline agencies began pressuring their political allies in organized labor to denounce the new group. "If the right wing of the church was attacking labor," one spokesman said, "you'd come to us for help. . . . We need the same support."[232]

A more substantive critique of IRD was delivered by Peter Steinfels, editor of *Commonweal* and author of a balanced appraisal of the neoconservatives. IRD's concentration on the "threat of totalitarianism" as "the most urgent truth to be said about secular politics," Steinfels suggested, could induce complacency toward other "urgent" truths, like the danger of nuclear war, mass starvation, and "terror of a brutal and old-fashioned sort." Steinfels took particular exception to IRD's claim to transcend usual ideological or partisan categories. At bottom, he charged, the new organization's platform was "a carefully crafted endorsement of the major premises of the Reagan administration's foreign policy."[233]

There is weight to Steinfels's criticism, despite Neuhaus's specific disavowal of the Reagan administration's selective approach to human rights. The institute's concentration on anticommunism inevitably produced a narrower agenda than seemed called for by the large reform principles set forth at Hartford. On the issues that it did deal with, IRD did not express a nonideological consensus of values rising above liberalism and conservatism, or left and right, as Neuhaus claimed, but a particular political point of view, namely that of contemporary moderate conservatism. Nevertheless, IRD has at least performed the worthwhile function of offering on some issues a moderate conservative alternative to the liberal-left policies that have generally held sway since the 1960s within mainline Protestantism.

The Underlying Issue

Some mainline leaders, including some among the most liberal, responded to the emergence of IRD and other expressions of ferment within the churches by opening up more basic questions concerning the role of religious institutions in politics.

Methodist Bishop James Armstrong, president of the National Council of Churches, who had himself in 1977 signed a statement that seemed to excuse political repression in Cuba, in 1982 brought Robb and Neuhaus to NCC headquarters in New York for an exchange on the ideological bias of the mainline churches. "We need to listen to critics," Armstrong said, while defending the overall record of the NCC. In a guest sermon at Riverside Church the following year, he declared, "If there are those who put ideology above the Gospel of Jesus Christ, the Gospel is betrayed." (In the midst of a personal emotional crisis toward the end of 1983, Armstrong resigned first as president of the NCC and as a Methodist bishop, and finally from the Methodist ministry.)[234]

James Wall, editor of the liberal *Christian Century*, told the NCC's Information Committee in 1983, "What is really needed is a change of attitude in the council and in the mainline denominations. We have repeatedly embraced causes without acknowledging their defects. That puts us in a weak position and makes it difficult to criticize them when their faults become obvious." Speaking later to a church gathering in Minnesota, he said, "the neoconservative IRD, the new religious right, and the liberal NCC have each on occasion followed tactics and strategy not from their religious base but from the political base of the coalitions to which they belong."[235]

At the 1984 United Methodist General Conference in Baltimore commemorating the two-hundredth anniversary of Methodism in the United States, Bishop William Cannon, in an address endorsed by the denomination's Council of Bishops, placed social action in a Wesleyan perspective: "People alone as individuals can be redeemed, not institutions, structures of society, or forms of government. . . . Neither the United States nor the Soviet Union will exist in heaven. . . . The church is not to be a mirror of the world but a reflection of heaven."[236]

Armstrong, Wall, and Cannon all were touching, in different ways, the underlying issue of what role churches, claiming to represent transcendent truth, may appropriately play in the politics of a pluralist democratic society like the United States. In the final section, I will examine more closely this issue, taking up first the question of the extent to which democracy depends on values transmitted by religion.

SEVEN

Religion and Democracy

ALMOST ALL of the principal founders of the United States, including Thomas Jefferson, were convinced that the health of republican government depends on moral values derived from religion. In more recent times some Americans have come to regard religion as a kind of consumer value, like sports or travel, that should be available in a pluralist society but that makes no essential contribution to the moral foundation of democracy. This latter view has been fed in part by skepticism among academic and cultural elites about whether religion of any traditional kind can possibly be accepted as true. But even apart from the question of the credibility of religion, democracy in this view requires no moral base beyond that supplied by purely secular values.

Religion, some civil humanists have pointed out, is not without social costs. Current controversies over religious values on issues like abortion and school prayer have created bitterly contested divisions within American society. The passions brought to politics by both the religious right and the religious left tend to impede the kind of pragmatic compromises that a pluralist democracy needs to function. Squabbles during the 1984 national campaign over which candidates were good Christians or good Catholics raised emotional heat without increasing substantive light. Some political leaders have become adept at wrapping religion around programs that have distinctly secular origins and substance.

The historical commitment of the American people to religion, broadly defined, can hardly be disputed. But perhaps this commitment is not beyond change. Some secularists look forward to the day when the mass of human beings, or at least the mass of inhabitants of the civilized West, will be free once and for all of the illusions of religion.

It is not enough, therefore, to say that the relationship between religion and democracy in the United States is simply a social fact that government, without supporting any particular religion, would be wise to accommodate. Perhaps a modern democratic government could get rid of religion, as governments in many totalitarian countries have tried to do, or at least could deprive religion of any hint of official respect or approval. The question therefore must be faced: can democracy flourish without support from religious values?

Neither ordinary Americans nor most of our political leaders devote much time to worrying about social philosophy. But if prevailing value systems offer no convincing answers to such questions as why individuals should under some circumstances be prepared to subordinate their particular ends to the common good or why there should be limits to the authority that civil society holds over its members, public confidence in standards of decency and fairness, on which democracy more than any other form of government depends for motivation and consent, must eventually crumble. All supporters of democracy and republican government, therefore, have a critical interest in maintaining values that legitimize free institutions.

Secular values must be based either on self-interest or on some kind of social interest. There are, therefore, three kinds of secular value systems: egoism (based wholly on self-interest), authoritarianism (based wholly on social authority), and civil humanism (based on some combination of self-interest and concern for the public good). Let us now consider the adequacy of each of these as a possible moral basis for democracy.

The Moral Foundation of Democracy

Some on both the left (Herbert Marcuse) and the right (Milton Friedman) have recently argued that egoism is by itself a sufficient value basis for a free and humane society (at least part of what is now meant by democracy). According to the tender-minded egoists of the left, human nature, once freed of sexual repression or economic deprivation, is so inherently benign that impulses rising from the individual self are sufficient to ensure social harmony. The tough-minded egoists of the right do not share this optimistic view of human nature, or at least do not depend on it. But through the "miracle of the marketplace," they argue, free competition among individuals, however naturally rapacious, will produce maximum achievable benefits for all.

The view of human nature assumed by the egoists of the left seems contradicted by almost every page of human history as well as by the daily newspaper and commonsense observation of practical experience. The darker aspects of human nature no doubt spring in part from various kinds of deprivations. But deprivation of one sort or another seems likely to be a prominent factor in the human condition for a very long time to come. Despite enormous economic growth, material appetites remain unsatisfied in even the richest nations, capitalist or socialist. Even if material scarcity were totally conquered, there would still be certain goods, as Fred Hirsch has pointed out, such as access to uncrowded beaches or admission to first-rank universities, that could not in the nature of things be made simultaneously available to all comers.[1] Besides, competition for mates will always produce substantial measures of anxiety, frustration, and disappointment. Even if human selfishness and cruelty were entirely traceable to deprivation—as seems unlikely—there is no prospect that the secular millennium forecast by Marcuse and Charles Reich, among others, would be achievable through natural means. Tender-minded egoism, therefore, though it serves as an unstated premise for much contemporary advertising and entertainment as well as politics and does indeed lead to a certain amount of personal liberation, almost surely cannot over an extended period provide an adequate value base for democracy.

Tough-minded egoism, on the other hand, can point to the actual achievements of market economies—producing far more material goods, distributed broadly though unevenly, than any previous economic system. But experience in the industrial West during the nineteenth and early twentieth centuries indicated, and much in current economic practice continues to confirm, that unrestrained economic warfare of each against all will lead to a social situation in which, as Hobbes would have predicted, life will be brutish for many and nasty for most, though not necessarily solitary or short. Even Milton Friedman, writing with his wife, Rose, has felt driven to expand the concept of self-interest to include "the scientist seeking to advance the frontiers of his discipline, the missionary seeking to convert infidels to the true faith, the philanthropist seeking to bring comfort to the needy"—in effect cushioning the effects of unbridled egoism by coupling it with other value systems.[2] I shall consider more fully below the compatibility of market capitalism with Judeo-Christian ethics. But as with the tender-minded egoism of the left, the evidence of the daily news media and of commonsense observation are probably sufficient to discredit tough-minded egoism, unmitigated by other value systems, as an adequate foundation for a society that can fairly be considered humane or even, under any definition that includes liberality of spirit, free.

There remains the formulation of Hobbes himself: egoism, whether we like it or not, *is* the human condition, and the only way to deal effectively with this reality is through submission to very tough social controls. Hobbes's own prescription was for absolute monarchy, but some forms of modern secular dictatorship should meet the requirements of his argument. The Hobbesian solution, however, will not be mistaken for democracy under any definition.

Therefore, despite its correspondence with a part of the reality of human experience, its ability to produce short-term exhilaration, and its contribution to economic progress, egoism is not by itself a sufficient value base for democracy. In fact, if left unleashed for an extended time, as some on both the left and the right seem anxious to do, egoism is practically guaranteed to cause social disaster.

Authoritarianism is almost by definition hostile to democracy. Benevolent authoritarianism of the varieties that Marxists and some social behaviorists claim to sponsor purports to create a kind of democracy of result, though not of public participation (regarded by authoritarians as a sham). But because awareness of self-interest is inherently human, societies claiming to operate as organic wholes will always in fact allot disproportionate benefits and rewards to those holding social power—as both fascist and communist dictatorships in the twentieth century have shown. The division of societies into leaders and followers discerned by Peggy Billings is characteristic not only, or even particularly, of capitalist societies, but of all human societies of any considerable size or complexity. To maintain some measures of practical freedom and equity, therefore, all but the most powerful members of society require protective institutions such as representative government, private ownership of property, and constitutional rights defended through an independent judiciary. Societies that reject such formal liberties on the ground that they interfere with the pursuit of the collective interests of man conceived as *species-being* may be operating in accord with what they regard as higher standards. But they, too, cannot possibly be confused with democracies.

What democracy needs is a value system that legitimizes both individual rights and social authority and establishes a balance between the two. This is precisely what civil humanism, the third of the secular value systems, purports to do. Civil humanism and theist-humanism agree in valuing personal freedom, distributive justice, citizen participation in social decisionmaking, and social discipline—the values on which democracy is based. Where they differ is that theist-humanism derives these values in part from a transcendent standard, while civil humanism contends they are amply supported by a purely natural interpretation of existence.

Can civil humanism in fact meet democracy's value needs? The Enlightenment, the intellectual origin of much of modern civil humanism, developed two differing, and as it turned out competing, theoretic means for bridging the apparent gap between private interest and public good. The first of these, descended from Locke by way of the British utilitarians, draws on the libertarian side of humanism. It holds that the individual makes a limited, but irreversible, cession of his natural rights to society so that he may more securely enjoy the rights that remain. Under this formulation adherence to social order flows from application of rational self-interest. The second, descended from Rousseau by way of Hegel and Marx, emphasizes the communitarian side of humanism. It maintains that civil liberties are products of social evolution and therefore depend ultimately on the organic will of the social group. Under this formulation the freedom of the citizen is achieved through participation in the general will.[3]

Both lines of argument have propagated distinguished bodies of social philosophy and have influenced the formation of social institutions and political behavior. Neither, however, has fully escaped the bias toward destructive tendencies that tainted it at the start: among the libertarians tendencies toward atomistic selfishness, obsessive materialism, and personal alienation, and among the communitarians toward social indoctrination, state control, and group aggression. Social philosophies developing along the libertarian line, such as those of modern American liberalism and European social democracy, seem always to come down to trusting biological human nature and hoping it will turn out to be more benign or altruistic than was suggested by Hobbes (or St. Paul or Sigmund Freud). Philosophies descending from the competing communitarian line, such as democratic socialism, seem always to come down to trusting organized society and hoping it will be more respectful of personal liberties than any actual social establishment lacking constitutional checks has ever over long duration proven to be. At the end of the path coming down from the interpreters of Locke lies Jerry Rubin or Robert Vesco; at the end of that opened by Rousseau and Hegel, the modern totalitarian state.[4]

In *A Theory of Justice,* published in 1971, John Rawls makes an ingenious attempt to extract a Rousseauian sense of social fairness from the supposedly rational choices of a Lockean natural man. Rawls's person in the "original position" is placed behind a "veil of ignorance," where he may know nothing of his distinctive attributes, such as his intelligence, his physical strength, his "conception of the good," his "place in society," or even "the special features of his psychology such as his aversion to risk or liability to optimism or pessimism." The hypothetical person who remains, Rawls argues, will select a system of social justice dedicated to the realization of two principles: enjoyment by each person of "the most extensive basic liberty compatible with a similar liberty for others" and limitation of "social and economic inequalities, for example inequalities of wealth and authority," to those that "result in compensating benefits for everyone, and in particular for the least advantaged members of society."[5]

Rawls's formulation has usefully clarified important issues in modern democratic theory, such as establishing a balance between equality and economic efficiency. But it ultimately founders, to the extent that it purports to provide a basis for democratic values rooted in human nature, because Rawls's person behind the veil of ignorance is so deprived of particular attributes that he has lost essential qualities of personhood—has become, in short, a simple computer, programmed by its creator to make choices based on values that have been obtained from some other source.

One other formulation of secular civil humanism maintains a

flickering half-life in the modern world: that which comes down from the approach to social ethics developed by the classical philosophers of antiquity, particularly Aristotle. (Aristotle's metaphysic does include a transcendent level of being, as a means for setting the physical universe in motion. But this transcendence is so remote, abstract, and indifferent to human interests that the real sources from which he obtains social values are essentially naturalistic.) The classical formulation rests on the belief that man is a goal-pursuing animal. "Political society exists," Aristotle wrote, "for the sake of noble actions, and not of mere companionship." Noble actions require participation in the grand enterprise of imposing rational direction on human behavior. "In the world both of nature and of art, the inferior always exists for the sake of the better or superior, and the better or superior is that which has a rational principle." Classical social ethics, Alasdair MacIntyre has observed, arises from the tension between "man-as-he-happens-to-be and man-as-he-could-be-if-he-realized-his-essential-nature." Man's "essential nature," dedicated to reason, depends for fulfillment on order, justice, and freedom. The moral authority of a free and humane society is founded, therefore, not on a social contract serving biological drives or on a convoluted metaphysic or on religion, but on the social and personal goals to which human beings by nature aspire.[6]

The classical formulation of humanism was taken over by Jewish, Christian, and Moslem scholars and philosophers into theist-humanism, where it continues to function fruitfully to the present. In this context the somewhat insubstantial classical concept of man's "essential nature" pursuing reason is replaced by the Judaic idea that man's true nature is determined by his relationship to God.

In its secular version, classical humanism maintains some presence in modern literature, philosophy, and even politics. It has formed an important part of the ideological equipment of that paragon of aristocratic virtue, the British gentleman, and of his emulators in the United States and elsewhere. In the novels of Joseph Conrad it defines the quality that enables morally upright men of affairs to recognize each other as "one of us." It serves as a moral touchstone for stoic heroes created by modern writers as different as Albert Camus and Joan Didion and provides the normative foundation for Jacques Monod's "ethic of knowledge."[7] To the extent that modern agnostic liberalism (of the kind conveyed, for instance, by the movie and television series, "M*A*S*H") possesses a coherent ethic, it probably reflects a dim echo of the classical formulation more than either utilitarianism or dialectical theories of history.

The persistent attraction of the classical formulation seems to grow out of two factors: it is compatible with the world view of natural science, and it confers membership in a kind of chivalric elite. Perhaps classical humanism has no conclusive rational argument against egoists or autocrats who, in pursuit of their own ends, reject concepts of social fairness or human rights. But egoists and autocrats who break the "rules of the game" must forfeit, at the least, the right to regard themselves as what humanists call human. MacIntyre offers the analogy of a participant in a game or sport who cheats in order to win: the cheater may obtain all the public and material rewards of victory, but the one thing he cannot have is the satisfaction of knowing in his own mind that he has played well.[8]

Yet the classical version of civil humanism by itself hardly provides an adequate value base for a democratic society. The question of whether any form of secularism can meet the deeper needs of the human spirit lies beyond the scope of this book (though spiritual as much as economic deprivation surely produces political consequences). But classical humanism has serious functional shortcomings from the more limited perspective of providing moral support for democracy.

As some of the above examples suggest, classical humanism is more congruent with an aristocratic than with a democratic approach to politics. Aristotle himself, though he saw some merit in democracy, subscribed to a mixed form of governance dominated in practice by financially independent upper-class statesmen. Classical humanism gains much of its emotive attraction, as has been noted, by drawing a circle. Those within the circle are "one of us." Perhaps the rules of the game call for a spirit of noblesse oblige toward those outside, but they certainly do not require much sharing of political or social power. In a democratic society, persons subscribing to a classical humanist ethic are driven to hypocrisy or cynicism—either pretending admiration or fellow-feeling for the masses that their value system does not sustain or scorning the political forms under which they live. In either case, social bitterness between humanist elites and the mass of working-class and middle-class citizens is bound to follow.

The fundamental flaw of secular civil humanism as a basis for democratic values is that it fails to meet the test of intellectual credibility. Either the self as an independent value source or organic society as an independent value source can reasonably be deduced from nature to be the ultimate origin of all human values, with the consequences described above. There is no logical inconsistency in arguing, as Hobbes did, that the self is the sole source of ultimate value or in claiming, with Marx, that all value comes finally from the social whole. (Empirical tests, I have argued, undermine the collectivist model.) But a combination of the self and society, held in balance as dual sources of ultimate value, cannot plausibly be found in nature without reference to a third value source. Using purely natural criteria, either the self or society must finally be regarded as sovereign. If the self, a rational individual will honor only those social values that serve his fairly immediate selfish interests. ("In the long run," as Keynes remarked, "we are all dead.") If society, personal freedom and the rights of individuals are left at the mercy of established secular authority. In either case, democracy lacks essential moral support. The classical approach comes closest to success. But the thinness of the classical formulation when divorced from religion turns it finally into an instrument for bolstering the self-esteem of a social class.

This brief discussion can hardly be regarded as conclusive. I hope, however, that it has suggested that the founding fathers after all were right: republican government depends for its health on values that over the not-so-long run must come from religion. Through theist-humanism, human rights are rooted in the moral worth with which a loving Creator has endowed each human soul, and social authority is legitimized by making it answerable to transcendent moral law. In a highly mobile and heterogeneous society like the United States, these values based on religion are even more essential to democracy than they may be in more traditional societies, where respect for freedom, order, and justice may be maintained for some time through social inertia or custom.

Religion, it must immediately be added, may pose very serious dangers to democracy and indeed to any kind of civilized existence. As the record of history shows and as recent troubles in Ireland, Iran, Lebanon, and India, among other places, clearly indicate, religious fanaticism may easily lead to social tragedy. Idealism and personalism have both in differing ways enriched human experience—the first by directing social authority toward loftier goals than mere survival and the second by inspiring personal creativity. Both, however, are at fundamental variance with the premises of democracy: idealism, as I have defined it, by rejecting the rights of the individual, and personalism by flouting the bonds of social civility and positive law, without which democracy cannot endure. Even monism encourages a social passivity that tends to undermine the political health of democracy. Among the religious value systems, therefore, only theist-humanism is fully congruent with values of both personal freedom and social responsibility. Democracy, while largely based on values that come ultimately from religion, must be ever on guard against abuses that some tendencies within religion foster.

The problem is made particularly difficult for democracy by the fact that, within the framework established by its own pluralist principles, democratic government can do very little to determine or even influence the kind of religion that churches in a free society may develop or practice. Democratic theorists since Locke have maintained that the state may ordinarily prohibit churches from violating civil laws without infringing on religious freedom. But even when religious beliefs clash with legal responsibilities or limits, democratic polities are sometimes moved by moral or prudential concerns to grant exemptions. People objecting on religious grounds to military service may be made legal exceptions; churches with divergent views on education, like those of the Amish, may be given judicial dispensations. On questions of church doctrine or of social policies advocated by the churches, democratic government can do almost nothing without taking on attributes of authoritarianism or absolutist idealism, the chief dangers against which the religion clauses of the First Amendment were meant to defend. Democractic government, therefore, finds itself bound by the uncomfortable but necessary condition that, while depending on religion for much of its moral sustenance, it must leave the churches and other religious institutions almost entirely free to develop and promote whatever values or beliefs their spiritual insights may inspire.

The key role of religion in maintaining the health of democracy gives all citizens, including those who are themselves without religious faith, a large stake in the way the churches carry out their roles in secular society. Most of the remainder of this chapter, therefore, will deal with the options now available to the churches in their approaches to public policy.

The Role of the Churches

"Why don't the churches just shut up?" Peter Berger has asked, expressing perhaps temporary exasperation over the recent flurry of social and political pronouncements issuing from church leaders and church bodies. Many, both within and outside the churches, agree that some religious groups have been drawn too deeply into secular politics. But the memory of events in Germany during the 1920s and 1930s sets an outer limit to the degree of political noninvolvement that most churchpersons now feel is morally acceptable for the churches.

Despite a few honorable exceptions, most German churches and church leaders made little effort to oppose, and some even actively supported, the rise to power and brutal performance of Adolf Hitler and the Nazi party. The Lutheran doctrine of the "two kingdoms" proved simply inadequate to deal with a situation in which the civil kingdom came to be dominated by a monster like Hitler. German Catholics or Calvinists, who lacked even the excuse of doctrinal inhibition, did little better in showing resistance to the Nazis.

There is now a consensus in virtually all churches that such noninvolvement must never be permitted to happen again: that the church must oppose clear social evil even at the risk of its own extinction. Some churchpersons have been led by this principle to detect incipient fascism among politicians or political groups who by more conventional standards seem simply to hold differing economic or social opinions. And some (sometimes the same persons) have developed remarkable tolerance for political repression carried out under the banners of the left. But whatever differences exist over its interpretation (and they are many), the principle is firmly established: the church is morally bound to do what it can to resist political despotism or terror.

Beyond this point of consensus, opinions swiftly diverge on the appropriate role for the churches in secular politics. Some church leaders and church bodies, holding that the churches should concern themselves primarily with salvation of individual souls, regard practically all political involvement by the churches beyond resistance to tyranny as irrelevant distraction. Others favor intense participation by the churches in all kinds of economic, social, and foreign policy issues, or even formation of a religious political party, perhaps modeled on the Christian Democratic parties in Europe or the religious parties in Israel.

The approaches taken by particular churches to political action are conditioned by their histories and by the current social needs and interests of their members. Most Jewish groups are naturally dedicated to support for Israel. The traditional role of the black churches as centers of social organization leads them to act as political advocates for black interests. Catholic concern that education be oriented toward religion produces a special outlook on church-state relations—now increasingly shared by evangelical churches sponsoring Christian academies. Catholics are tugged in opposite directions on the political spectrum by the issues of abortion and nuclear disarmament, though Catholic leaders maintain that concern for human life is the theme uniting their positions on the two issues. Evangelical Protestants are particularly aroused by the growing secularization of American society. Mainline Protestants are influenced by the precedents of church participation in the struggles for abolition, Prohibition, and women's suffrage. Historically, "peace" churches, like the Quakers and the Mennonites, are particularly active in the campaign for disarmament. Mormons join evangelical Protestants and conservative Catholics in support for traditional moral values.

Some versions of these differences among religious groups in their approaches to politics will no doubt continue into the indefinite future. To perform both their social and their more purely religious functions effectively, however, the churches need to define more carefully the level and nature of their political involvements. This work of definition requires thoughtful consideration of several conceptual and strategic questions.

Should the churches take stands on issues that are socially divisive? Some social issues that involve major moral questions, like abortion and civil rights, are profoundly divisive within the larger society. When the churches become politically active on these issues, they inevitably, if they are at all influential, push higher the emotional heat in what may already be an explosive social environment and may make pragmatic compromise more difficult.

Church leaders often speak of their responsibility to be socially prophetic in the manner of the prophets of ancient Israel. This formulation exaggerates the relevance of a precedent drawn from a very different social system. The Hebrew prophets operated in a nondemocratic polity that had no institutional equivalent of an elected opposition or a free press. Under a democratic system, primarily political institutions are normally available to represent most of the socially aggrieved.[9] Nevertheless, the churches can hardly avoid taking stands on issues that, according to the principles of their creeds, involve fundamental moral issues. This has been true for mainline Protestants, Catholics, and Jews on civil rights, for many church groups on the nuclear arms issue, for Catholics and evangelical Protestants on abortion, and for Mormons and fundamentalists in opposition to the Equal Rights Amendment.

The larger society must hope that the churches will express their positions on issues of this kind with due regard for the rights of citizens who do not share their convictions and for the continued viability of democratic processes. But a democratic polity cannot restrict and in fact should welcome, as a counterweight to necessary but potentially demoralizing pragmatism, churches' moral insights into debates over issues that raise important ethical questions.

On some issues churches have at times felt obliged to recommend or at least to countenance actual violation of civil law as a means of expressing protest against prevailing government policies. Examples include the abolitionists of the 1850s, the suffragettes of the early decades of the twentieth century, and the civil rights activists and antiwar protesters of the 1960s. Currently, some church groups threaten civil disobedience to halt abortion, and others offer "sanctuary" to illegal immigrants from Central America. Such actions obviously escalate the legal and political stakes—as the protesters intend. They are, however, absorbable by a system of government through law so long as they stop short of violence and so long as the protesters are prepared to accept prescribed civil or criminal penalties for their acts. Protesters breaking a civil law to make a political point are within a tradition that pluralist democracy under normal circumstances can accept and sometimes learn from. But protesters who break laws and then attempt to escape legally prescribed punishments are placing themselves in defiance of the entire system of government through law that is among democracy's essential supports.

Do outcomes matter? During my interviews with church leaders and activists in the early 1980s, I often heard a favorite maxim: "God does not call us to be successful but to be faithful." In the sense that no one can be expected to do better than his best, the sentiment conveyed by this aphorism is surely a worthy one. But there is another sense, which I think sometimes creeps into it, that is more open to dispute: the idea that acts should be judged on the basis of their intrinsic moral content only, and without reference to their likely results.

On the issue of nuclear arms, for example, church leaders at times come close to suggesting that the churches' primary objective should be not to prevent war by whatever means seem to have the best chance of success, but to make sure that if war should come, the churches will not be responsible. Some churches within the Judeo-Christian tradition, such as the Quakers and the Mennonites, have always held that use of military force—killing—or threat to use force is inherently sinful, and therefore can never be justified, no matter how bad the consequences that may follow if force is not available. During the 1980s, some leaders of American mainline churches have approached this kind of total pacifism. "We reject any system of security based on fear and intimidation," said a 1985 pronouncement signed by several mainline leaders.[10] Since *all* forms of military preparedness are aimed at inducing "fear and intimidation" among potential military adversaries, this position in effect rejects military defense or preparation for defense of any kind. The more usual Christian and Jewish traditions, like the Catholic doctrine of just wars, however, have maintained that acts bad in themselves may sometimes be approved as means for preventing outcomes that would be even worse, such as the conquest of one's country by a military aggressor. Most religious traditions have also regarded deterrence of war through maintenance of a strong military defense as justified, in fact praiseworthy.

Even within these traditions it may well be argued that some acts, like the destruction of heavily populated cities by nuclear weapons, are so horrible that even the threat to use them or the capacity to carry them out can never be justified, regardless of alternative

354 *Religion in American Public Life*

outcomes. But if it is conceded that outcomes matter—if it matters, in the case of the nuclear issue, whether democracy survives or whether the likelihood of war is increased or reduced—then questions of feasibility and of relative risk, which the churches have at times seemed to view with disdain, must be given weight in forming responsible public policy.

I generally asked church leaders or activists who advocated unilateral disarmament by the United States how they thought the Soviet Union would react. A few said that calculation of Soviet reaction had no moral bearing on the rightness of American disarmament, or that God would miraculously intervene and protect the United States against possible Soviet aggression—both positions that seem to me to deserve moral respect, whatever their intellectual shortcomings. But several replied that if the United States were to disarm, "world opinion" would somehow force the Soviet Union to follow—at which point the groans of millions of victims of totalitarianism all over the world seemed almost audible.

Is every political issue a moral issue? Practically every decision made by government, even if it involves no more than changing the physical location of a government office, touches moral concerns at some point. The extent of these moral dimensions, however, varies enormously. Some issues, such as civil rights or nuclear war or abortion, are fundamentally, though almost never exclusively, moral in nature. At the other extreme are issues like administrative reform or choice of government contractors that normally turn on questions that are primarily technical or pragmatic. In between these extremes lies a wide range of issues that raise significant moral questions but on which persons operating on similar moral assumptions may come down on different sides because of differing technical or empirical judgments.

If the churches advocate detailed positions on particular pieces of legislation or administrative policies in this middle range, which includes many important economic and foreign policy issues, they risk squandering their moral authority on questions on which their technical competence will usually be slight. When the mainline churches, for example, supported the Humphrey-Hawkins full employment bill in the late 1970s or when they opposed renewal of American support for the International Monetary Fund (on the ground that IMF "encourages development strategies that rely on foreign markets") in 1983, they advocated policies that most competent economists predicted would produce effects opposite those intended, causing great harm to the poor.[11] Similarly, when elements of the religious new right opposed return of sovereignty over the Panama Canal to Panama in 1977 or when they supported the Reagan administration's economic program at the beginning of the 1980s, they pronounced judgments that had no clear relation to their theological or moral principles.

The recent propensities of many churches to take detailed positions on issues on which they possess little technical competence were probably what chiefly provoked Peter Berger's expression of exasperation. Advocacy of one side or another, Berger has pointed out, by no means exhausts and may actually inhibit the useful and appropriate functions the churches may perform on such issues. By very reason of their broad and varied memberships and the moral standing they should naturally possess, the churches are well suited to act as mediators or fact-finders on many issues over which technical experts disagree. But to perform such roles, the churches would have to cultivate reputations for objectivity and openmindedness as to means. These qualities are hardly compatible with the positions that some churches have recently been taking as partisan combatants or propagandists for the political left or right.

Should the churches operate in politics like ordinary interest groups? Most economic, social, and ideological interest groups pursue their political objectives in part through pragmatic exchanges of favors with public officeholders and with other interest groups—in short, through political logrolling. When the churches become involved in politics, they are naturally tempted to play by standard political rules. Some conventional interest-group techniques, such as publishing tabulations of how legislators have voted on selected issues, can probably be adopted by the churches without undue danger to their moral standing. But if the churches enter very far into the game of practical politics as it is usually played, they risk compromising the claim to objective moral concern that is the chief resource most of them bring to the political arena.

When the mainline church establishments began feeling heat from the Institute on Religion and Democracy in 1983, some church agencies called on their allies in organized labor to denounce the IRD on the ground that the churches had stood by the unions in the past and now deserved a favor in return. Some went so far as to make support for unions in current economic negotiations contingent on the unions' assailing the IRD. For economic or ideological interest groups, tactics of this kind would be commonplace and acceptable. But for the churches such resort to logrolling raises extreme practical as well as moral hazards.[12]

When the churches take a stand on a political or economic issue, that position should be perceived to represent independent moral judgment, not an exchange for past political favors. Otherwise there will be no moral distinction between positions taken by the churches and those promoted by the Pipefitters Union, the National Association of Realtors, or, for that matter, the Fifth Ward Political Jobholders Club.

Should religious groups become directly involved in political campaigns? Federal tax laws prohibit churches that enjoy tax exemptions from endorsing or actively supporting candidates for public office. Many black churches, and more recently some conservative fundamentalist preachers, have operated on the edge of this prohibition. Some church leaders, both liberal and conservative, argue that tax laws should be changed so that churches in the United States can participate directly in politics as their counterparts do in many European countries.

Some of the operations of the religious new right indicate the dangers that such participation can bring, both for the churches and for the political system. Particularly in the South, involvement by fundamentalist churches in political campaigns has produced some bitterly polarized local communities. The "moral report cards" issued by right-wing religious groups condemning some members of Congress for their liberal votes on economic and foreign policy issues while approving others who had conservative voting records but were involved in personal or political scandals has stirred up irrelevant emotions and at times made the religious groups look ridiculous.[13]

On occasion churches may feel obliged to give tacit support to particular candidates or parties as the only practical means for advancing their moral objectives. But as a rule the more deeply churches become involved in the electoral side of government the greater the dangers of unleashing tendencies to religious absolutism, which, as has been noted, are dangerous to civil liberties and to the political system's capacity for achieving practical compromise.

The case of the black churches is particularly difficult. Black ministers took up political responsibilities because other sources of social leadership in the black community were scarce. In some instances, black ministers have indeed played roles resembling those of the ancient Hebrew prophets, giving voice to social complaints that would not otherwise have been heard. But as other institutions, such as the political parties, become increasingly effective in providing social leadership, the specifically political role of the black churches probably will and should decline.

To what extent does the Judeo-Christian ethic imply a particular ideology (or anti-ideology)? "Christianity," it used to be said by left-wing Christians, "is the religion of which socialism is the practice." Socialism espouses the goal of human mutuality, which is also one of the social objectives of theist-humanism, the other two being reverence for God and his creation, and respect for the dignity of the individual human soul. Some socialists, such as the proponents of liberation theology, profess religious ideals, but the socialist movement has generally traced its origins to the secular traditions of the French and Russian revolutions. Socialist governments in power have usually been hostile to religion. On the question of personal freedom, some socialists have claimed that liberation of individual personality is an important long-run goal of economic collectivization. But such liberation is to be achieved through a process that requires sacrifice of "formal" or middle-class economic and social freedoms. Most socialists seem ultimately to accept Marx's solution of dissolving individual interests into the collective interest of humankind. Christianity, Judaism, Islam, and other religions descended from Judaic roots thus have important value differences with orthodox socialism.

The practical economic performance of state socialism where it has assumed political power (which is not to be confused with the policies of governing social democratic parties in countries like Sweden and West Germany that usually have limited themselves to maintaining welfare-state capitalism) has been so dismal and its record of political repression so consistent that socialism as such no longer seems to exert much attraction for even radical religious groups in the United States. The prevailing ideology among leftist Christians and Jews whom I interviewed seemed to be not so much socialism as anticapitalism. Many were anxious to deflect criticism of the Soviet Union, but this inclination seemed usually to grow out of concern that such criticism provides part of the rationale for the American military buildup rather than out of positive admiration for the Soviet system. Some expressed admiration for the kind of socialism they believed exists in, for instance, Sweden or Tanzania. But most went no further than the conviction that capitalism is bad (exploits the poor, plunders third world countries), and that social evolution will somehow produce something better.

Capitalism's emphasis on individual acquisitiveness and its tendency to produce extreme differences in the distribution of wealth certainly appear to be at odds with the goal of mutuality prescribed by Judeo-Christian values. On the other hand, if outcomes matter, market capitalism has the merit of meeting economic needs more efficiently than any other system yet devised. Also, capitalism has been found to complement a political system based on representative government and constitutionally guaranteed civil liberties.

Robert Benne, in *The Ethic of Democratic Capitalism,* and Michael Novak, in *The Spirit of Democratic Capitalism,* have recently argued that, as Benne writes, "there is much to say from a moral point of view for capitalism." Neither contends that "democratic capitalism is the practice of which Christianity and Judaism are the religions." But both maintain that in an inherently imperfect world, market capitalism, modified by democracy and religion, has demonstrable moral advantages over rival ideologies.[14]

Capitalism, Novak writes, has "lengthened the life span, made the elimination of poverty and famine thinkable, enlarged the range of human choice." It has achieved these triumphs by putting "ineradicable sin to creative purposes." Benne finds support for capitalism in a Niebuhrian sense of the moral limitations of bureaucratic authority: "Agape as a quality of human interaction is possible only among persons or very small groups. The character of larger group relations can be described only rarely by mutuality but is more likely a balance of power."[15]

Unlike such simple egoists as Friedman, however, both Benne and Novak regard the self-assertive drives unleashed by capitalism as potentially destructive as well as useful. To achieve beneficial results, capitalism must be conditioned by a "moral-cultural system" that encourages "self-restraint, hard work, discipline, and sacrifice for the future" and also motivates "generosity, compassion, integrity, and concern for the common good."[16]

Capitalism and theist-humanist religion will always be to some degree in tension—as capitalism and democracy or democracy and religion are in tension. But the analyses of Benne and Novak suggest that this tension need not be hostile and may be both socially and morally productive. To the extent that it promotes theist-humanist values, religion supplies moral qualities that capitalism needs for survival and that counter its dehumanizing tendencies. Capitalism, in turn, creates the economic base on which may be built, with guidance from religion and democracy, a more humane society of the kind called for by both Christian and Jewish traditions.

From the standpoint of the public good, the most important service churches offer to secular life in a free society is to nurture moral values that help humanize capitalism and give direction to democracy. Up to a point, participation by the churches in the formation of public policy, particularly on issues with clear moral content, probably strengthens their ability to perform this nurturing function. If the churches were to remain silent on issues like civil rights or nuclear war or abortion, they would soon lose moral credibililty. But if the churches become too involved in the hurly-burly of routine politics, they will eventually appear to their members and to the general public as special pleaders for ideological causes or even as appendages to transitory political factions. Each church must decide for itself where this point of political and moral peril comes. But it is in all our best interests that the churches not be frivolous in testing the limits of public tolerance.

"A Religious People"

"Religious nations," Tocqueville wrote, "are naturally strong on the very points on which democratic nations are most weak; which shows of what importance it is for men to preserve their religion as their condition becomes more equal."

The social usefulness of religion to democracy does not of course mean that it will be available. Human beings, for the most part, are drawn to religion not to fill the moral gaps of a political or economic system but to get in touch with what William James called man's "germinal higher part," which is "operative in the universe outside," and which the individual can "in a fashion get on board and save himself when all his lower being has gone to pieces in the wreck."

Fortunately for the health of free institutions, Americans remain, despite recent incursions by civil humanism among cultural elites and relentless promotion of egoism by advertising and entertainment media, overwhelmingly, in Justice Douglas's words, "a religious people." By all the indices of public opinion surveys, most Americans regard religion as either "very important" (56 percent in 1984 according to Gallup) or "fairly important" (30 percent) in their personal lives. More than 90 percent of Americans indicate some kind of religious attachment, all but about 2 percent within the Judeo-Christian tradition.[17] How much deep religious experience these figures represent is open to question—probably more than many academic commentators assume. After several decades of decline, the share of youth expressing some form of religious faith in the 1980s has begun to rise. A new religious awakening seems well within the realm of possibility.

From the beginning of American history, religion and the practice of democracy have been closely intertwined. This relationship, despite changes in structure and recurring tensions, shows no signs of breaking. "Of all the dispositions and habits which lead to political prosperity," George Washington said in his farewell address, "religion and morality are indispensable supports. In vain would that man claim the tribute of patriotism, who should labor to subvert these great pillars of human happiness, these firmest props of the duties of men and citizens." Most Americans continue to believe that Washington was right.

NOTES

Chapter 1. The Religious Issue

1. *Religion in America: 50 Years, 1935–1985*, Gallup report no. 236 (May 1985), pp. 39, 56.

2. Richard John Neuhaus, *The Naked Public Square* (Grand Rapids, Mich.: Eerdmans, 1984) points out the risks of insulating public life against religion.

3. Robert N. Bellah and others, *Habits of the Heart: Individualism and Commitment in American Life* (University of California, 1985) argues that the growing influence of egoism, which he calls individualism, is pushing the United States toward a cultural crisis.

4. *Cantwell v. Connecticut*, 310 U.S. 296 (1940); and *McCollum v. Board of Education*, 330 U.S. 15 (1946). The earlier *Everson* decision (1946) had laid the judicial groundwork for *McCollum* (see chapter 4).

Chapter 2. Religion, Politics, and Human Values

1. For other proposed value typologies, see Charles Y. Glock and Rodney Stark, *Religion and Society in Tension* (Rand McNally, 1965), pp. 11–38; William C. McCready and Andrew M. Greeley, *The Ultimate Values of the American People* (Sage, 1976), pp. 15–29; and Ronald Inglehart, *The Silent Revolution* (Princeton University Press, 1977), pp. 39–71.

2. For discussions of the evolution of self-consciousness, see Peter J. Wilson, *Man the Promising Primate* (Yale University Press, 1980), pp. 85–97; Steven Rose, *The Conscious Brain* (Weidenfeld and Nicolson, 1973), pp. 141–47; and Gordon G. Gallup, Jr., "Self-awareness in Primates," *American Scientist*, vol. 67 (April 1979), pp. 417–21.

3. Alexis de Tocqueville, *Democracy in America*, vol. 1 (Vintage, 1945), p. 320.

4. Gen. 1:21.

5. Lewis Brown, ed., *The World's Great Scriptures* (Macmillan, 1946), p. 30; and *Works of Mencius*, translated by James Legge (Dover, 1970), p. 79.

6. Reinhold Niebuhr, *The Nature and Destiny of Man* (Scribner's, 1941), vol. 1, p. 150; and Erich Fromm, *The Anatomy of Human Destructiveness* (Holt, Rinehart, and Winston, 1973), p. 208.

7. James H. Breasted, *The Development of Religion and Thought in Ancient Egypt* (Scribner's, 1912), p. 183; *World's Greatest Scriptures*, p. 12; Werner Jaeger, *Paideia: the Ideals of Greek Culture* (Oxford University Press, 1945), vol. 1, p. 127; and Euripides, *The Bacchae*, in David Greene and Richard Lattimore, eds., *Complete Greek Tragedies* (University of Chicago Press, 1958), vol. 4, p. 581.

8. Wilhelm Reich, *The Mass Psychology of Fascism* (Farrar, Strauss, and Giroux, 1970), pp. 29, 55.

9. Ernest Mandel, *Marxist Economic Theory* (London: Merlin, 1968), p. 668; and Charles A. Reich, *The Greening of America* (Random House, 1970), p. 383.

10. Herbert Marcuse, *Eros and Civilization* (Vintage, 1962), p. 205.

11. Ibid., p. 137.

12. Jerry Rubin, *Do It! Scenarios of the Revolution* (Simon and Schuster, 1970), p. 98.

13. Quoted in a somewhat different form in James Hastings Nichols, *Democracy and the Churches* (Westminster, 1951), p. 72: "We must exhort all Christians to gain all they can; that is, in effect, to grow rich. What way then can we take, that our money may not sink us to the nethermost hell? . . . If those who gain all they can, and save all they can, will likewise give all they can."

14. Milton Friedman, *Capitalism and Freedom* (University of Chicago Press, 1962), pp. 2, 133.

15. George Gilder, *Wealth and Poverty* (Basic Books, 1981), p. 265; and Michael Novak, *Toward a Theology of the Corporation* (American Enterprise Institute, 1981), p. 43. Novak concedes, however, that "corporations are of this world. They are *semper reformanda*—always in need of reform."

16. Wilson, *Promising Primate*, pp. 54, 167.

17. Jaquetta Hawkes, *Prehistory* (New American Library, 1963), p. 194; and Joseph Campbell, *The Masks of God: Primitive Mythology* (Viking, 1959), p. 118.

18. Hawkes, *Prehistory*, p. 194; and Peter Farb, *Man's Rise to Civilization as Shown by the Indians of North America from Primitive Times to the Coming of the Industrial State* (Dutton, 1968), p. 18.

19. Breasted, *Development of Religion*, p. 193; and G. Maspero, *The Dawn of Civilization* (Appleton, 1897), p. 637.

20. Jaeger, *Paideia*, p. 83; *Confucian Analects*, translated by James Legge in *The Chinese Classics* (Clarendon Press, 1893), vol. 1, p. 258; and *World's Great Scriptures*, p. 227. For a discussion of the enduring influence of Confucianism, see H.G. Creel, *Chinese Thought: From Confucius to Mao Tse-Tung* (University of Chicago Press, 1953).

21. Michael Harrington, *Socialism* (Saturday Review Press, 1970), p. 24.

22. Karl Marx, *Essential Writings*, Frederic L. Bender, ed. (Harper and Row, 1972), p. 176.

23. Ibid., p. 261.

24. Ibid., p. 66.

25. Harrington, *Socialism*, p. 174.

26. Jacques Maritan, *Man and the State* (University of Chicago Press, 1951), p. 192.

27. Adolf Hitler, *Mein Kampf* (New York: Reynold and Hitchcock, 1939), p. 600.

28. William James, *The Varieties of Religious Experience* (New American Library, 1958), p. 42. Definitions by Durkheim, Weber, and Tillich are quoted in Robert N. Bellah and Phillip E. Hammond, *Varieties of Civil Religion* (Harper and Row, 1980), p. 142; those of Berger, Dupré, and Bell are quoted in Mary Douglas, "The Effects of Modernization on Religious Change," *Daedalus*, vol. 3 (Winter 1982), p. 6. For a discussion of the etymology of the word *religion*, see Wilfred Cantwell Smith, *The Meaning and End of Religion* (Harper and Row, 1978), particularly pp. 204–05.

29. Alfred North Whitehead, *Science and the Modern World* (Macmillan, 1925), p.

56. Whitehead wrote, "Nature is a dull affair, soundless, scentless, colourless; merely the hurrying of material, endlessly, meaninglessly. . . . No alternative system of organizing the pursuit of scientific truth has been suggested. It is not only reigning, but it is without a rival. And yet—it is quite unbelievable."

30. Tocqueville, *Democracy in America*, vol. 1, p. 321.

31. Ernst Cassirer, *The Myth of the State* (Yale University Press, 1946), p. 23.

32. James, *Varieties of Religious Experience*, p. 384.

33. Luke, 11:9.

34. Farb, *Man's Rise to Civilization*, p. 182; Robert R. Wilson, *Prophecy and Society in Ancient Israel* (Philadelphia: Fortress Press, 1980), pp. 24–26; and Max Weber, *The Sociology of Religion* (Beacon Press, 1964), p. 30.

35. Breasted, *Development of Religion*, p. 326.

36. Sir Leonard Wooley, *The Beginnings of Civilization* (New American Library, 1963), p. 475.

37. For discussions of Hinduism and Buddhism, see Nancy Wilson Ross, *Three Ways of Asian Wisdom* (Simon and Schuster, 1966); and W. Norman Brown, *India and Indology* (Delhi: Motilal Bansidass, 1978), pp. 3–119.

38. *World's Great Scriptures*, p. 141.

39. Quoted in Douglas, "Effects of Modernization," p. 4.

40. Campbell, *Primitive Mythology*, p. 467.

41. Ibid., p. 291.

42. Joel 2:1.

43. Plato, *The Republic*, translated by Allan Bloom (Basic Books, 1968), p. 275.

44. Plato, *The Laws*, translated by Trevor J. Saunders (Penguin, 1970), p. 437; and *The Republic*, pp. 101, 153.

45. 1 Cor. 12:12–13.

46. Rom. 12:2 and 13:1–3; and Acts 5:29.

47. Augustine, *The City of God* (Random House, 1950), p. 112.

48. Reinhold Niebuhr, *Beyond Tragedy: Essays on the Christian Interpretation of History* (Scribner's, 1941), p. 121.

49. Quoted in R. Freeman Butts, *The American Tradition in Religion and Education* (Beacon Press, 1950), p. 13.

50. *Koran*, 2d and 4th surahs.

51. The recent revival of Islamic fundamentalism in Iran and elsewhere in reaction to modernizing regimes has shown that when confronted by a hostile state, the faith possesses a capacity for developing utopian idealism, which, if successful, swiftly converts to absolutist idealism.

52. Roy Pascal, *The Social Basis of the German Reformation: Martin Luther and His Times* (New York: Augustus Kelley, 1971), pp. 146, 187.

53. Karl Holl, *What Did Luther Understand by Religion?* (Philadelphia: Fortress Press, 1977), pp. 105–08; and John M. Headley, *Luther's View of Church History* (Yale University Press, 1963), pp. 2–10.

54. Ernst Troeltsch, *The Social Teaching of the Christian Churches* (Macmillan, 1931), vol. 2, p. 515.

55. John Calvin, *On God and Political Duty*, John T. McNeill, ed. (Bobbs-Merrill, 1956), pp. 45, 46.

56. Ibid., pp. 59, 65.

57. Ibid., p. 81.

58. W. H. Longridge, *The Spiritual Exercises of Ignatius Loyola* (Robert Scott, 1919), p. 199.

59. Edmund Wilson, *To the Finland Station* (Doubleday, 1940), p. 320.

60. Quoted in Niebuhr, *Nature and Destiny of Man*, vol. 2, p. 221.

364 *Notes (pages 36–46)*

61. Frederick Watkins, *The Political Tradition of the West* (Harvard University Press, 1948), p. 61. Watkins is chiefly interested in the social and material effects of dualism, but his argument can be applied to the development of moral and spiritual values as well.

62. Friedrich Nietzsche, *The Birth of Tragedy,* translated by Francis Golffing (Doubleday, 1956), p. 92.

63. Henry Adams, *Mont-Saint-Michel and Chartres* (Doubleday, 1905), p. 381; and Soren Kierkegaard, *Fear and Trembling,* translated by Walter Lowrie (Doubleday, 1941), p. 64.

64. Matt. 5:48; and H. Richard Niebuhr, *Christ and Culture* (Harper, 1951), p. 88.

65. H. Richard Niebuhr, *The Kingdom of God in America,* (Harper, 1937), p. 26.

66. As a broad cultural force and a theological point of view, pietism exerted influence within Lutheranism, Calvinism, and Anglicanism as well as through the Anabaptist movement. But emphasis on the individual's direct experience of God's grace, which forms the essence of pietism, while shared to some degree by all branches of Protestantism, was the defining characteristic of Anabaptism and of such related movements as Quakerism and the later Baptist churches in Britain and America.

67. Thomas G. Sanders, *Protestant Concepts of Church and State* (Holt, Rinehart, and Winston, 1964), p. 82.

68. H. R. Niebuhr, *Kingdom of God in America,* p. 92.

69. Nichols, *Democracy and the Churches,* p. 72.

70. Aristotle, *Politics,* translated by Benjamin Jowett (Random House, 1943), p. 55; and John Stuart Mill, *On Liberty* (Macmillan, 1926), p. 14.

71. Jaeger, *Paideia,* p. 8; and Edith Hamilton, *The Greek Way* (Norton, 1942), p. 35. In the fifth century the advice of Phoenix was often quoted to make the point that words alone are not enough. But within the Homeric context the revolutionary departure was that words were given parity with acts.

72. Milton C. Nahm, ed., *Selections from Early Greek Philosophy* (Crofts, 1934), p. 239.

73. Gilbert Murray, *History of Ancient Greek Literature* (Frederick Ungar, 1966), p. 373.

74. Heinrich Zimmer, *The Arts of Indian Asia* (Pantheon, 1955), vol. 1, p. 131; and Jaeger, *Paideia,* p. 217.

75. Aristotle, *Politics,* p. 233.

76. Lewis Mumford, *The City in History* (Harcourt, Brace, and World, 1961), p. 147.

77. John Finnis, *Natural Law and Natural Rights* (Clarendon Press, 1980), p. 397.

78. Aeschylus, *Agamemnon,* in *Complete Greek Tragedies,* vol. 1, p. 78. Aeschylus tries to solve the problem by proposing the possibility of fulfillment through a kind of civic idealism, but his diagnosis remains more impressive than his cure.

79. Will Durant, *The Age of Faith* (Simon and Schuster, 1950), pp. 477, 950.

80. Kenneth Clark, *Civilization* (Harper and Row, 1969), p. 108.

81. Galileo, *Discoveries and Opinions,* translated by Stillman Drake (Doubleday, 1957), p. 183.

82. Niccolo Machiavelli, *Discourses* (Modern Library, 1950), pp. 285, 528.

83. Some recent commentators, particularly Richard Cox and Robert Goldwin, have argued that Locke proceeded on an essentially Hobbesian view of human nature and placed no real dependence on Christian values. Cox acknowledges that Locke claimed to base his theory on the "law of God and nature" and specifically cited sources in the Bible for such "important points" as "the sanctions for punishment of murder, the beginnings of political society, the origins and limits of property, the nature of

parental power, and the right of rebellion against an unjust conqueror." All of this, however, Cox maintains was no more than window dressing employed by Locke to protect himself against political persecution. Cox's case, though richly detailed, comes down to the view that a man as smart as Locke in the seventeenth century could not possibly have believed what Locke said he believed—a dubious assumption. Goldwin argues that Locke's underlying conception of human nature is almost as bleak as Hobbes's. He concedes, however, that "Locke's state of nature is *not* as violent as Hobbes's." See Richard C. Cox, *Locke on War and Peace* (University Press, 1982), pp. 34–49; and Robert A. Goldwin, "John Locke," in Leo Strauss and Joseph Cropsey, eds., *History of Political Philosophy* (University of Chicago Press, 1972), pp. 457–60.

84. Alasdair MacIntyre, *After Virtue* (Notre Dame Press, 1981), p. 36.

85. Leo Pfeffer, "The Triumph of Secular Humanism," *Journal of Church and State,* vol. 19 (Spring 1977), p. 211.

86. Sophocles, *Oedipus the King,* in *Complete Greek Tragedies,* vol. 2, p. 47.

87. Sophocles, *Oedipus at Colonus,* in *Complete Greek Tragedies,* vol. 2, p. 148.

88. Amos, 5:21–24.

89. Isa. 10:1–2.

90. Jer. 22:13–16.

91. Robert Benne, *The Ethic of Democratic Capitalism* (Philadelphia: Fortress Press, 1981), p. 35.

92. John, 15:12.

93. Matt., 5:18; and Mark, 2:27.

94. Matt., 5:44; 6:34; and 7:1.

95. Matt., 22:21; and John, 18:36.

96. Luke, 4:18–19.

97. C. H. Dodd, *The Founder of Christianity* (Macmillan, 1970), p. 28.

98. Arthur A. Cohen, "Human Fraternity: The Liturgy of Theological Enmity," in Nahum N. Glatzer, ed., *Modern Jewish Thought* (Schocken, 1977), p. 180.

Chapter 3. Intentions of the Founders

1. Sydney E. Ahlstrom, *A Religious History of the American People* (Doubleday, 1975), vol. 1, p. 169.

2. Ernst Troeltsch, *Social Teachings* (Macmillan, 1931), vol. 2, p. 599; and Perry Miller quoted in Ahlstrom, *Religious History,* vol. 1, p. 174.

3. Quoted in Samuel P. Huntington, *American Politics: The Promise of Disharmony* (Harvard University Press, 1981), p. 153.

4. John Coolidge, *The Pauline Renaissance in England* (Oxford University Press, 1970), pp. 63, 101, 104.

5. Quoted in Thomas G. Sanders, *Protestant Concepts of Church and State* (Holt, Rinehart, and Winston, 1964), p. 243.

6. Paul E. Lauer, *Church and State in New England* (Johns Hopkins University Press, 1982); and George Lee Haskins, *Law and Authority in Early Massachusetts* (Macmillan, 1960).

7. Perry Miller, ed., *The American Puritans: Their Prose and Poetry* (Doubleday, 1956), p. 98.

8. George Armstrong Kelly, "Politics and the American Religious Consciousness," *Daedalus,* vol. 3 (Winter 1982), p. 132.

9. Robert N. Bellah and Phillip E. Hammond, *Varieties of Civil Religion* (Harper and Row, 1980), p. 150.

10. Perry Miller, *Jonathan Edwards* (Greenwood Press, 1949), p. 11; and Coolidge, *Pauline Renaissance*, p. 69.

11. Miller, ed., *American Puritans*, p. 85; and H. Richard Niebuhr, *The Kingdom of God in America* (Winnetka, Ill.: Willett, Clark, 1937), p. 80.

12. Miller, ed., *American Puritans*, p. 89.

13. Perry Miller, *The New England Mind: From Colony to Province* (Harvard University Press, 1953), pp. 56–59.

14. Miller, ed., *American Puritans*, pp. 171–72.

15. Miller, *New England Mind*, p. 59.

16. Ibid.

17. Ibid., p. 128.

18. Quoted in Samuel S. Hill and Dennis E. Owen, *The New Religious Political Right in America* (Abingdon Press, 1982), p. 113.

19. Miller, *New England Mind*, pp. 246–47.

20. Miller, ed., *American Puritans*, p. 129; and Alan Heimert, *Religion and the American Mind: From the Great Awakening to the Revolution* (Harvard University Press, 1966), p. 19. Like the nineteenth century populists, Wise regarded himself not as an innovator but as a traditionalist, maintaining the Puritan ethic of brotherhood against the new commercialism represented by the Brattles.

21. Quoted in John Demos, "Underlying Themes in the Witchcraft of Seventeenth Century New England," in John M. Mulder and John F. Wilson, eds., *Religion in American History* (Prentice-Hall, 1978), p. 86.

22. Miller, *New England Mind*, pp. 410–11; and Miller, ed., *American Puritans*, pp. 215–19.

23. Mencken is quoted in Cushing Strout, *The New Heavens and New Earth: Political Religion in America* (Harper and Row, 1974), p. 1; Morison is quoted in Charles L. Wallis, ed., *Our American Heritage* (Harper and Row, 1970), p. 53; and Dawson is quoted in James Hastings Nichols, *Democracy and the Churches* (Westminster, 1951), p. 30. Other commentators have argued that the Enlightenment was more important than Puritanism in shaping American beliefs in progress and individual rights, but for the mass of Americans, Puritanism seems to have been the stronger source. In any case the Enlightenment itself, in its Scottish and English embodiments, was in part derived from Puritanism.

24. Bellah and Hammond, *Varieties of Civil Religion*, p. 149.

25. Ibid.; and Jacob C. Meyer, *Church and State in Massachusetts from 1740 to 1833* (Western Reserve, 1930), p. 1.

26. Quoted in Niebuhr, *Kingdom of God*, p. 47.

27. Meyer, *Church and State in Massachusetts*, p. 5; and Sidney E. Mead, *The Nation with the Soul of a Church* (Harper and Row, 1975), p. 27.

28. Anson Phelps Stokes, *Church and State in the United States* (Harper Brothers, 1950), vol. 1, pp. 195, 759; and Sanders, *Protestant Concepts*, p. 179.

29. Quoted in Irwin H. Polishok, *A Controversy in New and Old England* (Prentice-Hall, 1967), pp. 34, 78.

30. Ahlstrom, *Religious History*, vol. 1, p. 219.

31. Quoted in Polishok, *Controversy*, p. 74.

32. Ibid., p. 67.

33. Mark DeWolfe Howe, *The Garden and the Wilderness: Religion and Government in American Constitutional History* (University of Chicago Press, 1965), pp. 5–6.

34. Ahlstrom, *Religious History*, vol. 1, p. 233.

35. Quoted in J. C. Murray, *We Hold These Truths* (Sheed and Ward, 1960), p. 56.

36. Miller, *New England Mind,* pp. 234–35; Miller, *Jonathan Edwards,* pp. 10–11.

37. Miller, *Jonathan Edwards,* p. 155.

38. Ibid.

39. Miller, *New England Mind,* pp. 286–87.

40. Harold P. Simonson, ed., *Selected Writings of Jonathan Edwards* (Frederick Ungar, 1970), p. 106.

41. Miller, *Jonathan Edwards,* pp. 147, 271.

42. Quoted in William James, *The Varieties of Religious Experience* (New American Library, 1958), p. 191.

43. Miller, *Jonathan Edwards,* pp. 147, 194.

44. Heimert, *Religion and the American Mind,* pp. 65, 102, 303.

45. Ibid., pp. 304, 307.

46. Ahlstrom, *Religious History,* vol. 1, pp. 349–51.

47. Martin E. Marty, *Righteous Empire: the Protestant Experience in America* (Dial, 1970), p. 265.

48. Heimert, *Religion and the American Mind,* p. 61.

49. Ahlstrom, *Religious History,* vol. 1, pp. 351, 355.

50. *Letter to Hezekiah Niles* quoted in Dean M. Kelley, "Religion in the American Revolution," *Christianity and Crisis,* vol. 34 (June 10, 1974), pp. 123–28.

51. John Webb Pratt, *Religion, Politics, and Diversity: The Church-State Theme in New York History* (Cornell, 1967), pp. 4, 5.

52. Ibid., p. 10.

53. Ibid., p. 6.

54. Ibid., pp. 29–31; and John Tracy Ellis, *American Catholicism* (University of Chicago Press, 1969), p. 30.

55. Pratt, *Religion, Politics, and Diversity,* p. 36.

56. Ray Allen Billington, *The Protestant Crusade* (Rinehart, 1938), p. 8.

57. R. Freeman Butts, *The American Tradition in Religion and Education* (Beacon Press, 1950), p. 24.

58. Pratt, *Religion, Politics, and Diversity,* p. 76.

59. Leo Pfeffer, *God, Caesar, and the Constitution* (Beacon Press, 1975), pp. 55, 56.

60. Thomas G. Sanders, *Protestant Concepts of Church and State* (Holt, Rinehart, and Winston, 1964), p. 128.

61. Ibid., p. 129.

62. Quoted in Frederick B. Tolles, *Meeting House and Counting House, The Quaker Merchants of Colonial Philadelphia, 1682–1763* (University of North Carolina, 1948), p. 3.

63. Albert C. Applegarth, *Quakers in Pennsylvania* (Johns Hopkins, 1892), p. 40.

64. Ibid., pp. 34, 35.

65. Sanders, *Protestant Concepts,* p. 132; and Christine M. Totten, *Roots in the Rhineland: America's German Heritage* (German Information Center, 1983), p. 57.

66. Ahlstrom, *Religious History,* vol. 1, p. 292.

67. E. Digby Baltzell, *Puritan Boston and Quaker Philadelphia* (Free Press, 1979).

68. Quoted in Applegarth, *Quakers,* p. 41.

69. Frederick B. Tolles, *Quakerism and Politics* (Guilford College Press, 1956), p. 17.

70. Jackson Turner Main, *Political Parties Before the Revolution* (University of North Carolina, 1973), p. 8.

71. Herbert Stroup, *Church and State in Confrontation* (Seabury, 1967), p. 41.

72. James Hennesey, *American Catholics* (Oxford University Press, 1981), p. 39.

73. Ahlstrom, *Religious History,* vol. 1, p. 407.

74. Ibid., p. 408; and George Petrie, *Church and State in Early Maryland* (Johns Hopkins, 1892).

75. Ahlstrom, *Religious History*, vol. 1, p. 408; and Ellis, *American Catholicism*, p. 27.

76. Stokes, *Church and State*, vol. 3, p. 567.

77. Ibid., vol. 1, pp. 163–65.

78. Philip Schaff, *Church and State in the United States or the American Idea of Religious Liberty and Its Practical Effects* (Arno Press, 1972), p. 28.

79. A. E. Dick Howard, "Up Against the Wall: The Uneasy Separation of Church and State," paper delivered at the Conference of Roscoe Pound—American Trial Lawyers Foundation, Cambridge, Mass., 1981.

80. Stokes, *Church and State*, vol. 1, p. 303.

81. Paul J. Weber and Dennis A. Gilbert, *Private Churches and Public Money: Church-Government Fiscal Relations* (Greenwood Press, 1981), pp. 10, 11.

82. Ibid.

83. James Madison, *Papers* (University of Chicago Press, 1973), vol. 8, pp. 299–300.

84. Ibid., pp. 299–301.

85. Ibid., pp. 301–03.

86. Ibid., p. 304.

87. Walter Berns, *The First Amendment and the Future of American Democracy* (Basic Books, 1970), p. 20.

88. Strout, *The New Heavens*, p. 85.

89. Gary Wills, *Inventing America: Jefferson's Declaration of Independence* (Vintage, 1978), p. 361. Wills argues that Hutcheson rather than Locke was the primary source of much of Jefferson's political philosophy, but concedes that in "the area of religious tolerance," Jefferson was much influenced by Locke; see p. 171. See also Sanford Kessler, "Locke's Influence on Jefferson's 'Bill for Establishing Religious Freedom,'" *Journal of Church and State*, vol. 25 (Spring 1983), p. 233.

90. John Locke, *Of Civil Government* (Dutton, 1924), pp. 12, 180–82.

91. Troeltsch, *Social Teaching*, vol. 2, p. 638; and Locke, *Civil Government*, p. 132. Locke cites biblical sources more than eighty times in the *First Treatise*, and twenty-two times in the *Second Treatise*.

92. John Locke, *The Reasonableness of Christianity* (Stanford University Press, 1958), pp. 57–59. For a contrary interpretation of Locke, see Richard Cox, *Locke on War and Peace* (University Press, 1982); see also the discussion in chap. 2, note 83 of this book.

93. John Locke, *A Letter Concerning Toleration*, in *Great Books of the Western World* (Encyclopedia Brittanica, 1935), vol. 35, p. 4.

94. Ibid., pp. 3, 4.

95. Ibid., pp. 15, 16.

96. Ibid., pp. 18, 19.

97. Berns, *First Amendment*, p. 205.

98. Sidney Mead, "Neither Church nor State: Reflections on James Madison's 'Line of Separation,'" *Journal of Church and State*, vol. 10 (Autumn, 1968), p. 349. Paul Weber argues that Madison's veto messages suggest that he would not have disapproved if the intended benefits had come to the churches through more general legislation; see "James Madison and Religious Equality: the Perfect Separation," *Review of Politics*, vol. 44 (April 1982), pp. 179–83. Walter Berns, Carey McWilliams, and others have maintained that Locke, Madison, Jefferson, and even Washington were not in "any meaningful sense Christians." With regard to Jefferson, this may well be so. The other three, if they are to be taken at their words, certainly *believed* they were Christians, and

were, in my terminology, theist-humanists. Though they may not have been strictly orthodox in all their religious beliefs, they adhered to broad tenets of Judeo-Christian doctrine.

99. Robert M. Healey, *Jefferson on Religion in Public Education* (Yale University Press, 1962), pp. 26, 27, 34; and Berns, *First Amendment*, p. 31.

100. Healey, *Jefferson on Religion*, p. 122.

101. Nat Hentoff, *The First Freedom* (Delacorte, 1980), p. 163; and Stokes, *Church and State*, vol. 1, p. 335.

102. Stokes, *Church and State*, vol. 1, p. 339; and Healey, *Jefferson on Religion*, pp. 134, 135.

103. Thomas Sieger Derr, "The First Amendment as a Guide to Church-State Relations," paper delivered at the Conference of Roscoe Pound—American Trial Lawyers Foundation, Cambridge, Mass., 1981.

104. Robert N. Bellah, "Civil Religion in America," *Daedalus*, vol. 96 (Winter 1967), pp. 7–8; and Stokes, *Church and State*, vol. 1, p. 338. An anonymous reader of this chapter has suggested that the reference to "Israel of old" may be read more as desanctification of Israel than as sanctification of the United States. But then what was Jefferson's point in introducing the parallel?

105. Stokes, *Church and State*, vol. 1, p. 338.

106. Strout, *New Heavens*, p. 54; Catherine L. Albanese, *Sons of the Fathers: The Civil Religion of the American Revolution* (Temple, 1976), p. 12; and Heimert, *Religion and the American Mind*, p. 1.

107. Albanese, *Sons of the Fathers*, p. 49.

108. Ibid., p. 28.

109. Carl Bridenbaugh, *Mitre and Sceptre: Transatlantic Faiths, Ideas, Personalities, and Politics: 1689–1775* (Oxford University Press, 1962), p. 313.

110. Billington, *Protestant Crusade*, pp. 18–19.

111. Donald E. Boles, *The Bible, Religion, and the Public Schools* (Iowa State University Press, 1963), p. 13; and Albanese, *Sons of the Fathers*, p. 56.

112. Ibid., p. 194.

113. Ibid., pp. 14, 86.

114. Ibid., pp. 52, 30.

115. Ibid., pp. 115–19; and G. Adolf Koch, *Republican Religion: The American Revolution and the Cult of Reason* (Holt, 1933), pp. 38, 39, 50.

116. Albanese, *Sons of the Fathers*, p. 114.

117. Ibid., p. 131.

118. Benjamin Franklin, *Autobiography* (Putnam, n.d.), pp. 185, 223.

119. Derr, "First Amendment," p. 9.

120. Franklin, *Autobiography*, p. 186; and Schaff, *Church and State*, p. 123.

121. Paul F. Boller, Jr., *George Washington and Religion* (SMU Press, 1963), pp. 27–29.

122. Ibid., pp. 52, 53, 62.

123. *Annals of America*, vol. 3 (Encyclopedia Brittanica, 1968), p. 612.

124. Boller, *Washington and Religion*, p. 156.

125. Stokes, *Church and State*, vol. 1, p. 276; and Albanese, *Sons of the Fathers*, p. 203.

126. Stokes, *Church and State*, vol. 1, p. 509.

127. Ibid., p. 512.

128. Ibid., p. 424.

129. Kathleen Orange, "Religion and the American Founding," paper delivered at

the annual meeting of the American Political Science Association, Washington, D.C., 1984; and Bellah and Hammond, *Civil Religion,* p. 17.

130. *The Federalist* (Modern Library, 1937), pp. 232, 337; and Charles W. Dunn, "The Theological Foundations of American Public Policy," paper delivered at annual meeting of the American Political Science Association, New York, 1981, p. 5.

131. James Bryce, *The American Commonwealth* (Chicago: Sergel, 1891), vol. 1, p. 299.

132. Berns, *First Amendment,* p. 31.

133. Schaff, *Church and State,* p. 21.

134. *Documents Illustrative of the Formation of the Union of American States* (Government Printing Office, 1927), p. 716.

135. Ibid., pp. 1030, 1035.

136. *Annals of the Congress of the United States* (Gales and Seaton, 1834), vol. 1, pp. 444, 451.

137. Ibid., p. 452; Berns, *First Amendment,* p. 5; and Irving Brant, *James Madison: Father of the Constitution* (Bobbs-Merrill, 1950), p. 273.

138. *Annals of Congress,* vol. 1, pp. 729, 730.

139. Ibid., p. 730.

140. Ibid., p. 731.

141. Ibid., p. 766.

142. *Journal of the Senate,* vol. 77 (September 9, 1789); and Brant, *Madison,* p. 271.

143. Ibid.

144. Meyer, *Church and State in Massachusetts,* pp. 218, 219.

145. Butts, *American Tradition,* pp. 84, 87.

146. Ibid., p. 41; *Annals of Congress,* vol. 1, p. 730; and Berns, *First Amendment,* pp. 7–8.

147. Koch, *Republican Religion,* p. 242.

148. Ibid., p. 278.

149. Ibid., pp. 280–81.

150. Alexis de Tocqueville, *Democracy in America* (Vintage, 1945), vol. 1, p. 316; and Albanese, *Sons of the Fathers,* p. xi.

Chapter 4. Interpreting the First Amendment

1. Anson Phelps Stokes, *Church and State in the United States* (Harper, 1950), vol. 3, pp. 150–51.

2. *Barron v. Baltimore,* 32 U.S. 487 (1833); and *Permoli v. New Orleans,* 44 U.S. 609 (1845).

3. *Congressional Globe,* 39 Cong., 1 sess., p. 2459.

4. Ibid., p. 806.

5. Ibid., p. 1088.

6. Ibid., p. 2462.

7. Ibid., p. 1088.

8. Charles Fairman, "Does the Fourteenth Amendment Incorporate the Bill of Rights?" *Stanford Law Review,* vol. 2 (December 1949), p. 76.

9. Ibid., pp. 87, 98, 112, 113.

10. Ibid., pp. 86, 87, 99; and J. R. Pole, *The Pursuit of Equality in American History* (University of Chicago Press, 1978), p. 95.

11. Some recent scholars have argued that Fairman's account understates the intention of Bingham and Howard to extend the Bill of Rights to the states. But

Fairman's case regarding the general understanding of Congress and of the ratifying state legislatures has not been shaken. See Alfred H. Kelly and Winfred A. Harbison, *The American Constitution: Its Origin and Development* (Norton, 1970), p. 463; and Henry J. Abraham, *Freedom and the Court* (Oxford University Press, 1977), pp. 36–48.

12. Franklin Hamlin Littell, *From State Church to Pluralism: A Protestant Interpretation of Religion in American History* (Macmillan, 1962), pp. 100–01.

13. Will Herberg, *Prostestant, Catholic, Jew* (Doubleday, 1960), p. 109.

14. *Reynolds v. United States,* 98 U.S. 150 (1878).

15. Ibid., 164.

16. *Davis v. Benson,* 133 U.S. 334, 344 (1890).

17. Philip B. Kurland, *Religion and the Law: Of Church and State and the Supreme Court* (Aldine Press, 1961), p. 24.

18. *Bradfield v. Roberts,* 175 U.S. 291 (1899).

19. *Quick Bear v. Leupp,* 210 U.S. 76 (1907).

20. *O'Neil v. Vermont,* 144 U.S. 363 (1892).

21. Ibid., 370.

22. *Meyer v. Nebraska,* 262 U.S. 402, 403 (1922).

23. *Pierce v. Society of Sisters,* 268 U.S. 535 (1924). The Court insisted, however, on "the power of the state reasonably to regulate all schools, to inspect, supervise and examine them, their teachers and pupils; to require . . . that teachers shall be of good moral character and patriotic disposition, that certain studies plainly essential to good citizenship must be taught, and that nothing be taught which is manifestly inimical to the public welfare."

24. *Gitlow v. New York,* 268 U.S. 625 (1925).

25. *Cantwell v. Connecticut,* 310 U.S. 296 (1940).

26. *Minersville School District v. Gobitis,* 310 U.S. 586 (1940).

27. *West Virginia State Board of Education v. Barnette,* 319 U.S. 641 (1942).

28. Ibid., 659.

29. *Murdock v. Pennsylvania,* 319 U.S. 112 (1942).

30. *Prince v. Massachusetts,* 321 U.S. 170 (1943).

31. *Braunfeld v. Brown,* 366 U.S. 607 (1960).

32. *Sherbert v. Verner,* 374 U.S. 404 (1962).

33. Leo Pfeffer, *God, Caesar, and the Constitution: The Court as Referee of Church-State Confrontation* (Beacon Press, 1975), pp. 150–52.

34. Ibid., pp. 153–55; *Seeger v. United States,* 380 U.S. 163 (1964); and *Welsh v. United States,* 398 U.S. 333 (1970).

35. *Gillette v. United States,* 401 U.S. 437 (1971).

36. *Wisconsin v. Yoder,* 406 U.S. 227 (1971).

37. Ibid., 240.

38. Ibid., 248.

39. Walter Berns, "Ratiocinations," *Harper's* (March 1973), p. 36.

40. *Heffron v. International Society for Krishna Consciousness,* 452 U.S. 640 (1981).

41. *Larson v. Valente,* 457 U.S. 1111 (1982).

42. Paul A. Freund, *The Supreme Court of the United States: Its Business, Purposes, and Performance* (World, 1949), p. 58.

43. Edward S. Corwin, *A Constitution of Powers in a Secular State* (Charlottesville, Va.: Michie, 1951), p. 114.

44. Perry Miller, ed., *The American Puritans: Their Prose and Poetry* (Doubleday, 1956), p. 218; and Donald E. Boles, *The Bible, Religion, and the Public Schools* (Iowa State University Press, 1963), p. 9.

45. Boles, *Bible, Religion and Public Schools*, p. 6; James Hennesey, *American Catholics* (Oxford University Press, 1981), p. 107; and Stokes, *Church and State*, vol. 2, p. 503.

46. Stokes, *Church and State*, vol. 2, pp. 549, 550; and Robert N. Bellah and Phillip E. Hammond, *Varieties of Civil Religion* (Harper and Row, 1980), p. 72.

47. Hennesey, *American Catholics*, pp. 107, 123.

48. Ibid., pp. 108–09; and John Webb Pratt, *Religion, Politics, and Diversity: The Church-State Theme in New York History* (Cornell University Press, 1967), pp. 178–89.

49. Stokes, *Church and State*, vol. 2, pp. 68–69.

50. Albert J. Menendez, *Religion at the Polls* (Westminster, 1977), p. 29.

51. Hennesey, *American Catholics*, p. 185; and Pfeffer, *God, Caesar, and the Constitution*, p. 259.

52. John Tracy Ellis, *American Catholicism* (University of Chicago Press, 1969), p. 111.

53. Pfeffer, *God, Caesar, and the Constitution*, p. 181; and Stokes, *Church and State*, vol. 2, p. 529.

54. Pfeffer, *God, Caesar, and the Constitution*, p. 182.

55. *Cochran v. Board of Education*, 281 U.S. 374 (1929).

56. *Everson v. Board of Education*, 330 U.S. 15 (1946).

57. Ibid., 19.

58. *McCollum v. Board of Education*, 333 U.S. 237 (1947).

59. Ibid., 247.

60. Stokes, *Church and State*, vol. 3, p. 565, vol. 2, p. 748; Fairman, "Fourteenth Amendment," pp. 79–80; and Corwin, *Constitution of Powers*, p. 115.

61. *Zorach v. Clausen*, 343 U.S. 313 (1951).

62. Ibid., 325.

63. Kurland, *Religion and the Law*, p. 98.

64. *McGowan v. Maryland*, 366 U.S. 442, 445 (1960).

65. Ibid., 575.

66. Ibid., 506.

67. Stokes, *Church and State*, vol. 2, p. 551; and Robert Booth Fowler, "The Constitutional Connection," paper delivered at the annual meeting of the American Political Science Association (September, 1982), p. 24.

68. Boles, *Bible, Religion and Public Schools*, p. 110.

69. Philip B. Kurland, "The School Prayer Cases," in Dallin H. Oaks, ed., *The Wall Between Church and State* (University of Chicago Press, 1963), pp. 147–49.

70. *Engel v. Vitale*, 370 U.S. 425, 435, (1961).

71. Ibid., 437.

72. Ibid., 445.

73. Kurland, "The School Prayer Cases," p. 143.

74. Pfeffer, *God, Caesar, and the Constitution*, p. 201.

75. Kurland, "The School Prayer Cases," pp. 144–45.

76. *Abington School District v. Schempp*, 374 U.S. 222 (1962).

77. Ibid., 257.

78. Ibid., 304.

79. Ibid., 313.

80. *National Center for Education Statistics Bulletin* (U.S. Department of Education, December 20, 1984); and *Washington Post*, February 3, 1985.

81. *1980 Republican Platform* (Republican National Committee, 1980), p. 15; and *Washington Post*, May 18, 1982.

82. *Congressional Quarterly*, March 24, 1984, p. 643; *Washington Post*, July 27, 1984;

Congressional Quarterly, October 6, 1984, p. 2460; and Charles H. Whittier, *Religion and Public Policy: Background and Issues in the 80's* (Congressional Research Service, 1984), pp. 27–31.

83. *Washington Post,* May 22, 1982.

84. *Congressional Quarterly,* September 25, 1982, p. 2359.

85. Gen. 47:26; and Pfeffer, *God, Caesar, and the Constitution,* p. 66.

86. *Walz v. Tax Commission,* 397 U.S. 669, 670 (1969).

87. Ibid., 674.

88. Dean M. Kelley, *Why Churches Should not Pay Taxes* (Harper and Row, 1977), p. 81; and *Bob Jones University v. United States,* slip no. 81-3 U.S. 29 (1983).

89. *Board of Education v. Allen,* 392 U.S. 247 (1967).

90. *Lemon v. Kurtzman,* 403 U.S. 625, 622 (1970).

91. *Tilton v. Richardson,* 403 U.S. 678, 689 (1970).

92. Ibid., 693.

93. *Committee for Public Education v. Nyquist,* 413 U.S. 794, 814 (1972).

94. *Committee for Public Education v. Regan,* 444 U.S. 646 (1981).

95. John Hart Ely, *Democracy and Distrust: A Theory of Judicial Review* (Harvard University Press, 1980), p. 25.

96. Ibid., pp. 1, 43. As far as I can tell, the chief advantage of "noninterpretivism" over "judicial activism" is that only lawyers know, or can guess, what the former means.

97. Lawrence M. Friedman, "The Conflict Over Constitutional Legitimacy," in Gilbert Y. Steiner, ed., *The Abortion Dispute and the American System* (Brookings, 1983), pp. 20, 21.

98. *Stone v. Graham,* 499 U.S. 39 (1980).

99. *Florey v. Sioux Falls,* 449 v. 987 (1980); and *Widmar v. Vincent,* slip no. 80-689 U.S. (1981).

100. *Marsh v. Chambers,* slip no. 82-23 U.S. 5 (1983).

101. *1980 Republican Platform,* p. 15; and *Congressional Quarterly,* April 24, 1982, p. 911.

102. Kurland, *Religion and the Law,* p. 18; Paul J. Weber and Dennis A. Gilbert, *Private Churches and Public Money: Church-Government Fiscal Relations* (Greenwood Press, 1981), pp. 185–89; and Denis P. Doyle, "A Din of Inequity: Private Schools Reconsidered," *Teachers College Record* (Summer 1981), p. 670.

103. *Mueller v. Allen,* slip no. 82-195 U.S. 9 (1983).

104. *Lynch v. Donnelly,* slip no. 82-1256 U.S. 7 (1984).

105. *Grand Rapids v. Ball,* slip no. 83-812 U.S. (1985); and *Aguilar v. Fenton,* slip no. 84-237 U.S. 11 (1985).

106. *Wallace v. Jaffree,* slip no. 83-812 U.S. 7 (1985).

107. *Mueller v. Allen,* 15.

Chapter 5. The Churches and Political Action: 1790 to 1963

1. Sidney Mead, *The Nation with the Soul of a Church* (Harper and Row, 1975). Mead adapted the phrase from an expression by G. K. Chesterton.

2. Sydney E. Ahlstrom, *A Religious History of the American People* (Doubleday, 1975), vol. 1, p. 622.

3. G. Adolf Koch, *Republican Religion: The American Revolution and the Cult of Reason* (Holt, 1933), p. 39.

4. Ibid., p. 246.

5. Ibid., p. xii; and Seymour Martin Lipset and Earl Raab, *The Politics of Unreason* (Harper and Row, 1970), p. 36.

6. Koch, *Republican Religion*, pp. xii, 113.

7. Ibid., pp. 134–35.

8. *Compendium of the Seventh Census* (Printer of the United States Senate, 1854), pp. 138, 140. Statistics on denominational membership have always been notoriously inexact. Figures gathered by the 1850 census, however, probably give a reasonably accurate basis for determining rank.

9. Timothy L. Smith, *Revivalism and Social Reform in Mid-Nineteenth Century America* (Abingdon, 1957), p. 23.

10. Ibid., p. 102.

11. Quoted in Anson Phelps Stokes, *Church and State in the United States* (Harper, 1950), vol. 1, pp. 653, 662.

12. John Tracy Ellis, *American Catholicism* (University of Chicago Press, 1969), p. 49.

13. James Hennesey, *American Catholics* (Oxford University Press, 1981), pp. 95–100.

14. Vergilius Ferm, *The Crisis in Lutheran Theology* (Century, 1927), pp. 129–51; and E. Clifford Nelson, *Lutheranism in North America* (Minneapolis: Augsburg, 1972), pp. 10–17.

15. Ronald P. Formisano, "Federalists and Republicans," in Paul Kleppner, ed., *The Evolution of American Electoral Systems* (Greenwood Press, 1981), p. 63.

16. Stokes, *Church and State*, vol. 1, pp. 673, 676; and Koch, *Republican Religion*, p. 272.

17. Stokes, *Church and State*, vol. 1, p. 675; and Thomas G. Sanders, *Protestant Concepts of Church and State* (Holt, Rinehart, and Winston, 1964), p. 250.

18. Alan Heimert, *Religion and the American Mind: From the Great Awakening to the Revolution* (Harvard University Press, 1966), p. 536.

19. Stokes, *Church and State*, vol. 1, p. 675.

20. Formisano, "Federalists and Republicans," p. 63.

21. Robert M. Healey, *Jefferson on Religion in Public Education* (Yale University Press, 1962), p. 123.

22. Formisano, "Federalists and Republicans," p. 64.

23. Sanders, *Protestant Concepts*, pp. 192, 193.

24. It is often forgotten that the burning parsonage in Epworth from which the child John Wesley was almost miraculously plucked had been set on fire by a radical mob that resented the outspoken Toryism of the child's father, the rector of the local Anglican church. Wesley was throughout his life a loyal supporter of the Tory party. He advocated social reform, attacked slavery, and took religion to the people in the streets and fields, but in politics he was a conservative, opposing the American Revolution and supporting the forces of established order in Britain against the radical Wilkesites.

25. Koch, *Republican Religion*, p. 11.

26. Sanders, *Protestant Concepts*, p. 192; and Stokes, *Church and State*, vol. 1, p. 676.

27. Smith, *Revivalism and Social Reform*, p. 60.

28. William G. Shade, "Political Pluralism and Party Development," in Kleppner, ed., *Evolution of American Electoral Systems*, pp. 102, 103.

29. *Historical Statistics of the United States* (Government Printing Office, 1960), p. 57.

30. Stokes, *Church and State*, vol. 1, pp. 693–98. In his personal religious practices and beliefs, Jackson was a devout evangelical, the first to hold the presidency; see

Robert V. Remini, *Andrew Jackson and the Course of American Democracy, 1833–1845* (Harper and Row, 1984), pp. 74, 184.

31. James Hastings Nichols, *Democracy and the Churches* (Westminster, 1951), pp. 58, 96.

32. John Webb Pratt, *Religion, Politics, and Diversity: The Church-State Theme in New York State History* (Cornell, 1967), p. 125.

33. Hennesey, *American Catholics*, pp. 145–46.

34. Stokes, *Church and State*, vol. 1, p. 826; and Hennesey, *American Catholics*, p. 119.

35. Stokes, *Church and State*, vol. 1, p. 826.

36. Ibid., p. 832.

37. Hennesey, *American Catholics*, p. 124.

38. Ronald P. Formisano, *The Birth of Mass Political Parties: Michigan, 1827–1861* (Princeton University Press, 1971), pp. 137–64; and Shade, "Political Pluralism," p. 102. See also Lee Benson, *The Concept of Jacksonian Democracy: New York as a Test Case* (Princeton University Press, 1961), pp. 198–207.

39. Joseph R. Gusfield, *Symbolic Crusade: Status Politics and the American Temperance Movement* (University of Illinois, 1963), pp. 40–52; Benson, *Jacksonian Democracy*, p. 199; and Stokes, *Church and State*, vol. 2, p. 41.

40. Formisano, *Mass Political Parties*, p. 154; and Shade, "Political Pluralism," p. 102.

41. Stokes, *Church and State*, vol. 1, p. 836.

42. Ibid., p. 837.

43. Ray Allen Billington, *The Protestant Crusade* (Rinehart, 1938), p. 389.

44. During the late 1830s and the 1840s, some of the planter class, particularly in Virginia and Georgia, supported the Whigs as the party most dedicated to the defense of property. According to an old Virginia saying, "Whigs know each other by the instinct of gentlemen." But when the Republicans replaced the Whigs in the 1850s, most of the slaveholders closed ranks behind the southern Democracy. See Arthur Charles Cole, *The Whig Party in the South* (American Historical Association, 1914), pp. 39–63, 68–69, 327–36.

45. St. Augustine, *The City of God* (Random House, 1950), p. 694.

46. Ahlstrom, *Religious History*, vol. 2, p. 93.

47. Nichols, *Democracy and the Churches*, p. 70.

48. Stokes, *Church and State*, vol. 2, p. 129.

49. Ibid., pp. 134–36; and Martin E. Marty, *Righteous Empire: The Protestant Experience in America* (Dial, 1970), p. 119.

50. Ahlstrom, *Religious History*, vol. 2, pp. 96–98.

51. Smith, *Revivalism and Social Reform*, p. 191; and Stokes, *Church and State*, vol. 2, p. 165.

52. Paul J. Weber, "Examining the Religious Lobbies," *This World* (Winter/Spring 1982), p. 97; and Smith, *Revivalism and Social Reform*, p. 180.

53. Mark DeWolfe Howe, *The Garden and the Wilderness: Religion and Government in American Constitutional History* (University of Chicago Press, 1965), p. 63.

54. Ahlstrom, *Religious History*, vol. 2, p. 120.

55. "The Lincoln-Douglas Debates," *Annals of America*, (Encyclopaedia Brittanica, 1968), vol. 9, p. 16.

56. Lincoln probably would have won even if the Democrats had remained united and a fourth party, the Constitutional Unionists, composed largely of former southern Whigs, had not entered the contest. He won absolute majorities over all three of his

opponents combined in 14 northern states with 169 electoral votes, 12 more than a majority in the electoral college. The Republicans' low percentage of the total popular vote occurred because Lincoln received almost no support in 14 of 16 states in which slavery was legal. The 1860 election was almost a clean sectional split; differing perceptions of slavery overrode all previous economic or ideological attachments.

57. Garry Wills, *Inventing America: Jefferson's Declaration of Independence* (Vintage, 1979), pp. xxi, xxii.

58. Stokes, *Church and State*, vol. 3, p. 113; and Abraham Lincoln, "First Inaugural Address," *Annals of America*, vol. 9, p. 255.

59. Cushing Strout, *The New Heavens and New Earth: Political Religion in America* (Harper and Row, 1974), p. 197.

60. Lincoln, "Second Inaugural Address," *Annals of America*, vol. 9, p. 556.

61. Ahlstrom, *Religious History*, vol. 2, pp. 118–21.

62. Ibid.; and Philip Schaff, *Church and State in the United States or the American Idea of Religious Liberty and its Practical Effect* (Arno Press, 1972), p. 39.

63. Smith, *Revivalism and Social Reform*, p. 78; and *Historical Statistics of the United States*, p. 229.

64. Louis Hacker, *The Triumph of American Capitalism* (Columbia University Press, 1940), pp. 361–73.

65. Paul Kleppner, "Partisanship and Ethnoreligious Conflict," in *The Evolution of American Electoral Systems* (Greenwood Press, 1981), p. 124; and Kleppner, *Parties, Voters, and Political Cultures* (University of North Carolina, 1979), p. 146.

66. Kleppner, *Parties, Voters, and Political Cultures*, p. 182–85.

67. Ibid., pp. 154–56.

68. William A. Gudelmas, Jr., and William G. Shade, *Before the Molly Maguires: The Emergence of the Ethno-Religious Factor in the Politics of the Lower Anthracite Region, 1844–1872* (Arno Press, 1976), pp. 50–82.

69. Kleppner, *Parties, Voters, and Political Cultures*, p. 194; and E. Digby Baltzell, *Philadelphia Gentlemen* (University of Pennsylvania, 1958), pp. 234–35.

70. Kleppner, *Parties, Voters, and Political Cultures*, p. 328; and Kirk H. Porter and Donald Bruce Johnson, eds., *National Party Platforms, 1840–1968* (University of Illinois, 1970), pp. 83, 109.

71. Kleppner, *Parties, Voters, and Political Cultures*, p. 328; and Kleppner, *The Cross of Culture: A Social Analysis of Midwestern Politics: 1850–1900* (Free Press, 1970), p. 90.

72. Richard Jensen, *The Winning of the Midwest* (University of Chicago Press, 1971), p. 287. Jensen's figure is based on examination of railroad records.

73. Kleppner, *Parties, Voters, and Political Cultures*, p. 196.

74. Leonard D. White, *The Republican Era: 1869–1901* (Macmillan, 1958), p. 4.

75. Ibid.

76. Leon Festinger, Henry W. Reicken, and Stanley Schachter, *When Prophecy Fails* (University of Minnesota, 1956), pp. 12–23.

77. Michael Lienesch, "The Role of Political Millennialism in Early American Nationalism," *Western Political Quarterly*, vol. 36 (September 1983), p. 448.

78. George M. Marsden, *Fundamentalism and American Culture: The Shaping of Twentieth Century Evangelism: 1870–1925* (Oxford University Press, 1980), pp. 36–37.

79. Harold Lindsell, *The Battle for the Bible* (Grand Rapids, Mich.: Zondervan, 1976), pp. 28–29.

80. Marsden, *Fundamentalism*, pp. 118–26.

81. Cushing Strout, *The New Heavens and the New Earth: Political Religion in America* (Harper and Row, 1974), pp. 242–43; and Walter Rauschenbusch, *A Theology for the Social Gospel* (Macmillan, 1917), pp. 55, 62.

82. Rauschenbusch, *Theology for the Social Gospel*, pp. 25, 36, 48, 50.

83. Ibid., pp. 60, 131.

84. Ibid., pp. 55, 140.

85. All quoted in Marty, *Righteous Empire*, pp. 144–50.

86. Ibid., pp. 177–79.

87. Jensen, *Winning of the Midwest*, pp. 283–85.

88. Ibid., pp. 284–85.

89. Hennesey, *American Catholics*, pp. 198–200.

90. Jensen, *Winning of the Midwest*, p. 285. In thirteen predominantly Polish Catholic precincts in Chicago, Jensen found that McKinley received 33 percent of the vote, 21 percent more than the share of the presidential vote won by the Republican ticket in 1892. In twelve Bohemian Catholic Chicago precincts, the Republican vote was 42 percent, also 21 percent over 1892.

91. James L. Sundquist, *Dynamics of the Party System: Alignment and Realignment of Political Parties in the United States* (Brookings, 1983), p. 163.

92. Kleppner, *Cross of Culture*, pp. 358–59; Sundquist, *Dynamics*, p. 166; and Edgar Eugene Robinson, *The Presidential Role, 1896–1932* (Octagon, 1970), table IX.

93. Sundquist, *Dynamics*, p. 168.

94. *National Party Platforms*, pp. 175–83.

95. John Milton Cooper, Jr., *The Warrior and the Priest* (Harvard University Press, 1983), pp. 130–32; and Will Herberg, *Protestant, Catholic, Jew* (Doubleday, 1960), p. 79.

96. Ray H. Abrams, *Preachers Present Arms* (Wellesley, Mass.: Round Table Press, 1933), p. 69.

97. Gusfield, *Symbolic Crusade*, p. 151.

98. Ahlstrom, *Religious History*, vol. 2, p. 347.

99. Gusfield, *Symbolic Crusade*, pp. 92–97.

100. Ahlstrom, *Religious History*, vol. 2, pp. 350–52; and Peter Odegard, *Pressure Politics: the Story of the Anti-Saloon League* (Columbia University Press, 1928).

101. Gusfield, *Symbolic Crusade*, pp. 118–19.

102. Ellis, *American Catholicism*, p. 141.

103. David J. O'Brien and Thomas A. Shannon, eds., *Renewing the Earth: Catholic Documents on Peace, Justice and Liberation* (Topeka, Kan.: Image, 1977), pp. 30–37.

104. Hennesey, *American Catholics*, p. 229; and Hugh J. Nolan, ed., *Pastoral Letters of the American Hierarchy, 1792–1970* (Huntington, Ind.: Our Sunday Visitor, 1971), pp. 199–211.

105. Ibid.

106. Hennesey, *American Catholics*, p. 230.

107. Ellis, *American Catholicism*, p. 142.

108. Ibid., p. 143.

109. Marilyn Sheffer, "Regional Receptivity to Reform: The Legacy of the Progressive Era," *Political Science Quarterly*, vol. 98 (Fall 1983), pp. 479–80. Not all Catholics, however, were Democrats. The redoubtable Republican machine in Philadelphia, for example, included many Catholics among both its leaders and its foot soldiers. Where Irish Catholics dominated the Democratic party, as they did in much of the Northeast, Italian Catholics often supported the Republicans; see Robert A. Dahl, *Who Governs?* (Yale University Press, 1961), p. 39.

110. Edgar Eugene Robinson, ed., *Presidential Vote, 1896–1932* (Octagon, 1947), table IX.

111. Hennesey, *American Catholics*, pp. 254–63.

112. Ibid., pp. 266–68.

113. Ibid., pp. 274–75.

114. Ibid., p. 275.

115. *The Gallup Poll: Public Opinion 1935–1971* (Random House, 1972), vol. 2, p. 1202.

116. John R. Petrocik, *Party Coalitions: Realignment and the Decline of the New Deal Party System* (University of Chicago Press, 1981), pp. 82–83.

117. *Gallup Poll*, vol. 3, p. 1693.

118. Hennessey, *American Catholics*, p. 308.

119. Sundquist, *Dynamics*, p. 216.

120. Robert N. Miller, *American Protestantism and Social Issues, 1919–1939* (University of North Carolina, 1958), p. 75.

121. Ibid., p. 68.

122. Ibid., pp. 118–25.

123. Reinhold Niebuhr, *The Nature and Destiny of Man: A Christian Interpretation* (Scribner's, 1941), vol. 1, pp. 150, 246; and vol. 2, p. 148.

124. Reinhold Niebuhr, *Beyond Tragedy: Essays on the Christian Interpretation of History* (Scribner's, 1931), p. 121.

125. Reinhold Niebuhr, *Nature and Destiny of Man*, vol. 1, p. 299; and vol. 2, pp. 87–88.

126. R. Niebuhr, *Nature and Destiny of Man*, vol. 2, p. 178.

127. H. Richard Niebuhr, *The Kingdom of God in America* (Harper, 1937), p. xiii.

128. Sundquist, *Dynamics*, p. 90.

129. Gerhard Lenski, *The Religious Factor* (Doubleday, 1963), p. 175. John Petrocik's analysis of survey data gathered from 1952 through 1960 shows that 56 percent of middle-status and high-status northern white Protestants identified themselves as Republicans, 22 percent as Democrats, and 22 percent as independents. The same data indicate that only 42 percent of low-status northern white Protestants thought of themselves as Republicans; but this was still a considerably larger share than the 31 percent who considered themselves Democrats and the 27 percent who were independents. See Petrocik, *Party Coalitions*, pp. 82–83.

130. Lenski, *Religious Factor*, pp. 89–93, 166.

131. Lawrence H. Fuchs, *The Political Behavior of American Jews* (Free Press, 1956), p. 26; and Stokes, *Church and State*, vol. 1, p. 858.

132. Fuchs, *Political Behavior*, p. 32. Fuchs's observation is based on Robert Ernst, *Immigrant Life in New York City, 1825–1863* (New York: King's Crown Press, 1949), p. 167.

133. Lipset and Raab, *Politics of Unreason*, p. 95.

134. Stephen D. Isaacs, *Jews and American Politics* (Doubleday, 1974), p. 141. Roosevelt's own attitude toward his Jewish supporters had its pragmatic side: "When Theodore Roosevelt named Oscar Straus to his cabinet as Secretary of Commerce and Labor, Jacob Schiff, banker and high panjandrum of German-American Jewry, threw a testimonial dinner. The President was the guest of honor, and he made a speech designed to reassure his listeners that Straus had been named for all the right reasons. 'I did not name him because he was a Jew. I would despise myself if I considered the race or the religion of a man named for high political office. . . . Merit and merit alone dictated his appointment.' These comforting remarks were warmly applauded. The only trouble was that no one bothered to tell Schiff what the President had said, and Schiff was deaf. So when he got up, he let the cat out of the bag: 'Before making up his cabinet, President Roosevelt sent for me and informed me that he wished to appoint a Jew as a member of his cabinet and asked me to recommend the ablest Jew who would be most acceptable to my race. I recommended Oscar Straus. He was appointed, and he has more than justified the recommendation.' The crowd, we are told, applauded nervously. Roosevelt stared into space." See David S. Landes, "New Zion, Old Zion," *The New Republic* (December 31, 1983), p. 26.

135. Nathan Glazer, *American Judaism* (University of Chicago Press, 1972), p. 24.

136. Ibid., pp. 25, 40.

137. Ibid., pp. 36–49.

138. Ibid., pp. 55–56.

139. Ibid., pp. 62–63.

140. Ibid., p. 45.

141. Ibid., p. 105; and *The American Jewish Yearbook, 5698* (Philadelphia: Jewish Publication Society, 1937), vol. 39, pp. 69–70.

142. Isaacs, *Jews in American Politics*, pp. 140–41; Glazer, *American Judaism*, pp. 136–37.

143. Fuchs, *Political Behavior*, p. 63.

144. Isaacs, *Jews in American Politics*, p. 151.

145. Ibid., p. 152.

146. Cited by Fuchs, *Political Behavior*, p. 75.

147. V. O. Key, *Public Opinion and American Democracy* (Knopf, 1961), p. 513.

148. Fuchs, *Political Behavior*, p. 99.

149. M. S. El Azhary, *Political Cohesion of American Jews in American Politics* (University Press of America, 1980), pp. 23, 40.

150. Frank J. Sorauf, *The Wall of Separation: The Constitutional Politics of Church and State* (Princeton University Press, 1976), p. 47.

151. W. E. B Du Bois, *The Souls of Black Folk* (Fawcett, 1961), p. 141.

152. *Census of Religious Bodies: 1936* (Government Printing Office, 1941), vol. 1, p. 851.

153. Lenski, *Religious Factor*, pp. 91, 166.

154. James Deotis Roberts, *Black Theology Today: Liberation and Contextualization* (Lewiston, N.Y.: Mellen, 1983), p. 130.

155. Interview with Walter Fauntroy, April 8, 1982.

156. Nancy J. Weiss, *Farewell to the Party of Lincoln: Black Politics in the Age of FDR* (Princeton University Press, 1983), pp. 3–5.

157. Ibid., pp. 34–59.

158. Ibid., pp. 207–10.

159. Black support for the Democrats had less impact than it might have because of low electoral participation. In much of the South blacks were effectively barred from voting, and elsewhere high levels of rootlessness or disinterest limited turnouts. In 1952, for example, reported voting among black Protestants was only 40 percent, compared to 81 percent among Jews, 78 percent among Catholics, and 79 percent among white Protestants. After the passage of civil rights legislation in the 1960s, however, black turnout began to rise, while voting among other groups generally declined. In 1968, reported voting among black Protestants was 55 percent, still 12 percentage points behind white Protestants and 21 points behind Jews.

160. Theodore H. White, *The Making of the President, 1960* (Athenium, 1961), pp. 321–23.

161. Martin Luther King, Jr., "Letter from Birmingham Jail," *Annals of America*, vol. 18, pp. 143–49.

162. Ibid., p. 159.

Chapter 6. Time of Turmoil: 1964 to 1985

1. Luke Eugene Ebersole, *Church Lobbying in the Nation's Capital* (Macmillan, 1951), p. 25.

2. Ibid., pp. 30–39.

3. *Yearbook of American and Canadian Churches, 1981* (Abingdon, 1981), p. 5. Martin Marty observes that in common usage, "mainline" religion came to mean the "traditional, inherited, normative, or median style of American spirituality and organization, over against the 'marginal' or 'fringe' or 'curious' groups that drew so much attention in the story-telling of the late 1960s and early 1970s." See his *A Nation of Behavers* (University of Chicago Press, 1976), pp. 53.

4. Interview with James Hamilton, June 24, 1982; and James L. Adams, *The Growing Church Lobby in Washington* (Grand Rapids, Mich.: Eerdmans, 1970), p. 258.

5. Ebersole, *Church Lobbying*, pp. 97–100.

6. Adams, *Growing Church Lobby*, pp. 4–5.

7. Ibid., pp. 5–6.

8. Ibid., p. 7.

9. Ibid., p. 10.

10. Ibid., p. 11.

11. Ibid., p. 3.

12. Ibid., p. 34.

13. Ibid., pp. 2, 24, 25.

14. Ibid., p. 34.

15. Ibid., p. 26.

16. Ibid., p. 3.

17. Memorandum from Paul Kittlaus, Director, Washington Office, Office for Church in Society, United Church of Christ, October 13, 1982.

18. Adams, *Growing Church Lobby*, p. 213.

19. James Hennesey, *American Catholics: A History of the Roman Catholic Community in the United States* (Oxford University Press, 1981), p. 319.

20. Adams, *Growing Church Lobby*, p. 208.

21. Ibid., p. 237.

22. Ibid., p. 221.

23. Ibid., p. 238.

24. Ibid.

25. Hennesey, *American Catholics*, p. 321.

26. Adams, *Growing Church Lobby*, pp. 208–09.

27. Ibid., p. 231.

28. J. Elliott Corbett, "Should the Church Lobby?" *Engage/Social Action* (October 15, 1970), p. 8. Corbett expanded on his views in an interview, December 29, 1981.

29. Ibid., p. 6.

30. Adams, *Growing Church Lobby*, p. xii.

31. Corbett, "Should the Church Lobby?" p. 8.

32. *Internal Revenue Code* (Lawyers Co-operative, 1974, with cumulative supplement, issued May, 1984) 26 USCS 501(c)(3), 170(b)(1)(a)(A)(i), and (c)(2)(D). Deductibility of charitable gifts from the gift tax is covered by 2522(a) and (b).

33. Dean M. Kelley, *Why Churches Should Not Pay Taxes* (Harper and Row, 1977), p. 79.

34. Ibid., pp. 80–82.

35. Ibid., p. 82.

36. Ibid.

37. Liberation theology has some of its roots in the political theology developed in Europe during the 1960s by such writers as Jurgen Moltmann and Johannes Metz. In the United States, however, the Latin American version has been perceived as more original and dynamic and has had greater influence.

38. David J. O'Brien and Thomas A. Shannon, eds., *Renewing the Earth: Catholic Documents on Peace, Justice, and Liberation* (Image, 1977), p. 34.

39. Ibid., p. 547.

40. Ibid., pp. 549–51.

41. Ibid., pp. 553, 563.

42. Ibid., pp. 550. 553.

43. Robert McAfee Brown, *Theology in a New Key: Responding to Liberation Themes* (Westminster, 1978), pp. 52–57.

44. Gustavo Gutiérrez, *A Theology of Liberation: History, Politics and Salvation*, translated by Sister Caridad Inda and John Eagleston (Orbis, 1973), pp. 15, 27, 236–37.

45. Ibid., pp. 26, 88.

46. Ibid., pp. 227–28.

47. Juan Luis Segundo, *Liberation of Theology*, translated by John Drury (Orbis, 1976), pp. 44, 71, 110–11.

48. José Miguez Bonino, *Christians and Marxists: The Mutual Challenge to Revolution* (Grand Rapids, Mich.: Eerdmans, 1976), pp. 81, 89, 90.

49. Ibid., pp. 92, 115, 116. In the final quotation Bonino approvingly paraphrases the communist theorist, Juan Rosales.

50. Ibid., p. 135.

51. Brown, *Theology*, pp. 15, 69, 178.

52. Ibid., 181.

53. James H. Cone, *Black Theology and Black Power* (Seabury, 1969), p. 38.

54. Ibid. pp. 56, 137, 143.

55. Ibid., p. 151. For a more recent formulation of black theology, see James Deotis Roberts, *Black Theology Today: Liberation and Contextualization* (Lewiston, N.Y.: Mellen, 1983), particularly pp. 151–60, 179–86.

56. Jane Redmont, "Theologies of Liberation," *Harvard Divinity Bulletin* (September–October 1980), p. 9.

57. Rosemary Radford Ruether, *Liberation Theology: Human Hope Confronts Christian History and American Power* (Paulist Press, 1972), pp. 7, 12.

58. Ibid., p. 190.

59. Mary Daly, *Beyond God the Father: Toward a Philosophy of Women's Liberation* (Beacon Press, 1973), pp. 72, 190.

60. Else M. Adjali and Carolyn D. McIntyre, *LIBERATION as an aim of the church's educational work* (Division of Education, United Methodist Board of Discipleship, 1975), pp. 11, 23.

61. Rael Jean Isaac and Enrich Isaac, "Sanctifying Revolution: Protestantism's New Social Gospel," *American Spectator* (May 1981), p. 7.

62. "Angela and the Presbyterians," *Christian Century* (July 7, 1971), p. 823; *Presbyterian Panel* (Research Division of the United Presbyterian Church, July 1974), p. 28.

63. "Statement of Church Persons after Visiting Cuba" (United Methodist church, Dakotas Area, 1977).

64. Interview with Robert Campbell, November 12, 1981.

65. *A Time for Candor: Mainline Churches and Radical Social Witness* (Institute for Religion and Democracy, 1983), p. 41. Bishop White did not respond to several efforts to check this quotation during the fall of 1984.

66. *Wall Street Journal*, June 10, 1982.

67. Brown, *Theology*, p. 15.

68. *Breaking Barriers* (Official Report of the World Council of Churches, Nairobi, 23 November–10 December, 1975).

69. *Fact Book on Theological Education* (American Association of Theological Schools), various years. According to Harry Adams, who was a student at the Yale Divinity School during the Vietnam war and is now (1985) assistant dean, "A lot of [his fellow

students] figured the way to stay out of Vietnam was to go to divinity school. They came here to avoid the draft. They preferred to be here [rather] than in Vietnam, but they weren't very happy here, either." *Wall Street Journal*, February 28, 1985.

70. Harvey Cox, *The Secular City* (Macmillan, 1965). See also J. A. T. Robinson, *Honest to God* (Westminster, 1963).

71. *Washington Report*, vol. 8 (January 1979). Published by the Office for Church in Society, United Church of Christ.

72. Interview with Kittlaus, November 5, 1981. Followup interviews were conducted on August 11, 1982, and August 1, 1984.

73. Ibid.

74. Corbett, "Should the Church Lobby?" p. 7.

75. *Presbyterian Panel* (July 1974), pp. 32–33.

76. *Presbyterian Panel* (March 1976), p. 25.

77. Carl F. Reuss, *Profiles of Lutherans in the U.S.A.* (Augsburg Publishing House, 1982), p. 49.

78. James Foyle Miller, *A Study of United Methodists and Social Issues* (General Council on Ministries, United Methodist church, 1983), p. 10.

79. *Religion in America, 1982* (Princeton Religion Research Center, 1982), p. 164.

80. Data supplied by CBS News. Percentages do not always add to 100 because some votes went to minor candidates. The popular vote for the electorate as a whole showed Reagan, 51 percent; Carter, 41 percent; Anderson, 7 percent.

81. Data supplied by Institute for Social Research, University of Michigan. People who identified themselves as Congregationalists were included with the United Church of Christ, although there is a small Association of Congregational Christian churches that did not join the merger with the Evangelical and Reformed church in 1957. The samples for some denominations were small and therefore present only the general contours of political preferences.

82. A. James Reichley, "A Change in Direction," in Joseph A. Pechman, ed., *Setting National Priorities: The 1982 Budget* (Brookings, 1981), p. 257.

83. "The Re-Making of America: A Message to the Churches from the Governing Board of the NCCC in the U.S.A.," adopted May 15, 1981.

84. Peggy Billings, "Standing with Those Who Suffer," *Engage/Social Action*, vol. 9 (July–August 1981), pp. 16–23.

85. *New York Times*, November 8, 1984. For voting distribution, see Everett Carll Ladd, "Secular and Religious America," paper delivered at the conference of Center on Religion and Society, January 24, 1985, table 28. Differences in polling methods may account for some of the differences in results found by this poll and the one taken by the ISR in 1980.

86. Letter to the author from Carolyn D. McIntyre, associate general secretary, General Board of Church and Society, United Methodist church, November 2, 1983. McIntyre also set forth her position in an interview, October 21, 1981.

87. Interview with Lee Rank, January 29, 1982.

88. Richard G. Hutcheson, Jr., *Mainline Churches and the Evangelicals: A Challenging Crisis?* (John Knox Press, 1981), pp. 41–43.

89. Richard G. Hutcheson, paper delivered at the Conference on Hunger, Washington, D.C., February, 1983.

90. "NCC's Tangled Power Lines," *United Methodist Reporter*, April 8, 1983.

91. "Mainline Churches Lost Flocks in Droves in '70s," *Washington Post*, October 3, 1982.

92. Studies of several denominations are presented in Dean A. Hoge and David A Roozen, eds., *Understanding Church Growth and Decline: 1950–1978* (Pilgrim Press, 1979).

93. Dean M. Kelley, *Why Conservative Churches Are Growing: A Study in Sociology of Religion* (Harper and Row, 1977), pp. ix–xx, 134–35.

94. Interview with Martin Marty, February 19, 1982.

95. Rael Jean Isaac, "Do You Know Where Your Church Offerings Go?" *Readers' Digest* (January 1983), p. 120.

96. Interviews with Kittlaus; Charles Bergstrom, October 6, 1981; and Joyce Hamlin, January 13, 1982.

97. Interviews with Hamilton and Hamlin.

98. Interview with Randolph Nugent, June 24, 1982.

99. "Barry, Clarke Receive Bishop's Blessing," *Washington Post,* August 23, 1982; "Jackson Gets Backing of Black Church Head," December 2, 1983.

100. *Wall Street Journal,* July 21, 1982; and interview with Frank Watkins, aide to Jesse Jackson, February 19, 1982.

101. Thomas E. Cavanaugh and Lorn S. Foster, *Jesse Jackson's Campaign: The Primaries and Caucuses* (Joint Center for Political Studies, 1984), pp. 9–14; *United Methodist Reporter,* March 23, 1984; and "Follow the Money," *New Republic,* February 20, 1984.

102. Dom Bonafede, "The Jackson Factor," *National Journal,* March 24, 1984; and "Follow the Money."

103. Curtis B. Gans, *Non-Voter Study '84–'85* (Committee for the Study of the American Electorate, 1985); Ladd, "Secular and Religious America," table 27; and "Portrait of the Electorate," *New York Times,* November 8, 1984. Other states in which relatively large portions of Mondale voters reported Democratic recommendations by their preachers included Mississippi, 24 percent; Texas, 19 percent; North Carolina, 15 percent; Michigan, 11 percent; and Illinois, 9 percent. In all of these states the share of Reagan voters reporting Republican endorsements by their preachers was substantially smaller. Only seventeen states across the nation were polled on the question.

104. Thomas E. Cavanaugh, "Black Mobilization and Partisanship: 1984 and Beyond," paper delivered at the 1985 conference on the Joint Center for Political Studies on the 1984 Elections and the Future of Black Politics.

105. John Courtney Murray, *The Problem of Religious Freedom* (Newman Press, 1975), pp. 13–14.

106. John A. Ryan and Francis J. Boland, *Catholic Principles of Politics* (Macmillan, 1940), pp. 314–21.

107. Hennesey, *American Catholics,* pp. 302–03.

108. John Courtney Murray, "Law or Prepossession?" *Law and Contemporary Problems,* vol. 14 (1949), p. 25; and *We Hold These Truths: Catholic Reflections on the American Proposition* (Sheed and Ward, 1960), pp. 157, 247.

109. Murray, *We Hold These Truths,* p. 23.

110. Ibid., pp. 28–29; and Murray, *Problem of Religious Freedom,* pp. 28–31.

111. Hennesey, *American Catholics,* pp. 309–11; and John Tracy Ellis, *American Catholicism* (University of Chicago Press, 1969), p. 240.

112. Walter J. Burghardt, *Religious Freedom, 1965 and 1975* (Paulist Press, 1977), p. 69.

113. Richard P. McBrien, "Roman Catholicism: E Pluribus Unum," *Daedalus,* vol. 3 (Winter 1982), p. 75. (Winter 1982), p. 75.

114. James Hitchcock, *Catholicism and Modernity: Confrontation or Capitulation* (Seabury, 1979), p. 37.

115. Rosemary Ruether, *The Church Against Itself* (New York: Herder and Herder, 1967), p. 152.

116. Hennesey, *American Catholics,* p. 314; and Burghardt, *Religious Freedom,* p. 71.

117. Hennesey, *American Catholics,* p. 329.

118. J. Brian Benestad and Francis J. Butler, eds., *Quest for Justice: A Compendium of Statements of the United States Catholic Bishops on the Political and Social Order, 1966–1980* (National Conference of Catholic Bishops, 1981), pp. 102–05, 373–85. In November 1984 the bishops began consideration of the first draft of a letter on market capitalism.

119. Ibid., p. 106; and "Statement on Central America" issued by National Conference of Catholic Bishops, October 30, 1981.

120. Hitchcock, *Catholicism and Modernity,* pp. 96–99.

121. Andrew M. Greeley, *The American Catholic: A Social Portrait* (Basic Books, 1977), p. 149.

122. Gilbert Y. Steiner, *The Futility of Family Policy* (Brookings, 1981), pp. 54–58; and Betty Sarris and Hyman Rodman, *The Abortion Controversy* (Columbia University Press, 1974), pp. 27–54.

123. *Roe v. Wade,* 410 U.S. 152 (1973); and John Hart Ely, "The Wages of Crying Wolf: A Comment on Roe v. Wade," *Yale Law Journal,* vol. 82 (April 1973), p. 935.

124. Raymond Tatolovich and Byron W. Daynes, "The Trauma of Abortion Politics," *Commonweal* (November 20, 1981), pp. 646–47. What the actual outcome of continued reform through legislation would have been remains, of course, speculative.

125. Stephen D. Johnston and Joseph B. Tanney, "The Christian Right and the 1980 Presidential Election," *Journal for the Scientific Study of Religion,* vol. 21 (June 1982), p. 129.

126. John E. Jackson and Maris A. Vinovskis, "Public Opinion, Elections, and the 'Single-Issue' Issue," in Gilbert Y. Steiner, ed., *The Abortion Dispute and the American System* (Brookings, 1983), p. 69.

127. Interviews with Francis Lally, December 9, 1980, and February 2, 1982; and *Political Responsibility: Choices for the 1980s* (United States Catholic Conference, 1979), p. 5.

128. Interview with Bryan Hehir, October 8, 1981.

129. Ibid.

130. *The Pastoral Constitution, 80,* cited in *Pastoral Letter on War and Peace* (National Conference of Catholic Bishops, 1983), p. iii.

131. *Political Responsibility,* p. 7; and Cardinal John Krol, "SALT II: A Statement of Support," *Origins* (September 13, 1979), p. 197.

132. Vincent A. Yzermans, "A Catholic Revolution," *New York Times,* November 14, 1981.

133. Marjorie Hyer, "Group Within Catholic Hierarchy Highly Critical of Nuclear Policy," *Washington Post,* December 25, 1981; and John J. Fialka, "Atom Weapons Issue Stirs Divisive Debate in the Catholic Church," *Wall Street Journal,* June 9, 1982.

134. Kenneth A. Briess, "Religious Leaders Objecting to Nuclear Arms," *New York Times,* September 8, 1981; and "Texas Catholic Bishops Reject Neutron Bomb," *New York Times,* September 13, 1981.

135. *Pastoral Letter of the National Conference of Catholic Bishops on War and Peace,* second draft (October 1982).

136. "West Germans Address Nukes," *National Catholic Reporter,* May 6, 1983.

137. Peter Hebblethwaite, "Rome Meeting Blow to National Conference," *National Catholic Reporter,* April 29, 1983; and Michael Novak, "The Bishops Speak Out," *National Review* (June 10, 1983), p. 678.

138. Amendments to Third Draft, *NCCB Pastoral Letter on War and Peace* (May 1983).

139. Accounts of the meetings of the bishops in 1981, 1982, and 1983 are from

my own reporting, supplemented by news accounts and analyses in the *New York Times, Washington Post, Chicago Tribune, National Catholic Reporter, New Republic,* and *National Review.*

140. Hennesey, *American Catholics,* pp. 289–91.

141. Frances Fitzgerald, "A Disciplined, Charging Army," *New Yorker* (May 18, 1981), p. 124; and *1980 Republican Platform* (Republican National Committee, 1980), pp. 13, 15.

142. James M. Penning, "Changing Partisanship and Issue Stands among American Catholics," paper delivered at the 1984 meeting of the American Political Science Association, Washington, D.C. Particularly among Irish Catholics, survey evidence suggests a two-step conversion process, first from Democratic to independent, and then from independent to Republican. For surveys from 1972 to 1974 average Democratic identification was 49 percent; independent, 34 percent; and Republican, 17 percent. For 1976 to 1978 Democratic identification was 41.4 percent; independent, 41 percent; and Republican, 17 percent. For 1980 to 1983 Democratic identification was 40.6 percent; independent, 34 percent; and Republican, 25 percent.

143. Penning, "Changing Partisanship"; and Gans, *Non-Voter Study of '84–'85.*

144. "Portrait of the Electorate"; and A. James Reichley, "Religion and Political Realignment," *Brookings Review* (Fall 1984), pp. 31–32.

145. Reichley, "Religion and Political Realignment," pp. 31–32.

146. *Religion in America, 1982,* pp. 161–64; and John H. Simpson, "Moral Issues and Status Politics," in Robert C. Liebman and Robert Wuthnow, eds., *The New Christian Right* (Aldine, 1983), p. 193.

147. Interview with Archbishop Thomas Kelly, January 12, 1982.

148. *New York Times,* May 26, 1985.

149. Norman Podhoretz, "The State of World Jewry," *Commentary,* vol. 76 (December 1983), p. 39.

150. Nathan Glazer, *American Judaism* (University of Chicago Press, 1972), p. 178.

151. Ibid., pp. 180–83.

152. Ibid., pp. 180–81.

153. Ibid., pp. 178–82.

154. Stephan D. Isaacs, *Jews in American Politics* (Doubleday, 1974), p. 158.

155. For Kristol's account of neoconservatism (a term apparently coined by the socialist theorist, Michael Harrington), see Irving Kristol, *Reflections of a Neoconservative* (Basic Books, 1983). For a critical but reasonably objective appraisal, see Peter Steinfels, *The Neoconservatives* (Simon and Schuster, 1979). For the roots of neoconservatism in the politics of the 1930s through the 1950s, see Gillian Peele, *Revival and Reaction: The Right in Contemporary America* (Oxford University Press, 1984), pp. 19–31.

156. Interview with Nathan Perlmutter, January 21, 1982.

157. Donald Feldstein, *The American Jewish Community in the 21st Century* (American Jewish Congress, 1984), pp. 23, 26.

158. Interview with Perlmutter.

159. Interview with Hyman Bookbinder, January 18, 1982.

160. Ibid.

161. Feldstein, *American Jewish Community,* p. 27.

162. Interview with Bookbinder.

163. Interview with Warren Eisenberg, November 19, 1981.

164. Interview with Marty.

165. Interview with Bookbinder.

166. Interview with David Saperstein, October 29, 1981.

167. *Congressional Quarterly* (August 22, 1981), p. 1526.

168. David Shribman, "Presidential Choice Perplexes Jews," *Wall Street Journal,*

September 19, 1984; Jack W. Germond and Jules Witcover, "Church-State Issue May Swing Jewish Voters Back into Democratic Column," *National Journal*, October 6, 1984; and Reichley, "Religion and Political Realignment," pp. 32–33.

169. Feldstein, *American Jewish Community*, p. 27.

170. James Davison Hunter, *American Evangelicalism: Conservative Religion and the Quandary of Modernity* (Rutgers, 1983), p. 41.

171. Ibid.

172. Ibid., pp. 50–54.

173. Ibid., pp. 43-44.

174. Ibid., pp. 44–45.

175. Ibid., p. 46; and Joe McGinniss, *The Selling of the President, 1968* (Trident, 1969), p. 163.

176. Robert Wuthnow, "Political Rebirth of American Evangelicalism," in *New Christian Right*, p. 168.

177. Ibid., p. 169.

178. Fitzgerald, "Disciplined, Charging Army," pp. 54–59.

179. Wuthnow, "Political Rebirth," p. 173; and George Gerbner and others, *Religion and Television* (Annenberg School of Communications, 1984), p. 3.

180. Fitzgerald, "Disciplined, Charging Army," p. 63.

181. "Homes Headed by Unwed Mothers Up 356%," *Washington Post*, June 18, 1982; Victor R. Fuchs, "The Soaring Rate of Unwed Mothers," *Wall Street Journal*, January 29, 1982; Bruce Chapman, "Seduced and Abandoned: America's New Poor," *Wall Street Journal*, October 5, 1982; and Philip J. Hilts, "Drinking Found to Trouble One in 3 Families," *Washington Post*, November 16, 1982.

182. Pamela Johnston Conover, "The Mobilization of the New Right: A Test of Various Explanations," *Western Political Quarterly*, vol. 36 (December 1983), p. 632–46.

183. Tim LaHaye, *The Battle for the Mind*, (Old Tappan, N.J.: Revell, 1980), p. 59; and Francis A. Schaeffer, *A Christian Manifesto* (Westchester, Ill.: Crossway, 1981), p. 54.

184. Michael Johnson, "The New Christian Right in American Politics," *The Political Science Quarterly*, vol. 53 (April–June 1982), p. 184; and interviews with William Billings, president of the National Christian Action Coalition, October 22, 1980, and Gary Jarmin, legislative director, Christian Voice, November 13, 1980.

185. Interview with Ronald Godwin, October 27, 1981.

186. George G. Higgins, "The Prolife Movement and the New Right," *America* (September 1980), p. 227.

187. For ties between the secular new right and its religious counterpart, see Peele, *Revival and Reaction*, pp. 101–16.

188. Fitzgerald, "Disciplined, Charging Army," p. 60.

189. Interviews with Godwin; Paul Weyrich, December 9, 1980; Richard Viguerie, November 12, 1980; Robert Billings, September 30, 1981; and Howard Phillips, December 18, 1984.

190. Robert C. Liebman, "Mobilizing the Moral Majority," in *New Christian Right*, p. 67.

191. James L. Guth, "The New Christian Right," in *New Christian Right*, p. 32.

192. Joseph B. Tanney and Stephen D. Johnson, "The Moral Majority in Middletown," *Journal for the Scientific Study of Religion*, vol. 22 (June 1983), p. 150.

193. Interview with Morton Blackwell, December 3, 1981; and Guth, "New Christian Right," pp. 37–38.

194. Margaret Ann Latus, "Mobilizing Christians for Political Action: Campaigning

with God on Your Side," paper delivered at 1982 meeting of the Society for the Scientific Study of Religion, Providence, R.I., pp. 2–5; and interviews with Jarmin and E. E. McAteer, December 17, 1981.

195. Guth, "New Christian Right," p. 36.

196. Wuthnow, "Political Rebirth," p. 182; and Donald Heinz, "The Struggle to Define America," in *New Christian Right,* p. 136.

197. Tina Rosenberg, "How the Media Made the Moral Majority," *Washington Monthly* (May 1982), pp. 26–32.

198. Samuel S. Hill and Dennis E. Owen, *The New Religious Right in America* (Abingdon, 1982), p. 78.

199. Seymour Martin Lipset and Earl Raab, "The Election and the Evangelicals," *Commentary* (March 1981), pp. 25–31; Robert Zwier, "The Moral Majority in the 1980 Elections: The Cases of Iowa and South Dakota," paper delivered at the 1981 meeting of the American Political Science Association, New York City; Tanney and Johnson, "Moral Majority in Middletown"; James L. Guth, "The Politics of Preachers: Southern Baptist Ministers and the Christian Right," paper delivered at the 1982 Citadel Symposium on Southern Politics, Charlestown, S.C.; Richard V. Pierard, "No Hoosier Hospitality for Humanism: The Moral Majority in Indiana," paper delivered at 1982 meeting of the Society for the Scientific Study of Religion, Providence, R.I.; Anthony Oberschall and Steve Howell, "The Old and New Christian Right in North Carolina," paper delivered at 1982 meeting of the Society for the Scientific Study of Religion, Providence, R.I.; and Greeley quoted by Arthur H. Miller and Martin D. Wattenberg, "Religious Orientations and the 1980 Elections," paper dated June 1982, p. 18.

200. Miller and Wattenberg, "Religious Orientations."

201. Fred Barbash, "Court Bars 2 Schools' Tax Break," *Washington Post,* May 25, 1983.

202. Interviews with R. Billings and Blackwell.

203. Jerry Falwell, *Listen, America!* (Doubleday, 1980), p. 13; interview with Godwin; and "Interview with Jerry Falwell," *Christianity Today* (September 4, 1981), p. 27.

204. Haynes Johnson, "A Preacher for 'Peace Through Strength,'" *Washington Post,* April 3, 1983; and Falwell, *Listen, America!* p. 106.

205. Gans, *Non-Voter Study of '84–'85;* Ann Cooper, "Voter Turnover May be Higher on Nov. 6," *National Journal,* November 3, 1984; and Adam Clymer, "Religion and Politics Mix Poorly for Democrats," *New York Times,* November 25, 1984.

206. Falwell, *Listen, America!* p. 113.

207. Schaeffer, *Christian Manifesto,* p. 108; and interview with Cal Thomas, May 10, 1982.

208. Interview with Thomas.

209. Dinesh D'Souza, "Jerry Falwell's Renaissance," *Policy Review* (Winter 1984), p. 39.

210. Hill and Owen, *New Religious Political Right,* p. 17; Peggy L. Shriver, *The Bible Vote* (Pilgrim Press, 1981), p. 54; and interview with Robert Dugan, October 21, 1981.

211. Interview with Jim Wallis, editor of *Sojourners,* January 13, 1982.

212. Phillip E. Hammond, "Another Great Awakening," in *New Christian Right,* p. 219.

213. John H. Simpson, "Moral Issues," pp. 193–94. The survey tested attitudes on homosexual relations between adults; the Supreme Court rulings on prayer and Bible reading in the public schools; the statement, "It is much better for everyone involved if the man is the achiever outside the home and the woman takes care of the home and the family"; and abortion for any reason.

214. Dean M. Kelley, "How Much Freedom of Speech Is Allowed to the Churches?" *Christianity and Crisis,* vol. 41 (October 5, 1981), p. 264.

215. Interview with Godwin.

216. Guth, "New Christian Right," p. 37; Hill and Owen, "New Religious Political Right," p. 109; LaHaye, *Battle for the Mind,* p. 78; interview with McAteer; Fitzgerald, "Disciplined, Charging Army," p. 107; and James David Fairbanks, "The Evangelical Right: Beginning of Another Symbolic Crusade," paper delivered at 1981 American Political Science Association meeting, p. 16.

217. Peter L. Berger and John Neuhaus, eds., *Against the World For the World: The Hartford Appeal and the Future of American Religion* (Seabury, 1976), pp. 4–5.

218. Peter L. Berger, "For a World with Windows," in *Against the World,* pp. 10–11.

219. Richard John Neuhaus, "Calling a Halt to Retreat," in *Against the World,* p. 151.

220. Ibid., p. 154.

221. Interview with William Sloan Coffin, January 21, 1982; and interview with Richard John Neuhaus, January 19, 1982.

222. Peter L. Berger and Richard John Neuhaus, *To Empower People* (American Enterprise Institute, 1977), p. 33.

223. *Preliminary Inquiry Regarding Financial Contributions to Outside Political Groups by Boards and Agencies of the United Methodist Church,* privately circulated paper by David Jessup, dated April 7, 1980.

224. Interview with David Jessup, December 14, 1981.

225. Interview with Penn Kemble, December 14, 1983.

226. Interview with Edmund Robb, May 15, 1982.

227. Interviews with Jessup; Kemble; Robb; Neuhaus; Carl Henry, October 29, 1981; and James Schall, October 12, 1981.

228. *Christianity and Democracy* (Institute on Religion and Democracy, 1981), p. 11.

229. Ibid., pp. 1–4.

230. Ibid., pp. 4–10.

231. Ibid., p. 12.

232. Steve Asken, "Church Groups Urge Union 'Distance' Itself from IRD Connection," *National Catholic Reporter,* July 29, 1983.

233. Peter Steinfels, "Neoconservative Theology," *Democracy,* vol. 2 (April 1982), pp. 20–23.

234. *Christian Democracy and the Churches Today* (Institute on Religion and Democracy, 1982); and *United Methodist Reporter,* April 1, 1983.

235. Sharon Mielke, "Church Told 'Get House' in Order," *United Methodist Reporter,* March 25, 1983; and Willmer Thorkelson, "Church Coalition Ties Challenged," *United Methodist Reporter,* June 24, 1983.

236. John A. Lovelace, "Twin Foci Featured in Episcopal Address," *United Methodist Reporter,* May 4, 1984.

Chapter 7. Religion and Democracy

1. Fred Hirsch, *Social Limits to Growth* (Harvard University Press, 1976), pp. 5–6.

2. Milton Friedman and Rose Friedman, *Free to Choose: A Personal Statement* (Harcourt Press, 1980), p. 27.

3. For a useful comparison of Hegel and Locke, see Lewis P. Hinchman, "The Origins of Human Rights: A Hegelian Perspective," *Western Political Quarterly,* vol. 37 (March 1984), pp. 7–29.

4. Another side of Rousseau, the side that produced the *Discourse on the Origin and Foundation of Inequality*, is a major source of modern tender-minded egoism. Rousseau has the distinction of pointing, in different aspects, toward both totalitarianism and Jerry Rubin.

5. John Rawls, *A Theory of Justice* (Harvard University Press, 1971), pp. 60–83, 136–42.

6. Aristotle, *Politics*, translated by Benjamin Jowett (Modern Library, 1943), pp. 144, 308; and Alasdair MacIntyre, *After Virtue* (Notre Dame, 1981), p. 50.

7. Jacques Monod, *Chance and Necessity* (Random House, 1972), pp. 176–80.

8. MacIntyre, *After Virtue*, pp. 175–76.

9. Robert R. Wilson, *Prophecy and Society in Ancient Israel* (Philadelphia: Fortress Press, 1980), p. 252.

10. "Group Opposes 'Star Wars' Funding," *Washington Post*, May 14, 1985. Signers of the statement, which was prepared and circulated by the American Friends Service Committee, included the Reverend Dwain Epps, director for international affairs of the National Council of Churches; Avery Post, president of the United Church of Christ; and Catholic Bishops Thomas Gumbleton of Detroit and Walter Sullivan of Richmond.

11. For the involvement of the churches in the IMF controversy, see "Church-Led Alliance Opposes $8.4 Billion Infusion for IMF," *United Methodist Reporter*, May 20, 1983.

12. Steve Askin, "Church Groups Urge Union Distance Itself from IRD Connection," *National Catholic Reporter*, July 29, 1983; and Robert S. Greenberger, "Divided Unions," *Wall Street Journal*, October 25, 1983. The churches' tactic worked, several church lobbyists pointed out to me, in the sense of forcing the unions to issue the desired attacks on the IRD. But this kind of success for the churches can turn out to be Pyrrhic indeed.

13. "Evangelical Conservatives Move from Pews to Polls," *Congressional Quarterly* (September 6, 1980), pp. 2627–34.

14. Robert Benne, *The Ethic of Democratic Capitalism: A Moral Reassessment* (Forrest Press, 1981), p. viii; and Michael Novak, *The Spirit of Democratic Capitalism* (American Enterprise Institute, Simon and Schuster, 1982), p. 13.

15. Novak, *Spirit of Democratic Capitalism*, p. 82; and Benne, *Ethic of Democratic Capitalism*, p. 82.

16. Novak, *Spirit of Democratic Capitalism*, p. 57.

17. *Religion in America: 50 Years, 1935–1985*, Gallup report no. 236 (May 1985), p. 22.

Index